EARLY S:

MONTGOMERY COUNTY, OHIO

Genealogical Abstracts from Common Pleas Court Records, Civil and Probate

Compiled and Edited by

Shirley Keller Mikesell

Heritage Books, Inc.

Published 1992 By

HERITAGE BOOKS, INC.
1540-E Pointer Ridge Place
Bowie, MD 20716
(301) 390-7709

ISBN 1-55613-601-3

A Complete Catalog Listing Hundreds of Titles on
History, Genealogy & Americana
Free on Request

Dedicated to

RUBY BOWSER KELLER

whose BOWSER and BOWMAN ancestors

helped settle Montgomery County

TABLE OF CONTENTS

INTRODUCTION

The purpose of this book is to supplement the substitute "census" of Montgomery County's early years begun in the previous volume. Land and tax records were the primary sources; now we take an in-depth look at court records. Many individuals, not previously named in land records, have been entered in these pages as members of juries or purchasers at auctions if not actually participants in lawsuits and estate matters. Since Court records were abstracted extending later than Volume 1 cut-off points (1814 tax lists and 1816 land records), the opportunity to discover early settlers has been greatly expanded. Over 600 family names appear in Volume II, not given in the first book. And so the "census" continues to grow with these additions.

The first courts were created with statehood -- the Circuit courts. The First Circuit was composed of Hamilton, Clermont, Butler, Green, Warren and Montgomery counties. Since Hamilton County began at the Ohio river and Montgomery County ended at the northern state line, this was a lot of territory to cover. The Circuit President was assisted at each local court by not less than two nor more than three associate judges.

The early court system operated on several levels, far different from present day divisions. The basis was the court of the Justice of the Peace, a local elected official with jurisdiction over small claims and misdemeanor cases. Records of these Courts were kept by the individuals; most have been lost over the passage of time. Chancery cases were heard by selected Justices of the Peace and the Clerk of Courts, known as Masters of Chancery.

The next level -- and records of most general interest -- was the Common Pleas Court, hearing cases of debt, slander, bastardy, assault & battery, probate, guardianships and appeals from the lower JP and Chancery courts. (Probate Court did not exist as an entity until 1851.) The Supreme Court, also created in 1803, heard appeals from Common Pleas, land disputes, etc.

Criminal cases are touched upon slightly in Common Pleas records. The earliest criminal records have been lost over the years, mostly in moving to a new Courthouse.

Montgomery County's first Courts were held in Newcom's Tavern, a four room log cabin with attached kitchen. One room served as the Courtroom, but the largest was used for sleeping quarters for judges and lawyers alike. Newcom also furnished the first jail -- variously one room of the house, a dry well on the lot, or the corn crib, site probably depending upon the character of the prisoner.

By 1805, the Court had moved to larger quarters at McCollom's Inn. Hugh had lured the court business by building a chimney with fireplace for winter sessions. He provided the room, firewood, benches and candles for $25 a year, later raised to $37.64. A jail had also been built -- a 30 x 16 ft log cabin, divided into two rooms. The smaller held criminals; the larger room, for debtors, had two windows and the fireplace.

Advertisements were let in 1805 to build a permanent courthouse. The contract was awarded to associate judge Benjamin Archer. Although incomplete, the building was first occupied in 1807. It was not truly finished until 1816 when a bell was installed in the courthouse cupola.

****

Abbreviations used in the abstracts--

Acct... account
Adm ... administration
Admr... administrator
Appt... appoint
Appr... appraisal, appraiser
Assoc.. associate
Chgd... charged
Dec ... deceased
Dfnt... defendant
Dism... dismissed

Disc... discontinued
Exec... executor
Inv.... Inventory
JP..... Justice of the
                    Peace
Plntf.. Plaintiff
rcvr... recover
Sec.... security
Twp.... township
(X).... signature mark

I. Common Pleas Civil Law Record Books

Early Common Pleas Court documents are found in two sets of books: the Civil Law Records and the Probate and Testamentary Docket books. The first section of this book abstracts the law records.

The Common Pleas civil law records contain a synopsis of each case, from service of the writ until judgement was rendered. The first five volumes covering the time period from 1803 until 1824 are held in the Ohio Archives of Wright State University Library near Fairborn, Ohio. Several of the volumes are not indexed and so are difficult to use.

What may the genealogist learn from these law records? Land and tax records located only to find those wealthy enough to own property. Civil cases name the tenant farmer, the small merchant, the craftsman and the constable who served the writ --the common folk who left few footprints for genealo-gists to trace. In rare instances, civil records spell out relationships as definitively as probate records.

Proof of residency are in these records as well. While either plaintiff or defendant might not be resident of Montgomery County, the jurors were! Jury service may give an earlier entry in Ohio than the date on a land sale. Unfortunately, witnesses were not named in the synopsis or the records would be even more valuable for research purposes.

A word of warning: some suits, as in courts today, were given continuances, taking several years to work through the system. The name of a Grand Juror recorded in the term of 1814, for example, is not proof of his existence in 1814. That case probably began several years earlier and the Grand Juror may have been deceased before the trial was held.

The historian will find an interesting overview of pioneer society in the following abstracts. The rough and tumble frontier lives on in records of knife fights, etc. The genealogist will find a more human side of our ancestors in these records, more than simply born/married/died. That "more human side" may have warts, but that only makes genealogy even more fascinating!

Common Pleas Court convened 4th Tuesday, July, 1803, first term after erection of Montgomery County on evening of the same day, being the 27th of July. Officers of the court were FRANCIS DUNLAVY, president of the First Circuit; BENJAMIN ARCHER, ISAAC SPINNING & JOHN EWING, associate judges; BENJAMIN VAN CLEVE, clerk pro tempore; GEORGE NEWCOM, sheriff; JAMES MILLER, coroner; DANIEL SYMMES, prosecutor pro tempore.

Grand jurors called for July term: JOHN McCABE, WILLIAM HAMER, WILLIAM SNODGRASS, JOHN DEVOR, JAMES MILLER JR, WILLIAM WAUGH, JOHN McGREW, WILLIAM LAMME, AARON NUTT, JOHN MIKESELL, ALEXANDER SCOTT, DANIEL C. COOPER, JOHN HOUSTON, JOHN BRADFORD, BENJAMIN ROBBINS, HENRY YOUNT, SAMUEL MORISON.

Term of November, 1803

Case 1. State vs PETER SUNDERLAND. Charged SUNDERLAND of Washington Twp with assault on BENJAMIN SCOTT on 10 June, 1803. SUNDERLAND admitted guilt, fined $9.00. pp 2, 3

Case 2. State vs JEREMIAH YORK. Charged YORK of Dayton Twp with assault on PATRICK LAFFERTY on 10 June. YORK admitted guilt, fined $11.35. pp 3, 4, 5

Case 3. RALPH STAFFORD vs DAVID LUCAS. Damages, suit disc. p 5

Case 4. JESSE DAVENPORT vs SAMUEL ARCHER. Damages, suit disc. p 5

Case 5. JEROM HOLT vs WILLIAM MASON. Slander, suit disc. p 5

Case 6. WILLIAM ORR vs JAMES MILLER. Suit to remove cause before JOHN FOLKERTH, JP of Montgomery Co, suit disc. p 5

Case 7. JOHN HOLLAND vs JAMES THOMSON. Suit to remove cause before JOHN FOLKERTH, JP of Montgomery Co, suit disc. p 5

Term of June, 1804

ARTHUR ST. CLAIR prosecuting attorney.

Case 1. State vs BENJAMIN SCOTT. On June 10, 1903, SCOTT of German Twp charged with assaulting PETER SUNDERLAND; plea of not guilty. Jury summoned: HENRY

Term of June, 1804 continued

ATCHISON, BARNABUS BLUE, BENJAMIN BOWMAN, ROBERT EDGAR, BENJAMIN IDDINGS, JOSEPH KINGREY, GEORGE KOONS, WILLIAM MASON, JOHN McCABE, ALEXANDER SNODGRASS, JOHN VANSEL, GEORGE YOUNT. Jury acquited SCOTT. pp 6, 7

Case 2. State vs WILLIAM CONCANNON. CONCANNON of Dayton Twp charged by November Grand Jury [JAMES MILLER, JAMES PETTICREW, WILLIAM DODDS, GEORGE GIL-LESPIE, SWANSY WHITING, WILLIAM CLARK, JACOB LONG, JOHN MIKESELL, ROBERT EDGAR, LEONARD WOLF, THOMAS JOHN, JOHN CRAWFORD, JOHN MILLER] with assault upon JOHN GUILE on 25 Oct, 1803. CONCANNON admitted guilt, fine and costs total $4.28. pp 8, 9

Case 3. State vs JOHN S. RIGGS. Charged RIGGS of Dayton Twp with stealing grindstone belonging to JAMES MILLER; plea of not guilty. Jury summoned: BARNABUS BLUE, BENJAMIN BOWMAN, JAMES HANNA, BENJA-MIN IDDINGS, JOSEPH KINGREY, GEORGE KUNS, ELIHU SAUNDERS, ALEXANDER SNODGRASS, HENRY STANSEL, JAMES THOMSON, GEORGE WESTFALL, GEORGE YOUNT. Jury ac-quited RIGGS. pp 9, 10

Case 4. SARAH GREGG vs JAMES MILLER. GREGG repre-sented by JOSHUA COLLETT, atty, charged MILLER with debt of $90, note made 10 July, 1802. MILLER refused to pay. Suit brought for $130 damages. MILLER found guilty, ordered to pay $90 debt, $10.35 damages, $9.05 costs. pp 10, 11

Case 5. AMOS DOROUGH vs WILLIAM GAHAGAN. Case disc. p 11

Case 6. WILLIAM HAMER vs JAMES THOMSON. Case disc. p 11

Case 7. PAUL D. BUTLER vs JAMES THOMSON. Charged THOMSON with debt of $20 made 10 Sept, 1802, previous debt of $10, later debt of $25 for goods and merchan-dise, $10 for meat, drink and lodging for 16 days, $14 for work and labor -- total damages sought, $100. Thomson refuted debt. Jury summoned: BARNABUS BLUE, BENJAMIN BOWMAN, BENJAMIN EADINGS, DANIEL HOOVER, JONATHAN JUSTICE, JOSEPH KINGREY, GEORGE KUNS, WIL-LIAM MASON, JOHN MILLER, ALEXANDER SNODGRASS, HENRY STANSEL, GEORGE YOUNT. Found THOMSON guilty, ordered to pay $18.84 damages. pp 12, 13, 14, 15

Case 8. JOHN WILLIAMS vs JAMES THOMSON. Charged

Term of June, 1804 continued

THOMSON with $61 debt, note made 17 Aug, 1802. THOMSON, represented by JACOB BURNET, att'y, admitted debt. WILLLIAMS to recover $61, $6.66 damages, $8.36 costs. pp 15, 16

Case 9. ANDREW LOCK vs JONATHAN PARKS. Trespass, suit disc. p 16

Case 10. PETER JOHNSTON vs LEVI NUTT. Trespass, battery, suit disc. p 16

Case 11. JAMES LOWRY vs DANIEL FERREL. Charged FERREL with $10 debt, 12 Sept, 1803, witness WILLIAM PEERY. Defendant appeared before JOHN FOLKERTH, JP, on 3 Oct, bringing his witness, WILLIAM ELLIS. FOLKERTH upheld debt. Court ordered payt of debt, $7.65 damages. p 17, 18

Case 12. SAMUEL MORE vs SMITH GREGG. Horse, value of $100, suit disc. p 18

Case 13. WILLIAM VAN CLEVE vs JAMES THOMSON. 14 March, 1803, $30 debt for work done. Thomson refuted debt. Jury summoned: BARNABUS BLUE, BENJAMIN BOWMAN, BENJAMIN IDDINGS, JOSEPH KINGREY, GEORGE KUNS, WILLIAM MASON, JOHN MILLER, SAMUEL McCORMACK, ELIHU SAUNDERS, ALEXANDER SNODGRASS, HENRY STANSEL, GEORGE YOUNT. Found THOMSON guilty. VAN CLEVE to recover $12 damages, costs of $7.88. pp 18, 19, 20

Case 14. WILLIAM VAN CLEVE vs JAMES THOMSON. $500 damages, cause submitted to WILLIAM DODDS, JOHN MILLER, ROBERT WILSON for arbitration. VAN CLEVE to recover $12 damages, costs of $7.88. pp 20, 21

Case 15. JAMES THOMSON vs WILLIAM CONCANNON. Damages, suit disc. p 21

Case 16. CHRISTIANA LUCAS, appellee, vs ROBERT CUNNINGHAM CRAWFORD, appellant. Appeal from judgement of JOHN GERARD, JP, Elizabeth Twp. Suit disc. p 21

Case 17. SAMUEL THOMSON vs (blank). Suit disc. p 21

Clerk of Court's bond, dated 7 June, 1804: BENJAMIN VAN CLEVE. Securitors: DANIEL C. COOPER, JEROM HOLT. Witness: JAMES THOMSON, GEORGE F. TENNERY. p 21

Term of November, 1804

Case 1. JAMES CANNON vs JAMES THOMSON. Damages, suit disc. p 22

Case 2. PIERRE FELIX vs JACOB ROBINSON. Note written in French, 6 Dec, 1802, for $112.50, previous debt of $150. ROBINSON claimed pay't of $112 on 10 May, 1803, denied previous debt. Court ordered pay't of $125.44, $11.46 costs. ROBINSON gave bond, secured by JAMES THOMSON, ROBERT CUNNINGHAM CRAWFORD. pp 22, 23, 24, 25

Case 3. PETER FELIX vs JAMES MILLER. Undated - debt of $37.75, to be paid in good whiskey, further debt of $50 cash. First debt acknowledged by MILLER. Ordered to pay $37.75, $10.68 costs. pp 25, 26, 27

Case 4. WILLIAM ORR vs EBENEZER WEAD. ORR represented by EZRA FITTZ FREEMAN, att'y. Agreement made 14 Feb, 1802, for ORR to teach "art and mystery" of weaving to EBENEZER WEAD, son of EBENEZER. Cost to be 1 cow @ $18 + $50 at conclusion. Apprentice EBENEZER departed "without reasonable cause", absenting himself from his master's service for 18 months. Father EBENEZER pled not guilty, brought notice of previous suit between ORR and himself which had settled dispute. ORR failed to appear Nov term. Court found ORR to take nothing, WEAD to recover $14.34 costs. pp 27, 28, 29, 30

Case 5. JOSEPH MEEKER vs ANDREW LOCK. 1 Nov, 1802 agreement for MEEKER to live with, work for LOCK for 1 yr to be paid $100, later agreement for 2d yr. Unpaid, MEEKER sued for $200. LOCK held that MEEKER left service before expiration of term, on 10 Sept, 1803. MEEKER denied leaving. Court granted MEEKER $200 for services, $22.78 costs. pp 30, 31, 32, 33

Case 6. WILLIAM CONCANNON vs DANIEL C. COOPER. CONCANNON rep by WILLIAM CORRY, att'y. Agreement of 1 Oct, 1803: CONCANNON to deliver 14,000 bricks, COOPER to pay $4 per thousand, previous debt of $56 for bricks. COOPER denied dealings. Jury: DAVID BERNTRAGER, WILLIAM BLAIR, URIAH BLUE, JOHN CLAWSON, WILLIAM FINCHER, ISRAEL HARRIS, SAMUEL HUSTON, JOSEPH REYBURN, JOHN S. RIGGS, JOSEPH RORER, RALPH STAFFORD, JOHN WILLIAMS. CONCANNON granted $56, $17.87 costs. pp 33, 34, 35

Case 7. JAMES MacDONALD vs SAMUEL ARCHER. Agreement of 10 Aug, 1802 at Dayton, $26.00 to be paid in good,

Term of November, 1804 continued

merchantable whiskey on 1 March, 1803. THOMSON failed to deliver. MacDONALD to recover $28.62, $5.97 costs. Copy of original note signed by ARCHER, endorsed on reverse that "JAMES MacDANELD" assigned title and claim to JESSE DAVENPORT, witness: PETER SMITH. pp 35, 36, 37

Case 8. SAMUEL THOMSON & DANIEL FERREL vs STEPHEN LUDLOW. On 1 Apr, 1804 LUDLOW charged with running wagons, horses and cattle on THOMSON & FERREL's land, erecting a fence and pasturing his cattle for a period of six months. Sued for damages of $200, LUDLOW denied trespass. Jury: DAVID BERNTRAGER, WILLIAM BLAIR, URIAH BLUE, JOHN CLAWSON, WILLIAM FINCHER, ISRAEL HARRIS, SAMUEL HUSTON, JOSEPH REYBURN, JOSEPH RORER, RALPH STAFFORD, GEORGE WESTFALL, JOHN WILLIAMS. Found LUDLOW guilty, pay $200 damages, #13.97 costs. pp 37, 38, 39

Case 9. JOHN RHOADS vs DANIEL C. COOPER. On 16 Nov, 1801, during lifetime of ISRAEL LUDLOW, he and COOPER bound selves to $600 debt. LUDLOW's estate and COOPER both failed to pay. Exec's of estate not in jurisdiction of the court. COOPER denied debt. At trial COOPER failed to defend, RHOADS granted $600, $115.08 costs. pp 39, 40

Case 10. MATTHEWS & BROWN vs DANIEL FLINN. Debt, suit disc. p 41

Case 11. JOHN BARNET, ELIZABETH BARNET, SUSANNAH BARNET vs JOSEPH FERRIS. Defamation, suit disc. p 41

Case 12. WILLIAM HAMER vs JAMES THOMSON. Covenant damages, suit disc. p 41

Case 13. JOB GUARD vs DANIEL C. COOPER. Covenant damages, writ quashed, COOPER recovered against JOB GARD for costs of $6.40. p 41

Case 14. SAMUEL THOMSON vs DANIEL C. COOPER. Damages, award filed and settled. p 41

Case 15. SAMUEL ALEXANDER & SAMUEL CREIGH vs DANIEL FLINN. Debt and damages, suit disc. p 41

Term of February, 1805

Case 1. JONATHAN BALLINGER vs WILLIAM WILLIS. BALLINGER represented by RICHARD S. THOMAS, atty.

Term of February, 1805 continued

16 Oct, 1802, BALLINGER lost mare valued at $80, found and kept by WILLIS although aware of owner. WILLIS, defended by GEORGE F. TENNERY, atty, pled not guilty. Jury: JOSEPH CRANE, THOMAS CLAWSON, JOHN DEVOR, THOMAS HATFIELD, ZACARIAH HOLE, NICHOLAS HORNER, EDWARD HUSTON, DAVID MOYER, FREDERICK NUTTZ, JOSEPH REYBURN, MARTIN RUPLE, BENJAMIN WALLINGSFORD. Found WILLIS innocent, recover $24.57 costs. pp 42,43

Case 2. WILLIAM CHENOWITH vs DANIEL C. COOPER. Feb, 1795 at Dayton, COOPER indebted for $200 in labor, $250 in cash; CHENOWITH to receive title to 2 lots in town of Dayton, #'s 37, 38. COOPER, represented by ARTHUR ST. CLAIR, atty, denied debt. At trial, COOPER failed to defend. CHENOWITH to recover $500, $12.19 costs. pp 44, 45, 46

Case 3. ROBERT WILSON vs HENRY ATCHINSON. 27 Feb, 1802 at Dayton, note written for 125 bushels good corn to be delivered following season, 28 Nov, 1803, in exchange for 2 horses. ATCHINSON claimed payment made 15 Nov, 1803 and that mare was unsound, of no value. Jury: THOMAS CLAWSON, JOHN DEVOR, THOMAS HATFIELD, NICHOLAS HORNER, EDWARD HUSTON, EPHRAIM McKINNY, DAVID MOYER, FREDERICK NUTTZ, JOSEPH REYBURN, MARTIN RUPLE, BENJAMIN WALLINGSFORD, GEORGE WESTFALL. ATCHINSON found guilty of non-paymt, WILSON granted $30.25, $14.68 costs. pp 46, 47, 48

Case 4. JAMES THOMSON vs DAVID RIFFLE. 1 Nov, 1798, RIFFLE owed $55 + previous debt of $55, to give horse to THOMSON. Failure to pay, suit brought for $500. RIFFLE denied debt, offered proof horse was bought in VA. Jury: JOSEPH CRAIN, JOHN DEVOR, THOMAS HATFIELD, ZACARIAH HOLE, NICHOLAS HORNER, EDWARD HUSTON, DAVID MOYER, FREDERICK NUTTZ, JOSEPH REYBURN, MARTIN RUPLE, BENJAMIN WALLINGSFORD, GEORGE WESTFALL. Found RIFFLE guilty, THOMSON recovered $73.96, $8.78 costs. Papers filed in evidence: Hamilton Co, OH, 27 May, 1799, before JOHN GREER, JP, appeared JOHN CLAPP, JAMES REED, JAMES HAMILTON. CLAPP testified horse now in possession of THOMSON formerly property of Capt. JAMES HAMILTON about 4 yr previous, lost or stolen while grazing. REED saw horse in Hamilton Co in possession of EDWARD WEST, was then lost or stolen. HAMILTON stated horse was purchased winter (17)93, stolen or lost (17)96, and that he never sold or bartered the horse nor empowered others to do so. pp 48,49, 50,51

Case 5. WILLIAM VAN CLEVE vs SAMUEL THOMSON & DANIEL

Term of February, 1805 continued

FERREL. 24 Feb, 1802, at Dayton, agreement to transfer deed to 10 acres in Sec 9, bound by town of Dayton, SE corner of THOMSON & FERREL's tract. Possession to be had by VAN CLEVE until deed made, on or
before 1 Sept, 1807. Possession denied, VAN CLEVE
sued for damages of $300. THOMSON & FERREL failed to
defend, VAN CLEVE to recover $300, $11.15 costs. pp
51, 52, 53, 54

Case 6. DAVID LUCAS vs ROBERT CUNNINGHAM CRAWFORD.
6 Jan, 1803 at Dayton, LUCAS agreed to work for CRAW-
FORD 1 yr for $117.50 wages, food, lodging and wash-
ing. On 6 Aug, 1803, "a further discourse was had"
and LUCAS left CRAWFORD's employ, releasing CRAWFORD
from balance of agreement. LUCAS req. payt of $58.75
for time served; CRAWFORD refused. Suit brought for
$100. Jury found for LUCAS, recover $46.28, $23.61
costs. pp 54, 55, 56, 57, 58

Case 7. STATE vs JAMES THOMSON. Grand Jury: JONA-
THAN MUNGER, RICHARD MASON, JAMES FLINN, ROBERT CUN-
NINGHAM CRAWFORD, MICHAEL WILLIAMS, WILLIAM WILLIS,
WILLIAM HAMER, JOHN GILL, WILLIAM GAHAGAN, JACOB
FOUT, DAVID SQUIER, LEVI MARTIN, GEORGE GILLESPIE,
JAMES MILES, ROBERT GILCHRIST. THOMSON offered himself as candidate for Montgomery Co Rep to House of
the Assembly, State of Ohio, 11 Oct, 1804. At election, town of Dayton, he "did unlawfully and corrupt-
ly offer one gallon of whiskey...as a bribe to said
WILLIAM HUNTER" for his vote, THOMSON setting a "dan-
gerous and evil example". THOMSON pled not guilty,
acquited by jury. pp 58, 59

Case 8. STATE vs ROBERT PATTERSON. Petition of ED-
WARD PAGE, a black man, charged restraint and threat
to be taken to KY and sold, by PATTERSON, contrary to
laws of OH: sworn before JOHN FOLKERTH, JP, 6 Feb,
1805. Petition of LUCY PAGE, a black woman, charged
restraint and threat to be taken to KY and sold, by
PATTERSON, contrary to laws of OH: sworn before JOHN
FOLKERTH, JP, 6 Feb, 1805. Affidavit of SAMUEL HOP-
KINS, of lawful age, testifed EDWARD & LUCY were held
as slaves by PATTERSON, threatened with being sent to
"DR. McCALLA in KY" into slavery: sworn before JOHN
FOLKERTH, 6 Feb, 1805. PATTERSON appeared before
Court, testifed NED & LUCE had absconded from his
service; that they were hirelings for 1 yr from Dr.
ANDREW McCALLA of Lexington, KY and his legal proper-
ty. Court directed that EDWARD & LUCY were to be set
free in accordance with Ohio law. pp 60, 61, 62

Term of February, 1805 continued

Case 9. STATE vs ROBERT PATTERSON. Petition of MOSES, a black man, restrained by PATTERSON, held to service, threatened with sale in KY, dated 7 Feb, 1805: sworn before JOHN FOLKERTH, JP. PATTERSON replied MOSES was property of WILLIAM LINDSAY, Scott Co KY; contracted services of MOSES, age 18, to deliver household goods. MOSES had since absconded. Court found PATTERSON not guilty of restraint. pp 62, 63

Case 10. JAMES THOMSON vs JAMES MILLER (tanner). Damages, suit disc. p 63

Case 11. RICHARD SHAW vs WILLIAM BAY. Slander, suit disc. p 63

Case 12. MATTHEW NEWCOM vs CHARLES MURRAY. Debt, suit disc. p 63

Case 13. WILLIAM MADDAN vs JOHN BATTRIL. Damages, suit disc. p 64

Case 14. SAMUEL THOMSON vs JEROM HOLT. Feather bed, suit disc. p 64

Term of August, 1805

Case 1. STATE vs JAMES THOMSON & WILLIAM CONCANNON. Charged with disturbing the peace 25 Dec, 1804 at Dayton, creating terror and disturbance ... "an evil example". Both admitted guilt. Fined $3.00 each, $4.91 costs. pp 65, 66

Case 2. STATE vs DANIEL GRIFFIN, JOHN BRADY, JONA-THAN HIGGINS & JOHN ANDERSON. The four men, all of German Twp, "being wicked, malicious and evil persons of unruly minds", on 5 Nov, 1804, assembled and gathered together a riot, caused a violent assault to be made on ISAAC REED. All denied guilt. Jury: CHRIS-TOPHER EMRICK, JONATHAN JOHNSTON, PATRICK LAFFERTY, SAMUEL MOORE, CHRISTIAN MOYER, THOMAS NEWMAN, BENJA-MIN OVERFIELD, DANIEL PRESSEL, WILLIAM STUART, BOAZ THARP, JOHN WADE, GEORGE WORTHINGTON. Found ANDER-SON innocent, others guilty. GRIFFIN, BRADY, HIGGINS protested verdict, requested judgement to be set aside and new trial ordered. pp 67, 68, 69

Case 3. STATE vs SAMUEL MORRISON. SAMUEL of Eliza-beth Twp, on 7 Aug, 1804, assaulted DAVID HAMILTON MORRIS, pled not guilty. Suit dropped by prosecutor ARTHUR ST. CLAIR. pp 70, 71

Term of August, 1805 continued

Case 4.   STATE vs SAMUEL MORRISON.   10 Apr, 1803,
MORRISON charged with erecting a fence on a common
highway, stopping traffic unlawfully, causing damages
and nuisance to citizens.   Plea of not guilty.   Suit
dropped by prosecutor.   pp 71, 72, 73

Case 5.   STATE vs STEPHEN LUDLOW.   Petition of JANE
COOPER, a black woman, restrained of liberty by LUD-
LOW, dated 5 Feb, 1805, sworn before JOHN FOLKERTH,
JP, 6 Feb, 1805.   LUDLOW responded that he had a
contract with DANIEL C. COOPER, in whose service she
had been, LUDLOW knowing nothing of her agreement
with COOPER.   LUDLOW acquited.   pp 73, 74

Case 6.   STATE vs THOMAS CUMBERFORD. (spelled CUMMI-
FORD in text)   Charged with "holding criminal conver-
sation" with wife of ELISHA WILCOX.   Grand Jury:
DAVID REID, WILLIAM KING, JOHN MILLER, JAMES HANNA,
JOSEPH PORTER, JOHN PENTECOST, JAMES McGREW, JAMES I.
NISBET, PHILIP SAYLOR, JOHN SIMMON, JACOB MULLENDORE,
ROBERT CUNNINGHAM CRAWFORD, JAMES GILLESPIE, JOHN
RICHEY, JOHN VANOSDALL.   CUMBERFORD of Elizabeth Twp
on 30 May, 1805, assaulted MARGARET WILCOX "to utter
discomfort and distraction of ELISHA WILCOX, her husband" and to the "displeasure of Almighty God and
contrary to his commandments".   CUMBERFORD failed to
appear, bail of $100 forfeit.   pp 74, 75

Case 7.   STATE vs STEPHEN MARSHAL & JEREMIAH YORK.
MARSHAL of Dayton Twp, YORK of Greene Co, OH, on 12
Apr, 1805 assaulted JOHN McKAIG.   MARSHAL admitted
guilt, fined $2.00, $4.38 costs.   Sheriff charged to
find and hold YORK.   pp 76, 77

Case 8.   STATE vs FRANCIS DILTS.   20 Aug, 1805, DILTS
of Washington Twp charged with selling whiskey without a license.   Admitted guilt, DILTS fined $1.00,
costs of $1.88.   pp 77, 78

Case 9.   STATE vs GEORGE W. SMITH.   20 Aug, 1805,
SMITH of Dayton Twp charged with selling merchandise
not the growth or manufacture of State of Ohio without a license.   Admitted guilt, SMITH fined $1.00,
costs of $1.88.   pp 78, 79

Case 10.   STATE vs ROBERT PATTERSON.   Assessed $8.16
when convicted in the EDWARD PAGE restraint trial,
PATTERSON requested writ be set aside as no costs
were adjudged at that time.   Court ordered writ
quashed, PATTERSON to pay nothing.   pp 79, 80

Term of August, 1805 continued

Case 11. STATE vs ROBERT PATTERSON. Assessed $8.16 when convicted in the LUCY PAGE restraint trial, PAT-TERSON requested writ be set aside as no costs were adjudged at that time. Court ordered writ quashed, PATTERSON to pay nothing. pp 80, 81

Case 12. STATE vs WILLIAM CONCANNON & ROBERT HUEY. JOHN McCLURE was arrested, held in jail by the sher-iff. CONCANNON of Washington Twp & HUEY of Dayton Twp charged with plotting and assisting in McCLURE's escape on 5 Feb, 1805. Both admitted guilt, fined $1.00 each, $4.27 costs. pp 82, 83, 84

Case 13. MATHEW HUSTON vs JAMES MILLER (tanner). In 1792 at Dayton, MILLER contracted debt of $44 for work done by HUSTON plus 24 June, 1801, $30.80 money recvd from HUSTON. No payment made, HUSTON filed suit for damages of $100. MILLER admitted debt, HUS-TON to recover $74.80, costs of $8.99. pp 84, 85, 86

Case 14. JOHN MATHEWS & HENRY BROWN vs DANIEL FLINN. 1 June, 1799 "at Lorimies,* to wit at Dayton" FLINN indebted to MATHEWS & BROWN for $125, further debt of $80 for hogs, sued for damages of $300. FLINN denied 1st debt, claimed he paid for hogs. Jury: THOMAS COPPOCK, TIMOTHY COUVAULT, CHRISTOPHER EMRICK, JONA-THAN JOHNSTON, SAMUEL MOORE, CHRISTIAN MOYER, DANIEL PRESSEL, WILLIAM STUART, BOAZ THARP, JOHN WEAD, GEORGE WORTHINGTON. Found FLINN guilty, MATTHEWS & BROWN to recover $225.62 damages plus $17.53 costs. Copy of original note, dated June 1, 1799 for 76 lbs, 17 sh, 6 pence PA money; endorsement on reverse signed JOHN SUTHERLAND. pp 86, 87, 88, 88, 89, 90 (*reference probably to Fort Loramie, now in Shelby Co, then in Elizabeth Twp, Montgomery Co and a trade center. MATHEWS, BROWN, SUTHERLAND all well-known traders of the day)

Case 15. SAMUEL ALEXANDER & SAMUEL CREIGH vs DANIEL FLINN. In 1793, ALEXANDER & CREIGH of Cincinnati loaned $833.33 to FLINN, WILLIAM BARNES & THOMAS BARNES. (BARNES & BARNES no longer in Montgomery Co jurisdiction 1805.) FLINN denied debt, to show evi-dence of payment. At hearing, FLINN admitted debt of $1294.51. ALEXANDER & CREIGH to recover debt, costs of $13.43, damages of $886.74. Copy of original note dated 12 Sept, 1793: "WILLIAM BARNS, THOMAS BARNS and DANIEL FLINN of Columbia, NW of the Ohio". Witness: HENRY THORKELL, JAMES BARNS, ELLIS MEMNALL. pp 90, 91, 92

Term of August, 1805 continued

Case 16. DANIEL GRIFFIN vs ISAAC REED. Charged with slander: on 3 Oct, 1804, REED said GRIFFIN committed perjury, caused damage to reputation. Sued for damages of $500. REED pled not guilty, maintained truth of accusation. Jury summoned, REED found innocent of slander, GRIFFIN to take nothing, pay court costs of $37.73. pp 93, 94, 95

Case 17. BENJAMIN FLINN vs DANIEL C. COOPER. FLINN a volunteer settler in Dayton, performed as required by COOPER by 4 Dec, 1797 to earn one lot of 10 acres, #17 on plat map. COOPER failed to transfer title as requested. Suit undefended, FLINN to recover damages of $200, costs of $15.91. pp 95, 96

Case 18. DANIEL KIRKENDALL vs WILLIAM HAMER. On 15 March, 1803, agreement for KIRKENDALL to have use of HAMER's field to grow corn, wheat, in return for one-third the crop. On 25 Aug, 1803, HAMER, charged with destroying the crop with his teams, ploughs and wagons, promised to reimburse KIRKENDALL $60. Unpaid, KIRKENDALL brought suit for $100. HAMER, represented by JOSHUA COLLETT, atty, denied promise of restitution. KIRKENDALL failed to appear at trial, to take nothing on bill, HAMER to recover costs of $18.66. pp 97, 98

Case 19. MATTHEW NEWCOM vs PETER FELIX. On 4 Dec, 1803, agreement made that NEWCOM would serve FELIX in keeping a store in Dayton, to be paid $300 and a suit of clothes at year's end. Unpaid, suit brought for $400. FELIX charged NEWCOM with failure to attend to business as a clerk, keeping the store shut, failing to deliver skins, furs and produce. Jury summoned, found FELIX guilty, awarded damages of $114 to NEWCOM, costs of $35.53. pp 98, 99, 100, 101

Case 20. JAMES THOMSON vs WILLIAM CONCANNON. 25 Dec, 1804, THOMSON charged CONCANNON with assault, sued for $1000 damages. CONCANNON pled not guilty, self-defense. Jury: THOMAS COPPOCK, CHRISTOPHER EMRICK, JONATHAN JOHNSTON, PATRICK LAFFERTY, SAMUEL MOORE, CHRISTIAN MOYER, THOMAS NEWMAN, BENJAMIN OVERFIELD, DANIEL PRESSEL, WILLIAM STUART, BOAZ THARP, GEORGE WORTHINGTON. CONCANNON found guilty, THOMSON to recover $50 damages, $28.14 costs. pp 101, 102

Case 21. THOMAS WILSON vs PETER FELIX. 2 July, 1804, note of $219,50 debt signed, FELIX refused to pay. At trial, FELIX did not appear, WILSON to recover

Term of August, 1805 continued

$235 damages, $10.24 costs. pp 102, 103, 104

Case 22. JACOB PICKELSIMER vs WILLIAM CLARK. On 10 May, 1804, note of $60 debt signed. CLARK failed to pay, failed to appear at trial. PICKELSIMER to recover debt of $60, cost of $11.48. pp 104, 105

Case 23. EDWARD TIFFIN, Governor of State of Ohio vs JAMES PATTERSON, JOHN PATTERSON SR, & JOHN DEVOR. On 27 Aug, 1803, debt of $3000. The defendants failed to pay, failed to appear in court. TIFFIN to recover $3000, $11.72 costs. pp 105, 106

Case 24. CORNELIUS WESTFALL vs GEORGE F. TENNERY. On 18 June, 1804, WESTFALL, a school teacher, made agreement to teach for one year, board at own expense, for cost of $2.00 per child per three month term, firewood and school house to be provided. TENNERY's three children attended for four terms; WESTFALL, unpaid, sued for $24. Jury: PAUL D. BUTLER, TIMOTHY COUVAULT, WILLIAM DONNEL, PETER FELIX, DANIEL FLINN, JOHN GERRARD, CALEB HUNT, JONATHAN JOHNSTON MAXFIELD LUDLOW, STEPHEN LUDLOW, JAMES McKINNY, JOHN RICHEY. Found for WESTFALL, to recover $12.00 damages, $18.74 costs. pp 106, 107, 108

Case 25. ARCHIBALD STEELE vs JOHN BRADY. STEELE sued BRADY for debt of $24 before JOHN FOLKERTH, JP. Court directed FOLKERTH to send writ of action. Dated 31 Dec, 1804, writ testified BRADY owed $24.67 as of 6 Feb, 1805. Court ordered BRADY to pay $24.67 debt, $10.26 costs. pp 108, 109

Case 26. JOHN BARNET, ELIZABETH BARNET & SUSANNAH BARNET vs JAMES THOMSON. Plaintiffs recovered $10.98 against JOSEPH FERRIS by compromise in Court, June Term, 1804, action of defamation. THOMSON had been security for FERRIS, responsible for damages if FERRIS failed to pay. One year later, plaintiffs held THOMSON accountable for damages. THOMSON failed to appear; plaintiffs to recover $10.98 damages, $10.11 costs. pp 110, 111

Case 27. SAMUEL THOMSON ads SUTHERLAND & BROWN. Court directed DANIEL C. COOPER, JP, to send notice of suit in which SUTHERLAND & BROWN were plaintiff, THOMSON defendant, in action of debt. Writ sent by Cooper. THOMSON failed to appear at trial, to take nothing in his suit, SUTHERLAND & BROWN to recover debt of $15.88, $9.56 costs. pp 111, 112

Term of August, 1805 continued

Case 28. JAMES MILLER & ROBERT MILLER vs BARNHART SPECK. Court directed DANIEL C. COOPER, JP, to send writ of suit in which plaintiffs appeared, suing SPECK for $9.38 debt. SPECK admitted guilt, ordered to pay debt. Court called trial, SPECK failed to appear. Plaintiffs to recover $9.38 debt, $10.44 damages, $5.60 costs. pp 112, 113

Case 29. JOHN FOLKERTH vs BARNHART SPECK. Court directed DANIEL C. COOPER, JP, to send writ of suit in which FOLKERTH sued SPECK for $6.00 debt. SPECK admitted guilt, ordered to pay debt. Court called trial, SPECK failed to appear. FOLKERTH to recover $6.00 debt, $10.44 damages. pp 113, 114

Case 30. MAXFIELD LUDLOW vs BARNHART SPECK. Court directed DANIEL C. COOPER, JP, to send writ of suit in which LUDLOW sued SPECK for $13.66 debt. SPECK admitted guilt, ordered to pay debt. Court called trial, SPECK failed to appear. LUDLOW to recover $13.66 debt, $10.44 damages. pp 114, 115

Case 31. AMOS DURROUGH* vs JOHN FREEMAN. Court directed DANIEL C. COOPER, JP, to send writ of suit in which FREEMAN was plaintiff, DURROUGH defendant in debt action. Writ stated DURROUGH confessed judgement for $25 debt before JOHN FOLKERTH, JP. Trial called, DURROUGH failed to appear, FREEMAN to recover $25 debt, $10.50 costs. p 115 *name alternatively spelled DOROUGH in text

Case 32. SAMUEL FREEMAN ads AMOS DURROUGH*. Court directed DANIEL C. COOPER, JP, to send writ of suit in which FREEMAN was plaintiff, DURROUGH defendant in debt action. COOPER issued execution against DURROUGH of Greene Co on transcript from JOHN FOLKERTH, JP, in favor of FREEMAN for $50. Trial called, Durrough failed to appear, FREEMAN to recover $50.00 debt, $10.44 damages. p 116 *name alternatively spelled DOROUGH in text

Case 33. JAMES GILLESPIE vs CATHARINE HENRY. suit disc. p 117

Case 34. STEPHEN MARSHAL vs JOHN McKAIG. Battery, suit disc. p 117

Case 35. THOMAS WILSON vs CHARLES MURRAY. damages. WILSON's suit quashed for lack of endorsement, MURRAY to recover $11.44 costs. p 117

Term of August, 1805 continued

Case 36. STATE vs DANIEL FERREL. Habeas corpus, recognizance forfeited. p 117

Case 37. SAMUEL THOMSON & DANIEL FERREL vs STEPHEN LUDLOW. Damages, suit disc. p 117

Case 38. JOHN FOLKERTH vs ROBERT --. Debt, damages, suit disc. p 117

Case --. STATE vs THOMAS CUMBERFORD. Indictment for Adultery, recognizance forfeited. p 117

Term of December, 1805

Case 1. STATE vs DANIEL C. COOPER. Grand Jury: DAVID REID, WILLIAM KING, JOHN MILLER, JAMES HANNA, JOSEPH PORTER, JOHN PENTICOST, JAMES McGREW, JAMES I. NISBET, PHILIP SAYLOR, JOHN SIMMONS, JACOB MULENDORE, ROBERT CUNNINGHAM CRAWFORD, JAMES GILLESPIE, JOHN RICHEY, JOHN VANORDALL. On 3 July, 1805, COOPER assaulted DANIEL FERREL, illegally detained FERREL for 1 day. COOPER pled not guilty. Jury summoned: JOHN ALEN, JAMES L. CRAWFORD, STEPHEN DAVIS, RALPH FRENCH, ROBERT MILLER, EDWARD MITCHEL, CHRISTIAN NOOP, RICHARD SHAW, GEORGE SINK, PETER SUNDERLAND, JOEL WESTFALL, FREDERICK YOUNT. Found COOPER guilty, fined $20.00, $2.87 costs. pp 118, 119

Case 2. STATE vs DANIEL FERREL. On 6 July, 1805, FERREL of Dayton Twp threatened life of DANIEL C. COOPER. Jury summoned, FERREL pled not guilty. Indictment quashed, lack of evidence. pp 119, 120

Case 3. STATE vs JOSEPH LAYTON. On 3 June, 1805, LAYTON of Elizabeth Twp threatened life of CONRAD MANN. LAYTON pled not guilty, indictment quashed. p 120, 121

Case 4. BARNHART SPECK vs THOMAS ROBISON. Court directed DANIEL C. COOPER, JP, to send writ of suit in which ROBISON sued for debt of $30. SPECK acknowledged debt, failed to pay. Trial called, SPECK failed to appear, ROBISON to recover $30.00 debt, $11.82 damages. pp 121, 122

Case 5. BARNHART SPECK vs ABRAHAM MANNIER. Court directed DANIEL C. COOPER, JP, to send writ of suit in which MANNIER sued for debt of $8.25. SPECK acknowledged debt, failed to pay. Trial called, SPECK failed to appear; MANNIER to recover $8.35

Term of December, 1805 continued

debt, $11.82 damages. pp 122, 123

Case 6. BARNHART SPECK vs JAMES MILLER SR. Court directed DANIEL C. COOPER, JP, to send writ of suit in
which MILLER sued for debt of $4.87. SPECK acknow-
ledged debt, failed to pay. Trial called, SPECK
failed to appear, MILLER to recover $4.87 debt,
$10.80 costs. pp 123, 124

Case 7. JOSEPH HECK vs GEORGE F. TENNERY. On 9
Aug, 1804, note for debt of $75. HECK claimed non-
payment, sued for damages of $50. TENNERY claimed
payment. Jury summoned. TENNERY admitted debt of
$61.00. HECK to recover debt, $2.99 damages, $9.68
costs. pp 124, 125, 126

Case 8. JACOB BUSBY vs ANDREW DYE JR. BUSBY represented by ETHAN STONE, atty. On 4 Nov, 1804, note
written for $75 debt. DYE admitted owing $67.95.
BUSBY to recover $67.95 debt, $9.73 damages. p 126

Case 9. STATE vs FRANCIS PATTERSON & ROBERT PATTER-
SON. Indictment for misdemeanor. JAMES WELSH recognized in $1000 for appearance of FRANCIS at next
term. p 127

Case 10. DANIEL ROBISON vs JACOB ROBISON & HUGH
ROBISON. damages, suit disc. p 127

Case 11. PAUL D. BUTLER vs JOHN TAYLOR. Damages,
suit disc. p 127

Case 12. JOHN COPPOCK vs BARNHART SPECK & MARY DAVIS
adm of estate of THOMAS DAVIS, dec. Debt of $69.50,
damages. Suit disc. p 127

Case 13. JOHN COMPTON JR vs GEORGE NEWCOM, Sheriff
of Montgomery Co. Sundries: books, clothes, grocer-
ies, etc - $4000, damage $1100. Suit disc. p 127

Case 14. JONAS WADE vs DAVID BRUEN. Trespass, damages. suit disc. p 127

Case 15. STATE vs HENRY LINDSAY. Indictment for
misdemeanor. Nonappearance. p 127

Case 16. STATE vs THOMAS CUNNINGHAM. Indictment for
adultery. Nonappearance. p 128

Case 17. BENJAMIN MULFORD vs DANIEL GRIFFIN. Cove-

Term of December, 1805 continued

nant broken, damages. Nonappearance. p 128

Case 18. ISAAC REED vs DANIEL GRIFFIN. Trespass, damages. Nonappearance. p 128

Case 19. REYNARD SNIP vs ABRAHAM CLAPMIRE. Damages, nonappearance. p 128

Term of April, 1806

Case 1. STATE vs DANIEL COOPER. Debt of $50 acknow-ledged by COOPER and THOMAS CUMMIFORD before DANIEL SYMMES, Judge of Supreme Court at Dayton. Appearance bond for CUMMIFORD, Common Pleas Court, August 1805 term. CUMMIFORD failed to appear; neither he nor COOPER paid bond. Judgement of Court that COOPER to pay $50 bond, $7.64 costs. pp 129, 130

Case 2. STATE vs FRANCIS PATTERSON & ROBERT PATTER-SON. On 20 August, 1805, the defendants assaulted EDWARD PAGE in Dayton Twp, aided HENRY LINDSAY in attempting to remove PAGE, a free black man, from State of Ohio. FRANCIS pled not guilty, jury sum-moned. ROBERT gave notice of intent to file in Su-preme Court, term of November, 1806. No disposition. pp 130, 131, 132

Case 3. STATE vs JEREMIAH YORK. STEPHEN MARSHAL of Dayton Twp, YORK of Green Co on 12 Apr, 1805, assaulted JOHN McKAIG. YORK admitted guilt, fined $2.00, $6.36 costs. p 132, 133

Case 4. ROBERT HUEY vs WILLIAM ELLIS. On 2 Jan, 1805 at Dayton, agreement to exchange $10 and horse belonging to ELLIS for HUEY's mare and colt. HUEY charged horse was unsound, nonpayment of $10, sued for damages of $125.00. ELLIS refuted agreement. Jury summoned: JAMES HANNA, AMOS HIGGINS, SAMUEL HOWARD, THOMAS JOHN, DANIEL LEARY, ANTHONY LOGAN, MAXFIELD LUDLOW, CHARLES MORGAN, DAVID H. MORRIS, WILLIAM NEWCOM, MATTHIAS PARSON, MATTHEW PATTON. Found ELLIS guilty, HUEY to recover $20.00, $33.60 costs. pp 133, 134

Case 5. ANDREW HAYS vs JAMES THOMSON. On 28 Dec, 1804 at Dayton, debt of $400. THOMSON pled not guilty of failure to pay. Jury summoned: LUTHER BRUEN, AMOS HIGGINS, SAMUEL HOWARD, THOMAS JOHN, DANIEL LEARY, ANTHONY LOGAN, MAXFIELD LUDLOW, JOHN MILLER, CHARLES MORGAN, WILLIAM NEWCOM, MATTHIAS

Term of April, 1806 continued

PARSON, MATTHEW PATTON. Found THOMSON innocent, HAYS to take nothing, THOMSON to recover $19.64 costs. pp 135, 136

Case 6. RALPH FRENCH vs JAMES MILLER. On 10 July, 1804, MILLER & AMOS DOROUGH signed note for $96.50; failed to pay. DOROUGH not found by sheriff to answer summons. MILLER failed to appear in court to defend; FRENCH to recover entire debt of $96.55 from MILLER, costs of $4.58. pp 136, 137

Case 7. JONATHAN TULLIS JR vs GEORGE F. TENNERY & WILLIAM CLARK. On 7 Jan, 1804, defendants signed note of $88.00; failed to pay. TENNERY & CLARK admitted guilt, TULLIS to recover debt, $8.18 damages, $10.05 costs. pp 137, 138, 139

Case 8. ALMERINE MARSHALL vs GEORGE SMITH. On 2 Feb, 1803, SMITH owed $416.26, refused to pay. In court, SMITH failed to appear. MARSHALL to recover his debt, $68.16 damages, $11.06 costs. pp 139, 140

Case 9. STEPHEN LUDLOW vs DANIEL C. COOPER. On 1 March, 1805, LUDLOW had worked for COOPER at rate of $12.50 per mo, amounting to $108.50, plus previous debt of $100. COOPER admitted fault, charged LUDLOW with damages of $53.82. LUDLOW to recover $53.82 debt, $10.62 costs. pp 140, 141, 142

Case 10. PEYTON SHORT vs DAVID LUCAS. on 12 Oct, 1804, signed note for $107, failed to pay. LUCAS admitted guilt. SHORT to recover debt, $9.81 damage, $11.65 costs. pp 142, 143

Case 11. PEYTON SHORT vs MICHAEL WILLIAMS. On 12 July, 1804, signed note for $202.50, failed to pay. WILLIAMS admitted guilt. SHORT to recover debt, $18.30 damage, $12.45 costs. pp 144, 145

Case 12. PEYTON SHORT vs STEPHEN DAVIS. On 3 Oct, 1804, signed note for $60.00, failed to pay. DAVIS admitted guilt. SHORT to recover debt, $5.40 damage, $12.29 costs. pp 145, 146, 147

Case 13. JOHN DENN on demise of SAMUEL THOMSON & DANIEL FERREL vs DANIEL C. COOPER. on 1 Jan, 1802, DENN demised land (200 acres in Sec 10, Twp 1, R 7) for term of 10 yrs. COOPER ejected DENN from land on 2 Jan, 1802. DENN sued for damages of $100.00; COOPER failed to defend. DENN to recover possession

Term of April, 1806 continued

of property, damages and costs totalling $9.81. pp 147, 148, 149

Case 14. SAMUEL THOMSON vs MARTIN MYERS. On 12 Nov, 1804, note for $220 debt made, failure to pay. MYERS claimed partial payment, outstanding balance of $121.48. THOMSON to recover debt, $12.19 costs. pp 149, 150

Case 15. PEYTON SHORT vs JAMES CORY. On 2 Aug, 1804 signed note for $80.00, failed to pay. CORY admitted guilt. SHORT to recover debt, $8.28 damage, $10.53 costs. pp 150, 151

Case 16. ARCHIBALD LOGAN vs DAVID REID & ROBERT PAT-TERSON. On 10 Sept, 1804, note for $173.45 debt signed, failed to pay. Suit brought, charging $16.90 damages. REID & PATTERSON admitted guilt, LOGAN to recover debt, $16.59 damages, $8.56 costs. Copy of original note: "ARCHIBALD LOGAN of State of KY..." pp 152, 153

Case 17. JAMES THOMSON vs DAVID RIFFLE. Suit disc. p 153

Case 18. GEORGE KUNS vs GEORGE SHEIDLER & MARY, his wife. Damages, suit disc. p 153

Case 19. GEORGE KUNS vs MICHAEL MOYERS. Damages $1000, suit disc. p 153

Case 20. STATE vs HENRY LINDSAY. Indictment for misdemeanor. Absent from court baliwick. p 153

Case 21. BENJAMIN MULFORD vs DANIEL GRIFFIN. Damages. Absent from court baliwick. p 154

Case 22. PEYTON SHORT vs JESSE EDWARDS. Debt, damages. Absent from court baliwick. p 154

Case 23. ISAAC REED vs DANIEL GRIFFIN. Trespass, damage. Absent from court baliwick. p 154

Term of August, 1806

Case 1. STATE vs DAVID M. SHARP. Case heard before CHRISTOPHER CURTNER, JP. On 27 Jan, 1806, SHARP, ROBERT PATTERSON & DAVID REID appeared before DANIEL C. COOPER, JOSEPH REYBURN & CURTNER, all JP's, to acknowledge debt of $500 each to state if SHARP did

Term of August, 1806 continued

not appear at next court session. Grand Jury: CHRISTOPHER CURTNER, JOHN AINSWORTH, JOB WESTFALL, DANIEL KREIB, LEONARD WOLF, JOHN PAULLY, ROBERT WILSON, JOHN MIKESELL, DAVID LAMME, JAMES THOMSON, SAMUEL McCORMACK, SAMUEL FREEMAN, PAUL D. BUTLER, JAMES MILLER, SAMUEL MORRISON. SHARP of State of KY on 27 Jan, 1806 assaulted JEROM HOLT with loaded pistol, attempting murder. SHARP failed to appear for trial in April, bound over to August term. SHARP pled not guilty. Cause removed to Supreme Court, change of venue to Warren Co, OH. pp 155, 156, 157

Case 2. STATE vs DAVID M. SHARP. Writ from CHRISTOPHER CURTNER as above, posting appearance bond. On 27 Jan, 1806, SHARP assaulted EDWARD PAGE, a free black man, attempting to remove PAGE to State of KY. SHARP failed to appear at April term, bound over to August. SHARP pled not guilty. Cause removed to Supreme Court, change of venue to Warren Co, OH. pp 157, 158, 159

Case 3. STATE vs PETER CLAWSON. Grand Jury: ROBERT PATTERSON, JONATHAN MOTE, JAMES FRAZER, DAVID SQUIER, ROBERT EDGAR, JOHN HUSTON, JOHN STUART, JOHN HARRIS, JAMES McCABE, TOBIAS WHITESEL, GEORGE WESTFALL, ANDREW HAYS, JACOB CRULL, JAMES PORTER, JOHN BAILEY. On 29 July, 1806, CLAWSON of Washington Twp assaulted SAMUEL HOPKINS in Dayton Twp. CLAWSON admitted guilt fined $2.08. p 160, 161

Case 4. STATE vs ALEXIS DUBOIS & FELIX DUBOIS. On recognizance, suit disc. p 161

Case 5. STATE vs JOHN TAYLOR. On recognizance, suit disc. p 161

Case 6. THOMAS BROWN vs JOHN MANNING. Debt, damage. Abated by death of plaintiff. p 161

Case 7. NICHOLAS HORNER vs WILLIAM BROOKIE. Debt, damage. Suit disc. p 161

Case 8. JOB WESTFALL vs JACOB BROWN. On 5 Jan, 1797 bond of $100 owed plaintiff. BROWN absconded. Sheriff ordered to find BROWN, hold for term of Dec, 1805. In Dec, 1805, sheriff reported he had levied right of preemption on east quarter Sec 5, Twp 1, R 6, valued at $300. Defendant did not appear in Dec nor in April, 1806, notice having been given in newspapers, etc. August, 1806, BROWN failed to appear,

Term of August, 1806 continued

in default. WESTFALL submitted claim against BROWN for debt and interest of $157.65. JAMES THOMSON submitted claim for money paid, work done; allowed $315 by auditors DAVID REID, JOHN FOLKERTH, ROBT. NEWCOM. Court ordered auditors to sell land to satisfy plaintiff, others. Copy of original 1797 note attached, granting land to WESTFALL if BROWN in default. Signed JACOB BROWN, JOB WESTFALL. Witness: JAMES THOMSON, ISAAC OSBORN. Endorsement of affidavit: statement of the claim entered in my office 9 Oct, 1801. JAMES FINDLAY. Note from WESTFALL, ceding land interest to THOMSON. $464.50 recvd by THOMSON on behalf of himself, as assignee of WESTFALL. pp 162, 163, 164, 165

Case 9. THOMAS WILSON vs CHARLES MURRAY. Damages, suit disc. p 165

Case 10. JAMES LAPELLE & FRANCIS LAPELLE vs JOHN BAPTISTE PETRIMOULX. On 1 Oct, 1804, note for $827.00 to be paid at Detroit. Plaintiffs sued for damages of $1600. PETRIMOULX admitted partial debt. Plaintiffs recover $627.26 debt, $13.23 costs. pp 165, 166, 167

Case 11. WILLIAM KING & JOHN McALLISTER vs GEORGE SMITH. KING & McALLISTER represented by JOHN ALEXANDER, atty. On 18 May, 1802, note signed for $1004 at Jonesboro, Washington Co, Tennessee. SMITH to repay in $251 increments or in marketable deer skins & furs, in the valuation of DAVID DEADERICK, merchant. Failure to pay, suit filed. SMITH claimed balance due only $168.75. Plaintiffs recover $168.75 debt, $13.14 costs. Copy of original note: SMITH a sadler by occupation, KING & McALLISTER identified as merchants of Jonesboro. Witness: MOSES RAWLINGS. pp 167, 168, 169, 170

Case 12. JAMES THOMSON vs ANDREW HAYS. on 28 Dec, 1804, agreemt to pay $100 in whiskey or horses. HAYS represented by ELIAS GLOVER, atty, said above agreemt not his act. Jury summoned: EVAN BALLINGER, HENRY BOWSER, ABIATHER DAVIS, WILLIAM HAMER, WILLIAM LUCE, WILLIAM MASON, JAMES MILLEGAN, WILLIAM NEAL, ANDREW SINK, ANDREW THARP, JONATHAN WATKINS, WILLIAM WILLIS. HAYS found guilty, THOMSON to recover $104 damages, $20.48 costs. Original note attached witnessed by ARCHIBALD GRAHAM, DANIEL BAXTER. pp 170, 171, 172

Case 13. JOHN COPPOCK vs BARNHART SPECK, surviving

Term of August, 1806 continued

obligor of SPECK & THOMAS DAVIS, dec. On 29 Oct, 1804, jointly signed note for $69.50, failed to pay. Suit brought for debt, $25 damages. SPECK failed to defend, COPPOCK to recover $69.50, $3.83 damages, $9.94 costs. Copy of original note signed BARNHART SPECK in german script, THOS. DAVIS. Witness: STEPHEN LUDLOW, JAMES NOLAN. pp 172, 173

Case 14. SAMUEL FREEMAN vs PETER McCREA & BARNHART SPECK. FREEMAN had recovered $50 debt, $10.44 damages against AMOS DOROUGH. McCREA & SPECK pledged to pay if DOROUGH failed. Sheriff GEORGE NEWCOM, JEROM HOLT & CHRISTOPHER FRITZ gave notice to SPECK & McCREA of debt, damages due. Both failed to appear in court to defend; FREEMAN to recover debt, $3.56 damages, $20.39 costs. pp 174, 175

Case 15. DAVID BAY vs FRANCIS DILTS. BAY sued for damages of $100, failed to appear in court, case continued to August term. BAY again failed to appear, in default. DILTS to recover $3.00 costs. p 176

Case 16. ARCHIBALD STEELE vs JAMES DENNISTON. Plaintiff had recovered against JOHN BRADY for $24.67 debt, $10.26 costs, failed to pay. DENNISTON, pledge for BRADY, now held responsible by STEELE. DENNISTON failed to appear, STEELE to recover debt, $1.24 damage, $20.59 costs. pp 177, 178

Case 17. ABNER SEABURN vs DAVID RIFFLE. In 1805, ABNER had horse valued at $100, became lost. On same day, DAVID found horse, knowing owner, converted horse to his use. RIFFLE pled innocent. Jury summoned, SEABURN failed to appear. RIFFLE to recover $12.77 costs. pp 180, 181, 182

Case 18. PEYTON SHORT vs WILLIAM MADDAN. In 1803, note for $50 + interest. MADDAN refuted debt, jury summoned. MADDAN admitted fault. SHORT to recover $99.60, $12.71 costs. Copy of original note signed WILLIAM MADDEN. pp 180, 181, 182

Case 19. PEYTON SHORT vs JOHN MANN. On 9 July, 1804 note for $120.00. MANN refuted debt, jury summoned. MANN admitted fault. SHORT to recover debt, $17.10 damages, $12.40 costs. Copy of original note signed JOHN MANN. pp 182, 183

Case 20. PEYTON SHORT vs JOHN BATRELL. On 10 June, 1804, note for $60.00. BATRELL refuted debt, jury

Term of August, 1806 continued

summoned. BATRELL admitted fault. SHORT to recover debt, $18.35 damages, $12.50 costs. Copy of original note, signed JOHN (x) BATRELL. pp 180, 181, 182

Case 21. PEYTON SHORT vs PETER SUNDERLAND. On 5 Oct 1804 note for $81.00. SUNDERLAND represented by JOSEPH H. CRANE, atty, admitted debt. SHORT to recover debt, $9.10 damages, $12.20 costs. Copy of original note signed PETER (x) SUNDERLAND, witness JONATHAN DONNEL. pp 185, 186

Case 22. PEYTON SHORT vs PETER SUNDERLAND. On 25 July, 1804 note for $320.00. Suit filed for $400 damages. SUNDERLAND admitted debt. SHORT to recover $340.80, $12.25 costs. Copy of original note signed PETER SUNDERLAND, witness ROBERT RENICKS, RALPH FRENCH. pp 186, 187

No case 23, misnumbered by clerks.

Case 24. PEYTON SHORT vs JONATHAN JOHNSTON. On 17 June, 1804, note for $65.00. Debt refuted by JOHNSTON. Jury summoned. JOHNSTON admitted fault. SHORT to recover debt, $8.55 damage, $12.45 costs. Copy of original note attached. pp 188, 189

Case 25. PEYTON SHORT vs JOHN CLINGAN. On 28 Dec, 1804, note for $100.00. Debt refuted by CLINGAN. Jury summoned. CLINGAN admitted fault. SHORT to recover debt, $10 damages, $12.30 costs. Copy of original note attached. Signed JOHN CLINGAN, witness JONATHAN DONNEL. pp 189, 190

Case 26. PEYTON SHORT vs PARKER ADKINS. On 9 July, 1804, note for $60.00. Debt refuted by ADKINS. Jury summoned. ADKINS admitted fault. SHORT to recover debt, $7.70 damages, $12.30 costs. Copy of original note attached. Signed PARKER ADKINS, witness JONATHAN DONNEL. pp 190, 191, 192

Case 27. PEYTON SHORT vs LEWIS WINTERS. On 1 June, 1804, note for $80.00. Debt refuted by WINTERS. Jury summoned. WINTERS admitted fault. SHORT to recover debt, $10.53 damages, $12.40 costs. Copy of original note attached. Signed LEWIS WINTERS, witness JONATHAN DONNEL. pp 192, 193

Case 28. PEYTON SHORT vs JOHN WILLIAMS. On 17 July, 1804, note for $100.00. Debt refuted by WILLIAMS. Jury summoned. WILLIAMS admitted debt of $57.00.

Term of August, 1806 continued

SHORT to recover debt, $12.91 costs. Copy of original note attached. Signed JOHN WILLIAMS, witness JONATHAN DONNEL. pp 194, 195

Case 29. PEYTON SHORT vs JOHN GERARD. On 4 Dec, 1804, note for 601.36 acres of land in Sec 1, Twp 1, R 10 at 37.5 cents per acre. Debt refuted by GERARD. Jury summoned. GERARD admitted fault. SHORT to recover debt and damages, total $256.00. Copy of original note attached. Signed JOHN GERARD, witness JONATHAN DONNEL. pp 195, 196, 197

Case 30. DAVID H. MORRIS vs WILLIAM WINTERS. On 9 Apr, 1805, agreement to allow MORRIS to plant corn in field, maintain fence and crops, split yield 1/3 to WINTERS. By 1 Nov, WINTERS to have harvested his share, give possession of field to MORRIS. WINTERS failed to uphold agreement, indebted for $50 for use and occupation of field. Suit for $100 damages, WINTERS refuted fault. Jury summoned, found WINTERS guilty. MORRIS to recover $8.57 damages, $30.49 costs. pp 198, 199, 200

Case 31. JOHN CLAWSON vs DAVID McCLURE. On 2 March, 1802, note for $224.00 to be paid to CLAWSON in 3 increments, to make pay't to JOHN EWING in 1805. Failed to pay, suit for $500 damages. McCLURE admitted guilt. CLAWSON to recover $104.04, $13.90 costs. Copy of original note. Title given to 100 in Sec 33, Twp 2, R 6 of Miami Purchase. signed JOHN (x) CLAWSON, DAVID McCLURE. Witness: JOHN EWING, NATHAN TOLBERT. pp 201, 202

Case 32. JACOB SPITLER vs HENRY KINZEA. On 27 Jan, 1806, note for $260.00. Signed by HENRY KINZEA & DAVID KINZEA, who is no longer in area. Suit for nonpayment; HENRY admitted debt of $132.60. SPITLER to recover $132.60, $9.47 costs. Copy of original note signed DAVID KINSEY, HENRY KINSEY, both in German script. Witness: SAMUEL BOLTIN, FREDERICK HICK. pp 203, 204

Case 33. GEORGE LARRISON vs MAXFIELD LUDLOW. On 12 Aug, 1804, note for $80.00. Suit brought for nonpayment; LUDLOW admitted guilt. LARRISON to recover debt, $3.20 camages, $9.23 costs. Copy of original note, signed MAXFIELD LUDLOW, witness ARCHIBALD McMULLEN. Note assigned to MOSES OFFERREL on 2 Jan, 1805, signed GEORGE LARRISON, witness JOHN WINTERS. Note assigned to CHARLES MOORE on 25 Feb, 1805,

Term of August, 1806 continued

signed MOSES OFFERREL, witness BUSTARD MOORE. pp 205, 206

Case 34. ELIZABETH JOHN & JOHN JOHN vs JAMES FLIN & ABRAHAM BARNET. On 22 Oct, 1804, note for $51.00. Suit for nonpayment, FLIN & BARNET admitted fault. Plaintiffs recover debt, $2.55 damages, $10.60 costs. Copy of original note witnessed by JOHN PATTERSON, DAVID HUSTON. pp 206, 207

Case 35. JOHN SHIDAKER vs SAMUEL MORRISON. $70 damages sought. SHIDAKER failed to appear, MORRISON to recover $9.23 costs. pp 207, 208

Case 36. Petition by DANIEL BOUZER & ANNA BOWSER. HENRY MOYERS of German Twp, dec, held title to land in Sec 36, T 4, R 4 containing 640 acres; in Sec 18, T 5, R 4 containing 640 acres; in Sec 26, T 3, R 5 containing 250 acres; in Sec 35, T 3, R 5 containing 278 acres. MOYER left 9 children: ANN, wife of DANIEL BOWSER; CHRISTINA, wife of JACOB BOWMAN, both daughters of full age; JOHN, JACOB, PETER, DANIEL, BETSEY & JONAS, minors. Petition requests land (except dower land of 150 acres in Sec 26) to be divided. Heirs to be notified prior to Dec term of court. Division to be made by JOHN SIMMONS, DANIEL PRESSEL, MATTHIAS RIGAL. Maps of divisions made, descriptions of the bounds included, signed JOHN (x) SIMMONS, DANIEL PRESSEL, MATHIAS RIGAL in German script, JAMES WILSON, surveyor of Montgomery Co. pp 208, 209, 210, 211, 212, 213.

Case 37. JOSEPH HARRIS vs HENRY GULLION. Damages; abated by death of defendant. p 214

Case 38. Petition by GEORGE W. SMITH under "An act for relief of insolvent Debtors". Court decided SMITH not eligible, assessed costs of $9.12. p 214

Case 39. ABRAHAM BARNET vs NATHAN SHAW. 2 horses, valued at $150. Discontinued. p 214

Case 40. ISAAC REED vs DANIEL GRIFFIN. Trespass, damages $100. Griffin not found in baliwick. p 214

Case 41. BENJAMIN MULFORD vs DANIEL C. COOPER. Damages, defendant not found. p 214

Case 42. PETER BANTA vs JAMES THATCHER & GEORGE

Term of August, 1806 continued

DOUGHERTY. Damages, def'dants not in baliwick. p 214

Term of December, 1806

Case 1. STATE vs DANIEL FISHER. On 24 Dec, 1805, FISHER assaulted and "carnally did know" ELIZABETH SPECK, wife of BARNHART SPECK. FISHER pled not guilty. Jury summoned: SAMUEL ARCHER, EVAN BALLINGER, ABIATHER DAVIS, JESSE FREIND, WILLIAM LUCE, WILLIAM MASON, JAMES MILLEGAN, WILLIAM NEAL, ANDREW SINKS, ANDREW THARP, JONATHON WATKINS, WILLIAM WILLIS. Found FISHER guilty of trespass and adultery, fined $6.00, costs of $17.63. pp 215, 216

Case 2. STATE vs DANIEL C. COOPER. Grand Jury: ROBT. PATTERSON, JONATHAN MOTE, JAMES FRAZER, DAVID SQUIER, ROBERT EDGAR, JOHN HUSTON, JOHN STEWART, JOHN HARRIS, JAMES McCABE, TOBIAS WHITESEL, GEORGE WEST- FALL, ANDREW HAYS, JACOB CRULL, JAMES PORTER, JOHN BAILY. On 5 July, 1806, COOPER assaulted STEPHEN LUDLOW. In Dec term, COOPER filed intention to appeal to Supreme Court. p 217

Case 3. STATE vs DANIEL FERREL. On 5 Aug, 1806, FERREL of Elizabeth Twp assaulted RODEY (RHODA) WOODS. FERREL admitted guilt, fined $1.00, $6.07 costs. pp 218, 219

Case 4. STATE vs THOMAS ASH. On 19 Apr, 1806, ASH of Dayton Twp assaulted JAMES GARNET. ASH pled guilty, fined $1.00, $4.08 costs. pp 219, 220

Case 5. STATE vs SAMUEL MORRISON. Grand Jury: JOHN FOLKERTH, JAMES BLUE, STEPHEN DYE, AARON TULLIS, OBE- DIAH WINTERS, BENJAMIN KNUP, JOHN NELSON, JOHN VAN- ORSDALL, JOHN H. WILLIAMS, PETER RACHER, JOHN MILLER, SAMUEL McCORMICK, DAVID VANDERPOOL, CALEB HUNT, MAT- THEW PATTON. On 21 May, 1806 and days afterward, MORRISON of Elizabeth Twp kept a publick Tavern with- out a license, and in the same house, did sell a spiritous liquor commonly called Peach Brandy by the half-pint, in contempt of the laws of the state of Ohio. MORRISON pled guilty, fined $6.00, $2.44 costs. pp 220, 221

Case 6. STATE vs BENJAMIN ARCHER. On 29 Sept, 1806, ARCHER of Washington Twp assaulted DANIEL C. COOPER. ARCHER pled guilty, fined $5.00, costs of $4.50. pp 221, 222

Term of December, 1806 continued

Case 7. JOHN FREEMAN vs PETER McCREA & BARNHART SPECK. FREEMAN had recovered $25, costs of $10.50 against AMOS DERROUGH. On 20 May, 1806, McCREA & SPECK stood bond for DERROUGH who failed to pay the judgement. Suit filed, McCREA & SPECK failed to appear and defend. FREEMAN to recover debt, damages and $16.33 costs. pp 222, 223, 224

Case 8. RUTH GREER vs DANIEL FERREL. On 2 Apr, 1805 at Dayton, note signed for $66.67. Failed to pay. FERREL failed to defend suit, GREER recovered $69.88, $12.27 costs. Copy of original note, witness AARON GREER. pp 224, 225, 226

Case 9. DAVID SQUIER & PAUL D. BUTLER vs MAXFIELD LUDLOW. On 18 March, 1805, note for $240.00. Failed to pay, suit for $100 damages. LUDLOW to show evidence of payment. Jury summoned: JOHN BRADFORD, ISAAC CLARK, HENRY CURTNER, JOHN DUNCAN, JESSE EDWARDS, SAMUEL IRVINE, DAVID JONES, CONRAD KASTER, WILLIAM MADDAN, SAMUEL MORRISON, JAMES RIDDLE, JAMES THOMSON. Court recognized partial payt of $65.60. Plaintiffs to recover residue of debt, $23.07 costs. Copy of original note attached. 226, 227, 228

Case 10. PEYTON SHORT vs JESSE EDWARDS. On 30 June, 1804, note for $60.00. Failed to pay. EDWARDS failed to appear, defend suit. SHORT to recover debt, $5.30 damages, $11.88 costs. Copy of original note attached. pp 229, 230

Case 11. JOHN HOLLAND & SARAH HOLLAND vs SAMUEL WARSON. Charge of defamation, damages of $500. Plaintiffs failed to appear at both Aug and Dec terms of court, WARSON to recover $5.00 costs. pp 230, 231

Case 12. SAMUEL ARCHER vs JOHN BIGGER, JAMES BAY & WILLIAM McCANN. On 3 May, 1805, defendants' note for $73.12 payable to WILLIAM CLARK. Note later assigned to FRANCIS DILS. On 26 Jan, 1806, DILS assigned note to ARCHER. Defendants failed to pay, suit brought, $100 damages charged. Defendants failed to defend. ARCHER to recover $77.40 debt and damage, $12.55 costs. Copy of original note, witness MATTHIAS PARSON & RIC'D. MASON. Assignments by CLARK, DILS. pp 231, 232, 233, 234

Case 13. NATHANIEL LYONS vs SAMUEL HA(W)KINS. On 23 Dec, 1805, HAWKINS & GEORGE LOY signed note for $53.78. Failed to pay. Suit filed, $50.00 damages.

Term of December, 1806 continued

LOY not to be found in sheriff's baliwick. HAWKINS failed to appear to defend. LYONS to recover $53.78, $3.22 damages, $11.65 costs. Copy of original note, witness: JAMES LEESEN, JONATHAN LYONS. pp 234, 235, 236

Case 14. BENJAMIN FLINN vs DANIEL C. COOPER. Case heard by Supreme Court at Dayton in Nov, 1806 by First Judge SAMUEL HUNTINGTON, Judges DANIEL SYMMES & GEORGE TOD. Case referred to JOHN MILLER, WILLIAM McCLURE, WILLIAM ROBISON for arbitration, report to Common Pleas next session. Decision: COOPER to bear all costs of suit, make proper title to FLINN or his assignees for Dayton outlot #17. FLINN to pay surveyors fees, purchase money. Court allowed FLINN to recover $37.51 costs. Copy of original note, granting land to FLINN in return of services as a settler. pp 236, 237

Case 15. JAMES THOMSON vs JOSEPH REYBURN, RICHARD STEVENS & JOHN CROY. CROY first charged with unlawful taking of a sorrel colt, 3 yrs old, valued at $60.00, plus horse gear (harness, etc) valued at $65.00. Writ of replevin second against all defendants. Cause referred for arbitration: CROY to pay $1.00, $11.45 costs in first case; all defendants to pay $1.00, $32.34 costs in second case. pp 238, 239

Case 16. PAUL D. BUTLER vs JOHN REID. Breach of contract, damages of $1000. Arbitrators GEORGE NEWCOM, MEEKER SQUIER, JAMES THOMSON: found BUTLER to recover $23.10 debt, $12.12 costs. pp 239, 240, 241

Case 17. SAMUEL WOODS & RHODA WOODS vs DANIEL FERREL. Defamation, damages of $1000. Suit disc. p 242

Case 18. ISAAC REED vs DANIEL GRIFFIN. Trespass, damages, $1000. Suit disc. p 242

Case 19. DANIEL H. FISHER vs PAUL D. BUTLER. Damages $1000, suit disc. p 242

Case 20. JAMES THOMSON vs WILLIAM VANORSDALL. 1 yoke of oxen, wagon, valued at $90, damages $90. Disc. p 242

Case 21. WILLIAM LUDLOW vs WILLIAM HUNTER. Damages $200, defendant not to be found. p 242

Term of April, 1807

Case 1. STATE vs MARTIN MYER. On 20 Nov, 1806, JOHN AIKENS of Dayton Twp, "not having the fear of God before his eyes but being moved and seduced by the devil" assaulted RACHEL AIKENS, beating her with both hands, inflicting mortal bruises. She languished until the next day, 21 Nov, dying of her injuries. MARTIN MYERS, knowing full well that AIKENS had murdered RACHEL, on 21 Nov attempted to hide the crime. MYERS pled not guilty. Indictment quashed, lack of evidence. pp 243, 244, 245

Case 2. STATE vs SAMUEL MORRISON. On 16 Nov, 1806, theft of 8 hogs, valued at $6.00, belonging to MARY LEWIS. MORRISON pled not guilty. Jury summoned: ABRAHAM BARNET, ANDREW BAYLEY, JOHN BENNET, WILLIAM CHENOWITH, DENNIS ENSY, VALENTINE EYLER, STEPHEN JAY, LUDOWICK KEMP, HENRY LEATHERMAN, LEWIS LECHLIDER, ROBERT WEAD, JOSEPH WILSON. Acquited MORRISON. pp 245, 246

Case 3. STATE vs FRANCIS DILTS. On 3 Dec, 1806, DILTS of Washington Twp assaulted GEORGE F. TENNERY at Dayton. DILTS pled guilty, fined $1.00, $4.33 costs. pp 247, 248

Case 4. JAMES THOMSON vs ANDREW HAYS. Defamation, damages of $1000. Case continued. ANDREW HAYS vs JAMES THOMSON. HAYS represented by ELIAS GLOVER, atty. Cases submitted to arbitration by WILLIAM ROBISON, WILLIAM McCLURE, JOHN MILLER & ALEXANDER TELFORD. CHRISTOPHER CURTNER chosen as umpire by arbitrators. THOMSON to pay costs of court, arbitrators. Each defendant to pay costs in case. HAYS to recover $30.73; THOMSON to recover $22.80. Any previous contracts, bonds or obligations between the two parties "from the beginning of the world until 9 March, 1807, shall cease and become void": CURTNER ruling. pp 248, 249, 250, 251

Case 5. ABNER SEABURN vs DAVID SQUIER. On 5 April, 1806, debt of $300 for work performed by SEABURN; SQUIER refuted agreement, claimed SEABURN owed $200 for board, lodging and cash advanced. Jury summoned. Found SQUIER had made agreement, that SEABURN did not perform as promised. SEABURN to recover damages of $17.35, $31.09 costs. SQUIER to appeal to Supreme Court. pp 251, 252, 253

Case 6. DANIEL FERREL vs JOHN SIDICKER. Charged conversion of brown yearling mare worth $120. FERREL

Term of April, 1807 continued

failed to appear, SIDICKER to recover $10.51 costs.
pp 254, 255

Case 7. JOSEPH RAYBURN vs SAMUEL HOPKINS. On 28
May, 1805, note for $68.50. Failed to pay, suit
filed, $25.00 damages. HOPKINS failed to appear to
defend. RAYBURN to recover $66.50 debt, $5.65 damages, $9.45 costs. Copy of original note attached.
pp 255, 256

Case 8. JOHN SIDICKER vs SAMUEL MORRISON. On 7 Aug,
1805, note for $50.00. Failed to pay. MORRISON ad-
mitted guilt. SIDICKER to recover $53.58 debt, costs
of $10.41. Copy of original note witnessed by EPH'M
MORRISON, A.D. BRIER. pp 257, 258

Case 9. BENJAMIN ARCHER vs DANIEL C. COOPER. On 1
Dec, 1806, debt of $200 for goods and merchandise,
previous debt of $100. COOPER failed to defend.
ARCHER amended debt residue to $89.01; to recover
debt, $10.43 costs. pp 259, 260, 261

Case 10. EDMUND MUNGER, JOHN DEVOR & JOHN FOLKERTH,
Commissioners of Montgomery Co vs SAMUEL HOPKINS,
SAMUEL HAWKINS & GEORGE F. TENNERY. HOPKINS, tax
collector of Montgomery Co, HAWKINS & TENNERY his
securitors. Plaintiffs charged balance of $574.04
due to county. Commissioners recovered against
HOPKINS & HAWKINS for $305.15 with 12% interest from
1 Feb, 1806 plus $10.58 costs. (No explanation of
reason TENNERY was excused) pp 261, 262

Case 11. Petition of DAVID LUCAS under "Act for re-
lief of insolvent Debtors". Assets included note due
from GEORGE YOUNT for $8.00. Creditors: JOHN WILLI-
AMS, JAMES McKINNEY, JON. DONNALDS, JOHN FOLKERTH,
JOHN WHINEN, DAVID MORRIS, WILLIAM MADDEN, PEYTON
SHORT. Signed DAVID (x) LUCAS. Relief granted.
JOHN COPPOCK named Trustee to distribute assets to
creditors. LUCAS to pay costs of $9.12. pp 263, 264

Case 12. AARON RICHARDSON vs JOSIAH CLAWSON, constable of Elizabeth Twp. Horse valued at $80. Indict-
ment quashed. CLAWSON to recover $9.27 costs. p 264

Case 13. PATRICK LAFFERTY vs SAMUEL HOPKINS, constable of Dayton Twp. Horse valued at $80. Indictment
quashed. HOPKINS to recover $2.11 costs. p 265

Case 14. JACOB HECK vs GEORGE F. TENNERY. Damages

Term of April, 1807 continued

$200. Case abated by death of plaintiff. p 265

Case 15. JOHN LYON vs WILLIAM TOPPIN. Damages $100, suit disc. p 265

Case 16. RALPH FRENCH vs PATRICK LAFFERTY. Defamation $500. Defendant not to be found. p 265

Term of August, 1807

Case 1. STATE vs THOMAS NOWLAND & JOSEPH DODDS JR. On 9 Dec, 1806, defendants, of Washington Twp, disturbed the peace in Dayton Twp. NOWLAND pled not guilty, DODDS admitted guilt. Jury found NOWLAND guilty. Each fined $5.00. NOWLAND to pay costs of $10.66, DODDS cost of $3.34. pp 266, 267, 268

Case 2. STATE vs JOSEPH H. CRANE, JOSEPH PEIRCE & GEORGE W. SMITH. Grand Jury: WILLIAM DODDS, HORATIO G. PHILLIPS, PETER LEHAMN, ROBERT EDGAR, JOHN BRADFORD, JAMES PATTERSON, JOHN PATTERSON, ROBERT CULBERTSON, CHARLES TULL, NOAH TIBBALS, ABIATHER DAVIS, JOHN NEWCOM, JAMES BROWN, JEROM HOLT, THOMAS CLAWSON. Defendants of Dayton Twp, charged with disturbing peace on 26 March, 1807, breaking windows in the Publick Schoolhouse. CRANE not found by sheriff; PEIRCE & SMITH pled guilty, fined $2.00 each, costs of $6.90. pp 268, 269

Case 3. STATE vs GEORGE LESLIE. On recognizance, discharged. p 270

Case 4. JOHN D. CAMPBELL vs JOHN AINSWORTH. Bay horse valued at $150, lost on 30 Dec, 1804. In AINSWORTH's possession the same day, knowing the owner of the horse. AINSWORTH pled not guilty. Case referred to JAMES MILLER Coroner, DAVID REID & WILLIAM McCLURE for arbitration. AINSWORTH to recover $36.69 costs from CAMPBELL. pp 270, 271, 272

Case 5. DANIEL C. COOPER vs STEPHEN LUDLOW. On 1 Jan, 1806, accused COOPER of treason, charged with slander, defamation. At trial, COOPER failed to appear; LUDLOW to recover $16.75 costs. pp 272, 273

Case 6. HEZEKIAH ROBISON vs SAMUEL McCORMICK. $400 damages. At trial, ROBISON failed to press charges, McCORMICK to recover $11.15 costs. pp 274, 275

Case 7. ICHABOD CORWIN vs JOHN OWINGS. On 8 Oct,

Term of August, 1807 continued

1806, note for $64.00. Failed to pay; OWINGS ad-
mitted guilt. CORWIN to recover debt, $2.60 damages,
$10.21 costs. Copy of original note signed JOHN
OWINGS, WILLIAM TILLY, witnesses PHILIP DEEBIN,
WILLIAM TELLY. pp 275, 276

Case 8. Petition of GEORGE W. SMITH in "Act for the
relief of an insolvent Debtor". Assets: debts owed
by WILLIAM DAVIS, WILLIAM FANE, JOHN MATTHEWS, PHILIP
A. SUBLETT, JONATHAN DAVIS, WILLIAM CHERVY, JOHN
COMPTON. Creditors: DAVID DEADERICK, ALMERINE MAR-
SHALL, JOHN McCALLESTER, HENRY FRANCIS, JAMES GILL-
INGHAM, PETER WITTLEBERGER, SUSANNAH STOCKDALE, ROB-
ERT BLAKELY, ROBERT HINEMAN, JOHN GARNET, - PRATER,
RICHARD CHURCHWELL, WILLIAM SAUNDERS, - OUSLEY, JOHN
CHESTER, SAMUEL ALCORN, ALEXANDER MATTHEWS, JOHN SUTH
- LEE, CAPT. NEWBY, DAVID BUCKHANNON, WILLIAM PAINE,
PHILIP SUBLETT, MAJ. STOCKDALE, FREDERICK LINDENBER-
GER & CO, JOHN ASHLEY. Petition granted. GEORGE
NEWCOM, sheriff, apptd Trustee, MATTHEW PATTON secur-
ity. SMITH to pay costs of $9.12.

No case 9, misnumbered by clerks.

Case 10. JOHN RHOADS vs DANIEL C. COOPER, surviving
obligor. $600 debt, damage $100. Writ quashed.
COOPER to recover $8.50 costs. p 279

Case 11. PAUL D. BUTLER & DAVID REID vs ROBERT PAT-
TERSON. Debt $280, damage $50. Suit disc. p 279

Case 12. DANIEL C. COOPER vs JOHN BODLY. Damage
$150, suit disc. p 279

Case 13. JOHN McCLELLAND vs JAMES FLINN. Horse
valued at $100. Suit disc. p 279

Case 14. SAMUEL MOORE vs GEORGE LONG. Damage $100,
suit disc. p 279

Case 15. JOHN GUEST, LEWIS ATTERBURY & CHARLES BANK-
ER vs JOHN COMPTON. Damages $1000. Suit disc. p 280

Case 16. ABNER SEABURN vs GEORGE CAN. Debt $70,
damages. Defendant not in jurisdiction. p 280

Term of December, 1807

Case 1. WILLIAM SNODGRASS vs WILLIAM ALLISON. SNOD-
GRASS represented by JOHN ALEXANDER, atty. On 1 May,

Term of December, 1807 continued

1806, agreement: ALLISON to use fenced field belonging to SNODGRASS, 25 acres in Sec 23, Twp 2, R 7, for 1/3 yield of corn, oats crops. ALLISON to occupy house on 1.5 acres for rent of flax crop on 1/2 acre. On 10 Aug, 1806, $50 debt for goods. Failure to pay. ALLISON claimed delivery of corn, payt of debt, gave evidence to show Plaintiff indebted for work done. Jury summoned: WILLIAM CASTOR, SAMUEL CRIPE, JAMES ENSY, JAMES EWING, WILLIAM GADDIS, JOHN MADDOCK, JOHN QUILLEN, JAMES SMALL, DAVID ULERY, SAMUEL ULRY, JOHN WAGGONER SR, LEONARD WOLF. Found ALLISON not guilty, to recover $49.80 costs. pp 281, 282, 283, 284, 285

Case 2. THOMAS HATCHER vs THOMAS NEWMAN. HATCHER represented by ISAAC G. BURNET. $100 debt, failure to pay. HATCHER failed to appear, NEWMAN to recover $9.92 costs. p 285, 286

Case 3. PAUL D. BUTLER & JEROM HOLT vs MATTHEW PATTON. On 1 May, 1807, horses, cattle and goods were seized, unjustly detained. Suit for $200 damages. PATTON failed to defend, BUTLER & HOLT to recover $.01 damages, $9.12 costs. p 287

Case 4. ABNER SEABURN vs MARTIN MYERS. Charged with taking calico, other materials worth $75.00. SEABURN failed to appear at the trial, MYERS to recover $9.73 costs. p 288

Case 5. DAVID SQUIER vs HUGH McCOLLOM. On 1 June, 1807, debt of $15.00 for work and labor by SQUIER & his servants, other materials. Failure to pay. McCOLLOM refuted debt, charged SQUIER owed $200 for goods before that time. Jury summoned: SAMUEL CRIPE SR, JAMES ENSY, JAMES EWING, WILLIAM GADDIS, WILLIAM KASTER, JOHN MADDOCK, JOHN QUILLEN, HENRY STRADER, SAMUEL ULRY, JOHN WAGGONER SR, LEONARD WOLF. Found SQUIER indebted to McCOLLOM as charged. McCOLLOM to recover $67.66. pp 289, 290, 291, 292

Case 6. ABNER SEABURN vs DAVID REID. $800 debt charged, failure to pay. SEABURN failed to appear; REID to recover $9.73 in costs. pp 292, 293

Case 7. MARTIN MYERS vs MATTHEW PATTON. Charged with unlawfully detaining wagon worth $80, damages of $20. MYERS failed to appear, PATTON to recover $9.87 costs. pp 293, 294

Case 8. FREDERICK JORDAN vs JOHN COMPTON JR. On 15

Term of December, 1807 continued

April, 1806 at Baltimore, to wit at Dayton, note for
$573.47. Failure to pay, suit for $1000 damages.
COMPTON failed to defend, JORDAN to recover $1000,
$12.03 costs. COMPTON to appeal to Supreme Court.
Copy of original note: no witnesses. pp 294, 295,
296

Case 9. JOHN GULLION vs MATTHEW PATTON. Unlawful
seizing and retaining of a grey mare valued at $40,
damages of $20. GULLION failed to appear, PATTON to
recover $7.98 costs. pp 296, 297

Case 10. MARTIN EARHART vs DAVID REID. On 12 Aug,
1806, note for $95.00. Refusal to pay. REID
admitted debt, EARHART to recover debt, $2.10 costs.
Copy of original note. Witness: GREEN B. FIELDS.
Endorsement on 3 Sept, 1806: EARHART transferred his
interest to ANDREW HAYS, witness JOHN GORDON & DAVID
HAYS. Endorsement of 28 Jan, 1807: HAYS assigned
note to JOHN COMPTON JR, witness ROBERT CLARK. pp
297, 298, 299

Case 11. Petition of JOHN BAPTISTE PETRIMOULX in
"Act for relief of insolvent Debtors". "Destitute of
property of every description..." Creditors: JAMES &
FRANCIS LAPELLE, JAMES & BAPTIST BABY, DAVID CLARK.
Court found PETRIMOULX entitled to relief, to pay
costs of $10.94. pp 299, 300

Case 12. Petition of JOHN OWINGS in "Act for relief
of insolvent Debtors". Creditors: MATHEW HEARBERD,
DANIEL HOLE, WILLIAM COMLEY & brother, WILLIAM ROBI-
SON, ICHABOD CORWIN, CAPT. B. ROBBS, HENRY & JOHN
McGEE, JOSHUA HOLBS, - ANDERSON, AMOS DOROUGH, -
WATTS, JOHN MARTIN, - TAYLOR, - PEW. Asset: horse
lent to WILLIAM TILLY, now in KY. Court found OWINGS
entitled to relief, to pay costs of $8.10. pp 300,
301, 302

Case 13. JAMES REYBURN ads JAMES RITTENHOUSE. Writ
requested of CHRISTOPHER CURTNER, JP in case where
plaintiff RITTENHOUSE sued REYBURN for debt. On 13
June, 1807, $10 note of judgement written. DAVID
RIFFLE & JOHN GULLION acknowledged bail for defendant
REYBURN who was to pay debt, $.25 interest, $1.67
costs. Writ from CURTNER dated 17 Dec, 1807. Proceedings quashed by court. RITTENHOUSE to recover
$8.91 costs. pp 302, 303

Case 14. JOHN GULLION vs JOHN LADLEY. Damages $100,

Term of December, 1807 continued

suit disc. p 304

Case 15. REBECCA COPUS vs JACOB HARTER. Damages
$1000, suit disc. p 304

Case 16. JAMES BIGGER vs JOSIAH CLAWSON, Constable
of Washington Twp. 2 silver watches, worth $50, suit
disc. p 304

Case 17. WILLIAM ROBISON vs JOSEPH REYBURN. Damages
$100, suit disc. p 304

Case 18. JOSEPH PEIRCE vs JOHN HUNT. Damages $60,
suit disc. p 304

Case 19. HEZEKIAH ROBISON vs SAMUEL McCORMICK.
Damages $400, McCORMICK not found by sheriff. p 304

Case 20. STATE vs SPARLING YOUNG, WILLIAM KYSER,
CHARLES McDONALD, GEORGE BOTKIN, GEORGE KIRKPATRICK &
WILLIAM McCORMICK. Indictment for riot at HUNTs,
defendants not to be found. p 305

Case 21. STATE vs SPARLING YOUNG, WILLIAM KYSER,
CHARLES McDONALD, GEORGE BOTKIN, GEORGE KIRKPATRICK &
WILLIAM McCORMICK. Indictment for riot at CLAWSONs,
defendants not to be found. p 305

Case 22. GEORGE F. TENNERY vs JOHN DRISCOL, admin.
of estate of JOHN AIKENS, dec. Debt of $50, damages
$25. Sheriff failed to summon. p 305

Term of April, 1808

Case 1. STATE vs JOSEPH H. CRANE, JOSEPH PEIRCE &
GEORGE W. SMITH. Recognizance dated 26 March, 1807,
made before CHRISTOPHER CURTNER, JP. Defendants,
HORATIO G. PHILLIPS & WILLIAM BOMBERGER appeared,
agreed to owe State $25.00 each as appearance bond
for the defendants. Grand Jury: WILLIAM DODDS,
HORATIO G. PHILLIPS, PETER LEHMAN, ROBERT EDGAR, JOHN
BRADFORD, JAMES PATTERSON, JOHN PATTERSON, ROBERT
CULBERTSON, CHARLES TULL, NOAH TIBBALS, ABIATHER
DAVIS, JOHN NEWCOM, JAMES BROWN, JEROM HOLT, THOMAS
CLAWSON. Defendants charged with disturbing peace on
26 March, 1807; broke 10 panes of glass in Publick
Schoolhouse. CRANE failed to appear at first hear-
ing, carried to next term, admitted guilt. Fined
$2.00, $1.45 costs. pp 305, 306

Term of April, 1808 continued

Case 2. STATE vs JOHN ENOCH & ABRAHAM HILDERBRAND. Grand Jury: JOHN COMPTON, JOHN WEBB, THOMAS McNUTT, JAMES MILLER, JAMES MILES, ABRAHAM HILDERBRAND, ABRAHAM NEFF, WILLIAM GRIFFIN, JAMES AIKEN, SAMUEL BROADBERY, OLIVER VOORHES, JACOB MULLENDORE, CALEB HUNT, JOHN VANORSDALE, GEORGE FRYBERGER, ANTHONY LOGAN. HILDERBRAND of German Twp, ENOCH of Dayton charged with disturbing the peace by fighting on 25 Aug, 1807 in Dayton Twp. HILDERBRAND pled guilty, ENOCH not guilty. Jury summoned: OWEN --, LUTHER BRUEN, HENRY CURTNER, DAVID DUNCAN, SMITH GREGG, JOHN GRIMES, GEORGE GROVE, JOHN HUNT, JAMES NOLAN, RICHARD SUNDERLAND, JOHN VANORSDALL, BAZEL WILLIAMS. Found ENOCH innocent. HILDERBRAND to pay $4.00 fine, $10.84 costs. pp 309, 310, 311

Case 3. STATE vs JOHN WEAVER. Grand Jury: ABRAHAM HILDERBRAND, JACOB KUNS, WILLIAM MASON, JOHN MIKESELL, DANIEL MILLER, JOHN MILLER, AARON NUTT, MATHEW PATTON, JOSEPH REYBURN, CHARLES ROE, CHRISTIAN SHIVELY, LUDWICK SPEECE, JOHN VANELY, JAMES WILSON, NATHAN WORLEY. On 20 March, 1808 and times thereafter, WEAVER sold whiskey without a license. Plea of guilty, fined $.25, $9.42 costs. pp 311, 312

Case 4. STATE vs THOMAS CLAWSON. Assault on JAMES RIDDLE. Dismissed. p 313

Case 5. WILLIAM SWISHER vs JAMES DENNISTON. On 27 March, 1805, note for debt of $288.35. Failure to pay. At trial, DENNISTON failed to defend. SWISHER to recover debt, $35.50 damages, $26.19 costs. DENNISTON to appeal to Supreme Court. Copy of original note; witness JOEL SHILTON, JOHN (x) CLAWSON, GEORGE (x) MIXELL (MIKESELL). pp 313, 314, 315, 316, 317

Case 6. GEORGE RIFFLE vs MARTIN MYERS. Accused of stealing suit of cotton clothes, vests, overalls, other goods, held for one month as surety from 15 Feb, 1807 until 16 March. At trial, MYERS failed to defend. RIFFLE to recover $.01 damages, $10.33. pp 317, 318

Case 7. SAMUEL THOMSON vs MATTHEW PATTON. Detained goods belonging to THOMSON against pledges on 30 June, 1807; held wagon, 4 oxen. Damages of $200 claimed. At trial, PATTON failed to defend, THOMSON to recover $.01 damages, $11.37 costs. pp 319, 320

Case 8. CHRISTIAN NULL vs DANIEL C. COOPER. On 17

Term of April, 1808 continued

Nov, 1801, note for $260 debt. Pre-emptive land purchased from J. C. SYMMES, repayment of debt based on payments due Congress. COOPER refuted debt as not his deed. Jury summoned; COOPER failed to defend. NULL to recover debt, $53 damages, $11.52 costs. Copy of original note, witness WILLIAM WILLS, C. KILGORE. pp 320, 321, 322

Case 9. JOHN DODSON vs DAVID SQUIER. DODSON represented by N. (NICHOLAS) LONGWORTH, atty. Agreement to do work on house of HUGH McCOLLUM (which SQUIER had undertaken to finish). DODSON to recv $500, Cincinnati wages for house carpenter. Failure to pay. SQUIER charged money owed him for goods, a mare, medicine, board for DODSON and his apprentices including JAMES BLAIR, tools destroyed. At trial, SQUIER failed to defend suit, present his evidence. DODSON to recover $500 damages, $15.02 costs. pp 323, 324, 325, 326

Case 10. JOHN RHOADS vs DANIEL C. COOPER, surviving obligor of COOPER & ISRAEL LUDLOW, dec. On 16 Nov, 1801, note for $600.00 signed at Cincinnati. Refusal to pay. At trial, COOPER failed to defend. RHOADS to recover debt, $232.00 damages, $12.48 costs. COOPER to appeal to Supreme Court. Copy of original note, witnessed by C. KILGORE, W. W. STUART. pp 326, 327, 328

Case 11. JAMES W. SLOAN vs JOHN COMPTON JR. On 5 Oct, 1804, note for $1198.62 signed at Baltimore, to wit at Dayton. Refusal to pay. COMPTON admitted debt of $598.62. SLOAN to recover $598.62, $124.33 damages, $12.68 costs. Copy of original note, witnessed by THOMAS BAXLEY. pp 328, 329, 330

Case 12. HUGH ANDREWS vs JOHN HUNT & NATHANIEL HUNT. On 1 Nov, 1807, enclosed tract at Sec 14, T 2, R 8, second tract at Sec 13, T 2, R 8, were broken into, timber cut down in value of $50. Defendants failed to defend suit. ANDREW to recover damages, value to be set by jury: JAMES ARCHER, JOHN BOWMAN, JACOB CROW, HENRY CURTNER, FREDERICK FOUTS, ANDREW HOOD, JAMES NOLAN, JAMES PORTER, HENRY SHEIDLER, RICHARD SUNDERLAND, ROBERT SWIFT, MARTIN WYBRIGHT. Damage set at $4.00, received by ANDREWS, $23.15 costs. pp 330, 331, 332

Case 13. JOHN GARTH vs JOSEPH REYBURN. On 29 July, 1805, $170.25 note signed. Refusal to pay. At Term of April, 1808 continued

trial, REYBURN failed to defend. GARTH to recover $140 on debt, $20.85 damages, $10.93 costs. Copy of original note: "JOHN GARTH of Scott Co, KY"; bond given for the season of a stud horse with five mares, ensurance of foals. Witnesses ARTHUR VOINTS, JAMES CORD. pp 332, 333, 334

Case 14. JACOB CRIPE vs WILLIAM McCANN. On 11 Dec, 1803, notes signed for $46 cash, "value received" to be repaid with 32 gal. whiskey @ $.75 each, further sum of $150. McCANN admitted debt of $85.00. CRIPE to recover $85.00, $11.32 costs. Copy of original notes, witness DAVID BAY. pp 335, 336, 337, 338

Case 15. PEYTON SHORT vs JOHN HUNT & NATHANIEL HUNT. On 15 July, 1805, $1500 note signed. Failure to pay. Defendants refuted debt. At trial, defendants admitted debt. SHORT to recover debt, $153.00 damages, $12.00 costs. Copy of original note, witness WILLIAM MILLAR. pp 338, 339, 340, 341

Case 16. JAMES McCLURE vs PETER MUSSELMAN. On 12 Nov, 1805, $150 note. Failure to pay, $25.00 damages. At trial, MUSSELMAN failed to defend. McCLURE to recover $41 debt residue, $7.29 damage, $11.45 costs. Copy of original note signed PETER MUSSELMAN in German script, witness JOSEPH REYBURN, DAVID MUSSELMAN. Endorsements of payt witnessed PETER SHOAFF. pp 341, 342, 343

Case 17. DAVID REID vs HUGH McCOLLOM. Writ of CHRISTOPHER CURTNER, JP, requested by court, certifying proceedings. REID had stood bail for default in McCOLLOM vs ABNER SEABURN. REID charged errors by CURTNER in hearing case. Affidavit filed by McCOLLOM. Court quashed suit. McCOLLOM to recover $10.09 costs. pp 343, 344, 345

Case 18. JOHN COMPTON JR vs AUSBORN COOPER. On 3 July, 1807, $44.89 note signed. Failure to pay. At trial, COOPER failed to defend. COMPTON to recover debt, $10.09 costs. Copy of original note, witness ROBERT CLARK. pp 347, 348, 349

Case 19. DANIEL C. COOPER vs ROBERT PATTERSON. On 26 Dec, 1803 at Cincinnati, $1000 note signed. Failure to pay, $150 damages. At trial, PATTERSON failed to defend. COOPER to recover $493.23 debt, $39.10 damage, $13.32 costs. PATTERSON filed notice of appeal to Supreme Court. Copy of original note, "RO-

Term of April, 1808 continued

BERT PATTERSON of State of KY"; witness JAMES FINDLEY
JAMES MARSHALL, MATTHEW PATTON. pp 347, 348, 349

Case 20. JAMES THOMSON vs PAUL D. BUTLER. On 1 Sept
1806, debt of $40 for work, use of THOMSON's horses,
oxen, wagons. Refusal to pay. BUTLER refuted agreement, claimed THOMSON owed $50 in goods and labor.
Jury summoned: JOHN BOWMAN, SAMUEL CAVENDIER, JACOB
CROW, FREDERICK FOUTS, WILLIAM GEORGE, ANDREW HOOD,
JOHN HUNT, JAMES NOLAN, JAMES PORTER, ROBERT SWIFT,
MARTIN WAYBRICHT. Found BUTLER not guilty, to recover $30.49 costs. pp 349, 350, 351, 352

Case 21. JOSHUA RUSSEL, RHODA RUSSEL & JOHN ROBB vs
SAMUEL THOMSON & BAZEL WILLIAMS. RHODA the wife of
JOSHUA. On 20 Feb, 1807, $30.25 note made to RHODA
RUSSEL before her marriage and to JOHN ROBB. Fail-
ure to pay. At trial, THOMSON & WILLIAMS failed to
defend. Plaintiffs to recover debt, $.80 damages,
$10.22 costs. Copy of original note: "promise to
pay to RHODA WOODS and JOHN ROBB", witness DAVID
SQUIER, MATT. PATTON. pp 353, 354

Case 22. WILLIAM D. JACKSON vs JAMES THOMSON & FRAN-
CIS DILTS. On 7 June, 1806, $25.06 note signed. Re-
fusal to pay. Defendants failed to appear in court.
JACKSON to recover debt, $.33 damages, $9.78 costs.
pp 355, 356

Case 23. DANIEL C. COOPER vs GEORGE WESTFALL. On 28
Aug, 1803, $28.97 note signed. Refused to pay, suit
for $20 damages. WESTFALL failed to defend. COOPER
to recover $27.97 balance of debt, $8.47 damages,
$9.83 costs. Copy of original note, witness WILLIAM
VAN CLEVE, RALTH LINES. pp 356, 357, 358

Case 24. JOHN COMPTON vs WILLIAM WESTFALL. On 6
Apr, 1807, $29.77 note signed. Failure to pay. WEST-
FALL failed to defend. COMPTON to recover debt,
$1.86 damages, $9.93 costs. Copy of original note,
witness ROBERT CLARK. pp 358, 359

Case 25. SARAH LOCK vs JOHN & NATHANIEL HUNT.
Damages $100. Abated by death of plaintiff. p 359

Case 26. WILLIAM REDICK vs WILLIAM CLARK. Disc. p
360

Case 27. JOHN IRVINE vs WILLIAM CLARK. Disc. p 360

Term of April, 1808 continued

Case 28. JOHN FLUCK vs WILLIAM HARRISON. Debt $60, damages $25. Suit disc. p 360

Case 29. PATRICK LAFFERTY vs JOSEPH REYBURN. Debt $68.50, damages $25. Suit disc. p 360

Case 30. HEZEKIAH ROBISON vs SAMUEL McCORMICK. Damages $400, defendant not to be found. p 360

Case 31. STATE vs SPARLING YOUNG, WILLIAM KYSER, CHARLES McDONALD, GEORGE BOTKIN, GEORGE KIRKPATRICK & WILLIAM McCORMICK. Indictment for riot at HUNTs, defendants not to be found. p 360

Case 32. STATE vs SPARLING YOUNG, WILLIAM KYSER, CHARLES McDONALD, GEORGE BOTKIN, GEORGE KIRKPATRICK & WILLIAM McCORMICK. Indictment for riot at CLAWSONs, defendants not to be found. p 361

Case 33. SAMUEL FREEMAN vs HENRY MULKINS. Damages $150. Suit disc. p 361

Case 34. PHILIP GUNCKLE vs DANIEL GRIFFIN. Slander, damages $2000. Defendant not to be found. p 361

Case 35. PHILIP GUNCKLE vs MARTIN EARHART. Slander, damages $2000. Defendant not to be found. p 361

Case 36. THOMAS WILLIAMS vs JOHN HUNT. Damages $300. Defendant not to be found. p 361

Case 37. GEORGE BEARD, assignee of WILLIAM BEARD JR, vs JOHN SEWELL & CHRISTIAN CALLENDINE. Debt $189.57, damages. Defendants not to be found. p 361

Case 38. REBECKA COPUS vs JACOB HARTER. Sheriff's return nihil. p 361

Case 39. JOHN McKEEN vs HENRY ENOCH. Damages $100. Defendant not to be found. p 362

Case 40. JOHN DENNY vs JOHN WOODEMAN. Debt $51, damages $25. Defendant not found. p 362

Case 41. ANDREW LOCK vs DAVID MILLER. Damages $150, defendant not found. p 362

Case 42. HENRY TAYLOR vs WILLIAM CLARK. Debt $40. Sheriff's return nihil. p 362

Term of September, 1808

Case 1. STATE vs JAMES STEELE & JOSEPH PEIRCE.
Grand Jury: JAMES HANNA, DAVID SQUIER, DANIEL
McDONALD, WHITLEY HATFIELD, JAMES ANDERSON, PETER
KELLER, JAMES MILES, JOHN BROWER ST, JOHN RISINGER,
JONATHAN JUSTICE, CHARLES ROE, HENRY KINSEY, JERE-
MIAH MOTE, WILLIAM KING, ANTHONY LOGAN.   On 1 Nov,
1808 and other times, sold foreign goods without a
license. Pled guilty. Fined $.25, costs of $8.58.
pp 363, 364

Case 2. STATE vs JOHN COMPTON JR.   On 1 Sept, 1808
and other times, sold foreign goods without license.
Pled guilty. Fined $.25, costs of $8.58. pp 364, 365,
366

Case 3. STATE vs BENJAMIN ARCHER.   On 1 Sept, 1808
and other times, sold foreign goods without license.
Pled guilty. Fined $.25, costs of $8.58. pp 366, 367

Case 4. STATE vs HUGH McCOLLOM. On 1 Sept, 1808 and
other times, sold foreign goods without license. Pled
guilty. Fined $.25, costs of $8.58. pp 367, 368

Case 5. STATE vs FRANCIS DILTS. On 1 Sept, 1808 and
other times, sold spiritous liquor (whiskey) without
license. Pled guilty. Fined $.25, costs of $8.58. pp
369, 370

Case 6. STATE vs JACOB BRANNER. On 1 Sept, 1808 and
other times, sold spiritous liquor (whiskey) without
license. Pled guilty. Fined $.25, costs of $8.58. pp
370, 371

Case 7. STATE vs GEORGE SOURBRAY.   On 1 Sept, 1808
and other times, sold spiritous liquor (beer) without
license. Pled guilty. Fined $.25, costs of $8.58. pp
372, 373

Case 8. JOSEPH WHITING vs WILLIAM MADDEN. WHITING
presented letters testamentary appt'g him as exec of
will of JOHN WHITING. On 5 Feb, 1807, MADDEN unjustly held livestock against pledges: sorrel horse
worth $80; sorrel horse worth $90; sorrel mare worth
$70; bay mare worth $150; bay mare worth $40; 1 yoke
oxen worth $50; 2 cows worth $30; 10 sheep and 10
geese worth $40; $550 damages caused by detainment.
MADDEN failed to defend, WHITING to recover $.01
damages, $13.52 costs. No explanation of bearing
executorship had on the case unless debt (and livestock) was that of JOHN WHITING. pp 373, 374, 375

Term of September, 1808 continued

Case 9. GEORGE BOTKIN vs NATHANIEL HUNT & JOHN HUNT.
On 10 Feb, 1807, debt of $66. Failed to pay. Suit
filed, damages of $50. Def'nts refuted debt, sub-
mitted affidavit that BELINDA BOTKIN, a material witness, was "wanting", case continued. At trial,
def'nts failed to defend. BOTKIN to recover debt,
$6.66 damamges, $11.76 costs. pp 375, 376, 377

Case 10. SAMUEL THOMSON & DANIEL FERREL vs PAUL D.
BUTLER & WILLIAM CHENOWETH. On 5 May, 1806, debt of
$60. Failed to pay. Suit filed, damages of $30.
Def'nts refuted debt, to give evidence plntfs indebted $100 for goods and merchandise, money lent. Jury
summoned: WILLIAM BOMBERGER, SOLOMON HAMER, SAMUEL
IRVINE, HENRY MARQUART, JAMES MILLER, JAMES MILLER,
CHRISTIAN MOYER, JOSEPH OWENS, WILLIAM REEDER, NATHAN
SILVER, ADAM SWINEHART, NATHAN TOLBERT. Found
def'nts guilty. THOMSON & FERREL to recover $28.04
debt, $5.28 damages, $22.73 costs. Copy of original
note, witness JAMES WAIRUM, WILLIAM W. D. ELLIOT. pp
377, 378, 379, 380

Case 11. TIMOTHY SQUIER vs PAUL D. BUTLER. On 9
Nov, 1807, $112.40 note. Failed to pay. Suit filed,
damages $200. BUTLER failed to defend, SQUIER to
recover $116 damages, $10.11 costs. Copy of original
note, witness JOHN OWINGS. pp 381, 382, 383

Case 12. BENJAMIN ARCHER vs HUGH McCOLLOM. On 20
Feb, 1807, $864.27 debt. Failed to pay. Suit filed,
damages $150. McCOLLOM refuted debt, claimed ARCHER
indebted for $200 for goods, money lent. April term,
jury summoned: HENRY ATCHINSON, JOHN BOWMAN, SAMUEL
CAVENDER, JOSEPH COLMAN, JACOB CROW, FREDERICK FOUTS,
WILLIAM GEORGE, ANDREW HOOD, JAMES PORTER, HENRY
SHEIDLER, ROBERT SWIFT, MARTIN WEYBRIGHT. Found
McCOLLOM guilty, ARCHER recover $615.40 debt, $34.57
costs. Def'nt charged verdict erroneous, requested
verdict be set aside, retrial given. Sept term,
McCOLLOM admitted debt of $600. ARCHER to recover
$600, $6.69 costs. Copy of original note, witness
JAMES SNOWDEN. pp 383, 384, 385, 386

Case 13. GEORGE F. TENNERY vs JOHN DRISCOL, adm of
estate of JOHN AIKENS, dec. On 22 Nov, 1806, $50
note. Failed to pay. Suit filed, damages of $25.
DRISCOL failed to defend, TENNERY to recover debt,
$5.37 damage, $10.68 costs. Copy of original note,
witness MARTIN MYERS. Endorsement, assigning note to
RALPH FRENCH, undated. pp 387, 388

Term of September, 1808 continued

Case 14.   PETER CLAWSON vs EDMUND VANSEL.   On 23 Jan,
1808, VANSEL assaulted "with sticks, clubs, knives
and fists" CLAWSON at Washington Twp.   On same day,
VANSEL made 2d assault, cutting CLAWSON on face,
body, arms and wrists.   On same day, VANSEL made 3d
assault, beating CLAWSON again. CLAWSON suffered pain
and torment for 3 months, forced to pay $100 for cur-
ing his wounds, prevented from carrying on his lawful
business. VANSEL, defended by WILLIAM CORRY, atty,
pled not guilty to first and second counts, self-de-
fense in the third, presented affidavit that JOHN
VANSEL, a material witness, is "wanting", asked con-
tinuance. Sept term, jury summoned: WILLIAM BLAIR,
WILLIAM BOMBERGER, HENRY BUTT, JOHN CROY, JAMES MIL-
LER late coroner, JAMES MILLER, CHRISTIAN MOYER,
JOSEPH OWEN, WILLIAM REEDER, NATHAN SILVER, ALEXANDER
SNODGRASS, ADAM SWINEHART.   Found VANSEL guilty on
first, second charges, not guilty on third. CLAWSON
to recover $50 damages, $29.56 costs.   pp 389, 390,
391, 392

Case 15. PETER LEMON vs BENJAMIN KISER. On 3 March,
1807, $31.50 debt, to be repaid in cash or merchant-
able rye @ 37.5 cents/bushel. Failed to pay. Suit,
damages $100. KISER failed to defend; LEMON recover
debt, $1.97 damages, $11.21 costs. Copy of original
note, witness JOHN BAIN. pp 392, 393, 394

Case 16. JONATHAN DONALD vs JAMES ARCHER.   On 6
June, 1804, $67.58 debt. Failed to pay. Suit filed,
$40 damage. ARCHER refuted debt, to offer evidence
DONNEL indebted $100. ARCHER failed to defend. DON-
NEL recover $57.48 debt residue, $4.72 damage, $10.82
costs. Copy of original note, witness WILLIAM MASON,
JOHN MILLER. Endorsement of partial payt: J. DONNEL.
pp 394, 395, 396

Case 17.   JONATHAN DONNEL vs WILLIAM MASON.   On 6
June, 1804, note for $184.68. Failed to pay. Suit
filed, damages $50.   MASON refuted debt, to give
evidence that DONNEL owed $100.   Trial: MASON ad-
mitted debt of $95.27.   DONNEL to recover $95.27,
$11.33 costs.   Copy of original not, witness JAMES
ARCHER, JOHN MILLER. pp 396, 397, 398, 399, 400

Case 18.   JOHN DRISCOL vs JAMES THOMSON & DAVID
SQUIER. On 9 Jan, 1807, $75.58 note. Failed to pay.
Suit filed, damages $30. Def'nts refute debt. Jury
summoned: JAMES BAXTER, HENRY BUTT, HENRY CLARK,
JOHN CROY, JOHN HIMES, SAMUEL HOPKINS, WILLIAM Term

43

of September, 1808 continued

McCLURE, SAMUEL MOORE, JOHN SHANK, LUDWIG SPEECE, WILLIAM VAN CLEVE, WILLIAM VANDERSLICE. Found def'nts guilty. DRISCOL to recover debt, $16.30 costs. Copy of original note. pp 401, 402, 403

Case 19. JOHN DRISCOL vs JOHN GULLION & BAZEL WILLIAMS. $76 note, failed to pay. Suit filed, damages $30. Def'nts failed to defend. DRISCOL to recover debt, $10.71 costs. pp 403, 404

Case 20. SAMUEL MORE vs DAVID REID. On 4 Dec, 1806, $35 note; to be paid with saddle and bridle @ $17, 2 neck collars @ $4.50, 2 breech bands @ $6, 2 blind bridles @ $4, $3.50 cash. Refused to pay. Suit filed, $20 damages. REID failed to defend; MORE to recover debt, $.20 damages, $10.83 costs. Copy of original note, witness ABNER SEABURN. Endorsement, assigning note to JAMES NOLAN on 6 Apr, 1807, signed SAMUEL MOORE. pp 404, 405, 406

Case 21. JOHN DEVOR, EDMUND MUNGER & JOHN FOLKERTH, Commissioners of Montgomery Co, vs JAMES THOMSON & PAUL D. BUTLER. On 9 Sept, 1805, $110 note given by DEVOR, MUNGER & then-commissioner SAMUEL HAWKINS. Failed to pay. Suit filed. Def'nts claimed they had been sued previously on the debt, judgement obtained and paymt made. Trial: def'nts admit debt. Plntfs recover $40.73 debt residue, $10.37 costs. Copy of original note: THOMSON to erect building on lot 183 in town of Dayton within 1 yr, pay $18.33 to County by 1 June, 1806, pay $36.37 to County before expiration of 1 yr, then this obligation is void, otherwise remains in full force. Endorsement of $18.33 payt. pp 406, 407, 408, 409, 410

Case 22. JOHN DEVOR, EDMUND MUNGER & JOHN FOLKERTH, Commissioners of Montgomery Co, vs JAMES THOMSON & GEORGE F. TENNERY. On 14 June, 1806, $50 note given by DEVOR, MUNGER & then-commissioner SAMUEL HAWKINS. Failed to pay. Suit filed. Def'nts failed to defend. Plntfs recover $21.93 debt residue, $10.95 costs. Copy of original note: TENNERY to erect building on lot 234 in town of Dayton before 1 Nov, 1807, pay $10.25 to County by 1 Jan, 1807, pay $10.25 to County by 1 Jan, 1808, then this obligation is void, otherwise remains in full force. pp 410, 411, 412, 413

Case 23. HENRY ENOCH vs BENJAMIN COX. On 12 Sept, 1807, agreement to pay ENOCH for fixing houses, value

Term of September, 1808 continued

to be agreed upon by 2 men, ENOCH to have use of qtr section #17 until 1 Apr, 1808, allowed to gather his crops and firewood. ENOCH charged failure to pay money owed from fixing houses. COX submitted original note of terms, claimed he was not bound by law to answer, money owed by agreement unclear, indefensable. Trial: COX admitted guilt, set money owed at $35. Court ordered ENOCH to recover $35, each to pay own costs. pp 413, 414, 415, 416

Case 24. JOHN GULLION vs ELIJAH OWINGS. On 15 March, 1808, $41.50 debt owed for sorrel mare. Failure to pay. Suit filed, $90 damages. Jury summoned: WILLIAM BOMBERGER, JOHN CROY, SAMUEL IRWIN, PETER LEHMAN, JAMES MILLER late coroner, JAMES MILLER, CHRISTIAN MOYER, JOSEPH OWEN, JONATHAN SHAW, NATHAN SILVER, ADAM SWINEHART, WILLIAM VANDERSLICE. Found OWING guilty. GULLION to recover $41.50, $19.31 costs. pp 416, 417, 418

Case 25. DANIEL C. COOPER vs HENRY CURTNER. On 26 Aug, 1806, $60.40 debt. Failure to pay. Suit filed, damage $25. Def'nt refuted debt, to offer evidence COOPER owed larger debt for work performed, offset. Trial: CURTNER admitted debt. COOPER to recover debt, $.95 damages, $10.89 costs. Copy of original note, witness GEORGE NEWCOM, WILLIAM VANDERSLICE. pp 419, 420, 421

Case 26. WILLIAM BUNDY vs PAUL D. BUTLER. On 3 July, 1807, $32.71 note. Failed to pay. Suit filed, $30 damages. BUTLER failed to defend. BUNDY recover debt, $1.96 damages, $10.07 costs. Copy of original note, witness THOMAS BUTLER. pp 421, 422, 423.

Case 27. THOMAS GUIER & WILLIAM DIEHL vs BENJAMIN ARCHER. On 3 Oct, 1807, note for $2000, goods and merchandise. (GUIER & DIEHL partners in trade at Philadelphia.) Failed to pay. ARCHER refuted debt. Trial: ARCHER failed to defend. Plntfs recover $1495.22 damages, $11.80 costs. Copy of acct rendered on which suit was based: first entry 8 Nov, 1804; last entry 17 Sept, 1807. pp 423, 424, 425

Case 28. GEORGE McCULLOUGH vs JOHN COMPTON JR. On 18 July, 1806, agreement of partnership in merchandising, buying and selling. Copartnership based on value of stock delivered by COMPTON of 2271 pounds, 13 sh, 7 p 3 farthings; delivered by McCULLOUGH of 307 pounds, 4 sh, 5 p, aforesaid money valued at 7

Term of September, 1808 continued

sh, 6 p to the dollar. Expenses, profits to be
shared equally. Partnership since dissolved, COMPTON
charged with debt of $600, refusal to pay, refusal to
execute partnership contract in writing, verbal deni-
al of partnership. COMPTON ordered to answer complaint at April term, 1808. Defn't agreed that he
had entered into partnership. Stock entered by
def'nt worth $6100, by plntf worth $800. Profit and
loss to be shared equally. Maintained he was always
willing to sign contract; admitted refusal to sign
articles of agreement offered considerable time after
commencement of partnership as offering was wholly
variant from original. Cost of hogs purchased by
McCULLOUGH, expenses of taking drove to Baltimore for
sale, amounted to $2525.90; McCULLOUGH sold drove
for $2240.40. Whole sum from sale was supposed to be
applied to claims against COMPTON at Baltimore. In-
stead, McCULLOGH gave COMPTON $1000, used balance of
sale money to pay off debt of McCULLOUGH's father.
Plntf also collected debts due partnership, of which
he refused to give acc'ting. McCULLOUGH recv'd much
more than original stock, actually owed COMPTON a
considerable amount. Response to original complaint
sworn before CHRISTOPHER CURTNER, JP, on 5 March,
1808, filed with Court April, 1808. Trial: McCUL-
LOUGH failed to appear. COMPTON to recover costs of
$14.78. pp 427, 428, 429, 430, 431, 432, 433, 434

Case 29. HENRY TAYLOR vs WILLIAM CLARK. TAYLOR
appeared before JOHN McCABE, JP of Washington Twp,
recovered judgement of $40 debt, $.12 costs. CLARK
failed to pay, summoned by Court to answer judgement.
CLARK failed to defend, TAYLOR to recover debt, costs
plus $5.30 damages, $10.74 court costs. pp 435, 436

Case 30. STATE vs SPARLING YOUNG, WILLIAM KYSER,
CHARLES McDONALD, GEORGE BOTKIN, GEORGE KIRKPATRICK &
WILLIAM McCORMICK. Indictment for riot at HUNT's.
Def'nts not to be found. p 436

Case 31. STATE vs SPARLING YOUNG, WILLIAM KYSER,
CHARLES McDONALD, GEORGE BOTKIN, GEORGE KIRKPATRICK &
WILLIAM McCORMICK. Indictment for riot at CLAWSON's.
Def'nts not to be found. p 437

Case 32. JOHN GULLION vs PRESIDENT, RECORDER & TRUS-
TEES, TOWN OF DAYTON. Damages $150. Disc. p 437

Case 33. ADAM KUCKLER vs JOHN HUNT. Debt $210,
damage $50. Disc. p 437

Term of September, 1808 continued

Case 34.   REBECKAH COPUS vs JACOB HARTER.   Disc. p 437

Case 35.   GEORGE SHOUB vs JACOB RUDY.   Trespass, damage $1000. Disc. p 437

Case 36.   PHILIP GUNCKLE vs MARTIN SHUEY.   Slander, damages $2000. Disc. p 438

Case 37.   JOSEPH BURROWS & EDEN BURROWS vs SAMUEL BECK. Damages $100, disc. p 438

Case 38.   JOHN WEAVER vs GEORGE MAIN.   Damages $56, disc. p 438

Case 39.   THOMAS WILLIAMS vs JOHN HUNT.   Damages $300, disc. p 438

Case 40.   SWANCY WHITTING vs EDMUND ADAMS.   Trespass, damage. Disc. p 438

Case 41.   JACOB PHILLIPSON vs BENJAMIN LEHMAN.   Covenant, damage $300. Disc. p 438

Case 42.   JACOB PHILLIPSON vs BENJAMIN LEHMAN.   Covenant, damage $200. Disc. p 438

Case 43.   JOHN ENOCH vs GEORGE MAIN.   Debt $48, damage $20. Disc. p 439

Case 44.   OLIVER ORMSBY & WILLIAM STANLEY, partners, vs SAMUEL BECK. Damages, $100. Not found. p 439

Case 45.   OLIVER ORMSBY & WILLIAM STANLEY, partners, vs SAMUEL BECK. Damages, $70. Not found. p 439

Case 46.   ZACARIAH ARCHER, STEPHEN McFARLAND & ARTHUR ST. CLAIR JR vs JAMES MILLER.   Debt $364, damages $100. Disc. p 439

Case 47.   WILLIAM NICOL vs SAMUEL BECK.   Debt $82, damages $30. Def'nt not found. p 439

Case 48.   SAMUEL TOMMIS vs SAMUEL BECK.   Debt $82, damage $30. Def'nt not found. p 439

Case 49.   JAMES ANDERSON vs PETER CLAWSON.   Damages $130. Disc. p 440

Case 50.   DAVID SQUIER VS DAVID VANDERPOOL.   Not to

Term of September, 1808 continued

be found. p 440

Case 51. PHILIP GUNCKLE vs DANIEL GRIFFIN. Slander, damages $2000. Def'nt not found. p 440

Case 52. DANIEL CHRISMAN vs JOHN WAGNER & WILLIAM EMRICK. Debt $716, damages $100. Disc. p 440

Term of January, 1809

Case 1. STATE vs JOHN COMPTON JR. Grand Jury: WILLIAM McCLURE, ROBERT EWING, JOHN SHUPART, MARTIN SHUEY SR, ANDREW SMALL, JAMES WILLSON, JONATHAN HATFIELD, ROBERT ELLIOT, BENJAMIN SMITH, WILLIAM WILSON, GEORGE LONG, CHRISTOPHER CURTNER, ALEXANDER SNODGRASS, ROBERT McCLEARY, LUTHER BRUEN. On 24 Nov, 1808, assaulted FABIAN EAGLE in Dayton Twp. Pled guilty. Fined $5.00, costs of $9.00. pp 441, 442

Case 2. STATE vs JAMES CAMMACK. Grand Jury: JAMES HANNA, DAVID SQUIER, DANIEL McDONALD, WHITLEY HATFIELD, JAMES ANDERSON, PETER KELLER, JAMES MILES, JOHN BROWER SR, JOHN RISINGER, JONATHAN JUSTICE, CHARLES ROE, HENRY KINSEY, JEREMIAH MOTE, WILLIAM KING, ANTHONY LOGAN. On 6 Sept, 1808 and other times CAMICK of Washington Twp sold spiritous liquor (beer) without a license. Pled not guilty. Jury summoned: JOHN CROY, JOHN ENOCH, JACOB KUNS, PETER LEHMAN, MARTIN MYERS, JOHN RICHEY, AARON RICHISON, HEZEKIAH ROBISON, JAMES THOMSON, WILLIAM VANDERSLICE, JOHN VANORSDALL, JOHN WOODEMAN. Found not guilty. pp 442, 443, 444

Case 3. STATE vs GEORGE BODKIN. Grand Jury: JOHN COMPTON JR, JOHN WEBB, THOMAS McNUTT, JAMES MILES, ABRAHAM HILDERBRAND, ABRAHAM NEFF, WILLIAM GRIFFIN, JAMES AIKEN, SAMUEL BROADBERRY, OLIVER VOORHEIS, JACOB MULLENDORE, CALEB HUNT, JOHN VANORSDALE, GEORGE FRIBERGER, ANTHONY LOGAN. On 12 Aug, 1807, CHARLES McDONALD, WILLIAM KIZER son of PETER KIZER, SPARLING YOUNG, GEORGE BODKIN, GEORGE KIRKPATRICK, and WILLIAM McCORMICK son of JAMES McCORMICK, all of Green County, rioted at Dayton Twp, armed with guns and other weapons, did disturb the peace at the house of JOHN HUNT. Sheriff ordered to take McDONALD, KIZER, YOUNG, BODKIN, KIRKPATRICK & McCORMICK. Case continued through several terms; Sheriff unable to locate def'nts in his baliwick. GEORGE BODKIN brought to court, pled not guilty. Jury summoned: JOHN AINSWORTH, LUTHER BRUEN, FRANCIS DILTS, WILLIAM DODDS,

Term of January, 1809 continued

JACOB KUNS, SIMPSON McCARTY, JAMES McGREW, THOMAS PATTERSON, JOHN PICKET, DAVID RIFFLE, DAVID SQUIER, TIMOTHY SQUIER. Found BODKIN not guilty. pp 445, 446, 447, 448

Case 4. STATE vs EDMUND VANSEL. On 28 Jan, 1808, assaulted PETER CLAWSON with a knife. Bondsmen for VANSEL, Sept term: JOHN VANSEL, JOHN STEELE. EDMUND VANSEL pled not guilty. EDMUND & JOHN VANSEL stood bond for January appearance of $200. VANSEL failed to appear, bond forfeit. pp 448, 449, 450, 451

Case 5. BETSEY WEAVER vs JAMES BARNET. On 18 Apr, 1808, JAMES BARNET, DANIEL C. COOPER & GEORGE HARRIS appeared before CHRISTOPHER CURTNER, JP, to post appearance bond of $300 for April court term. ELIZABETH WEAVER charged JAMES with being the father of a "bastard child she lately delivered". BARNET presented affidavit to court that HENRY CLARK, a material witness, was missing; continuance sought. Trial: pled not guilty. Jury summoned: JOHN AINSWORTH, HENRY BUTT, ROWLAND ELLIS, THOMAS JOHN, DAVID MUSSELMAN, ROBERT PARKS, GEORGE W. SMITH, IRA SMITH, PETER SUNDERLAND, ROBERT TAYLOR, JOHN VANNIMAN, CHRISTIAN WELDY. Found BARNET guilty, to pay BETSEY WEAVER $75 in increments until child is 3 years old, to assure that child would not be financial burden on township. pp 452, 453, 454

Case 6. JEROM HOLT vs JOHN VANORSDALL & CORNELIUS VANORSDALL. On 1 March, 1808, set dogs on a horse belonging to HOLT, chased and killed it. HOLT sued for damages of $100. Def'nts represented by NATHANIEL HUNT, atty.; pled not guilty, gave affidavit that ABIA MARTIN, a material witness, was not found, asked continuance. January term, CORNELIUS acquited, to recover costs of $22.04. pp 454, 455, 456

Case 7. JOHN WEAVER vs EDMUND ADAMS. On 1 March, 1808, agreement made for ADAMS to farm 10 acres located in Dayton Twp, one third of crop to go to WEAVER. ADAMS refused to take possession and fulfill agreement. Suit filed, $50 damages. Def'nt refuted agreement. Jury found ADAMS guilty. WEAVER to recover ·$5.00 damages, $23.92 costs. pp 456, 457, 458, 459

Case 8. JOHN WEAVER vs HUGH McCOLLOM. On 1 Apr, 1808, sold 142 pounds bacon to McCOLLOM. Failure to pay. Suit filed, $50 damages. Jury: JESSE CLARK,

Term of January, 1809 continued

OWEN DAVIS, JAMES HENDERSON, SIMPSON McCARTY, DAVID MILLER, MARTIN MYERS, HORATIO G. PHILIPS, HEZEKIAH ROBISON, ALEXANDER SNODGRASS, GEORGE WESTFALL, JOB WESTFALL, GEORGE WOLLASTON. Juror PHILLIPS withdrawn by Court for unexplained connection to plntf, rest of panel discharged. WEAVER to take nothing, McCOLLOM recover $32.89 costs. pp 461, 462

Case 9. JAMES CHATHAM vs JAMES THOMSON. On 30 Nov, 1807, agreement that CHATHAM would teach school for term of 3 months beginning 7 Dec, 1807 and would do THOMSON's part of the repairs, amounting to $9. Refusal to pay debt, further debt of $20. Children of THOMSON attending school: BETSY, MOSES, MATTHEW, POLLY, WILLIAM & NEAL. THOMSON refuted terms of agreement. Jury summoned: HENRY BUTT, ROWLAND ELLIS, THOMAS JOHN, DAVID MUSSELMAN, ROBERT PARKS, JOHN REGANS, JOHN RICHEY, IRA SMITH, CHARLES TULL, JOHN VANNIMAN, CHRISTIAN WELDY, GEORGE WESTFALL. Acquited THOMSON. CHATHAM to take nothing, THOMSON recover $29.03 costs. pp 463, 434, 465, 466

Case 10. EDMUND MUNGER, JOHN DEVOR, JOHN FOLKERTH, Commissioners of Montgomery Co, vs GEORGE NEWCOM, Sheriff of Montgomery Co. Judgement of $327.91 obtained by Commissioners against SAMUEL HOPKINS & SAMUEL HAWKINS. NEWCOM failed to enact judgement. Failed to defend. Commissioners to recover amount of judgement, $38.80 damages, $7.79 costs. pp 467, 468

Case 11. JOHN SUTHERLAND & HENRY BROWN vs HENRY CURTNER. On 13 Jan, 1806, note for $19.09, to be paid in hats. 2d note, 1 June, 1806 for $66.00. 3d note, 19 July, 1808 for $116.00, goods and merchandise. SUTHERLAND & BROWN represented by WILLIAM CORRY, atty. Def'nt refuted debts of the 1st, 2d counts; balance of charges: at the time mentioned, he and CHRISTOPHER CURTNER carried on business of manufacturing hats. Goods involved were purchased for the business. Since CHRISTOPHER was not named in the indictment, HENRY requested charges be quashed. Trial: HENRY failed to appear, defend. SUTHERLAND & BROWN to recover $129.07 debt residue, $12.01 costs. Copy of original notes and accounts, witness WILLIAM MILLAR, THOMAS STEWART. pp 468, 469, 470, 471, 472, 473

Case 12. ARTHUR ST. CLAIR JR vs JAMES MILLER. On 25 Dec, 1806, note for $40. Refusal to pay. Suit filed, damages of $80. MILLER admitted debt. ST.

Term of January, 1809 continued

CLAIR to recover debt, $7.25 damages, $10.80 costs. Copy of original note. pp 474, 475

Case 13. JAMES FINDLEY, surviving obligor of JAMES FINDLEY & CHARLES KILGORE, vs DANIEL C. COOPER. On 8 Sept, 1804, at Cincinnati, note for $109.35, for certificates issued in name of MATTHIES DENMAN. COOPER refuted debt, to give evidence the plntfs were indebted for $200 for money paid and advanced. COOPER faied to defend. FINDLEY to recover debt, $28.43 damages, $10.36 costs. Copy of original note. pp 475, 476, 477

Case 14. JOHN DENNEY vs JOHN WOODEMAN. On 6 July, 1807, note for $51. Failure to pay; suit filed. WOODEMAN failed to defend. DENNEY recover debt, $3.82 damages, $10.91 costs. Copy of original note, witness HORATIO G. PHILLIPS. pp 477, 478

Case 15. ANDREW LOCK vs DAVID MILLER. On 1 Jan, 1804, debts for $35 money, $33.33 for 100 bushels corn. Failure to pay. MILLER refuted debt. Jury found MILLER guilty. LOCK to recover damages of $7.50, $26.54 costs. pp 479, 480, 481, 482

Case 16. JOHN KENNEDY vs DAVID REID. On 12 Jan, 1807, $42.33, previous debt of $50. Failed to pay. Suit filed, damages of $80. REID failed to defend. KENNEDY to recover $47.35 debt residue, $10.38 costs. Copy of original note, witness JAS. NOLAN. Endorsement assigned note to WILLIAM HUFF, undated; witness BENNY BROWN. pp 483, 484.

Case 17. GEORGE F. TENNERY vs MARTIN MYERS. On 1 June, 1808, $105 debt for work as atty. Failure to pay. Debt refuted by MYERS, charged TENNERY indebted for more money than due: $60 cash, $30 goods, $30 work performed at plntf's business. Jury found MYERS guilty. TENNERY to recover $28.19 damages, $30.69 costs. pp 485, 486, 487

Case 18. DAVID SIMMON vs ISAAC DAVIS. On 25 Dec, 1807, note promising to pay $50 to EDWARD PAGE. Note assigned to F. FISHER who then assigned note LANSON SHAW. Note last assigned to SIMMONS, who attempted to collect debt. Case sent to arbitrators HENRY DISBROW, JAMES THOMSON, DAVID REID. Found SIMMONS had not established claim against DAVIS, as DAVIS had proved payment of demand, witnessed by WILLIAM M. SMITH. SIMMONS to pay costs of suit and arbitration.

Term of January, 1809 continued

DAVIS recover $18.98 costs. pp 487, 488, 489, 490

Case 19 missing, misnumbered by clerks.

Case 20. GEORGE KUNS vs OWEN DAVIS. On 11 Aug, 1808, assaulted KUNS at Dayton. Suit filed, damages of $2000. DAVIS, represented by WILLIAM M. SMITH, atty, pled not guilty, self-defense. Jury summoned: FRANCIS DILTS, JOSEPH EWING, JOHN FOLKERTH, GEORGE GROVE, ALBERT HUEY, THOMAS JOHN, SIMPSON McCARTY, DAVID MUSSELMAN, THOMAS REID, GEORGE SMITH, IRA SMITH, JAMES THOMSON. Acquited DAVIS, to recover $75.75 costs. pp 491, 492

Case 21. CHARLES ELLET vs BENJAMIN ARCHER. On 5 Nov, 1804 at Philadelphia, note for $397.38, further sum of $1000. On 23 Oct, 1805, debt for $300 in goods. Failure to pay. ARCHER refuted debt, to give evidence to prove ELLET indebted for $1200. Trial: ARCHER failed to defend. ELLET to recover $661.13 debt residue, $13.98 costs. Copy of original note; listing of merchandise delivered by ELLET. Statement signed Mayor of Philadelphia ROBERT WHARTON. pp 492, 493, 494, 495, 496

Case 22. CONRAD KASTER vs BENJAMIN ARCHER & PETER SUNDERLAND. On 30 March, 1807, note for $143.00. Refusal to pay. Def'nts failed to defend suit. KASTER to recover $98.58 debt residue, $13.15 costs. Copy of original note, witness JOHN DAY. pp 496, 497, 498

Case 23. JOHN FLAICK vs EBENEZER WEAD. Unlawfully taking and detaining a wagon for debt, causing FLAICK damages of $50. Writ quashed. WEAD to recover $8.49 costs. p 498

Case 24. JOHN ENOCH vs CHRISTOPHER CURTNER. Assault and battery, false imprisonment. Damages $500. Disc. p 498

Case 25. CONKLIN MILLER vs JOSIAH CORBILL & WILLIAM VAN CLEVE. Covenant damages $100. Disc. p 499

Case 26. GEORGE SOURBRAY vs JOSHUA RUSSEL. Trespass, assault and battery. Damages $200. Disc. p 499

Case 27. JOHN MIKESELL vs NATHANIEL LYON. Grey mare & colt $100, damages $25. Disc. p 499

Term of January, 1809 continued

Case 28. EDMUND ADAMS vs HENRY LEATHERMAN. Damages $50. Disc. p 499

Case 29. Trustees of the Dayton Academy vs CHRISTIAN FRITZ & DAVID SQUIER. Debt $642, damages $100. Disc. p 499

Case 30. WILLIAM ALLISON vs WILLIAM NEWCOM. Trespass, damage $1000. Disc. p 499

Case 31. PHILIP GUNCKEL vs DANIEL GRIFFIN. Slander damages $2000. Def'nt not found. p 499

Case 32. JACOB YECKI vs FREDERICK AIGENBREGHT. Slander, damages $500. Def'nt not found. p 500

Case 33. JOSEPH HALE vs ALEXANDER SCOTT. Debt $120, damages $50. Def'nt not found. p 500

Case 34. JOHN COMPTON JR vs DAVID REID. Debt $199.32, damages $50. Def'nt not found. p 500

Case 35. SUTHERLAND & BROWN vs MARTIN SHUEY & MARTIN EARHART. Damages $2000. Def'nts not found. p 500

Term of May, 1809

Case 1. STATE vs BENJAMIN LEHMAN. Grand Jury: DANIEL HOOVER JR, DANIEL SHIVELY, JONATHAN HARSHMAN, CHRISTIAN BROWER, JACOB MULLENDORE, STEPHEN ULERY, ROBERT SCOTT, JOHN AINSWORTH, JOHN DAY, ANDREW BAY, JOSEPH COOPER, WILLIAM FARMER, CHARLES MORGAN, JOHN ARCHER, JOSEPH EWING. On 16 June, 1808, LEHMAN of Dayton Twp forged due bill, purporting to be note of JAMES NOLAN, requiring payt of $19.83, witnessed by THOMAS LENNAN: intent to defraud. LEHMAN pled not guilty. Jury summoned: DANIEL C. COOPER, WILLIAM HOLE, ALEXANDER McCONNEL, GEORGE NEWCOM, JOHN NOFFZINGER, JAMES STILLIKEN, JOHN TAYLOR, PHILLIP WAGGONER, JOHN WAYMIRE, JOHN H. WILLIAMS, JAMES WILSON, ROBERT WILSON. Acquited LEHMAN. pp 501, 502, 503

Case 2. STATE vs PHILIP GUNCKEL. On 1 Sept, 1808 and other times, GUNCKEL of German Twp sold goods of foreign manufacture without a license. Prosecutor dropped suit. pp 503, 504

Case 3. STATE vs PETER CLAWSON. On 13 Aug, 1808, at Washington Twp, assaulted JOHN EWING. Def'nt and

Term of May, 1809 continued

DANIEL C. COOPER stood appearance bond of $100.
Def'nt pled not guilty. January Court term: since
EWING, the victim, was a judge of Common Pleas, there
was no quorum present. Case continued until May.
Trial: CLAWSON changed plea to guilty, fined $5.00,
costs of $12.27. pp 504, 505, 506

Case 4. STATE vs GEORGE BOTKIN. On 12 Aug, 1807,
CHARLES McDONALD, WILLIAM KIZER son of PETER KIZER,
SPARLING YOUNG, GEORGE BODKIN, GEORGE KIRKPATRICK,
and WILLIAM McCORMICK son of JAMES McCORMICK, all of
Green County, did stone and disturb the peace at the
dwelling house of FREDERICK CLAWSON. Sheriff ordered
to take McDONALD, KIZER, YOUNG, BODKIN, KIRKPATRICK &
McCORMICK. Case continued through several terms;
Sheriff unable to locate def'nts in his baliwick.
GEORGE BODKIN brought to court, pled not guilty. In-
dictment dropped by prosecutor ISAAC G. BURNETT. pp
507, 508, 509

Case 5. ISAAC VANNEST vs HENRY ENOCH. On 8 Sept,
1806, $171 note signed by HENRY ENOCH & HENRY ENOCH
JR. The son was not found by the Sheriff to answer
the indictment. Refusal to pay. Suit filed, damages
of $50. ENOCH refuted debt, to offer evidence of
agreement of land rental. Plntf failed to keep up
fences; defn'ts crops damaged to extent of $200, off-
set debt. Jury summoned: SAMUEL ARCHER, JOHN COX.
WILLIAM HALE, ANDREW HOOD, GEORGE KUNS, ALEXANDER
McCONNEL, WILLIAM NEWCOM, JOHN NOFFZINGER, JOHN
TAYLOR, WILLIAM VANDERSLICE, JOHN WAYMIRE, ROBERT
WILSON. Found ENOCH guilty. VANNEST recover $153.57
debt residue, $22.62 costs. Copy of original note,
witness JAMES BARNET, ABNER ENOCH. pp 509, 510, 511,
512

Case 6. EDMUND VANSEL vs FRANCIS DILLS, HENRY ATCHI-
SON, JOHN HOLE. On 5 Feb, 1808, VANSEL assaulted and
imprisoned 24 hours. Suit filed, damages of $1000.
Def'nts pled not guilty. At trial, VANSEL failed to
appear and proceed, def'nts to recover $16.31 costs.
pp 512, 513

Case 7. JOHN WEAVER vs JAMES BARNET. On 1 Jan,
1807, assaulted and seduced ELIZABETH WEAVER, daughter of JOHN, when she was in BARNET's employment, got
her with child. From 1 Nov, 1807 until 1 Apr, 1808,
father JOHN lost the benefit and advantage of the
services of ELIZABETH. He also was "put to great
expense" in providing for her delivery and lying in,

Term of May, 1809 continued

amounting to $100. BARNET pled not guilty. Jury
summoned: JOHN BONNER, JOHN BRADFORD, DANIEL C.
COOPER, OSBORN COOPER, JOHN CROY, FRANCIS DILTS,
ROBERT ELLIOT, JOHN GRIPE, PHILIP GUNCKEL, PETER
LEHMAN, AARON NUTT, PHILIP WAGGONER. Found BARNET
guilty. WEAVER to recover $45 damages, costs of
$34.47. pp 513, 514, 515

Case 8. JACOB SLY vs JOHN DOVE. On 18 March, 1806,
$45 note, to be paid in good, merchantable corn, to
be delivered to JOHN SMITH's or HEGAR MAN's mills
(HEGARMAN?) at market price on or before 25 Dec,1806.
Failure to pay. DOVE failed to defend. SLY recover
$37.53 debt residue, $11.38 costs. Copy of original
note, witness JOHN ARMSTRONG. pp 515, 516, 517

Case 9. JAMES FINDLEY, surviving obligor of FINDLEY
& CHARLES KILGORE, vs DANIEL C. COOPER. On 12 Sept,
1804 at Cincinnati, note for $104 for certificate
delivered to heirs of ISRAEL LUDLOW. Partial paymt
made when GENERAL FINDLEY accepted quarter section of
Sec 7, T 2, R 7 for $40. Failure to pay balance.
Suit filed, damages $120. Debt refuted by COOPER, to
give evidence of indebtedness by KILGORE of $80,
expended on behalf of both plntfts. Trial: COOPER
admitted debt. FINDLEY to recover $81.87 debt,
$10.61 costs. Copy of original note. pp 517, 518,
519

Case 10. ZACARIAH ARCHER, STEPHEN McFARLAND & ARTHUR
ST. CLAIR JR, adm of CHARLES KILGORE, vs DANIEL C.
COOPER. On 11 May, 1807 at Dayton, $45 note. Failed
to pay. Suit filed, damages $80. COOPER refuted
debt, to give evidence KILGORE indebted for $100 in
goods and merchandise. Trial: COOPER admitted debt.
Plntffs to recover $36.45 debt, $11.07 costs. pp
519. 520. 521

Case 11. HEZEKIAH ROBISON vs SAMUEL McCORMICK. $400
damages. Case referred to GEORGE NEWCOM, WILLIAM
McCLURE & JOHN MILLER for arbitration. Found ROBISON
had no cause for action. McCORMICK recover $11.70
costs. pp 521, 522

Case 12. JOHN WODEMAN vs ROBERT CULBERTSON. On 18
Apr, 1807, $50 debt. Refusal to pay. Suit filed,
damages $25. CULBERTSON refuted debt, to give evi-
dence of plntf's indebtedness of $30 in goods, $30 in
cash. Trial: CULBERTSON admitted debt. WODEMAN to
recover $40.37 debt residue, $13.27 costs. Copy of

Term of May, 1809 continued

original note, witness ABRAHAM DARST.   pp 522, 523,
524

Case 13.   SAMUEL REED vs JOHN AINSWORTH.   On 20 Oct,
1806, 3 steers, valued at $50, lost.   On same day,
found in possession of AINSWORTH, knowing them to be
property of REED.   Suit for damages of $100 by con-
version.   AINSWORTH pled not guilty.   Jury acquited
def'nt.   REED to take nothing, AINSWORTH to recover
costs of $22.46.   pp 524, 525

Case 14.   WILLIAM LAMB vs USUAL CRANE.   On 15 Sept,
1802, at Chillicothe, debt of $63.70.   Refusal to
pay.   Suit filed, damages $25.   CRANE failed to de-
fend.   LAMB to recover debt, $25 damages, $10.30
costs.   Copy of original account: Docter USUAL
CRANE, witness JOHN SHERER.   Statement of JOHN SHERER
concerning his knowledge of debt, signed JOHN HUTTS,
JP, Ross Co, OH, 16 Oct, 1806.   pp 526, 527

Case 15.   JACOB WOLF vs WILLIAM McCANN.   On 22 Jan,
1803, $80 note.   Failure to pay.   Suit filed.   McCANN
failed to defend.   WOLF to recover $100.83 damages,
$10.39 costs.   Copy of original note, witness DANIEL
McDONALD.   pp 527, 528

Case 16.   OLIVER ORMSBY & WILLIAM STANLEY vs SAMUEL
BECK & CONRAD KASTER.   Plntfs are partners in trade
at Cincinnati.   On 16 Nov, 1807, at Cincinnati, not
for $35, further debt of $16.   Failed to pay.   Suit
filed, damages of $100.   Def'nts failed to defend.
Plntffs to recover $54.62 damages, $12.16 costs.
Copy of original note, witness LEWIS HOWELL.   pp 528,
529, 530, 531

Case 17.   OLIVER ORMSBY & WILLIAM STANLEY vs SAMUEL
BECK.   On 21 Dec, 1807, note for $16.50.   On 22 Dec,
1807, note for $14.58.   On 20 Dec, 1807, note for
$4.44.   Failure to pay.   Suit filed, damages of $70.
BECK failed to defend.   Plntfs recover $38.53 damage,
$12.12 costs.   Copies of original notes, witness W.S.
HATCH.   pp 531, 532

Case 18.   WILLIAM NICOL vs SAMUEL BECK.   On 25 Dec,
1807, note for $103.   Failure to pay.   Suit filed,
damages $50.   BECK failed to defend.   NICOL to recov-
er debt, $8.41 costs.   Copy of original note, witness
JOSEPH BECK, JOHN BECK.   pp 532, 533

Case 19.   SAMUEL TOMMIS vs SAMUEL BECK.   On 7 Dec,

Term of May, 1809 continued

1807, note for $82. Failure to pay. Suit filed, $50 damages. BECK failed to defend. TOMMIS to recover debt, $4.17 damages, $12 costs. pp 533, 534

Case 20. FABIAN EAGLE vs JOHN COMPTON JR. On 24 Nov, 1808. Defn't assaulted EAGLE. Suit filed, $100 damages. COMPTON pled not guilty. Jury acquited def'nt. EAGLE to take nothing, COMPTON to recover $11.11 costs. pp 534, 535

Case 21. FABIAN EAGLE vs JOHN COMPTON JR. On 24 Nov, 1808, $40 debt for labor done at business place of COMPTON, $20 debt for hire of a horse. COMPTON refuted debt. Trial: COMPTON found guilty, EAGLE to recover $17 damage, $12.81 costs. pp 535, 536, 537

Case 22. DAVID SQUIER vs DAVID VANDERPOOL. Case heard before CHRISTOPHER CURTNER, JP: SQUIER to recover debt of $55.74, $5.23 interest, 2d debt of $53.00, $4.90 interest. Failed to pay. SQUIER brought suit to Common Pleas Court. VANDERPOOL summoned 15 Oct, 1808, refuted debt. Def'nt to present evidence that on 17 May, 1808, SQUIER took transcript of Curtner's judgement to Hamilton County, OH, where VANDERPOOL resides. JOHN MAHARD, JP for Hamilton Co, on 16 June, 1808, upheld judgement which still remains in force. Trial: VANDERPOOL failed to defend, SQUIER to have execution of debt by default, costs of $11.93. pp 537, 538, 539

Case 23. DAVID ARCHER vs JOSIAH CLAWSON. Charged taking and detaining of grey mare, valued at $75. Trial: ARCHER failed to appear, writ quashed. CLAWSON recover $10.15 costs. p 539

Case 24. HUGH McCOLLOM vs BENJAMIN ARCHER & DAVID SQUIER. On 1 June, 1808, $400 debt for goods and merchandise (whiskey, brandy, wine and cider), $50 for work and labor, $400 debt for cash. Failed to pay. Suit filed, $500 damages. Def'nts refute suit. Jury found ARCHER & SQUIER guilty. McCOLLOM recover $312.76 debt, $44.20 costs. ARCHER & SQUIER gave notice of appeal to Supreme Court. Bail entered by JOHN ARCHER & DAVID REID. Copies of original notes. pp 539, 540, 541, 542, 543

Case 25. GEORGE WOLLASTON vs JOHN DODSON. On 28 Dec, 1807, $46.37 debt. DODSON admitted debt. WOLLASTON to recover $37.76, $10.94 costs. Copy of original note, witness IRA SMITH. pp 543, 544

Term of May, 1809 continued

Case 26. JOSEPH HOUGH, THOMAS BLAIR, ROBERT CLARK, NEIL GILLISPIE vs MARTIN SHUEY. Plntffs partners in trade at Hamilton, Butler Co, OH. On 15 Aug, 1805, $1280.17 note for value recvd. SHUEY refuted debt. Suit filed. Trial: SHUEY failed to defend. Plntfs recover $1157.61 debt residue, $12.02 costs. Copy of original note, witness MARTIN SHUEY JR. pp 544, 545, 546

Case 27. WILLIAM VANDERSLICE vs DAVID REID. On 1 Jan, 1807, $60.96 note. Refused to pay. Suit filed, $90 damages. REID failed to defend. VANDERSLICE recover $51.62 debt residue, $10.47 costs. Copy of original note, witness JOHN KEITH. Goods received included saddle for HENRY DEAN and cider. pp 546, 547

Case 28. WILLIAM RYON vs JEROM HOLT & HUGH McCOLLOM. On 19 Nov, 1807, $100 note. Failed to pay. Suit filed, failed to defend. RYON recover debt, $3.06 damage, $10.94 costs. Copy of original note. pp 548, 549

Case 29. Trustees of Dayton Academy vs JAMES THOMSON & HUGH McCOLLOM. On 29 April, 1808, $302 debt. Failed to pay. Suit filed, $50 damages. Failed to defend. Trustees recover $75.50 debt residue, $1.20 damages, $12.82 costs, and remaining payments as they come due. Copy of original note, witness WILLIAM BOMBERGER JR, BENJAMIN BAYLIS. pp 549, 550

Case 30. Trustees of Dayton Academy vs WILLIAM PATTERSON, BENJAMIN BAYLIS, CHRISTOPHER CURTNER & CHARLES TULL. On 29 April, 1808, $362.50 debt. Failed to pay. Suit filed, $50 damages. Failed to defend. Trustees recover $90.62 debt residue, $1.43 damages, $12.31 costs, and remaining payments as they come due. Copy of original note, witness JAMES THOMSON, HUGH McCOLLOM. pp 550, 551

Case 31. Trustees of Dayton Academy vs PETER SUMAN & JOHN GRIMES. On 29 April, 1808, $344.00 debt. Failed to pay. Suit filed, $50 damages. Failed to defend. Trustees recover $86.00 debt residue, $1.36 damages, $12.13 costs, and remaining payments as they come due. Copy of original note, witness JOHN ELLIOT, WILLIAM BOMBERGER JR. pp 552, 553

Case 32. MARTIN MYERS vs GEORGE F. TENNERY. MYERS, professing himself to be of unblemished character and

Term of May, 1809 continued

held high in his neighbors' esteem, charged TENNERY
with slander.   MYERS testified in a case, SAMUEL
FREEMAN vs JOHN DRISCOL, adm of the estate of JOHN
AIKENS, held at Xenia (Greene Co), heard 25 Aug, 1808
in the Supreme Court before SAMUEL HUNTINGTON & WIL-
LIAM SPRIGG.   TENNERY called MYERS a perjurer.   Suit
filed, $1000 damages. TENNERY pled innocent, claiming
that since the accusation was made in the course of
the trial, it was lawful for him to do so.   Jury
found TENNERY guilty.   MYERS to recover damage of
$.01, costs of $27.66.   pp 553, 554, 555

Case 33.   SAMUEL IRVINE vs DAVID ARCHER.   On 8 April,
1806, $50 debt.   Refusal to pay.   Suit filed, $80
damages. ARCHER refuted debt, claiming IRVINE had
recovered in a suit heard before ABNER GERARD, JP,
Washington Twp on 6 Dec, 1807.   Trial: ARCHER admitted debt.   IRVINE recover $48.28 debt, $11.25 costs.
Copy of original note, witness ANN IRVINE.   pp 555,
556

Case 34.   ZACARIAH HOLE vs FRANCIS DILTS.   On 12 Feb,
1807, $61 debt.   Failure to pay; suit filed.   DILTS
failed to defend.   HOLE to recover $55.57 debt resi-
due, $10.87 costs.   Copy of original note.   pp 556,
557

Case 35.   EDMUND ADAMS vs HENRY LEATHERMAN.   On 13
June, 1808, PAUL D. BUTLER made $27.37 note, payable
to LEATHERMAN, to settle an account.   On 24 June,
1808, the note was assigned to STEPHEN JAY, who then
on 7 Nov, 1808, assigned the note to ADAMS.   Both
BUTLER & JAY refused to pay the note when due and
LEATHERMAN became liable.   Def'nt refuted the debt.
Jury found LEATHERMAN guilty.   ADAMS to recover
$28.84 debt and damages, $23.32 costs. Copy of original note, witness   JOHN MILLER.   Endorsements as
noted.   pp 557, 558

Case 36.   WILLIAM WAUGH vs HENRY LEATHERMAN.   On 19
Oct, 1807, LEATHERMAN received at the grist mill a
bag belonging to WAUGH, marked with his initials and
containing 4 bushels wheat to be ground.   LEATHERMAN
failed to deliver the ground wheat and/or the marked
bag.   Def'nt refuted agreement.   Jury summoned: JOHN
BONNER, ROBERT ELLIOT, WILLIAM HOLE, GEORGE KUNS,
ALEXANDER McCONNEL, WILLIAM NEWCOM, JOHN NOFFZINGER,
JOHN TAYLOR, PHILIP WAGNER, JOHN WAYMIRE, ROBERT
WILSON, JOHN WOLF.   Found LEATHERMAN guilty.   WAUGH
to recover $4.55 damages, $12.26 costs.   Copy of

COMMON PLEAS (CIVIL) LAW RECORD BOOK A-1

Term of May, 1809 continued

statement of testimony of JOHN FLUCK, mill employee, heard by JOHN FOLKERTH, JP. pp 558, 559

Case 37.   JACOB PHILLIPSON vs HENRY MARQUARD.   On 1 Sept, 1808, $300 debt for goods.   Refusal to pay. Suit filed.   Def'nt refuted debt.   Jury summoned: JOHN BONNER, DANIEL C. COOPER, OWEN DAVIS, WILLIAM HOLE, ALEXANDER McCONNEL, JAMES MILLEGAN, WILLIAM NEWCOM, JOHN NOFFZINGER, JOHN TAYLOR, PHILIP WAGNER, JOHN WAYMIRE, ROBERT WILSON.   Found MARQUARD not guilty, to recover $38.20 costs. pp 560, 561

Case 38.   BENJAMIN LEHMAN vs HENRY MARQUART.   On 8 July, 1807, $50 note.   On 18 May, 1808, 2d $50 note. On 15 July, 1808, $70 note.   Failure to pay.   Suit filed.   Def'nt refuted debt, to offer evidence of indebtedness by LEHMAN for $30.   Jury found MARQUART guilty.   LEHMAN to recover $50.56 debt, $54.08 costs. Copy of original note.   HENRY MARQUART ads BENJAMIN LEHMAN.   Deposition made at Cincinnati before JAMES EWING, JP, on 8 March, 1809: testimony of SIMON PHILIPSON, of legal age, concerning a conversation he had with LEHMAN who denied that MARQUART owed money, but that he was indebted to MARQUART. pp 561, 562, 563

Case 39.   JOHN SUTHERLAND & HENRY BROWN vs MARTIN SHUEY & MARTIN EARHART.   On 16 Dec, 1808, SHUEY & EARHART, acting as partners in trade, signed note for $1845 for goods received.   Failed to pay.   Suit filed; EARHART was not found by sheriff.   SHUEY admitted debt.   Plntfs recover $1886.31 damages, $11.16 costs.   Copy of original note.   pp 563, 564

Case 40.   JOHN MIKESELL vs NATHANIEL LYON.   Unlawful detention of grey mare valued at $80 by LYON.   Sued for $25 damages.   Suit quashed; LYON to recover $9.19 costs. p 564

Case 41.   STATE vs JOSIAH CLAWSON.   Contempt.   Discharged. p 564

Case 42.   Commissioners of Montgomery County vs AUSBORN COOPER & PAUL D. BUTLER.   Debt $94, damages $20. Disc. p 564

Case 43.   JOHN COMPTON JR vs EZEKIEL HUTCHINSON. Damages $100.   Disc. p 565

Case 44.   HENRY DISBROW vs WILLIAM HEAH.   Damage $60. Disc. p 565

COMMON PLEAS (CIVIL) LAW RECORD BOOK A-1

Term of May, 1809 continued

Case 45. WILLIAM CLARK vs WILLIAM REDDICK. Sheriff's return nihil. p 565

Case 46. STATE vs MOSES BADGLEY. Sheriff's return nihil. p 565.

Case 47. JOHN RHOADS vs DANIEL C. COOPER. Sheriff's amendment. p 565.

COMMON PLEAS (CIVIL) LAW RECORD BOOK B-1

Term of September, 1809

Case 1. STATE vs PAUL D. BUTLER. On 23 Aug, 1808, writ of execution issued by JOHN FOLKERTH, JP. Judgement obtained by GEORGE KUNS against BUTLER for payt of $5.39 debt, $.55 costs. BUTLER was to be arrested, property seized, until debt was paid. On 26 Aug, 1808, writ given to Constable EBENEZER WADE of Dayton Twp who attempted to levy writ by taking BUTLER's table. BUTLER assaulted Constable WADE, pled not guilty. DAVID SQUIER & BUTLER stood appearance bond of $100 for Sept court term. Jury summoned: FRANCIS BROCK, JOHN BROWER JR, JOHN BUCHER, ANDREW FOUTZ, SMITH GREGG, GEORGE HARRIS, JOHN HIMES, ELIHU KELLOGG, GEORGE KERNS, CHRISTIAN NEFF, JOHN NOFFZINGER, JAMES THOMSON. Found BUTLER not guilty. pp 1, 2, 3

Case 2. STATE vs JACOB MULLENDORE. Grand Jury: DANIEL HOOVER JR, DANIEL SHIVELY, JONATHAN HARSHMAN, CHRISTIAN BROWER, JACOB MULLENDORE, STEPHEN ULRICH, ROBERT SCOTT, JOHN AINSWORTH, JOHN DAY, ANDREW RAY, JOSEPH COOPER, WILLIAM FARMER, CHARLES MORGAN, JOHN ARCHER, JOSEPH EWING. On 20 March, 1809, JACOB of Jefferson Twp assaulted JOHN MILLER. Def'nt pled not guilty. MULLENDORE & JOHN COMPTON JR stood appearance bond of $60. Jury summoned: JOHN BUCHER, JACOB DEAL, ANDREW FOUTZ, SMITH GREGG, GEORGE HARRIS, JOHN HIMES, SAMUEL HOWARD, ELIHU KELLOGG, GEORGE KERNS, CHRISTIAN NEFF, JOHN NOFFZINGER, JAMES THOMSON. Found JACOB guilty. Fined $18.21. pp 4, 5

Case 3. GEORGE FRIBERGER vs PATRICK LAFFERTY. On 12 March, 1806, $60 note. Failed to pay. Suit filed. LAFFERTY failed to defend. FRIBERGER to recover $51.85 debt, $10.81 costs. Copy of original note, witness VALENTINE WEAVER. pp 5, 6, 7

Term of September, 1809 continued

Case 4. JONATHAN JUSTICE vs SAMUEL HOPKINS & JAMES MILLER. On 27 Aug, 1805, $45.50 note. Copy of original note, witness WILLIAM ELLIS. Refused to pay. Suit filed. Def'nts refuted debt: case should have been taken to Justice of the Peace, the proper jurisdiction for the size of the debt. Trial: def'nts failed to defend. JUSTICE to recover $26.98 debt residue and damages. pp 7, 8, 9

Case 5. DANIEL C. COOPER vs HENRY DISBROW et al. Petition signed by DISBROW et al placed before Montgomery County Commissioners on 6 June, 1808, asking for road leading south, intersecting with state road to Cincinnati. Commissioners appt'd WILLIAM GEORGE, JOHN H. WILLIAMS & WILLIAM ROBINSON as viewers, JOSEPH WILSON, surveyor, to inspect for road, report back. At next meeting, agreed to proceed with road; petitioners filed bond conditioned upon building a bridge across a bayou. COOPER & PAUL D. BUTLER, his security, appealed the decision on 13 Sept, 1808. Suit brought; Court decided appeal should be quashed and dismissed suit. DISBROW et al to recover costs of $8.16. pp 10, 11

Case 6. JAMES MILLER, late Coroner of Montgomery Co, vs WILLIAM McCANN & PETER CLAWSON. On 5 Aug, 1807, debt of $200. Refused to pay. Suit filed. Failed to defend. MILLER to recover $120.90 debt residue, $11.11 costs. Copy of original note, witness HUGH McCOLLOM, ABRAHAM BARNET. pp 11, 12

Case 7. JOSEPH HALE vs ALEXANDER SCOTT. On 1 March, 1808, $120 debt. SCOTT failed to pay. HALE appeared before JOHN McCABE, JP of Washington Twp, for judgement against PETER CLAWSON. Suit taken to Supreme Court which supported judgement of $11.76 and costs. HALE charged nonpayment by CLAWSON and by SCOTT. Defendant failed to defend. HALE to recover $82.50 debt residue, $11.76 costs. pp 13, 14, 15

Case 8. JOHN COMPTON JR vs DAVID REID. On 18 March, 1807, $71 debt. On 5 April, 1808, $31 debt. On 31 Dec, 1808, $97.32 debt. Refusal to pay. Suit filed. REID failed to defend. COMPTON to recover $199.32 debt, $17 damage, $10.98 costs. REID to appeal to Supreme Court. Copies of original notes. pp 15, 16

Case 9. JOHN MIKESELL vs NATHANIEL LYON. Unlawful taking of bay colt, valued at $60, 100 bushel corn valued at $25, unjustly detained against pledges.

Term of September, 1809 continued

MIKESELL failed to appear. LYON recover $9.99 cost.
pp 16, 17

Case 10. STATE vs MOSES BADGELY. MOSES had sued
DANIEL GRIFFIN who was not found by the Sheriff to
respond; the suit was dismissed. Costs of $5.02
remain unpaid. BADGELY, not to be found in the baliwick, failed to defend. State to recover previous
costs of $5.02, $8.64 costs. pp 17, 18

Case 11. WILLIAM A. BEATTY DIRECTOR vs BENJAMIN
ARCHER. On 10 Sept, 1806, $173.50 note signed by
ARCHER & SAMUEL G. MARTIN (who was not found to
respond to writ). Failure to pay. Suit filed,
ARCHER failed to defend. DIRECTOR to recover debt,
$20.75 damage, $10.50 costs. Copy of original note,
witness GRAY GARY, WILLIAM GORDON. pp 18, 19

Case 12. THOMAS GRAHAM vs HENRY DISBROW. On 28 May,
1808, $311 note. Failed to pay. Suit filed. DIS-
BROW failed to defend. GRAHAM to recover $295.64
debt residue, $10.11 costs. DISBROW gave notice of
appeal to Supreme Court. Copy of original note,
witness DANIEL BAILEY. pp 19, 20

Case 13. JEROM HOLT, Sheriff of Montgomery Co, vs
DAVID RIFFLE. On 27 Aug, 1808, RIFFLE & PATRICK LAF-
FERTY signed note for $100. Failed to pay. Copy of
original note included, witness SAMUEL THOMSON. Note
covered appearance bond in case of GEORGE FRIBERGER
vs PATRICK LAFFERTY in which LAFFERTY failed to appear. Court found matters insufficient in law to
maintain action; suit dismissed. RIFFLE to recover
$11.05 costs. pp 20, 21, 22

Case 14. ANDREW LOCK vs WILLIAM ALLISON. On 1 May,
1807, agreement to rent land to ALLISON, payable in
corn. On 1 Dec, 1807, $15 debt for corn seed, $15
debt for pork sold. Failed to pay. Suit filed. AL-
LISON refuted debts. Jury summoned: JAMES BAXTER,
JOHN COMPTON JR, JACOB DEAL, JOHN DODSON, SAMUEL HOW-
ARD, PETER LEHMAN, HUGH McCOLLOM, JAMES MILES, JOHN
MILLAR, GEORGE STRADER, JAMES WELSH, ROBERT WILSON.
Acquited ALLISON. LOCK's atty charged verdict contrary to evidence, requested verdict be set aside,
new trial granted. Court ruled verdict was in no way
insufficient or erroneous, not to be set aside. LOCK
to take nothing, ALLISON recover $26.50 costs. pp 23
24, 25

Term of September, 1809 continued

Case 15. PAUL D. BUTLER vs ANDREW LOCK. On 10 Jan, 1809, $50 debt for lodging, board, services provided SARAH LOCK, wife of ANDREW, during her lifetime. Debt of $20 for services of BUTLER's wife SARAH as a seamstress for SARAH LOCK. Def'nt refuted debt. Jury summoned: FRANCIS BROCK, JOHN BROWER JR, JOHN BUCHER, ANDREW FOUTS, SMITH GREGG, GEORGE HARRIS, JOHN HIMES, ELIHU KELLOGG, GEORGE KERNS, CHRISTIAN NEFF, JOHN NOFFZINGER SR, JAMES THOMSON. Found LOCK guilty. BUTLER to recover $7.25 damages, $28.58 costs. pp 25, 26, 27

Case 16. JOHN MILLER vs JACOB MULLENDORE. On 1 Oct, 1808, $50 debt for labor. JACOB refuted debt, to give evidence of full payment. Jury found JACOB guilty. MILLER to recover $8 damages. JACOB's atty charged verdict was erroneous, requested retrial. Court found verdict sufficient, refused to grant new trial. MILLER to recover damages, $28.38 costs. pp 27, 28

Case 17. MAXFIELD LUDLOW vs PAUL D. BUTLER & DAVID SQUIER. On 26 Dec, 1804, LUDLOW contracted for the manufacture and delivery of 60,000 bricks, paying $4 per thousand. Gave note for $240. The defendants brought suit for payt, claiming they had delivered the bricks as agreed. The Supreme Court, term of Nov, 1807, issued a judgement in favor of BUTLER & SQUIER. Sheriff's sale of LUDLOW's home and lot caused financial injury and loss to LUDLOW. In this suit, LUDLOW charged failure to deliver bricks, breach of contract, conspiracy with unknown persons to cause financial ruin. The def'nts responded that the allegations were vague, unfounded, and requested judgement whether they should be compelled to answer further. Plaintiff, required by the Court to show cause, failed to appear for trial, failed to enter security for court costs. Suit dismissed by Court. pp 29, 30, 31

Case 18. JOHN MIKESELL vs JOHN COMPTON JR. PHILIP GUNCKEL, JP of German Twp, heard case COMPTON vs MIKESELL on 1 Sept, 1807. Judgement of $49.36 debt, $5.88 interest, $1.12 costs against MIKESELL. On 28 Nov, 1808, JOHN MIKESELL SR became securitor for plntfs court appearance. Plntf's atty charged errors in GUNCKEL's judgement, request that it be set aside. Writ quashed by Court. COMPTON to recover $9.38 costs. pp 31, 32

Term of September, 1809 continued

Case 19. PEYTON SHORT vs JOHN HUNT & NATHANIEL HUNT. Execution of judgement set aside in previous case, since that judgement was levied on a tract of land whose title remains with United States and since Jury considered value of a distillery which was personal chattels. Court set judgement aside. p 32

Case 20. MARTIN EARHART vs DAVID REID. Motion to set judgement aside; levied on parcel of land. p 33

Case 21. JOHN FREEMAN vs BARNHART SPECK & PETER McCREA. Judgement at Dec 1806 term for Plntf: costs remain unpaid. Plntf to pay $23.79 costs. p 33

Case 22. JOSEPH REYBURN vs SAMUEL HOPKINS. Judgement at Apr term, 1807 for Plntf: costs remain unpaid. Plntf to pay $11.16 costs. p 33

Case 23. PAUL D. BUTLER & DAVID SQUIER vs ROBERT PATTERSON. Case disc at Df'nt's cost Aug term, 1807. Costs of suit unpaid. Df'nt to pay $14.59. p 33

Case 24. JOHN McCLELLAND vs JAMES FLINN. Disc at Df'nt's cost Aug term, 1807. Costs unpaid. Df'nt to pay $9.97. p 33

Case 25, WILLIAM ROBISON vs JOSEPH REYBURN. Case disc 1807. Costs unpaid. Plntf to pay $2.02, atty having relinquished his fee. p 34

Case 26. PATRICK LAFFERTY vs JOSEPH REYBURN. Case disc Apr term, 1808. Costs unpaid. Plntf to pay $8.92. p 34

Case 27. JOHN MIKESELL vs NATHANIEL LYON. Case disc Jan term, 1809. Costs unpaid. Plntf to pay $7.71. p 34

Case 28. SAMUEL GRIPE vs DANIEL FETTERS. Damages $200. Disc. p 34

Case 29. GEORGE F. TENNERY vs PETER CLAWSON. Damages $50. Disc. p 34

Case 30. RHINEHART SNIPE, appellee, vs CYRUS THAXTON, appellant. Appeal from judgement, court of JOHN McCABE, JP. p 34

Case 31. JAMES MILLER late coroner vs JOHN COMPTON JR & DAVID REID. Debt $2200, damage $500. Disc. p 34

Term of January, 1810

Case 1.   STATE vs GEORGE BODKIN.   Grand Jury: WIL-
LIAM McCLURE, ROBERT EWING, JOHN SHUPART, MARTIN
SHUEY, ANDREW SMALL, JAMES WILSON, JONATHAN HATFIELD,
ROBERT ELLIOT, BENJAMIN SMITH, WILLIAM WILSON, GEORGE
LONG, CHRISTOPHER CURTNER, ROBERT McCLEARY, ALEXANDER
SNODGRASS, LUTHER BREWEN. On 1 Nov, 1808, BODKIN of
Green Co assaulted JOHN HUNT.   Dfnt pled not guilty.
BODKIN & JOSIAH CLAWSON posted appearance bond.   BOD-
KIN failed to appear 3 consecutive terms of court.
Bond forfeiture declared absolute.   pp 35, 36

Case 2.   STATE vs JOHN HUNT & NATHANIEL HUNT.   On 1
Nov, 1808, assaulted GEORGE BODKIN.   NATHANIEL pled
not guilty.   GEORGE NEWCOM & NATHANIEL posted appearance bond.   Jan term, indictment dropped by prosecutor ISAAC G. BURNET, dfnts dismissed.   pp 36, 37

Case 3.   STATE vs BENJAMIN LEHMAN.   Grand Jury:
DAVID REID, JOHN H. WILLIAMS, EDMUND MUNGER, HENRY
CRIST, MARTIN McCREA, WILLIAM EMRICK, NATHANIEL LYON,
ANDREW NOFFZINGER, ISAAC MILLER SR, WILLIAM HAMER,
WILLIAM P. SMITH, JOHN ULRICH, JAMES B. OLIVER, ISAAC
GRIFFIN, ABRAHAM TROXEL.   16 June, 1808, LEHMAN
"forged and counterfeited" a due bill, purported to
be that of JAMES NOLAN, intent to defraud.   Copy of
disputed note. Brought into Court, LEHMAN said State
should be barred from indictment; he had previously
answered the charge April term, 1810, and was acquit-
ed. Court found no record of indictment.   LEHMAN
pled not guilty. Jury summoned: LUTHER BRUEN, JOSEPH
CRIPE, JACOB CRULL, JOHN DODSON, DAVID DUNCAN, OWEN
HATFIELD, ALEXANDER SCOTT, WILLIAM STEPHENS, JOHN
TAYLOR, STEPHEN ULRICH, CHRISTOPHER WILSON, JOSEPH
WILSON.   Acquited LEHMAN.   pp 37, 38, 39

Case 4.   GEORGE SMITH vs NIMROD HADDIX & ROBERT BELL.
On 12 Jan, 1809, dfnts assaulted SMITH, held him
prisoner 24 hours.   HADDIX pled not guilty.   SMITH
failed to enter security for court costs; charges
dismissed. HADDIX & BELL recover $18.31 costs.   pp
39, 40

Case 5.   ISAAC REID vs JOHN ARCHER. On 25 July, 1806
at New Orleans, note for $400 signed. Refused to pay.
Suit filed, damages $60.   ARCHER failed to defend.
REID to recover $240.50 debt residue, $10.67 costs.
Copy of original note: "ISAAC REID of Pennsylvania"
Debt was to be paid at "port of Havana, ARCHER now
being lading for that port of board the Brig Blacka-
lunt".   Note endorsed by REID to ISAAC TODD of Phila-

Term of January, 1810 continued

delphia on 1 Dec 1807. Assigned by TODD to MAURICE WARTZ at Philadelphia, Apr, 1808. pp 40, 41

Case 6. SAMUEL ARCHER vs JOHN BIGGER, JAMES BAY & WILLIAM McCANN. ARCHER recovered $77.40 debt, $12.55 costs in previous suit. Dfnts failed to pay judgement. Failed to defend this suit. ARCHER to recover $17.90 damages, $9.98 costs. pp 42, 43

Case 7. JOHN BROWN vs BENJAMIN ARCHER. On 15 June, 1808, JOHN JUDY gave note for $90, ARCHER to pay BROWN on JUDY's behalf. Refused to pay. ARCHER failed to defend. BROWN recover $95.33 damages, $11.11 costs. Copy of original note. "To BENJAMIN ARCHER Sir pleas to pay or except to pay unto JOHN BROWN the some of ninety dollars and this shall be your receipt for the same and in so doing you will oblige your freind. JOHN JUDY." Witness, DAVID GRUMMAN. Endorsement: Accepted, BENJAMIN ARCHER. pp 43, 44

Case 8. JOHN COMPTON JR vs JEROM HOLT. On 29 July, 1808, $123.43 debt. Failed to pay. Suit filed, damages $50. HOLT admitted debt. COMPTON to recover debt, $10.50 damages, $9.15 costs. Copy of original note, witness NATHANIEL HUNT. pp 44, 45

Case 9. JOHN VANOSDALL vs BENJAMIN LEHMAN. Damages $600. Disc. p 45

Case 10. PEYTON SHORT vs JOHN BODLEY. Debt $1600, damages $400. Disc. p 45

Case 11. DAVID REID vs PETER WOOD. Damages $200. Disc. p 46

Case 12. BARNHART SPECK vs JOHN HENSEY. Bay horse, value $60. Settled. p 46

Case 13. EDWARD FLOOD vs GEORGE GEISAMAN & DANIEL RHUFF. Damages $200, dfnts not to be found. p 46

Term of May, 1810

Case 1. HENRY PURVIANCE vs SAMUEL FREEMAN. Disc. p 47

Case 2. WILLIAM ELLIS vs THOMAS STEWART. The plntf claimed he was man of unblemished character, slandered by STEWART. On 25 Dec, 1807, accused ELLIS of

Term of May, 1810 continued

stealing a handful of salt out of the barrel in "our cellar", meaning the cellar of traders JOHN SUTHERLAND & HENRY BROWN. ELLIS was taken before JPs DANIEL COOPER, CHRISTOPHER CURTNER where he was required to give bail for court appearance. STEWART pressed charges; grand jury refused to find bill of indictment against ELLIS. So cleared, ELLIS accused STEWART of injuring his reputation, hindering him from carrying out his business, and sued for $300 damages. STEWART pled not guilty and posted appearance bond of $100. HENRY BROWN posted bond for damages if STEWART convicted. ELLIS filed affidavit that JAMES BROWN, a material witness, was missing: case continued to next term. Jury summoned: JOHN ALLEN, JOHN BIGGER, JOSEPH FLORA, GEORGE KUNS, ALEXANDER McCONNEL, JACOB MULLENDORE, ROBERT PARK, JOSEPH RORER, JACOB RUDY, JACOB STETLER, SAMUEL WILLIAMSON, HENRY ZELLER. Acquited STEWART. ELLIS take nothing, STEWART recover $43.34 costs. pp 47, 48, 49,, 50, 51, 52

Case 3. STATE vs PETER CLAWSON. On 30 Aug, 1809, unlawfully threatened JOHN EWING, JOHN HOLE, RICHARD SHAW, JOHN PRICE and OWEN DAVIS. Dfnt claimed he was not bound to answer charge; threats aforesaid were not specified. Indictment quashed. pp 53, 54

Case 4. THOMAS NEWMAN vs JOSHUA CON. damages $150. Disc. p 54

Case 5. ABRAHAM HOSIER vs HENRY DISBROW. On 9 March, 1809, $300 debt. Failed to pay. Suit filed. Dfnt refuted debt. Jury summoned: LUTHER BRUEN, JOSEPH CRIPE, JACOB CRULL, JOHN DODSON, DAVID DUNCAN, OWEN HATFIELD, CHRISTOPHER MASON, ALEXANDER SCOTT, WILLIAM STEPHENS, JOHN TAYLOR, STEPHEN ULRICH, JOSEPH WILSON. Found DISBROW guilt. HOSIER to recover $122.76, $19.43 costs. copy of original notes: HOSIER assigned certificate on lot 200, town of Dayton, to DISBROW, witness DAVID MITCHEL. Note drawn by MATTHEW ULRIGHT, dated 28 March, 1808, assigned by DISBROW to HOSIER on March 1809, witness STEPHEN STULHEW. Note drawn by WILLIAM McCASEY, witness WASHINGTON PHARES, dated 5 Oct, 1807, assigned by DISBROW to HOSIER on 9 March, 1809. Note drawn by WILLIAM McCARTY, witness JOSEPH HUNT, dated 27 Nov, 1806, assigned by DISBROW to HOSIER on 9 March, 1809 pp 54, 55, 56

Case 6. JOHN DENN on demise of WILLIAM BROWN vs WILLIAM KING. On 1 April, 1809, DENN had agreement

Term of May, 1810 continued

with BROWN for 2 yrs use of 600 acres in Sec 16, T 2, R 5; term not expired. KING, on 2 April, 1809, with force and arms, ejected DENN from the farm. DENN sued for damages of $500. KING pled not guilty. Jury summoned: JOHN ALLEN, JOHN BIGGER, JOSEPH FLORA, PETER HOOVER, GEORGE KUNS, ALEXANDER McCONNEL, JACOB MULLENDORE, ROBERT PARK, JOSEPH RORER, JACOB RUDY, JACOB STETLER, HENRY ZELLER. Found KING guilty, DENN to collect $.05 damages, $18.69 costs. Copy of original indenture dated 19 Oct, 1805, made between JOHN McCABE & JAMES CAROTHERS, Trustees of Washington Twp, and WILLIAM KING. Land lease for 15 years if KING clears land, builds cabin, plants orchard. Witness NAHELL CAB, PETER BABB. Judgement in WILLIAM BROWN vs JOHN KING, WILLIAM KING, ALEXANDER WEID & JOSEPH PARKS JR, dated 11 March, 1809: property used to satisfy judgement was the above lease. Certified by JAMES McENREW, Warren Co. Endorsement assigning land rights in lease to JOHN KING, dated 31 Jan, 1807, signed WILLIAM KING. Certificate dated 31 March, 1809, delivered execution of judgement to WILLIAM BROWN, signed ROBERT WINSLOW, Constable of Franklin Twp, Warren Co, OH. Record for lease #470, Washington Twp Trustees to WILLIAM KING, recorded Bk A, p 376, on 18 June (1807), signed D. SUTTON for MICHAEL H. JOHNSON, recorder, Warren Co. pp 57, 58, 59

Case 7. WILLIAM LAMB vs DAVID SQUIER. On 4 Jan, 1809, DAVID & TIMOTHY SQUIER entered into recognizance in case of WILLIAM LAMB vs UZAL CRANE, $133.42 bond if CRANE convicted. LAMB recovered $66 debt, $25 damage, $2.31 costs, which CRANE failed to pay. Suit brought against securitor DAVID. Failed to defend suit. LAMB recover damages amounting to $102.02, costs of $10.19 this action. pp 60, 61

Case 8. ARTHUR ST. CLAIR vs DANIEL C. COOPER. On 15 June, 1804, discourse on right of preemption to Sec 32, T 4. R 8, which COOPER had previously sold to JOSEPH McCUNE, JOHN BLUE & JOHN IRWIN. Preemption granted to St. Clair by JAMES FINDLEY & CHARLES KILGORE, Commissioners appted to settle claims contracted by JOHN CLEVES SYMMES. Agreement: ST. CLAIR to transfer rights to McCUNE, BLUE & IRWIN for $200 which they owed COOPER, who would then convey title to 2 lots, town of Dayton, to ST. CLAIR. Suit filed when ST. CLAIR could not get title to lots. COOPER refuted agreement. Jury summoned; COOPER admitted debt. ST. CLAIR recover $144 damage, $12.73 costs. pp 61, 62, 63, 64

Term of May, 1810 continued

Case 9.   Petition of BARNHART SPECK in "an act for relief of insolvent Debtors".   Creditors: TIMOTHY GREEN, JOHN ALEXANDER, JOHN CROLL, JOHN VERNUM, JOHN GEPHART, ANDREW LOCK, ABRAHAM HOZIER, DANIEL LEARY. SPECK failed to appear at hearing. Judges dismissed petition.   SPECK to pay costs of $9.32.   p 65

Case 10. Petition of JOHN DOVE in "an act for relief of insolvent Debtors".   Creditors: JACOB SLY, JOHN LONG, HENRY STANCILL, AMOS MONRO, THOMAS KELSEY, WILLIAM LUCE, JEROM HOLT.   Assests: 1 bed.   DOVE failed to appear at hearing.   Judges dismissed petition.   DOVE to pay costs of $9.32.   p 66

Case 11. Petition of WILLIAM McCANN in "an act for relief of insolvent Debtors". No listing of assests, creditors. McCANN failed to appear at hearing, petition dismissed. p 67

Case 12.   WILLIAM RAMSAY vs MARTIN SHUEY.   Debt of $816.20, damages $100. Disc. p 67

Case 13.   Petition for partition by JOHN DRISCOL in the right of his wife MARY, sister to JOHN AIKEN who died intestate.   AIKENS owned 2 half-lots in town of Dayton, #13 & #14.   Heirs are JOHN DRISCOL in right of wife, WILLIAM AIKENS of Green Co, OH, ALEXANDER AIKENS & GEORGE AIKENS of Lancaster Co, PA.   WILLIAM McCLURE, JOHN GRIMES & HENRY DISBROW to make partition, found lots could not be divided equitably, report dated 5 May, 1809.   Court ordered lands to be sold by Sheriff. DRISCOL to pay costs of $23.65. [[68, 69

Case 14.   EDWARD FLOOD vs GEORGE GEISAMON & DANIEL RHUFF. Damages $200, dfnts not found. p 69

Case 15.   HENRY JENNINGS vs WILLIAM LUCE. Debt $150, damage $50. Disc. p 70

Case 16.   STATE vs GEORGE HOLDER & JOHN MORRIS.   On 1 March, 1810, dfnts, both of Wayne Twp, stole a beehive belonging to JACOB REPLOGEL.   JOHN MORRIS & TRAVIS MORRIS signed appearance bond before JOHN FOLKERTH, JP, 26 March, 1810.   HOLDER, detained in county jail, posted bond co-signed by TRAVIS MORRIS, on 30 March, 1810.   Indicted by Grand Jury: JOHN MILLER, WILLIAM WILLIS, JOHN MIKESELL ST, WILLIAM BOMBERGER JR, JOHN WEAD, JOHN LUCE, JOSEPH HANCOCK, JOHN DUNCAN, JAMES RUPEL,   THOMAS McNUTT, ROBERT WEAD,

Term of May, 1810 continued

JACOB REPLOGEL, ABRAHAM TROXEL, JOHN PETTICREW, DANI-
EL MILLER of Bear Creek. Dfnts failed to appear at
trial. Bonds forfeited. pp 70, 71

Case 17. STATE vs ISRAEL CROSS. On 9 Apr, 1810,
CROSS accused of killing a bull belonging to JOHN
DILLE, stealing the hide. Bond posted by SOLOMON
CROSS & MICHAEL YOUNG. At hearing, no one came for-
ward to accuse CROSS. Case dismissed. pp 71, 72

Case 18. STATE vs PETER CLAWSON. Assault on GEORGE
SOURBRAY. Dfnt escaped before writ served. p 72

Case 19. STATE vs GEORGE BODKIN. Offense not specified. BOTKIN pled not guilty. Jury: BOTKIN guilty.
BOTKIN charged indictment was insufficient, verdict
erroneous. Court agreed. BOTKINS discharged. p 72

Case 20. STATE vs FRANCIS DILTS. On 12 Feb, 1810,
assaulted JAMES HINTON at Washington Twp. DILTS pled
guilty. Fined $2.00, $8.87 costs. p 73

Case 21. Petition of GEORGE MOYER, CATHERINE MILLER,
DAVID MILLER & DANIEL MILLER. DANIEL MILLER & CATH-
ERINE GEPHART MILLER, wife of DAVID, were adm of estate of PETER GEPHART. 2 tracts of land in Sec's 9 &
10, Twp 2, R 5E were co-owned by MOYER & GEPHART. The
land was contracted for sale to JOHN SHUPART, CHRIS-
TOPHER SHUPART & DANIEL MANNBECK, possession already
granted, money already paid. Petition asked right to
execute deeds. Court so ordered. pp 73, 74

Case 22. Petition of GEORGE MOYER, CATHERINE MILLER,
DAVID MILLER & DANIEL MILLER. DANIEL MILLER & CATH-
ERINE GEPHART MILLER, wife of DAVID, were adm of es-
tate of PETER GEPHART. Tracts of land in Sec's 9 &
10, Twp 2, R 5E were co-owned by MOYER & GEPHART.
Agreement made to partition land between MOYER, GEP-
HART's heirs. Bounds of partition included. Request
to execute deeds. Court so ordered. pp 74, 75

Case 23. OLIVER ORMSBY & WILLIAM STANLEY, partners
in trade, vs. CONRAD KASTER & HENRY STRADER. $96.34
debt. Failed to pay. Suit filed. Dfnts admitted
debt. ORMSBY & STANLEY recover $96.34 debt, $9.25
costs. p 76

Term of September, 1810

Case 1. STATE vs BENJAMIN LEHMAN. Indictment for forging note on HENRY MARQUART. Records sent to Green Co for trial. p 77

Case 2. STATE vs BENJAMIN LEHMAN. Indictment for forging note on HENRY MARQUART. Records sent to Green Co for trial. p 77

Case 3. JAMES AIKEN vs HENRY STRADER. Words damage, $1000. Disc. p 77

Case 4. EDMUND ADAMS vs ABRAHAM BARNET. Appeal from judgement of JAMES THOMSON, JP. Disc. p 77

Case 5. ROBERT JOHNSTON vs THOMAS JOHNSTON. Assault & battery, $500 damage. Disc. p 77

Case 6. THOMAS NEWMAN vs JOSHUA COX. Damage $150. Disc. p 77

Case 7. THOMAS McNUTT vs AARON RICHISON. On 17 March, 1810, $500 note signed. RICHISON's son EPHRAIM put as apprentice to McNUTT, later left without permission. Matter to be arbitrated by MATTHEW PATTON, JAMES THOMSON, chose JOHN FOLKERTH to be umpire. Arbitrators found plntf, dfnt wrote mutual notes, ordered McNUTT to give up Articles of Indenture on EPHRAIM RICHISON, release claim for future service. RICHISON to pay $78 to McNUTT for loss of ap prentice service, $1.95 damages, $10.57 costs. pp 78, 79, 80

Case 8. Petition of HENRY CRIST & JACOB KULLMAN, adm of estate of MATTHIAS SCHWARTZEL, permission to convey deed in Sec 20, T 2, R 5E to PHILIP SCHWARTZEL. MATTHIAS, dec in 1805, had original grant on land above, had agreed with brother PHILIP to exchange parcels. Court so ordered. pp 80, 81

Case 9. HENRY ATCHINSON vs WILLIAM B. TODD. On 2 June, 1807, $247 debt. Failed to pay. Suit filed, $50 damages. Dfnt refuted debt, to present evidence that plntf owed $300 for work, goods and cash lent. TODD presented affidavit that JAMES RADCLIFFE, a material witness, was missing: case continued. Trial: TODD admitted debt of $74.07. ATCHISON to recover $74.07, $10.50 costs. Copy of original note co-signed by TODD & DANIEL RICHARDSON, witness HENRY BISHOP. Recpt signed by FREDERICK NUTTZ (german script) for whiskey delivered by RICHARDSON as partial payment of debt, witness PETER KESSLINGER (german script). 1808

Term of September, 1810 continued

note requesting "RITCHISON" to pay bearer DANIEL LAREY as discharge of debt to ATCHISON, witness SAMUEL BOLTON. pp 81, 82, 83, 84

Case 10. MARTHA PERRY vs HENRY DISBROW. Disc. p 84

Case 11. NATHANIEL HUNT vs DANIEL H. FISHER, late Constable of Dayton Twp. Notice that HUNT's property taken by FISHER on a search warrant for GEORGE HOLDER is to be returned. FISHER appeared in court, showed sufficient cause. Suit dismissed by Court. p 84

Case 12. ARCHIBALD McCLEAN vs WILLIAM McCLURE. On 9 Sept, 1808, $100 debt for printing press, type and labor. Failed to pay, dfnt claimed McCLEAN failed to perform labor as agreed. McCLEAN responded that charges are insufficient at law; he was not bound to make answer to McCLURE. McCLEAN to recover debt, $6.50 damages, $10.13 costs. pp 85, 86, 87

Case 13. SOLOMON HAMER vs ALEXANDER GUY. Judgement for $7 issued by JOHN FOLKERTH, JP. On 8 Dec, 1808, note for $8.33 signed; dfnt failed to pay. Suit filed. Dfnt refuted debt, to offer evidence of labor and payment, submitted affidavit that EDWARD FLOOD & JOHN COTTOM, material witnesses, were missing. Bond posted by GEORGE WOLLASTON for GUY. Jury summoned: PETER BANTA, HENRY BROWN, JAMES CAMMACK, NICHOLAS HORNER, BENJAMIN HUTCHINS, JAMES INSCO, THOMAS JAY, ISAAC MILLER SR, GEORGE NEWCOM, EPHRAIM OWEN, PETER SWINEHART, PHILIP WOLF. Found GUY guilty. HAMER to recover $2.25 debt residue, $40.66 costs. Copy of original note. pp 87, 88, 89

Case 14. STATE vs JACOB KUNS. On 29 March, 1810, KUNS & DAVID DUNCAN posted $100 appearance bond with JOHN FOLKERTH, JP. KUNS of Madison Twp, charged with fraud by counterfeit money, pled not guilty. KUNS, JOHN COMPTON, DAVID RIFFLE posted bond in case KUNS was convicted. Jury acquited KUNS. pp 89, 90, 91

Case 15. ARTHUR ST. CLAIR JR, appellant, vs DAVID RIFFLE, appellee. Disc. p 91

Term of January, 1811

Case 1. JOSEPH HACKNEY vs JOSEPH SLOAN. On 4 Aug, 1807, A.W. FOSTER of Crawford Co, PA, wrote bill of exchange which required SLOAN of same to pay $60.

Term of January, 1811 continued

Note accepted by HACKNEY. Refusal to pay. Suit
filed. Dfnt refuted debt, to present evidence plntf
indebted for $50. Trial: dfnt admitted debt. HACK-
NEY to recover $71.70 damage, $10.16 costs. Copy of
original note. pp 92, 93, 94

Case 2. THOMAS FREAM vs LUDWICK KEMP & PETER LEHMAN.
Debt $100, damage $100. Disc. p 94

Case 3. JOHN PAULEY vs PHILIP NEGLEY. Debt $2000,
damages $50. Settled. p 94

Case 4. DANIEL MONBECK & MARGARET MONBECK, his wife,
vs ABRAHAM PAULUS & CHRISTINA PAULUS, his wife. Word
damage $1000. Disc. p 94

Case 5. MARTIN BAUM & SAMUEL PERRY, partners, vs
PETER RUHFF. Suit filed for $192.42 debt, $40 damages. Failed to defend. BAUM & PERRY recover
$192.42, $6.86 damages, $10.24 costs. Copy of orig-
inal note. pp 95, 96

Case 6. DANIEL LEAS vs SAMUEL HOWARD. On 28 Oct,
1807, $50 debt. Failed to pay. Suit filed. HOWARD
failed to defend. LEAS recover debt, $13 damages,
$8.27 costs. Copy of original note, witness WILLIAM
LEAS. pp 96, 97, 98

Case 7. JOHN WEAVER, appellant, vs ABRAHAM MINNIEAR,
appellee. Disc. p 98

Case 8. HUGH STEELE vs JAMES STEELE, JOSEPH STEELE.
Settled. p 98

Case 9. JOHN SUTHERLAND & HENRY BROWN vs MARTIN SHU-
EY. Previous suit judgement gave SUTHERLAND & BROWN
to recover $1886.31 debt, $11.16 costs. SHUEY failed
to pay. Summoned to respond on failure to pay, SHUEY
failed to appear in court. SUTHERLAND & BROWN to
recover additional $7.12 costs. pp 99, 100

Case 10. SAMUEL GRIPE vs DANIEL FETTERS. On Sept,
1808, $2000 debt. Submitted to arbitration by DAVID
ULREY, JOHN GRIPE, PHILIP GUNCKEL umpire. Arbitrators
found FETTERS owed debt of 200 pounds PA currency or
$533.33, pay all costs if he fails to fulfill agree-
ment. Court hearing: FETTERS failed to appear. GRIPE
recover $443.96 debt residue, $7.90 costs. Recpts
filed for payments made between arbitration and court
hearing, witness SAMUEL KIMMEL. pp 100, 101, 102, 103

Term of January, 1811 continued

Case 11. STATE vs HENRY MARQUART. Grand Jury: ROB-
ERT EDGAR, JOHN GUNCKEL, EDWARD SULGROVE, JOHN SUL-
GROVE, DAVID WARD, DANIEL FETTER, IRA SMITH, RICHARD
BROWN, JOHN PATTERSON, WILLIAM VAN CLEVE, GEORGE
WESTFALL, JAMES THOMSON, ROBERT ELLIOT, JAMES BARNET,
RALPH WILSON. On 1 Jan, 1811, MARQUART assaulted
PETER CONNER in Dayton Twp. Pled guilty. Fined $1,
$2.69 costs. p 103

Notice of adjournment. p 104

Term of May, 1811

Case 1. WILLIAM RYAN, appellee vs OWEN DAVIS, appellant. Judgement of 26 Aug, 1809: RYAN to recover
$23.12 debt, $.97 costs. Appealed before JOHN FOL-
KERTH, JP. DAVIS pled not guilty; he had been unable
to pay in goods as RYAN had no house in Dayton to
make delivery, failed to meet other conditions.
Trial: DAVIS admitted debt. RYAN to recover $24.57
debt parcel, $15.26 costs. Copy of original note:
Debt was to be paid in whiskey at RYAN's house. RYAN
to provide half the whiskey barrels, witness AUSBURN
COOPER. pp 105, 106, 107, 108

Case 2. ARCHIBALD McCLEAN vs WILLIAM McCLURE. On 6
Sept, 1808, $100 debt. Failed to pay. Suit filed.
Dfnt refuted debt, McCLEAN failed to perform labor as
agreed. Plntf claimed matters insufficient in law,
not to be replied. McCLURE charged matters were sufficient, require response. Court found McCLURE's
case insufficient. McCLEAN to recover debt, $4.62
damage, $15.37 costs. pp 108, 109, 110

Case 3. ARTHUR ST. CLAIR JR vs BENJAMIN KISER. On 1
Jan, 1810, $20 debt for work as atty. KYSER failed
to pay. Suit filed. Jury summoned: ISAAC COOPER,
HENRY CRULL, JOHN DODSON, ROBERT ELLIOT, EDWARD
MITCHEL, ABRAHAM NEFF, HENRY NEFF, JOHN NEWCOM, JOHN
PATTERSON, JOHN RIGGANS, ROBERT STRAIN SR, STEPHEN
WHITE. KYSER failed to defend. ST. CLAIR recover $5
damages, $15.82 costs. pp 111, 112

Case 4. ARTHUR ST. CLAIR, appellant, vs JAMES BARN-
ET, appellee. On 1 Jan, 1810, $20 debt for work as
an atty. Failed to pay. Suit filed. BARNET failed
to defend. ST. CLAIR recover $8, $9.03 costs. pp
113, 114, 115

Term of May, 1811 continued

Case 5. HENRY WEAVER vs JOHN WAGNER. WEAVER of German Twp, assignee of HENRY WEAVER of Manheim Twp, Berks Co, PA. On 22 Sept, 1806, note signed for $56.34 plus interest. Note assigned 13 April, 180?. WAGNER failed to pay. Suit filed, $30 damages. Failed to defend. WEAVER to recover debt, $15.63 damages, $10.04 costs. pp 115, 116, 117

Case 6. NANCY MAXWELL & JACOB HAINES vs NATHANIEL HUNT & DAVID SQUIER. On 26 Oct, 1809, $144 Debt. Failed to pay. Suit filed, damages $100. Failed to defend. Plntfs recover debt, $4.68 damages, $9.93 costs. Recpt for payt dated 27 May, 1811 signed JACOB HANES. pp 118, 119

Case 7. NANCY MAXWELL & JACOB HAINES vs BENJAMIN SCOTT & JAMES THOMSON. On 26 Oct, 1809, $87.60 debt. Failed to pay. Suit filed. Dfnts admit debt. Plntfs recover $46.70 debt residue, $8.05 damage, $9.19 costs. pp 120, 121

Case 8. ADAM SWINEHART vs JOHN FOLKERTH. On 21 March 1808, $130 debt. Failed to pay in suit of JOHN A. MIKESELL ads ADAM SWINEHART on judgement before PHILIP GUNCKEL, JP German Twp. FOLKERTH stood $130 bond for MIKESELL. Suit filed, damages $50. FOLKERTH failed to defend. SWINEHART recover $22.31 damage, $1.52 costs. pp 121, 122, 123

Case 9. DAVID MILLER vs ANDREW LOCK. On 1 Oct, 1808 agreement for MILLER to farm LOCK's land, caring for livestock. LOCK to provide oxen, a boy to help MIL-LER. At year's end, LOCK & MILLER to divide increase in livestock. MILLER charged he performed duties as agreed. On 30 March, 180?, LOCK ousted MILLER from farm, refused to give MILLER stock, and sued for the price of several hundred bushels corn, causing $300 damage to MILLER. LOCK refuted agreement, to give evidence that MILLER destroyed property and was in debt for $100 in goods. At hearing, MILLER failed to appear. MILLER to take nothing, LOCK recover $29.71 in costs. pp 123, 124, 125, 126, 127, 128

Case 10. STATE vs ABRAHAM DEMOTT. Case brought in Preble Co Common Pleas Court, April term, 1810. Grand Jury (Preble): ALEXANDER PEW, DAVID FOUTZ, DAVID OSBORNE, WILLIAM GARRETT, ABRAHAM HAPNER, WILLIAM CAMPBELL, THOMAS CASSADY, BENEDICT STONER, DAVID VAN WINKLE, PETER OZIAS, SILAS DAVIS, JOHN CLOSSON (CLAWSON?), ALEXANDER STILE, WILLIAM LEES,

Term of May, 1811 continued

JESSE SWISHER. On 9 Jan, 1810, DEMOTT of Twin Twp
stole hogs, value of $12, property of JOSEPH SINGER.
Pled not guilty. Jury summoned (Preble): JACOB LOY,
JOHN NIFE, GEORGE MORNINGSTAR, HENRY FRENCH, WILLIAM
DAVIS, WILLIAM HICKSORD, JOHN SOMERS, HENRY PRICE,
SIMEON VANWINKLE, ADAM BONECRAKE, THOMAS MASSIE, JOHN
WARD. Found DEMOTT guilty. New trial requested and
granted. Place of venire changed as impartial trial
could not be held in Preble Co. DEMOTT, JACOB ROMAN
& WILLIAM BRUCE posted appearance bond. DANIEL REX,
MARTIN RICE, JOSEPH WALKER, DAVID GRISSUM on behalf
of MICHAEL PRICE, SAMUEL HAWKINS, ALBERT BANTA, JACOB
OZIAS & JOHN HART all posted bonds to appear and tes-
tify at trial. ALEXANDER LANIER, Clerk of CommonPleas
Court, Preble Co, 7 Jan, 1811. Montgomery County jury
summoned, found DEMOTT innocent. pp 128, 129, 130

Case 11. STATE vs WILLIAM ASHER. Champaign County
Court of Common Pleas at Urbana: FRANCIS DUNLAVY,
president, JOHN REYNOLDS, JOHN RUNYARD & JOHN GUT-
RIDGE, assoc. judges. Grand Jury (Champaign): BENJA-
MIN NEWELL, JOHN STEWART, JAMES SARGENT, WILLIAM DON-
ALD, JAMES LAMB, JOHN VANCE, JOSEPH SNODGRASS, SAMUEL
PENEE, JOHN GILLILAND, ROBERT MOORE, JOHN CRAIG,
HIRAM M. CURRY, THOMAS M. PENDLETON, ELNATHAN CORRY,
ISAAC VANDESSIN. On 31 March, 1810, ASHER of Zane
Twp assaulted CATHERINE ZANES, beating her with "in-
tent to ravish and carnally know". ASHER, arrested
by Sheriff SAMUEL M. CORD, pled not guilty. Bond
posted by ASHER, JOHN SHARP & SAMUEL SHARP. Prosecu-
tors.for STATE: EDWARD W. PIERCE & HENRY BACON.
Trial heard in Supreme Ct, Champaign Co, term of Dec,
1810. Ordered venire be changed to Montgomery Co.
Additional bond posted by ASHER, JOHN, SAMUEL & DAVID
SHARP, signed by WILLIAM WARD, Clerk, Champaign Co.
Trial jury (Montgomery): HENRY BOWSER, THOMAS COOP-
ER, HENRY CRULL, JOHN DODSON, ROBERT ELLIOT, EDWARD
MITCHEL, HENRY NEFF, JOHN NEWCOM, JOHN PATTERSON,
JOHN RIGGANS, ROBERT STRAIN SR, STEPHEN WHITE. Ac-
quited ASHER on 1st count, found guilty on 2d. Fined
$100, costs of $21.38. (Counts not specifically
given. 1st probably the assault, 2d the attempted
rape.) pp 131, 132, 133

Case 12. STATE vs CONKLIN MILLER. On 1 Jan, 1811,
assaulted JAMES JACKSON at Dayton Twp. Pled guilty.
Fined $2, costs of $6.56. pp 133, 134

Case 13. STATE vs THOMAS SHANKS. On 25 Dec, 1810,
at Washington Twp, assaulted JOHN HUESTON. Pled

Term of May, 1811 continued

guilty. Fined $2, costs of $5.83. pp 134, 135

Case 14. STATE vs PETER LEHMAN.. On 28 Oct, 1810
and other times, sold spiritous liquor (whiskey)
without license. Pled guilty. Fined $.50, $5.00
costs. pp 136, 137

Case 15. MARTIN McCREA vs HENRY ZELLER. Case heard
by PHILIP GUNCKEL, German Twp JP; judgement given 9
Apr, 1810. Writ did not follow within 15 days as
proscribed by law. Writ quashed, suit dismissed.
ZELLER recover $10.28 costs. pp 137, 138

Case 16. ABRAHAM MINNIEAR vs WILLIAM WILSON.
Replevin for black stud horse. Disc. p 138

Case 17. WILLIAM A. BEATY DIRECTOR vs DAVID SQUIER &
DAVID REID. Debt $347, damage $300. Disc. p 138

Case 18. STATE vs ABRAHAM HILDERBRAND. Charged with
contempt. Paid costs of attachment $3.50. p 138

Case 19. STATE vs WILLIAM BUNNEL. Bond posted by
BUNNEL, ELI COMPTON, FREEMAN SHAW before WILLIAM
SNODGRASS, JP, on 28 March, 1811. No one appeared to
press charges. BUNNEL released. p 139, 140

Case 20. STATE vs JOHN ALSPACH. Assault and battery.
Dfnt not found in Sheriff's baliwick. p 140

Case 21. STATE vs JAMES JACKSON. Assault and battery on C. MILLER. Dfnt not found in Sheriff's
baliwick. p 140

Case 22. STATE vs JOHN ROBB. Assault and battery on
JOHN ENOCH. Dfnt not found in baliwick. p 140

Case 23. STATE vs JOHN ENOCH. Assault and battery
on JOHN BELL. Dfnt not found in baliwick. p 140

Term of September, 1811

Case 1. JAMES MILES vs PETER MIKESELL. On 23 Apr,
1810, ABRAHAM HILDERBRAND, JP, Jefferson Twp, heard
case MIKESELL vs MILES. Requested by Common Pleas
Court to send transcript, HILDERBRAND failed to respond through 3 terms of court, to be charged with
contempt if no response by Jan term, 1811. Record of
judgement produced for Sept, 1811 term. On 26 March,
1810, MILES confessed judgement in favor of MIKESELL

78

Term of September, 1811 continued

for $54.45, granted by JP, plus $1.75 costs. Writ (MILES vs MIKESELL) dismissed, sent back to ABRAHAM TROXELL, JP, Jefferson Twp. MIKESELL to recover $11.65 costs. pp 141, 142

Case 2. MATTHIAS RIGAL vs JOHN BARLETT. Damages $500. Disc. p 142

Case 3. JACOB STETLER & BETSEY STETLER, his wife, vs PETER HOOVER. Damages $500. Disc. p 142

Case 4. JACOB STETLER vs PETER HOOVER. Damages $100. Disc. p 142

Case 5. STATE VS PETER SUNDERLAND. Appearance bond posted 4 Sept, 1810, by SUNDERLAND & GEORGE NEWCOM in court of JAMES THOMSON, JP. On 10 Sept, 1810, assaulted WILLIAM WILSON at Dayton Twp. Pled guilty. Fined $5, $7.55 costs. pp 142, 143, 144

Case 6. STATE vs JOHN ALSPACH. On 25 Nov, 1810, assaulted IRA SMITH. Pled guilty. Fined $5, $7.55 costs. pp 144; 145

Case 7. STATE vs JOHN ROBB. On 9 Oct, 1810, ROBB of Wayne Twp assaulted JOHN ENOCH. Pled guilty. Fined $5, $8.66 costs. p 145

Case 8. NICHOLAS SMALL SR vs ABRAHAM BARNET & JAMES BARNET. Debt $1500, damages $500. Setlted. p 146

Case 9. BETSY INDICOT (ENDICOT?) vs SOLOMON HAMER. Recognizance for bastardy. Discharged at dfnt's cost. p 147

Case 10. DAVID REID & WILLIAM GEORGE vs ELIZABETH PARKER & JAMES WELSH. Petition for partition of real estate. Petition withdrawn. p 147

Case 11. STATE vs JAMES JACKSON. Assault. Dfnt not found in Sheriff's baliwick. p 147

Case 12. JOSEPH DODDS vs JOHN McGREW. certiorari to McGREW, JP. Settled. p 147

Case 13. JOSEPH DODDS vs ISAAC CLARK. certiorari to McGREW, JP. Settle. p 147

Case 14. JEROM HOLT, Sheriff, vs DANIEL RHUFF & HENRY RHUFF. Debt $600, damages $50. Disc. p 147

COMMON PLEAS (CIVIL) LAW RECORD BOOK B-1

Term of September, 1811 continued

Case 15.   PHILIP GUNCKEL vs MARTIN SHUEY.   Damages
$2000. Disc. p 147

No #.   On 9 Sept, 1811, CATHERINE GEPHART of Washington Twp and HUGH McCOLLOM of Dayton applied for renewal of licenses to keep a tavern. p 147

No #.   On 11 Sept, 1811, STEELE & PEIRCE applied for
license to keep store at Dayton. DANIEL C. COOPER
applied for license to keep store at Dayton. ROBERT
GRAHAM applied for license renewal to keep tavern. p
147.

No #.   On 11 Sept, 1811, Bond of Clerk of Common
Pleas Court, BENJAMIN VAN CLEVE. Securitors HORATIO
G. PHILIPS, HENRY BROWN. p 148

No #.   On 11 Sept, 1811, Bond of Inspector of Montgomery County, WILLIAM GEORGE. Securitors DAVID
REID, JAMES THOMSON. Treasurer of Montgomery County
CHRISTOPHER CURTNER. Inspector to provide branding
irons: MESS PORK, CARGO PORK, M.C. INSPECTED, FINE,
S. FINE. Butter and lard to be marked on cask with
pencil or brush. p 148

Term of January, 1812

Case 1.   JOHN COMPTON JR vs GEORGE NEWCOM, Sheriff.
Dec term, 1805: COMPTON replevined $4000 worth of
merchandise unjustly detained by NEWCOM. (over 2
pages itemizing merchandise taken from COMPTON's
store, held against debts) Coroner JAMES MILLER
endorsed replevin, took possession of goods. NEWCOM
charged writ was vague, did not sufficiently list
chattels to be taken, need not respond. Court found
writ was sufficient, NEWCOM should respond. At
hearing, NEWCOM failed to appear. COMPTON to recover
$16.50 costs. pp 149, 150, 151, 152, 153, 154

Case 2.   STATE vs OWEN DAVIS. On 10 Aug, 1808, DAVIS
of Dayton Twp assaulted GEORGE KUNS. Pled not guilty.
Bond posted by DAVIS, ABRAHAM BARNET. Jury found
DAVIS guilty. Case continued through several terms
while Court decided upon judgement, finally dismissed
case. pp 154, 155, 156, 157

Case 3.   STATE vs JOHN MULLINIX. Grand Jury: AARON
NUTT, MICHAEL HAGAN, CONKLIN MILLER, SYLVANUS SWAL-
LOW, GEORGE YOUNT JR, JOSEPH COOPER, BENJAMIN OWENS,
DANIEL JONES, JOSEPH COLMAN, JACOB ARNOLD SR, WILLIAM

Term of January, 1812 continued

WILSON, EBENEZER WEAD JR, JOHN PRICE, JOHN HUNT, RALPH WILSON. On 15 --, 1811, MULLINIX of Randolph Twp assaulted BENJAMIN HUTCHINS. Pled guilty. Fined $1, $4.49 costs. pp 157, 158

Case 4. STATE vs JOHN HOLLINGSWORTH. On 1 May, 1811, THOMAS COOPER & HOLLINGSWORTH of Randolph Twp fought together at fisticuffs, an evil example for others. Sheriff failed to find dfnts. HOLLINGSWORTH voluntarily appeared, pled guilty. Fined $3, $3.60 costs. pp 158, 159

Case 5. PEYTON SHORT vs PETER RHUFF. $320 debt, $100 damages. Disc. p 159

Case 6. BETSEY INDICOT vs SOLOMON HAMER. execution. p 159

Case 7. BENJAMIN LEHMAN vs JAMES NOLAN. Slander, damages $1000. Settled. p 159

Case 8. JAMES McCLURE vs JOHN COMPTON JR. Settled. p 159

Case 9. DANIEL C. COOPER vs RALPH PHILLIPS. Damage $5000. Disc. p 160

Case 10. ABRAHAM BARNET vs PAUL D. BUTLER, HUGH McCOLLOM, JAMES BARNET. Damage $300. Settled. p 160

Case 11. DANIEL C. COOPER vs ROBERT CULBERTSON. Damage $100. Disc. p 160

Case 12. STATE vs JOHN ENOCH. On 9 Oct, 1810, ENOCH of Wayne Twp assaulted JOHN BELL. Pled not guilty. Jury summoned: JOHN BRADFORD, RICHARD GREY, WILLIAM LONG, DANIEL MARTIN, MARTIN McCREA, JOSEPH OWENS, JAMES RIDDEL, GEORGE SMITH, GEORGE SOURBRAY, LUDWICK SPEECE, ABRAHAM STONER. Found ENOCH guilty. Fined $1, $24.11 costs. pp 160, 161

Case 13. DANIEL C. COOPER vs ELIAS J. DAYTON. Slander, suit of $1000. Affidavit: DAYTON a citizen of NJ, requests change of venue to Chillecothe, OH, to be heard in US Circuit Court. Appearance bond posted on behalf of DAYTON by HORATIO G. PHILLIPS. Change of venire granted. pp 162, 163

Case 14. STATE vs HENRY LEHMAN. On 2 Nov, 1811, LEHMAN and JOHN ENSY posted appearance bond with

COMMON PLEAS (CIVIL) LAW RECORD BOOK B-1

Term of January, 1812 continued

JOHN FOLKETH, JP. Grand Jury: BENJAMIN ARCHER,
GEORGE GROVE, WILLIAM DODDS, HENRY CURTNER, CHRISTO-
PHER EMRICK, STEPHEN STUTZMAN, BENJAMIN MALTBIE,
JAMES MILES, ANDREW RAY, GEORGE ROUDEBUSH, DAVID
McCLURE, AARON BAKER, WILLIAM McCLURE, GEORGE FRI-
BERGER, JOHN PATTERSON. On 28 Sept, 1811, writ
issued in case of JOSHUA RUSSEL, RHODA RUSSEL & JOHN
ROBB vs SAMUEL THOMSON & BAZIL WILLIAMS. Judgement
for debt and damages in Plntfs' favor. Property of
dfnts to be sold to satisfy. JEROM HOLT, Sheriff,
authorized Constable DAVID STEELE to impound a cow to
be sold. LEHMAN assaulted STEELE, to prevent the cow
from being taken. LEHMAN pled guilty. Fined $5,
$10.77 costs. pp 163, 164, 165, 166

Case 15. JONATHAN TULLIS JR vs JEROM HOLT, Sheriff of
Montgomery Co. TULLIS produced execution docket of
Sept term, 1810, case 10: Suit for debt against
GEORGE TENNERY & WILLIAM CLARK. TULLIS moved to act
against HOLT for recovery. Court found TULLIS to
take nothing, HOLT recover $13.10 costs. pp 166, 167

Case 16. STATE vs DANIEL RHUFF, HENRY RHUFF, ADAM
RHUFF & FREDERICK PENTHER. Defnts and securitors
CHRISTIAN CARVER & WILLIAM STEWART appeared in Court.
Nothing exhibited against them by Grand Jury.
Dismissed. p 167

Case 17. STATE vs RICHARD D. GARDNER. On 6 Jan,
1812, assaulted THOMAS DISBROW, a black man, at Dayton Twp. Pled guilty. Fined $10, $9.33 costs. pp
167, 168

Case 18. LUDWICK CHRISTIAN vs JACOB KUNS. Case between KUNS & DANIEL DIETER heard 13 Sept, 1810, before DAVID HOOVER, JP, Randolph Twp. CHRISTIAN was
witness for DIETER. Accused of perjury by KUNS in
German language "ER HAT FALSH GESHWAREN", understood
by nearly all in hearing. Damage to reputation $500.
KUNS pled not guilty. Jury found KUNS guilty, gave
CHRISTIAN damages of $45. KUNS' atty charged verdict
erroneous, should be set aside. Court found verdict
was sufficient, not quashed. CHRISTIAN recover $45,
$24.37 costs. pp 168, 169, 170, 171

Case 19. SAMUEL REDDICK vs JONATHAN MUNGER.
Summoned to answer to suit for $500 damages, MUNGER
filed affidavit that he was served writ on 6 Jan,
1812. Court dismissed writ. p 171, 172

82

Term of January, 1812 continued

Case 20. HENRY DISBROW vs JOSEPH SLOAN & DAVID STEELE. Writ served 6 Jan, 1812 in presence of ROBERT GRAHAM by JEROM HOLT for SAMUEL ARCHER, Sheriff. WILLIAM M. SMITH posted bond for DISBROW. Affidavit filed that STEELE & SLOAN were served. Court dismissed writ. p 173

Case 21. HENRY DISBROW vs JOSEPH SLOAN. Writ served 6 Jan, 1812 in presence of ROBERT GRAHAM by JEROM HOLT for SAMUEL ARCHER, Sheriff. WILLIAM M. SMITH posted bond for DISBROW. Affidavit filed that SLOAN was served. Court dismissed writ. p 173

Case 22. SAMUEL TOMMIS vs DANIEL REEDER & JAMES CAM-MACK. Debt $82, damage $16.17. Not summoned by Sheriff. p 173

Term of May, 1812.

Case 1. HOUGH, BLAIR, CLARK & GILLESPIE vs BENJAMIN ARCHER. On 25 May, 1810 at New Orleans, note for $1561.27, to be paid in Philadelphia. Failed to pay. Suit filed. Failed to defend. Plntfs recover $1722.59 damages, $10.35 costs. pp 174, 175, 176

Case 2. LUDWICK CHRISTIAN vs DANIEL FETTERS JR. Damages $500. Disc. p 176

Case 3. Adm of HUEY's estate vs GUARDIANS of HUEY's estate. Settled. p 176

Case 4. JAMES BROWN vs WILLIAM COMPTON. BROWN filed transcript of judgement of JAMES MILLER, JP, 4 June, 1811. COMPTON to recover $1.45 costs, JOHN FILIBACK witness. BROWN filed notice of appeal; JACOB REPLO-GEL his security. Suit brought; mutually agreed to settle. Plntf & dfnt each to pay $8.07 costs. p 176

Case 5. JOHN DODSON vs HENRY DISBROW. Debt $132, damage. Disc. p 177

Case 6. PEYTON SHORT vs ANDREW LOCK. On 8 Oct, 1808 debt of $1333.33. Failed to pay. Suit filed. Dfnt refuted debt. Hearing: failed to defend. SHORT to recover debt, $127.50 damages, $10.37 costs. Copy of original note. pp 177, 178

Case 7. GEORGE YOUNG vs ADAM KOBLENTZ. On 19 Oct, 1808, $100 note written to JOSEPH COLEMAN. Assigned to YOUNG 21 Oct, 1811. KOBLENTZ failed to pay.

Term of May, 1812 continued

Suit filed. Failed to defend. YOUNG to recover debt, $25.50 damages, $11.67 costs. KOBLENTZ gave notice of appeal to Supreme Court. Copies of original note to COLEMAN. Endorsement to YOUNG, witness JAMES CHATHAM. pp 179, 180, 181

Case 8. HENRY COLEMAN vs JACOB COLEMAN. Debt $1000 on penal bond, damages. Disc. p 181

Case 9. SAMUEL IRWIN vs JAMES BARNET & ABRAHAM BARNET. On 25 March, 1811, note for $183.50. Failed to pay. Suit filed, damages $30. Defnts refuted debt. At hearing, failed to defend. IRWIN recover $95.43 debt residue, costs $11.33. Copy of original note, witness AMOS IRWIN. pp 181, 182, 183

Case 10. PETER SUNDERLAND vs FRANCIS DILTS. On 10 Sept, 1811, note to deliver 45 barrels flour to SUNDERLAND at WILLIAM WAUGH's mill. At time of delivery to be worth $180. DILTS refused to deliver goods, refused to pay debt. Suit filed, $250 damages. Jury summoned: JAMES C. ANDERSON, JACOB BOWER, JOSIAH CLAWSON, JOHN DODSON, EDWARD DYER, PETER EAGLE, ROBERT EDGAR, DAVID HENDERSON, ABRAHAM HOZIER, PETER RACHER, MARTIN WIBRIGHT, NATHAN WORLEY. Found DILTS guilty. SUNDERLAND to recover $167.37 debt, $18.38 costs. Deposition presented in evidence signed WILLIAM BRUCE, certified by DAVID E. HENDRICKS, Preble Co JP. pp 183, 184, 185

Case 11. JOHN HUNT vs DANIEL C. COOPER & JOHN COMPTON JR. On 1 March, 1811, dfnts were partners in trade, signed note for $1241. Refused to pay. Suit filed. Dfnts failed to defend. HUNT to recover $1329.42 damages, $9.81 costs. Copy of original note, witness C. R. GREENE. pp 185, 186, 187

Case 12. JOHN McCANN vs JOHN LOWE. damages $150. Disc. p 188

Case 13. NICHOLAS SMALL SR vs ABRAHAM BARNET & GEORGE HARRIS. On 10 Sept, 1811, $240 note. Refusal to pay. Suit filed. Dfnts refuted debt. Hearing: failed to defend. SMALL to recover debt, $9.67 costs. Copy of original note, witness JAMES HENDERSON, JAMES ELLIOTT. pp 188, 189

Case 14. CHARLES ELLET vs BENJAMIN ARCHER, JOHN DUNCAN, WILLIAM STEPHENS. On 26 Dec, 1810, $700.66 note. Fail to pay. Suit filed, damages $200. Dfnts

Term of May, 1812 continued

failed to defend. ELLET to recover debt, $57.22
damages, $7.66 costs. Copy of original note; witness
GEORGE HARRIS, ISAAC G. BURNET. pp 190, 191

Case 15. MICHAEL BAKER vs DAVID REID. On 15 Dec,
1808, REID, B. & J. ARCHER signed $75 note. Failed
to pay. Suit filed, damages of $20. Sheriff could
not find B. & J. ARCHER to serve writ. REID failed
to defend. BAKER to recover debt, $13.57 damages,
$8.84 costs. Copy of original note. pp 192, 193

Case 16. STATE vs FREEMAN SHAW. On 15 Sept, 1811,
SHAW of Wayne Twp assaulted WILLIAM PATTERSON, biting
off WILLIAM'S lower lip. SHAW and JOHN GILE posted
hearing appearance bond on 19 Sept. Pled not guilty.
SHAW, JOHN ENOCH & ELIJAH WOOD posted trial appearance bond. Jury found SHAW guilty of maiming, fined
$10.00 & $13.39 costs. pp 194, 195, 196

Case 17. HENRY DISBROW vs JOSEPH SLOAN in equity.
Suit filed in Chancery addressed to Court of Common
Pleas. On 10 July, 1810, DISBROW had dealings with
SLOAN. 25 Dec, 1811: SLOAN took attachment of $37
against DISBROW. SLOAN in debt to DISBROW at that
time, sought injunction to stay judgement against
Plaintiff DISBROW. Injunction allowed by associate
judge WILLIAM GEORGE on 19 Feb, 1812. At hearing:
injunction dissolved, bill dismissed at cost to com-
plaintant of $10.01. pp 196, 197

Case 18. STATE vs THOMAS COOPER. Indictment. Defnt
not found by sheriff. p 197

Case 19. STATE vs CHARLES CHEVALIER. Indictment for
assault and battery. Defnt not found. p 198

Case 20. STATE vs CHARLES CHEVALIER. Indictment for
resisting constable. Defnt not found. p 198

Case 21. STATE vs DANIEL McDANIEL. Assault on --
WEAD. Defnt not found. p 198

Case 22. STATE vs JOHN ARCHER. Selling whiskey
without a license. Defnt not found. p 198

Case 23. STATE vs JACOB BENNER. On 25 Dec, 1811 and
other days, BENNER of Washington Twp sold whiskey
without a license. Pled guilty. Fined $1, costs of
$7.25. p 198, 199

COMMON PLEAS (CIVIL) LAW RECORD BOOK B-1

Term of May, 1812 continued

Case 24.   STATE vs JACOB BENNER.   Charged with
selling goods not of United States manufacture
without license.   Pled guilty.   Fined $1, costs of
$7.25.   p 199, 200

Adjournment for the term.   p 201

Term of September, 1812

Case 1.   STATE vs MARTIN MYERS.   On 15 Nov, 1811,
MYERS of Dayton Twp charged with stealing one ewe,
value of $2, property of CHARLES TULL.   Appearance
bond posted 23 Nov, 1811 by MYERS & LAWRENCE ESPY.
Pled not guilty.   Jury summoned: JOHN BRADFORD, JOHN
BURNS, WILLIAM CALHOUN, WILLIAM LONG, DANIEL MARTIN,
RICHARD MASON, MARTIN McCREA, GEORGE SMITH, IRA
SMITH, LUDWICK SPEECE, JAMES STEELE, ABRAHAM STONER.
Found MYERS guilty.   MYERS claimed verdict erroneous,
contrary to directions of the court, requested a new
trial.   Affidavit filed by MYERS on 9 Jan, 1812:   The
sheep was property of an unknown person (residing) up
the Stillwater (river).   The unknown person will
prove sheep is his property, not that of TULL; MYERS
to prove by witness CAPTAIN ROBERT ROBERTSON that he
made enquiries as to ownership.   Verdict set aside.
New bond posted by MYERS, JAMES RITCHIE & JOSEPH
CONNOR.   New trial: MYERS failed to appear, bond
forfeited, costs of $26.38 levied.   pp 202, 203, 204

Case 2.   STATE vs JOHN ARCHER.   On 14 Dec, 1811 and
other times, ARCHER of Washington Twp sold spiritous
liquor (peach brandy) without license.   Pled guilty.
Fined $1, $5.90 costs.   pp 204, 205

Case 3.   STATE vs JAMES SCOTT & JAMES AIKENS, JR.   On
25 Dec, 1811 at Washington Twp, def'nts assembled,
rioted, fought and disturbed the peace.   Both pled
guilty.   Fined $5 each, costs of $10.28.   pp 206, 207

Case 4.   NATHANIEL HUNT vs DAVID REID, GEORGE PATTER-
SON, GEORGE G. BRADFORD.   On 9 April, 1811, def'nts
assaulted HUNT, imprisoning him for two hours.   Suit
filed, damages $500.   Def'nts pled not guilty, filed
affidavit that GEORGE MINICH, a material witness, is
missing.   At hearing, HUNT failed to appear.   Def'nts
to recover $23.46 costs.   pp 207, 208, 209

Case 5.   STATE vs JOHN GRIMES.   Grand Jury: DAVID
JOHN, MICHAEL MOYER, JOSEPH EVANS, ROBERT PART, DAVID
WAYMIRE, JOHN VANNIMAN, DAVID HARTMAN, HENRY CREAGER,

Term of September, 1812 continued

ALEXANDER SNODGRASS, LEWIS LECHLIDER, LUKE BRYAN, WILLIAM BRUMBAUGH, JOHN PATTERSON, JOHN WEAVER, PETER SUMAN. On 31 Aug, 1812 and other times, GRIMES sold a spiritous liquor (peach brandy) without license. Pled guilty. Fined $.50, costs $2.71. pp 209, 210

Case 6. STATE vs THOMAS COOPER. Indictment, def'nt not found in baliwick. p 210

Case 7. STATE vs CHARLES CHEVALIER. Indictment, assault and battery on JOHN McCANN. Def'nt not found in baliwick. p 210

Case 8. STATE vs CHARLES CHEVALIER. Indictment, resisting constable. Def'nt not found. p 210

Case 9. STATE vs DANIEL McDANIEL. Assault and battery on ALEXANDER WEAD. Def'nt not found. p 210

Case 10. DANIEL FUNDERBURG, assignee of JOHN STRAUSBURGER, assignee of JOHN HIMES, vs HENRY MARQUART. Debt $100, damages $20. Def'nt not found. p 211

Term of January, 1813

Case 1. HUGH McCOLLOM vs PAUL D. BUTLER. On 28 Jan, 1811, McCOLLOM obtained judgement of $31.21 against BUTLER in court of JOHN FOLKERTH, JP. BUTLER to appeal decision. At hearing, McCOLLOM, an innkeeper for many years in Dayton, gave evidence of indebtedness by 18 Dec, 1810: $80 for 3 years food and lodging, $80 for 3 years horse stabling and food, $80 for goods, $80 for cash lent. BUTLER refuted debt, to give evidence of plntf's indebtedness. Jury summoned: WILLIAM COX, SIDNEY DENISE, EMANUEL FLORY, LUDWICK KEMP, JOHN MILLER, JACOB MULLENDORE, CHARLES PATY, JOHN PRICE, DANIEL REPP, HENRY STALEY, WILLIAM WALTON, JOSEPH WILSON. Found BUTLER guilty, McCOLLOM to recover $57.21 damages, $28.87 costs. pp 212, 213, 214, 215

Case 2. STATE vs JOHN PRICE & HANNAH PRICE, his wife, late HANNAH DAVIS, adm. of THOMAS DAVIS. Summons to show cause why estate has not been settled. Disc. p 216

Case 3. SAMUEL SCOTT vs HENRY ATCHISON. On 27 Dec, 1808, $293 debt owed to SCOTT. Refused to pay. Suit filed, damages $50. At hearing, SCOTT failed to appear. ATCHISON to recover costs of $11. pp 216, 217

Term of January, 1813 continued

Case 4. CONKLIN MILLER vs JAMES MILLER. On 24 Sept, 1811, $101 note signed. JAMES failed to pay, failed to defend suit. CONKLIN to recover debt, $6.69 damages, $12.43 costs. pp 217, 218, 219

Case 5. STATE vs JOHN SISSEL. On 2 May, 1812, assaulted JONAS GRAHAM. Bond posted by SISSEL & BEN-JAMIN SCOTT. SISSEL pled guilty, fined $2, costs of $6.46. pp 219, 220

Case 6. STATE vs JOHN BROWER. Grand Jury: CHRISTIAN MILLER, JAMES MILLER, JACOB STUTZMAN, WILLIAM KING, ALEXANDER McCONNELL, JAMES HANNA, HENRY YOUNT, MAT-THEW PATTON, JOHN PATTERSON, FREDERICK NUTZ, JOHN DENISE, PETER MIKESELL, PETER LEHMAN, JOHN MILLER, EBENEZER WEAD JR. On 1 Feb, 1812 and at other times, BROWER of Jefferson Twp sold spiritous liquor (whis-key) without license. Pled guilty. Fined $.25, $6.50 costs. pp 220, 221

Case 7. JAMES GIBSON & SAMUEL GIBSON vs ANDREW BIKEL. The GIBSONS, partners in trade, represented by DAVID ESTE, atty. On 23 Jan, 1812, at Cincinnati, $127.75 note signed. BIKEL refused to pay, failed to defend suit. GIBSONs' to recover debt, $10.59 costs. BIKEL gave notice of appeal to Supreme Court. Copy of ori-ginal note, signed ANDREW BIKEL (in german), witness HENRY WALLICK, ALEX. PETTIT. pp 221, 222, 223

Case 8. GEORGE NEWCOM & PETER LEHMAN, exec's of last will and testament of GEORGE FRIBERGER, vs JEROM HOLT, sheriff. Plntfs represented by JOHN ALEXANDER, atty. FRIBERGER had brought suit for debt against PATRICK LAFFERTY, whom Sheriff JEROM HOLT took into custody, later released. At trial, LAFFERTY failed to appear. HOLT held responsible for judgement ob-tained against LAFFERTY: $51.85 damages, $10.81 costs. FRIBERGER died March, 1812; plntfs brought suit on behalf of estate. HOLT failed to defend. Plntfs to recover damages and costs aforesaid, addi-tional $8.11 costs. HOLT gave notice of appeal to Supreme Court. pp 223, 224

Case 9. HENRY WEAVER vs JAMES THOMSON. On 17 April, 1812, $100 debt. THOMSON refused to pay. Suit filed damages $30. THOMSON failed to defend. WEAVER to recover debt, $3.83 damage, $11.5 cost. Copy of original note, witness JOHN ELTZROTH, MOSES THOMSON. pp 225, 226

Term of January, 1813 continued

Case 10. JAMES RITCHIE vs ELIJAH SWAIM. No date given, SWAIM took bay horse, valued at $65, retained against pledges. RITCHIE brought suit, damages $100. SWAIM failed to appear at court. RITCHIE recovered $.01 damages, $8.94 costs. pp 226, 227

Case 11. JAMES KYLE vs MICHAEL BURNS. Damages $200. Disc. p 227

Case 12. HECTOR CRAIG vs WILLIAM P. SMITH. Debt $1270.90, damage $1000. Disc. p 227

Case 13. JAMES JOHN vs JOHN MILLER & JAMES MILLER. On 21 Sept, 1811, $127.80 debt. Failed to pay. Suit filed, damages $30. Failed to defend. JAMES JOHN to recover $123.48 debt residue, $10.29 costs. Copy of original note, witness EDWARD NEWCOM. pp 228, 229

Case 14. JOHN RUDY vs WILLIAM M. SMITH & CHARLES SMITH. On 2 Dec, 1811, note signed by def'nts & HENRY LEATHERMAN. Refused to pay. Suit filed, damages $25. (LEATHERMAN not found in baliwick) Failed to defend. RUDY to recover $90 debt, $3.67 damages, $10.04 costs. Copy of original note, witness GEORGE GROVE, DAVID STEELE. pp 230, 231

Case 15. ANDREW LOCK vs JOSEPH DODDS. In Sept term, 1812, judgement against DODDS & JAMES HENDERSON to pay $78.01 due on note written 22 Aug, 1811. HENDERSON not found by sheriff. DODDS, responsible for entire amount, failed to defend. LOCK to recover $78.01 debt, $1.75 damage, $10.98 costs. Copy of original note. pp 231, 232, 233

Case 16. STATE vs JAMES THOMSON, JEROM HOLT, IRA SMITH. On 22 Aug, 1812, the def'nts assaulted BETSY FITSHUE (FITZHUGH?), a black woman, beating her. Prosecutor ISAAC G. BURNET dropped charges against SMITH. THOMSON & HOLT pled not guilty. Jury summoned: GEORGE G. BRADFORD, WILLIAM COX. SIDNEY DENISE, EMANUEL FLORY, JOSEPH McKINNEY, JOHN MILLER, JACOB MULLENDORE, CHARLES PATY, HORATIO G. PHILLIPS, DANIEL REPP, JOSEPH WILSON. Acquited THOMSON, HOLT. pp 233, 234

Case 17. STATE vs JAMES THOMSON, JEROM HOLT, IRA SMITH. On 22 Aug, 1812, the def'nts assaulted JOSEPH FITSHUE (FITZHUGH?), a black man, beating him. Prosecutor ISAAC G. BURNET dropped charges against SMITH. THOMSON & HOLT pled not guilty. Charges dism. p 235

Term of January, 1813 continued

Case 18. Trustees of Dayton Academy vs JEROM HOLT, late sheriff of Montgomery Co. Judgement issued against PETER SUMAN & JOHN GRIMES to be held against HOLT (failure to perform his duty) plus interest and 10% damages. Court ruled HOLT had notice of action. Trustees recover $137.31 damages, $6.52 costs. p 236

Case 19. Trustees of Dayton Academy vs JEROM HOLT, late sheriff of Montgomery Co. Judgement issued against JAMES THOMSON & HUGH McCOLLOM to be held against HOLT (failure to perform his duty) plus interest and 10% damages. Court ruled HOLT had notice of action. Trustees to recover $154.44 total damages, $6.17 costs. p 236

Case 19*. Commissioners of Montgomery County vs JEROM HOLT, late sheriff of Montgomery Co. Judgement issued against JAMES THOMSON & PAUL D. BUTLER to be held against HOLT (failure to perform his duty) plus interest and 10% damages. Court ruled HOLT had notice of action. Commissioners to recover $88.04 total damages, $6.17 costs. p 237 *misnumbered by clerks

Case 20. GEORGE WOLLASTON vs JEROM HOLT, late sheriff of Montgomery Co. Judgement issued against JOHN DODSON to be held against HOLT (failure to perform his duty) plus interest and 10% damages. Court ruled HOLT had notice of action. WOLLASTON to recover $25.53 total damages, $6.17 costs. p 237

Case 21. ISAAC REED vs JEROM HOLT, late sheriff of Montgomery Co. Judgement issued against JOHN ARCHER to be held against HOLT (failure to perform his duty) plus interest and 10% damages. Court ruled HOLT had notice of action. REED to recover $25.53 total damages, $6.17 costs. p 238

Case 22. MARTIN BAUM & SAMUEL PERRY vs JEROM HOLT, late sheriff of Montgomery Co. Judgement issued against PETER RUHFF to be held against HOLT (failure to perform his duty) plus interest and 10% damages. Court ruled HOLT had notice of action. Plntfs to recover $123.02 total damages, $6.17 costs. p 238

Case 23. PEYTON SHORT vs GEORGE MINNICH. Debt $220 damage $80. Settled. p 239

Case 24. STATE vs JONATHAN NEWMAN. Assault and battery on EMANUAL COBAL. Def'nt not found. p 239

Term of May, 1813

Case 1. MOSES HATFIELD vs JOHN KERCHER. Debt $98.25 damages $50. Disc. p 240

Case 2. GEORGE KUNS vs FREDERICK ELSRODE. Rifle value $25, damages $75. Settled. p 240

Case 3. JOHN PRICE, assignee of JOHN BAIN, vs GEORGE GROVE & HENRY MARQUART, surviving obligors of SAMUEL SHOUB, GROVE & MARQUART. Debt $68, damages $50. Disc. p 240

Case 4. DANIEL DIETER, appellee, vs JACOB KUNS, appellant. Transcript of judgement by DAVID HOOVER, JP dated 19 Sept, 1808: DIETER vs KUNS. Debt was $50 for carpenter labor by DIETER. Judgement of $18 and costs; KUNS failed to pay. Suit filed. DANIEL HOOVER SR posted appearance bond for KUNS. DIETER failed to appear at hearing, to take nothing; KUNS to recover $14.04 costs. pp 240, 241, 242

Case 5. JAMES THOMSON, appellee, vs JONAS GRAHAM, appellant. Transcript of judgement by JOHN FOLKERTH, JP, dated 7 Apr, 1812. Judgement of $42.30 against GRAHAM who gave notice of appeal. At hearing, court found THOMSON to recover $44.86 damages, $18.68 costs. pp 243, 244

Case 6. ADAM SPITLAR vs LEARING MARSH. Damages $500. Disc. p 244

Case 7. JONAS GRAHAM vs JOHN CISSEL. Suit for $200 damages. GRAHAM failed to appear. CISSEL to recover $8.84 costs. p 245

Case 8. JESSE HUNT vs HENRY STALEY & GEORGE SHOUB. On 15 Sept, 1805, $230 note signed. Refused to pay. Suit filed. Failed to defend. HUNT to recover $68 debt residue, $5.05 costs. Copy of original note. Notice of letter from JOHN SMITH, senator, to JACOB BERGEPER, stating SAMUEL SHOUB had left $120 with BERGEPER, requesting that it be sent to him. (Letter probably offered as evidence.) pp 246, 247

Case 9. JOHN HUNT & NATHANIEL HUNT vs DANIEL LANDON. On 23 Oct, 1809, $236 note signed. Failed to pay. Suit filed, $350 damages. LANDON failed to defend. Plntfs to recover $276. 42 damages, $9.75 costs. Copy of original note. pp 247, 248

Term of May, 1813 continued

Case 10. WILLIAM D. McKIM vs JOHN COMPTON JR. On 26
Apr, 1808, at Baltimore, $1102.07 bill of obligation
signed. Failed to pay. Suit filed, $500 damages.
COMPTON failed to defend. McKIM to recover $229.35
debt residue, $10.40 costs. pp 249, 250

Case 11. DANIEL FUNDERBURGH, assignee of JOHN
STRAUSBERGER, assignee of JOHN HIMES, vs HENRY MAR-
QUART. On 9 Jan, 1812, note signed to HIMES. On 29
Apr, 1812, assigned to STRAUSBERGER. On 15 May, 1812
assigned to FUNDERBURGH. Def'nt refused to pay.
Suit filed, damages $20. Failed to defend. FUNDER-
BURGH to recover $100 debt, $5.50 damages, $11.61
costs. MARQUART gave notice of appeal to Supreme
Court. Copy of original note, witness JACOB SAUM,
SAMUEL HIMES. pp 250, 251, 252

Case 12. JAMES BAY vs JANE GRAY, adm of RICHARD
GRAY, dec. JP court judgement appeal. Disc. p 252

Case 13. WILLIAM BROMBAUGH vs JACOB KUNS. Damage
$150. Disc. p 252

Case 14. JOHN BERLOT vs CHRISTIAN WELDY. Debauching
plntf's daughter, damage $500. Disc. p 253

Case 15. ELIZABETH BERLOT vs CHRISTIAN WELDY.
Recognizance in bastardy. Disc. p 253

Case 16. STATE vs THOMAS COOPER. Indictment; new
writ awarded. p 253

Case 17. STATE vs JONATHAN NEWMAN. Assault & battery on EMANUEL COBAL. New writ awarded. p 253

Case 18. THOMPSON & HARRIS vs MARTIN SHUEY. Mortgage for $1556.80. p 253

Term of September, 1813

Case 1. STATE vs JOHN BERLOT. Summoned to answer
contempt charge. Failed to appear as State witness
on indictment of JACOB KUNS. Dismissed. p 254

Case 2. STATE vs BENJAMIN LEHMAN. Summoned on contempt charge. Failed to appear as State witness on
indictment of JACOB KUNS. Dismissed. p 254, 255

Case 3. DANIEL C. COOPER vs JOSEPH McCLEARY. Suit
filed for $100 damages. Dismissed by consent. p 255

Term of September, 1813 continued

Case 4. PETER DILTS, appellee, vs JOHN WEAVER, appellant. Transcript of suit heard in JP court, 3
Oct, 1812; judgement against DILTS. Appeal filed.
JOSEPH COLEMAN gave bail for DILTS, who failed to appear at hearing. WEAVER recover $13.25 costs. p 256

Case 5. ARTHUR ST. CLAIR JR vs ANDREW LOCK. On 20
Aug, 1808, $200 debt for work performed as atty.
Failed to pay. Def'nt refuted debt, to give evidence
of Plntf's indebtedness. Jury summoned: MICHAEL
BAKER, LUTHER BRUEN, JOHN BURNS, AMOS CLARK, DAVID
HARTER, GEORGE HARTER, JAMES KERR, JACOB KRULL, JOHN
MILLER, EBENEZER WEAD JR, SAMUEL WOODWARD, DANIEL
YOUNT. Acquited LOCK. ST. CLAIR to take nothing,
LOCK recover $20.67 costs. pp 257, 258, 259

Case 6. ADAM FUNK vs WILLIAM VANARSDAL. On 30 Jan,
1811, $420.07 note, to be paid in merchantable cat-
tle. Refused to pay. Suit filed, $100 damages.
Case disc by FUNK; VANARSDAL to pay costs $9.90. pp
259, 260, 261

Case 7. SAMUEL TOMMIS vs DANIEL REEDER & JAMES CAM-
MACK. January term, 1809, def'nts pledged bail for
SAMUEL BECK (TOMMIS vs BECK), who failed to pay
judgement levied by court. Summons served on def'nts
by JEROM HOLT, NICHOLAS SMALL JR. Def'nts claimed
BECK paid judgement; they should not be held responsible. BECK filed affidavit JOHN BENHAM, a material
witness, was missing, could prove payment of 70 gallons peach brandy to TOMMIS, plus offering other vouchers which BECK believed would show judgement was
satisfied. Court, after considering all evidence,
held TOMMIS to recover $19.38 debt residue, $12.18
costs from REEDER & CAMMACK. pp 261, 262, 263, 264

Case 8. JAMES I. NESBIT vs ADAM SPITLAR. On 7 May,
1811, agreement to deliver 240 gallons merchantable
whiskey in 7 barrels at ADAM'S stillhouse, value of
62.5 cents per gallon. Failed to deliver. Suit
filed, $300 damages. SPITLAR failed to appear in
court. Damages set by jury: MICHAEL BAKER, LUTHER
BRUEN, JOHN BURNS, SAMUEL GRIPE, DAVID HARTER, GEORGE
HARTER, OWEN HATFIELD, JAMES KERR, JACOB KRULL, JOHN
MILLER, GEORGE SNIDER, SAMUEL WOODWARD. NESBIT to
recover $116.90 damages, $19.50 costs. Copy of original note, witness WILLIAM HARRISON. pp 264, 265, 266

Case 9. WILLIAM SOURBRAY vs JAMES McDONALD & WILLIAM
WALLACE. Settled. p 267

Term of September, 1813 continued

Case 10. GEORGE PHILLIPS vs BENJAMIN MALTBIE. Plntf charged he was illegally detained by Lt. MALTBIE, U.S. Army as he had never legally enlisted. MALTBIE presented evidence of enlistment on 2 Sept, 1813, for period of 1 yr in 26 Regt, U. S. Infantry. MALTBIE to pay costs of $7.66. pp 267, 268

Case 11. JOHN COMPTON, JOHN HUNT & NATHANIEL HUNT, dba COMPTON & HUNTS, vs ROBERT RENNICK. Damages $6000, disc. p 268

Case 12. SUTHERLAND & BROWN vs JOHN DODSON. Disc. p 268

Case 13. JOHN GEPHART vs BARNHART SPECK. Disc. p 269

Case 14. THOMPSON & HARRIS vs MARTIN SHUEY. Mortgage against SHUEY's homesite on 1 July, 1811: 202 acres located Sec 19, T 2, R 5, bounded by lands of HENRY CRIST & ADAM SHUEY, and additional 100 acres in same section. SHUEY to pay $1556.80 plus interest. At hearing, SHUEY failed to appear. THOMPSON & HARRIS to recover $1556.80 debt, $204.71 damages, $11.20 costs. Copy of original mortgage: THOMPSON & HARRIS of Philadelphia, witness MARTIN EARHART, NICHOLAS LONGWORTH. Statement of Warren Co JP ENOS WILLIAMS: SHUEY acknowledged mortgage to be voluntary. pp 269, 270, 271, 272, 273

Case 14. JOSEPH McKINNEY & ELIZA McKINNEY vs REBECKAH MOONEY. Slander, damages $1000. "Staid by Plaintiff". p 273

Case 15. JOHN HUNT vs JOHN COMPTON JR & DANIEL C. COOPER. Motion withdrawn. p 273

Case 17. MAGDALENE NEFF & JOHN KERR, adm of HENRY NEFF, dec. Petition to execute contract between dec. and MARTIN HOUSER. 1808 contract to convey 22 acres @ $2.50 per acre. HOUSER paid $22, ready to pay balance. Permission granted. pp 273, 274

Case 18. DAVID REID & WILLIAM GEORGE vs JAMES WELSH & ELIZABETH PARKER in Chancery. GEORGE, assignee of ROBERT PATTERSON, REID, WELSH, & PARKER, assignee of LAWSON McCULLOUGH, were tenants in common of Secs 27, 28, 29, T 2, R 6E, patent from U. S. dated 10 Jan, 1812. Plntfs sought partition of land in May term, 1811. Def'nts responded, Sept term, 1881, saying agreement made by original purchasers differed from

Term of September, 1813 continued

partition now proposed. Plntfs refuted any previous
agreement. Case continued to next session as associate judge WILLIAM GEORGE was party to the suit. Jan,
1813, response of def'nt JAMES WELSH filed: The land
was originally seen by WELSH who made the initial
payment on it. Being unable to puchase such a large
tract himself, he returned to Lexington, KY, to seek
partners. Co-purchasers were given plat as surveyed,
with respective plots pointed out prior to purchase.
McCULLOUGH, dissatisfied with agreement, was persuaded by partners to sell his interest to PARKER, she
being willing to agree to terms of division. PATTER-
SON transferred his share to ANDREW McCALLA who later
transfered to GEORGE. New land division was sought
by REID & GEORGE who owned land adjacent to proposed
change in partition. WELSH, as agent for himself and
for PARKER, agreed to that minor change, accepted by
THOMAS GEORGE on behalf of his father WILLIAM. REID
had made improvements to his property and in order to
settle a judgement against him, sold some of his portion to JAMES HENDERSON; both facts indicated his ac-
ceptance of the original partition terms. Answer of
ELIZABETH PARKER, filed in same court: reviewed her
participation in land entry, agreed with WELSH's
version, signed ELIZA I. PARKER, Lexington, KY.
THOMAS McNUTT, witness for plntfs, testified WELSH
returned (to KY) from Dayton in 1803, stated intention to purchase land. McCULLOUGH agreed to purchase
until shown map, questioning WELSH's right to first
choice. REID persuaded McCULLOUGH to take portion
assigned to him. MATTHEW PATTON testified he was
present when PATTERSON requested PARKER's name be inserted on entry. JEROM HOLT testified he was directed as sheriff to levy judgement on REID's land, but
was not directed by REID as to what part of tract he
owned. Depositions of LAWSON McCULLOUGH, ASA FARROW
& ANDREW McCALLA taken at Lexington, KY. McCULLOGH
reviewed participation, disagreements over land division. FARROW testified as to original purchasers,
denied knowledge of partition agreement. McCALLA acknowledged agreement as outlined by WELSH & PARKER,
and had informed GEORGE at time of purchase. PATTER-
SON testified partition agreement outlined by WELSH
was understood by all parties. SIMPSON McCARTY testified he had rented land of REID who defined boundaries, agreeing with WELSH's version. Deposition of
MAXFIELD LUDLOW, taken in Hamilton Co, OH, 1813: testified to his understanding of partition agreement.
Had surveyed land at REID's request, witnessed REID's
improvements. Map gives complete land claim entries.

Term of September, 1813 continued

Copy of Articles of Agreement between REID & JAMES HENDERSON, dated 24 Oct, 1812, transferring 100 A., title to be conveyed when partition made. Court ordered tract to be divided by Col. JOHN GRIMES, JOHN H. WILLIAMS & Capt. JAMES STEELE. Costs of $54.18 paid by plaintiffs. Def'nts WELSH & PARKER gave notice of appeal to Supreme Court. pp 275 through 298

Term of January, 1814

Case 1. PETER HOOVER vs JACOB STETLER & ELIZABETH STETLER (his wife). Slander, $1000 damages. JACOB HOOVER security for costs of plntf. Disc. p 299

Case 2. HECTOR CRAIG vs WILLIAM M. SMITH. On August 6, 1806, the Supreme Court of state of New York at Albany gave judgement to CRAIG to recover debt of $1256.28, damages of $14.62. SMITH refused to pay. Suit filed in Dayton by CRAIG. Payment of $200 by CHARLES SMITH to gain release from judgement on WILLIAM's behalf. CRAIG acknowledged settlement. WILLIAM to pay costs of $6.97 and $1.89. Copy of settlement agreement, witness CHARLES SMITH, D. PIKER. pp 300, 301, 302

Case 3. WILLIAM FARMER JR vs ASA OWEN. Def'nt represented by WILLIAM M. SMITH, atty. FARMER gave notes to OWEN for collection, held against SAMUEL SHIPP of GA, (notes against MARK SULLIVAN, ELIJAH ECHOLS & REUBEN WALSINGHAM, CHARLES & JESSE ROBERTS put into SHIPP's hands for collection), recpt from SHIPP to JOHN SAUNDERS on note given by SAMUEL SULLIVAN. OWEN was to convey sums collected from SHIPP to FARMER; charged with failure to deliver. Suit filed, $500 damages. OWEN refuted agreement. FARMER disc suit, paid $9.88 costs. pp 302, 303, 304, 305

Case 4. JOHN JAY vs HENRY MARQUART, JOHN HUNT & JOHN COMPTON JR. ANDREW WAYMIER stood security for JAY. Writ also against MARTIN ROWZER & NATHANIEL HUNT who were not found in sheriff's baliwick. On 5 Aug, 1812 $744 note signed. On 5 March, 1813, additional $800 debt when JAY delivered 300 head cattle to def'nts. Failed to pay. Suit filed for $1000. MARQUART failed to defend suit and JAY to recover $698.74 damages, $10.50 costs from him. HUNT & COMPTON refuted the debt. Jury summoned: JOHN BAILEY, JACOB BENNER, SAMUEL BUCHER, WILLIAM CALHOUN, PETER CRUMVINE, JOHN DODSON, HENRY HEPNER, OWEN JONES, JACOB KUHN, JOHN NOFFZINGER, HEZEKIAH ROBINSON, ADISON SMITH. Found

Term of January, 1814 continued

HUNT & COMPTON guilty. JAY recover $698.74 damages, $23.17 costs. COMPTON & HUNT to appeal to Supreme Court. pp 306, 307, 308, 309, 310, 311

Case 5. JAMES HAMPSON vs JOHN COMPTON & NATHANIEL HUNT. Security for def'nts: AARON BAKER, coroner. HAMPSON disc suit. p 311

Case 6. HENRY CREAGER vs HENRY CRUMBAUGH. Slander, damages $500. Disc. p 311

Case 7. HORATIO G. PHILLIPS vs NOAH BEAUCHAMP. Damages $300. Def'nt not found in baliwick. p 312

Case 8. JOHN WAGENOR vs ROBERT DELAP. Debt $600, damages $200. Disc. p 312

Case 9. JOHN HUNT vs JOHN HANDY. On 1 Feb, 1813, assault and battery. Suit filed, $1000 damages. HANDY pled not guilty: at time of alleged assault, Df'nt was working in his stillhouse, making whiskey. HUNT entered and carried away still meal. HANDY requested that HUNT leave. Upon refusal, HANDY "gently laid his hands on said HUNT" to eject him. Jury summoned: JAMES ELLIOT, BENJAMIN JOHN, OWEN JONES, WILLIAM KING, JACOB KUHN, DAVID LEHMAN, EDMUND K. MUNGER, JAMES RUSSEL, BENJAMIN SCOTT, JAMES THOMSON, WILLIAM VANDERSLICE, JOHN H. WILLIAMS. Found HANDY guilty. HUNT to recover $3 damages, $21.21 costs. HUNT to appeal to Supreme Court. pp 312, 313, 314

Case 10. JACOB BRUMBAUGH vs GEORGE KUNS. On 1 Dec, 1812, BRUMBAUGH lent KUNS a mare to pull his wagon from Dayton to St. Mary's, Miami Co, and to return. KUNS, on 3 Dec, "immoderately drove, beat and abused" the mare so that she died. Suit for $200 damages. KUNS pled not guilty, filed affidavit that GEORGE LOY, a material witness, was missing. Jury summoned: JOHN BAILEY, JACOB BENNER, SAMUEL BUCHER, PETER CRUMVINE, JOHN FOLKERTH, HENRY HEPNER, JOHN NOFFZINGER, JOHN REGANS, HEZEKIAH ROBINSON, ADISON SMITH, JOHN (W)RIGHT, ELIJAH WOOD. Found KUNS guilty. BRUMBAUGH to recover $85 damages, $37.18 costs. pp 315, 316

Case 11. STATE vs JACOB GRIPE. April term, 1808, GRIPE recovered $96.12 judgement from WILLIAM McCANN. Costs of suit still unpaid, were paid to sheriff when served writ. Suit dismissed. p 317

Case 12. JAMES BARNET ads of JOHN WEAVER. On 11

Term of January, 1814 continued

Oct, 1811, paid WEAVER $50, amount of judgement and interest due on lawsuit. WEAVER refused to give recpt. Suit filed. WEAVER pled not guilty, filed affidavit: $50 applied toward note for $30 plus interest & toward a back acct held against BARNET & brother, ABRAHAM. When BARNET requested credit on the judgemt instead, WEAVER refused; he did not want to bring suit again to collect the $30 and the back acct. Would credit to judgemt if ABRAHAM would cosign $30 note; he refused. Petition to credit $50 to debts. Court so allowed, dismissed case. WEAVER recover $4.65 costs. pp 318, 319

Case 13. ROBERT EDGAR, guardian of RACHAEL GRAY & ROBERT GRAY, heirs of RICHARD GRAY, dec. Petition for partition of lands (164 acres, Sec 26, T 2, R 7) held in common by heirs and ROBERT GRAY. Commissioners to divide land: GEORGE NEWCOM, JAMES GILLESPIE SR & SAMUEL ARCHER. Map of partition. pp 319, 320, 321

Case 14. STATE vs JOHN McCANN. Suit for costs; dfndt not found in baliwick. p 321

Case 15. JOHN C. DEATH vs ADAM SPITLAR & MARTIN EARHART. Debt $80, damage $50. Dfndts not found. p 321

Term of May, 1814

Case 1. STATE vs JEREMIAH MILLS. Disc. p 322

Case 2. SUTHERLAND & BROWN vs HENRY MARQUART. AARON BAKER & HENRY CURTNER stood bail for MARQUART. Debt for goods & merchandise, work performed & material used. Refused to pay. Suit filed. Defnt refuted debt, to provide evidence plntfs owe $250 to him. Sent to arbitrators JOSEPH PEIRCE, JOHN FOLKERTH & BENJAMIN VAN CLEVE. Plntfs recover $90.54 damages, $13.19 costs. pp 322, 323, 324, 325, 326

Case 3. JOHN HUNT & NATHANIEL HUNT vs THOMAS HANDY & JOHN HANDY. On 8 April, 1812, leased farm to def'nts to raise corn and rye for distillery; plntfs to recve whiskey from 1/3 crop. Def'nts to have use of still house, 3 stills, utensils, 2/3 crop; to cut no green wood, maintain stillhouse, raise hay & store 1/2 for HUNTS in meadow which plntfs were to fence. THOMAS & JOHN were charged $500 for occupation of farm, misuse of farm and crop. Def'nts refuted agreement, charged plntfs failed to perform as promised; debts owed by HUNTS: $400 for erecting 2 log cabins, $100 for hogs

Term of May, 1814 continued

delivered. Suit disc by HUNTS. Each party to pay own costs. pp 327, 328, 329, 330, 331

Case 4. THOMAS HANDY & JOHN HANDY vs JOHN HUNT & NA-THANIEL HUNT. Disc by plntfs. p 331, 332

Case 5. FRANCIS WELLS vs JOHN BODLEY. WELLS represented by DAVID K. ESTE. Security on behalf of WELLS was CHARLES ESTE. Security on behalf of BODLEY: ELE-AZER GRIFFITH, OWEN JONES. On 14 June, 1813, note for $109.38 signed. Failed to pay. Suit filed; BOD-LEY failed to defend. WELLS recover debt, $5 damages $9.66 costs. Copy of original note: FRANCIS WELLS of Augusta, Bracken Co, KY. pp 332, 333

Case 6. ROBERT WEAD, appellee vs JAMES STEELE & JO-SEPH PEIRCE, applnts. Disc. p 334

Case 7. BARBARA OVERHOLSER vs DAVID BROMBAUGH. Bastardy. Deposition by plntf dated 6 Nov, 1813: pregnant since shortly after harvest. DAVID named as father. Security for def'nt: WILLIAM BROMBAUGH. Appearance bond posted by JACOB SMITH, DAVID & WIL-LIAM. Suit disc. Costs paid by defnt. pp 334, 335

Case 8. CALEB HAYS, assignee of ISAIAH BROWN, vs JACOB MILLER. HAYS represented by THOMAS R. ROSS, atty. On 22 Feb, 1813 at Washington Twp, two $125 notes signed in favor of BROWN. On 24 Aug, 1813, notes assigned to HAYS. Failed to pay. Suit filed. MILLER failed to defend. HAYS recover $250 debt, $12.50 damage, $10.87 costs. Copy of original notes & endorsements, witnesses BENJAMIN MALTBIE, JOSEPH PROUD. pp 336, 337, 338

Case 9. ISAAC McPHERSON vs DANIEL C. COOPER. On 6 June, 1812, $650 note signed. Refused to pay. Suit filed. COOPER failed to defend suit. McPHERSON to recover debt, $74.62 damages, $8.52 costs. Copy of original note, witness JAMES WALSH. pp 339, 340

Case 10. SAMUEL WARD vs JOHN JORDAN. Security for plntf: JAMES PETTICREW. Security for def'nt: JOHN WEAVER, GEORGE GROVE who transferred bond to ISAAC CLARK. On 2 Aug, 1813, $105 note signed. Refused to pay. Suit filed. JORDAN failed to defend. WARD to recover debt, $4.72 damage, $10.50 costs. JORDAN gave notice of appeal to Supreme Court. Copy of original note, witness CHRISTIAN PETTIFISH. pp 340, 341, 342

Term of May, 1814 continued

Case 11. PEYTON SHORT, assignee of THOMAS HELMS, vs WILLIAM ELLIOT. On 4 Jan, 1811, $224 note signed to HELMS. On 8 July, 1811, note assigned to SHORT. Failed to pay. Suit filed, damages $50. ELLIOT failed to defend. SHORT to recover $264 damages, $10.12 costs. Copy of original note, witness SAMUEL JESSE, WILLIAM KEMP. pp 342, 343, 344

Case 12. DAVID LONGHEAD, appellee, vs DAVID REID & THOMAS REID, appellants. Transcript presented of LONGHEAD, assignee of D. ARTHUR, administrix of JOHN ARTHUR, dec, vs DAVID REID & THOMAS REID; case heard in JP court. Judgement of $46.73 against def'nts who gave notice of appeal. Case settled. pp 344, 345

Case 13. BENJAMIN BLUMER vs JOHN MEYERS & JAMES RHEA. On 18 Nov, 1813, $361.20 note signed. Failed to pay. Suit filed. MEYERS & RHEA failed to defend. BLUMER to recover debt, $3.88 damages, $9.37 costs. Copy of original note, signed JOHN MYERS, JAMES RAY, witness ISAAC MYERS, JOHN CUTLER. Endorsed Urbana, OH (Champaign Co) pp 345, 346

Case 14. JOHN COMPTON vs FRANCIS DUCHOUQUET. Debt of $201.26, $150 damages. Settled 7 Feb, 1814. Case disc. p 347

Case 15. JOHN COMPTON JR vs JOHN HUNT & NATHANIEL HUNT. Writ presented from Chancery court. Def'nts indebted to PEYTON SHORT; judgement issued against them. COMPTON and DAVID SQUIER, since dec, pledged security. JOHN HUNT has moved from state, NATHANIEL preparing to move west; judgement balance of $900 unpaid. SHORT's atty threatens lawsuit against COMPTON to recover. Endorsement of AARON BAKER, coroner: On 4 Apr, 1814, NATHANIEL HUNT gave bond of $1800 to DANIEL C. COOPER, JP, to secure judgement. COMPTON dismissed suit. pp 347, 348, 349, 350

Case 16. DAVID REID & WILLIAM GEORGE vs JAMES WELSH & ELIZABETH PARKER. Writ of partition by commissioners on tract located Sec 27, 28, 29, T 2, R 6. Map of partition, defined boundaries. Court ordered recording of partition agreement, deeds to be executed. Costs distributed according to quantity of land held. WELSH: $3.60. PARKER: $5.43. REID: $1.50. GEORGE: $1.83. pp 350, 351, 352, 353, 354

Case 17. Heirs of MARTHA McCLURE vs heirs of WILLIAM McCLURE, DANIEL C. COOPER & MATTHEW PATTON. Heirs of MARTHA: petitioners JAMES STEELE, SAMUEL STEELE, JOHN STEELE, MARY STEELE, JANE STEELE, NANCY THOMSON (wife of JOHN THOMSON), SARAH GLASS, children of ELIZABETH BARR, dec (MARIA BARR, ENOCH BARR, ROBERT BARR & ISAAC ROSS BARR, all under 21 years), & children of MARGARET MOORE, dec, (not named), all infants under 21 years represented by JOHN STEELE, their next Friend. 15 Nov, 1805: dfnt MATTHEW PATTON to convey title to Dayton lot #186 to WILLIAM McCLURE & JAMES STEELE or their heirs when a patent could be obtained from U S govt. 13 Aug, 1803: dfnt DANIEL C. COOPER to convey Dayton lot #33 to DAVID SQUIER when patent obtained. In 1809, SQUIER transferred his right to ISAAC G. BURNET who then assigned to McCLURE & HENRY DISBROW in 1810. On 9 Oct, 1812, WILLIAM McCLURE died without issue. During his last illness, he directed his property to be given entirely to wife MARTHA. Knowing WILLIAM's intent, his heirs (wife MARTHA, JOHN McCLURE, JAMES McCLURE, DAVID McCLURE & ANTHONY LOGAN) drew the following disposition: MARTHA to have all Dayton property; brother JOHN to have deed to 190 acres where he lives; brother JAMES to have deed to 60 acres after paying balance due to JACOB BURNETT. Balance of land after paying debts to be divided equally among brothers and sisters. DAVID McCLURE & JAMES STEELE to administer. Signed MARTHA McCLURE, JOHN McCLURE, JAMES McCLURE, DAVID McCLURE, MARTHA McCLURE (#2, sister?), ANTHONY LOGAN. Witness by JOHN THOMPSON & JOHN STEELE. On 6 April, 1813, widow MARTHA McCLURE made her will, believing she had full rights to WILLIAM's property. Appt'd brother JOHN STEELE as exec, witness JAMES McCLURE, ALEXANDER LOGAN. Petitioners (heirs of MARTHA) believed defnt heirs of WILLIAM (signers of the property dispostion agreement) would direct PATTON & COOPER to convey deeds to them. Defnt heirs of WILLIAM claimed MARTHA had been given only life interest in property, not title, so could not convey land to her heirs. Petitioners requested Court to compel COOPER & PATTON to convey title. COOPER & PATTON refuse to convey title until dispute settled among heirs. Defnts refuted agreement, failed to remember hearing WILLIAM specify his directions as given in disposition. On evening of his funeral, his brothers and sisters were coerced to sign disposition agreement; did not believe that WILLIAM intended to convey title to widow, taking land from them. Claimed brothers JOHN & JAMES had equitable title (prior to WILLIAM's death) to land mentioned in disposition; terms granting title were unneccessary. Defnts request dismissal of suit. After deliberation, Court decreed heirs of WILLIAM to pay costs of $13.79; PATTON & COOPER to execute deeds

Term of May, 1814 continued

to JOHN STEELE, exec of MARTHA, before 1 Aug. STEELE
to sell lots, distribute proceeds to heirs named in
MARTHA's will. pp 355, 356, 357, 358, 359, 360, 361

Case 18. NATHANIEL HUNT vs JAMES MORROW. On 31
March, 1813, assaulted and imprisoned HUNT without
reasonable cause. MORROW pled not guilty: at time of
assault, he was 1st Lt, U. S. Infantry, recruiting
and enlisting men as ordered. HUNT, an Army contractor providing soldiers' rations, brought abstract of
rations issued for payment. MORROW questioned contract under which issue took place; HUNT replied if
MORROW would sign, he would insert contractor's name.
MORROW signed; HUNT refused to give name, started to
leave. MORROW "desired NATHANIEL to either insert
the name of the person" or strike out MORROW's signature. HUNT refused to obey. MORROW "gently lay his
hands upon said NATHANIEL & detained him" until HUNT
complied. MORROW, desiring to remove his name from
abstract, ordered his soldiers to "gently lay hands"
upon HUNT, keeping him in custody until paper was
surrendered. MORROW erased his signature and returned abstract to HUNT. NATHANIEL disc suit, recovered
$16.75 costs from MORROW. pp 362, 363, 364, 365, 366

Case 19. STATE vs JOHN McCANN. Costs remain unpaid
from disc suit against JOHN LOWE, May, 1812. Sheriff
unable to find McCANN. Defnt failed to appear.
State recover $13.87 costs. pp 366, 367

Case 20. JOHN ARCHER vs ROBERT RENICK. On 16 Jan,
1813, $250 debt for goods, namely 15 barrels of
flour. Failed to pay. Suit filed. Def'nt refuted
debt. Jury summoned: JESSE CLARK, JOHN COLMAN,
DANIEL C. COOPER, JOSEPH EWING, DANIEL H. FISHER,
ISAAC GRIFFITH, JONATHAN HERSHMAN, HENRY JENNINGS,
JOHN MENGAL, PETER SWANK, ABRAHAM SWARTZLEY, JAMES
THOMSON. Found RENICK guilty. ARCHER recover $86.69
damages, $18.88 costs. pp 367, 368, 369

Term of September, 1814

Case 1. ISAAC GRIFFITH vs JOHN BODLEY. OWEN JONES &
ELEAZER GRIFFITH stood bail for BODLEY. Disc. p 370

Case 2. JOHN C. DEATH vs MARTIN EARHART. Writ also
issued for ADAM SPITLAR; not found by sheriff. On 8
Dec, 1812, $80 note signed by EARHART & SPITLAR.
Failed to pay. Suit filed. EARHART failed to appear
at hearing. DEATH recover debt, $7.20 damages, costs

Term of September, 1814 continued

of $10.85. Copy of original note, witness CHARLES
LONG, BENJAMIN KELL. pp 371, 372

Supreme Court appeals, returned to Common Pleas for
execution of judgement:
1. JOHN JAY vs HENRY MARQUART, JOHN HUNT & JOHN
    COMPTON JR.
2. JOHN ARCHER vs ROBERT RENICK
3. PATRICK LAFFERTY vs GEORGE FRIBERGER -
    dism in error
4. JACOB KUNS vs LUDWICK CHRISTIAN - dism in
    error

Case 3. JONATHAN DONNEL vs JEROM HOLT. In Jan, 1813,
DONNEL came before Court, requesting former sheriff
HOLT be held responsible for judgement recovered
against JAMES ARCHER (plus interest and 10% damages);
HOLT failed to perform duty. Before case was heard,
DONNEL died in Champaign Co, leaving SARAH DONNEL &
DANIEL McKINNON as his adms & legal reps. HOLT failed
to appear. DONNEL to recover $108.07. p 373

Case 4. HENRY MARQUART vs MARTIN ROWZER. On 5 Feb,
1814, $90 note signed. Failed to pay. Suit filed.
ROWZER failed to appear. MARQUART recover $93.03
damages, $9.53 costs. Copy of original note, witness
ELIZABETH (x) MARQUART. pp 374, 375

Case 5. JOHN PETTICREW vs SAMUEL STEELE & HENRY JEN-
NINGS. Def'nts bail pledged by JONATHAN KNIGHT. On
27 Feb, 1813, $1200 note signed. Defnts failed to
pay. Suit filed. Def'nts failed to appear. PETTI-
CREW to recover $655 damages, $11.63 costs. Copy of
original note, witness SALLY JENNINGS, JAMES TUCKER.
pp 375, 376, 377.

Case 6. JOHN FOLKERTH, JOHN H. WILLIAMS & DAVID
McCLURE, Commissioners of Montgomery Co, successors
of FOLKERTH, JOHN DEVOR & DANIEL HOOVER JR, vs JEROM
HOLT, GEORGE GROVE, HUGH McCOLLOM, DAVID DUNCAN,
CONKLING MILLER & JAMES THOMSON. On 4 June, 1810,
the def'nts signed $4000 performance bond for JEROM
HOLT in the office of Montgomery Co Sheriff. Refused
to pay. Suit filed, damages $200. Def'nts claimed
bond was supposed to be signed by 12 persons, notably
DANIEL C. COOPER & WILLIAM McCLURE. The instrument
was sealed with several blanks, delivered to Commissioners, and so was not a legal instrument. Case
disc. HOLT to pay $16.77 costs. pp 377, 378, 379,
380, 381, 382, 383, 384, 385

Term of September, 1814 continued

Case 7. DANIEL C. COOPER vs DAVID ALSPACH. Suit for
$100 damages. On 20 Sept, 1813, ALSPACH forced entry
into closed field belonging to COOPER, treading crop,
destroying other herbiage. He then turned cattle and
horses into the field. ALSPACH pled not guilty. Jury
summoned: SAMUEL BROADAWAY, JESSE CLARK, JOSEPH FLORY
JOHN HARDMAN, ABRAHAM HOSIER, OWEN JONES, JOSEPH
PIERCE, HEZEKIAH ROBINSON, HENRY SHANK, JACOB SUMAN,
PHILIP WAGNER, ASHBERRY WOOD. Acquited ALSPACH. COO-
PER to pay $19.51 costs to ALSPACH. pp 385, 386, 387

Case 8. JAMES RITCHIE vs JOHN COMPTON JR. Def'nt's
bail pledged by ROBERT GRAHAM & NATHANIEL HUNT. On
10 Oct, 1813, $250 debt for labor at COMPTON's busin-
ess. Failed to pay. Suit filed, damages $300. Def'nt
refuted agreement, to give evidence plntf owes $1000
for goods, money lent, board and lodging. Jury summoned: DAVID ALSPACH, SAMUEL BROADAWAY, JESSE CLARK,
JOSEPH FLORY, ROBERT GRAHAM, ROBERT GRAY, JOHN HARD-
MAN, ABRAHAM HOSIER, JOSEPH PIERCE, HENRY SHANK,
NICHOLAS SMALL, PHILIP WAGNER. Found COMPTON guilty.
RITCHIE to recover $125 damages, $26.54 costs. pp
387, 388, 389, 390

Case 9. JOHN WEAVER vs CHRISTIAN YEAZEL. Damages
$300. Disc. p 391

Case 10. JOHN WEAVER vs ABRAHAM MINNIEAR. In suit
in JP court, WEAVER obtained judgement against defnt.
Failed to pay. Note: "DAVID SQUIER, Esq, Sheriff of
Montgomery Co having departed this life", writ was
served by AARON BAKER, coroner. MINNIEAR not found
in baliwick, failed to appear in court. WEAVER to
recover $3.15 costs. pp 391, 392

Case 11. JAMES THOMPSON vs COMMISSIONERS OF MONTGOM-
ERY CO. On 10 Nov, 1811, agreement for THOMPSON to
build stone jailhouse (full specifications included)
for $2147.91, plus $600 debt for previous work done.
Failed to pay. Suit filed. Def'nts refuted debt,
filed affidavit that WILLIAM M. LUKES, a material
witness, is missing. At hearing, def'nts claimed
THOMPSON did not perform work as requested (full list
included). Case sent to arbitration by ABNER GERRARD
BENJAMIN ARCHER & NATHANIEL HUNT. Found Commission-s
guilty. THOMPSON to recover $337.42 damages, $47.15
costs. pp 392, 393, 394, 395, 396, 397, 398

Case 12. Town of Dayton vs. CHARLES ESTE. Charged

with riding a horse on the sidewalk, fined $.50. ESTE
gave notice of appeal; WILLIAM PATTERSON stood bail.
Acquited by Court. Town of Dayton recover nothing,
to pay ESTE's costs of $6.29. p 398

Case 13. DAVID HOLE, heir of Dr. JOHN HOLE, petition
of partition of real estate. Father JOHN HOLE died,
holding land in Sec 32, T2, R6. Petitioners: DAVID,
BETSEY DODDS wife of WILLIAM, JANE MULFORD wife of
JACOB, NANCY HOLE, JOHN HOLE, MATILDA HOLE & PHOEBE
HOLE (last four all minors). JOHN TAYLOR, JOHN ALLEN
& RICHARD MASON to divide land. Map of partition.
DAVID HOLE to pay costs of $33.55. pp 399, 400

Term of January, 1815

Case 1. JOSEPH RYAN vs CHRISTIAN WELDY. On 1 June,
18-- and other times, WELDY assaulted KATHERINE, wife
of JOSEPH of German Twp, "ravished, lay with and carnally knew and begot with child" whereby JOSEPH suffered loss of companionship and was put to great expense. Suit for damages of $1000. WELDY pled not
guilty. RYAN filed affidavit that JESSE KELLY, a material witness, was missing. Settled by consent:
$14.46 costs paid by defendant. pp 401, 402

Case 2. RICHARD SPARKS vs JAMES RHEA. Writ also is-
sued for JOHN WRIGHT, not found by sheriff. Suit for
$75 damages, disc. Copy of original note. "JAMES
RHEA & JOHN WRIGHT of Alligany Co, PA" to RICHARD
SPARKS of same. Debt of $198 dated 16 Apr, 1791.
Obligation was to provide Capt. SPARKS with company
of 27 soldiers, capable of passing a review, on or
before 1 June, witness AARON APPLEGATE, ROBERT
WRIGHT. pp 403, 404, 405

Case 3. JOHN MOORE vs DAVID WEIDNER. On 10 Dec,
1804, JACOB EBERSOLE wrote note for $86 to WEIDNER.
Assigned to MOORE on 30 May, 1805; EBERSOLE refused
to pay. MOORE brought suit 19 Aug, 1805 in "Botte-
tourt" Co, VA; judgement given to recover debt, damages, costs. Writ returned "EBERSOLE not found". On
1 Jan, 1813, served notice on WEIDNER at Dayton.
Failed to pay. Suit filed. Case settled. Def'nt
pay $7.12 costs. pp 405, 406, 407, 408

Case 4. BENJAMIN LEHMAN vs JOSEPH ROHRER. Slander,
damages of $1000. Case disc by consent. pp 408, 409

Case 5. JOSEPH HEDGES & HENRY NEVILL (Hedges & Co)

Term of January, 1815 continued

vs NATHANIEL HUNT, JOHN HUNT & JOHN COMPTON JR.   On
10 March, 1813, def'nts indebted $200 for goods.
Failed to pay. Suit filed. Plntfs recover damages
of $130.48, $11.19 costs. pp 409, 410, 411, 412

Case 6.   JOHN HUNT & NATHANIEL HUNT vs ABRAHAM TEA-
GARDEN, HENRY ENOCH & HENRY ENOCH JR. Suit for $500
damages. Disc by consent. Def'nts pay $4.16 costs.
pp 412, 413

Case 7.   MOSES IRWIN, appellee vs OLIVER TALBERT,
appellant. ERWIN vs TALBERT heard by JAMES RUSSEL,
JP. Witness JOSEPH WALKER, JOHN TUCKER, WILLIAM
ERWIN for plntf; HENRY CREAGER for defnt. Judgement:
$10.24 for IRWIN. On 1 Nov, 1813, OLIVER assaulted
MOSES' horse (valued at $80) with poles and clubs,
rendering the horse incapable of working.   TALBERT
pled not guilty: the horse entered the stable of
RUTH TALBERT, feeding on hay, doing damage. OLIVER,
as servant of RUTH and at her command, gently struck
the horse to drive it away.   Jury summoned: JOHN
BROWER, HENRY BROWN, WILLIAM CALHOUN, WILLIAM COMP-
TON, JOSEPH HANCOCK SR, GEORGE HARRIS, DANIEL MILLER,
JOHN MILLER JR, HENRY MOYER, JOHN RIGGANS, JAMES
RITCHIE, HENRY SWARTZEL.   Found TALBERT guilty.
IRWIN to recover damages of $20, $32.73 costs. pp
413, 414, 415, 416

Case 8.   FREDERICK HAMMER vs JOHN COMPTON & DANIEL C.
COOPER. On 10 Dec, 1810 at Baltimore, MD, $289.19
note signed. Failed to pay. Suit filed, $500 dam-
ages. Failed to defend suit. HAMMER recover $351.10
damages, $9.35 costs. Def'nts gave notice of appeal
to Supreme Court. pp 416, 417, 418

Case 9.   HUGH McCOLLOM vs JAMES RITCHIE. Suit heard
in JP court gave McCOLLOM $43.30 judgement against
RITCHIE. Failed to pay. Suit filed. Writ served by
S. DAW & I. NOTT NONES; RITCHIE failed to appear.
McCOLLOM to recover damages. pp 418, 419, 420

Case 10.   JAMES McCORMACK, appellee vs JOHN AINSWORTH
appellant. Transcript of McCORMACK vs AINSWORTH,
heard by JOHN D. CAMPBELL, JP, on 28 June, 1813.
Witness JOHN ULERY, ROBERT YOUNG. Bail for plntf:
DAVID ARCHIBALD.   Plntf to recover $9.49 damages.
AINSWORTH, charged with driving away McCORMACK's bull
on 10 Apr, 1813, failed to pay judgement. Suit filed.
AINSWORTH pled not guilty. Jury summoned: JOHN BROWER

Term of January, 1815 continued

HENRY BROWN, WILLIAM CALHOUN, WILLIAM COMPTON, WILLIAM DOUGHERTY, DANIEL H. FISHER, JOSEPH HANCOCK, GEORGE HARRIS, DANIEL MILLER, JOHN MILLER JR, DAVID MOYER, HENRY SWARTZEL. Found AINSWORTH guilty of trespass. McCORMACK to recover $.01 damages, $28.10 costs. pp 420, 421, 422

Case 11. JOHN COMPTON JR vs PETER WEAVER. In Chancery. In Nov or Dec of 1812, COMPTON was drafted to serve 6 months in state militia. Agreed to pay WEAVER $50 to serve as sub or procure sub. Company, serving at Fort "Lorimies", was released early. WEAVER demanded $50; COMPTON refused to pay until given proof of substitution. Spring of 1813, COMPTON court-martialed and fined $150 for failing to serve so had reason to doubt Weaver. Suit brought in JP court; judgement against COMPTON. Plntf's petition asks Court to force WEAVER to give evidence of substitution, proof of muster. WEAVER: employed - MALOY who mustered company of Capt FRANCIS PATTERSON who provided certificate. WEAVER sent certificate, requesting payment. Col. HOLT supposed to have remitted fine to COMPTON as court martial was in error. Transcript of BENJAMIN VAN CLEVE, Master in Chancery: JEROM HOLT testifed fine was remitted. Col. DAVID REID testified plntf agreed to pay substitute. Capt PATTERSON testified JAMES MALOY was sub, had provided certificate. Court dissolved injunction, dismissed suit. pp 422 through 431

Case 12. MASSEY HOLE vs DAVID HOLE and other heirs of Dr. JOHN HOLE. (see Case 13, p 105) In 1813, the Court found personal property of Dr. JOHN HOLE was insufficient to pay debts, ordered sale of 36 acres in Sec 2 & 3, T 1, R 6 by adms MASSEY HOLE & JOHN EWING. Sold at auction 26 Feb, 1814. Purchased by plntf on terms; half in cash, half by note due in 2 yrs. Def'nts summoned to court to acknowledge payment of father's debts, legality of sale. RICHARD MASON guardian of minor heirs. Def'nts failed to respond to petition, ordered by court to convey title to plntf. pp 431, 432, 433, 434, 435, 436

Case 13. DAVID McCLURE & JAMES STEELE, adm of WILLIAM McCLURE. Petition to sell town of Dayton lot 86 to settle debts. Schedule of debts: To DANIEL CONNER & CO, P. SPINNING, WILLIAM KING, JAMES WELSH, JOSEPH H. CRANE, I.G. BURNET, ANTHONY LOGAN, ELLIOT & HENDERSON, ELIJAH GRANT, MARTHA McCLURE, AGNES STEELE

Term of January, 1815 continued

GEORGE GROVE. Notes due to estate: From ROBERT EWING, GEORGE DRUMMOND, WILLIAM VAN CLEVE, JAMES McCLURE, JEROM HOLT, WILLIAM SHAFER, GEORGE DRUMMOND (again), DAVID McCLURE, JOHN McCLURE. Note of disputed land sale in Butler Co between JESSE HUNT & C. R. SEDAN, hold bond of ELIJAH BOUDINOT for HUNT & SEDAN to give title or refund money. Appraisal of value of lot 86 for $1800 made by ISAAC BURNET, WILLIAM SMITH, HORATIO G. PHILLIPS. Ordered recorded by Court. pp 437, 438

Case 14. SOPHIA PLUMMER & GEORGE LINKS JR, adms of estate of PHILEMON PLUMMER, dec. Petition: estate insufficient to complete payments of Sec 13, T 5, R 5E; requesting authorization to assign certificate. DANIEL WAYMIRE has paid estate money which PHILEMON paid to U. S. on patent, has completed remaining payments due. Administrators need permission to convey title, which was granted. pp 439, 440

Case 15. CHRISTOPHER MOWREY, JOHN HIZER & BARBARA, his wife, adms of CHRISTIAN FOGELSONG. Petition for power to execute deed to PETER SOUDERS on behalf of heirs. On 28 Oct, 1805, agreement between FOGELSONG and SOUDERS for sale of land in Sec 24, T 4, R 4, except for portion sold previously to JACOB STIVER. SOUDER completed paying for land per schedule. Patent issued to heirs of FOGELSONG, all of whom are under legal age. (BARBARA identified as formerly BARBARA FOGELSONG, now HIZER, no relationship given to CHRISTIAN -- widow, sister, daughter?) Permission to convey title granted. pp 440, 441

COMMON PLEAS (CIVIL) LAW RECORD BOOK C-1: exerpts

Term of May, 1815

Case 7. STATE vs ELIZABETH CASTOR, adm of CONRAD CASTOR, dec. Dism. p 9

Case 8. Petition of ROBERT STRAIN JR, adm of JOHN STRAIN, dec. Authorization to convey real estate. JOHN owned Dayton lot #182; ROBERT SR owned lot #206. Agreement to trade south halves of respective lots. John died July, 1814, leaving widow, one child, said child has since died. Petition to exchange deeds. Authorization granted. pp 10, 11

Case 11. JOHN HUSTON, DOMINICK McGRATH & CATHERINE,

his wife, JACOB CROY, BETSEY CROY, ALEXANDER CROY,
MATHIAS CROY, JOHN CROY, BENJAMIN CROY, SARAH CROY,
SAMUEL CROY, JOSEPH CROY, McCLURE CROY & JAMES CROY
by JOHN CROY, their next friend, vs GEORGE NEWCOM &
JOHN EWING, adms of ALEXANDER HUSTON, dec, MARY ANN
HUSTON, SAMUEL HUSTON & EDWARD HUSTON. Petition:
ALEXANDER HUSTON died Feb, 1814, leaving children
JOHN HUSTON & CATHERINE McGRATH and grandchildren by
SUSANNAH CROY, dec dau of ALEXANDER. Will disputed,
gave 1/3 possessions to widow MARY ANN, land to sons
SAMUEL, ALEXANDER & EDWARD, daus RACHEL McCLURE &
SARAH OSWALT, money to sons JOHN & DAVID, dau SUSAN.
While in act of writing the will, father became
deranged, remained so until his death; writing
remained incomplete. Dfnts produced will, accepted
by Court; execution caused damage to petitioners.
Court set will aside as invalid. pp 19, 20, 21.

Court order: ISAAC G. BURNET appted County Commis-
sioner to fill vacancy of DAVID McCLURE who moved to
Indiana Territory. p 27

Term of September, 1815

Case 15. RACHEL HATFIELD & THOMAS HATFIELD, adms of
estate of JONAS HATFIELD. Petion to convey title to
land in Sec 20, T 3, R 4E to PHILIP GUNCKEL. Contract
by JONAS during his lifetime. Bond: JONAS HATFIELD
of Wayne Co, Indiana Territory. Witness: LEWIS SHUEY
dated 2 Apr, 1814. Court authorized conveyance. p 45

Case 23. Petition of JOHN ROHRER & ANN SHOWERS, adms
of ABRAHAM SHOWER, dec, sought to convey title to
land in Sec 24, T 6, R 4 to PETER WILL of Randolph
Twp. Contract made 1812. Permission granted. pp 54,55

Case 30. MARY WEAVER vs WILLIAM VAN CLEVE. Suit in
JP court, 15 May, 1815 for bastardy. Dfnt's testimo-
ny appears to attempt to shift responsibility onto
ABSOLEM WESTFALL. Suit filed. Jury summoned: JOHN
ANDERSON, BENJAMIN BARKALOW, JAMES BROWN, PATRICK
BRYSON, OBADIAH CONOVER, OWEN HATFIELD, JOHN HIZER,
JAMES MAJOR, MATHIAS PARSONS, JACOB ROHRER, MARTIN
SHEETZ, ROBERT STRAIN. Acquited VAN CLEVE. Dfnt
rcvr $17.72. costs from plntf. pp 62, 63.

Term of April, 1816

Case 3. (second #3, error by clerks). JOSEPH C.
SILVER & WILLIAM ROGERS, vs ROBERT SILVER. On 22
April, 1815, land in Sec 14, T 2, R 6 and in the VA
reservation was mortgaged for $535.63; suit filed to

COMMON PLEAS (CIVIL) LAW RECORD BOOK C-1: exerpts

foreclose. ROGERS died during the term of the case,
before Jan, 1816. ROBERT failed to defend; foreclos-
ure granted. Plntfs rcvr $535.63 debt, $31.25 damage
$12.29 costs. Original mortgage witness: DAVID
BAILEY, WILLIAM BLAIR JR. pp 126, 127, 128, 129

Case 25. CHRISTIANNA MILLER, adm of SAMUEL MILLER,
dec, vs ABNER HOBBS. Debt; dfnt not found. p 173

Term of August, 1816

Case 6. JOHN STUMP, heir of LEONARD STUMP. Petition
for partition of real estate. "with brother GEORGE
STUMP and sister ELIZABETH STUMP, heirs of father
LEONARD STUMP, dec". Land in Sec 4, T 2, R 5E & Sec
13, T 3, R 4E. WILLIAM EMRICK, guardian of GEORGE
STUMP. PHILIP GUNCKEL, guardian of ELIZABETH STUMP.
Valuation made by JOHN H. SCHENCK, ABRAHAM TROXELL &
CHRISTOPHER EMRICK. Found that after setting off
dower, land could not be divided without diminishing
value. Court ordered adms JULIANA STUMP & GEORGE
STUMP to sell land in German Twp. Purchased by JACOB
W. DECHANT: 60 acres, SEc 13, T 3, R 4. Purchased
by JOHN CASPER DILL: 26.5 acres, no S-T-R. Purchased
by SAMUEL LENICK: Sec 4, T 2, R 5E, no acres given.
pp 187, 188, 189, 190

Case 7. Application of JOHN MILLER, a native of Sax-
ony in Europe, for certificate of naturalization,
resident of 5 years & upward. p 190

Case 9. JOHN SCHENCK, PETER SCHENCK, WILLIAM B.
SCHENCK, DANIEL SCHENCK, CHRINEYANCE SCHENCK, sons of
WILLIAM SCHENCK, dec, JOSEPH TAPSCOTT & ANNE, his
wife, dau of WILLIAM SCHENCK, LYDIA ERICKSON (by her
next friend WILLIAM B. SCHENCK), dau of JOHN & ELLEN
ERICKSON, said ELLEN dau of WILLIAM dec, & SARAH
SCHENCK, widow of WILLIAM, vs DAVID SCHENCK. Father
WILLIAM, an original purchaser in Sec 28, T 2, R 5,
paid 1/2 money due at time of entry. Agreed to sell
100 acres to eldest son DAVID, later raised to 120
acres to include improvements on land. DAVID to pay
balance due on to US Govt, clearing title on father's
behalf, accountable to father for rest of money due
on 120 acre tract (difference between money due govt
and cost of tract). Father WILLIAM gave DAVID the
certificate to take to Cincinnati land office to pay
off entry, not realizing land paym't had been allowed
to lapse & land to come up for forfeiture. (Believed
the land advertised as being in danger of forfeiture
belonged to Admiral WILLIAM SCHENCK, not himself) At
Cincinnati, DAVID made new entry on land in his name.

110

He then refused to convey land over the agreed 120 acres to father or to pay balance of money due. Since father's death, DAVID refused to settle with rest of family, insisted he was still entitled to son's share of estate. Petition asked DAVID to give accounting and convey land not in original agreement to family. DAVID's response: at father's request, DAVID moved his family from western New York state to OH. He became security on father's debt to -ERICKSON of NJ & was arrested by - ERICKSON, had to pay $80 on father's behalf. Father agreed to convey deed when the govt patent was issued. DAVID, on learning of the forfeiture, paid balance due to avoid losing the land; was told by father to keep certificate until it was requested. Witness depositions made. WILLIAM COX: father admitted he had lost land in forfeiture. WILLIAM C. CONOVER SR: surveyed land father intended to sell to DAVID & testified to 120 acre agreement. JONATHAN ROBBINS: father blamed DAVID for allowing the land to be forfeited as father was capable of making payments. EDEN BURROWS: had proposed that if WILLIAM SCHENCK would pay debt to Burrows, he would then hire father and son to build barn. After land dispute, DAVID requested payment for his past work. DAVID SCHENCK ads WILLIAM B. SCHENCK and others -- testimony by WILLIAM MARTIN: father thought forfeiture notice an error, angry with DAVID for claiming land in own name. THOMAS CONOVER: father blamed blamed forfeiture on DAVID, signed THOMAS COVENHOVEN. Court found DAVID to pay JOSEPH TAPSCOTT & WILLIAM B. SCHENCK, adms of WILLIAM SCHENCK, $390 + interest from 1 Jan, 1812. EDMUND MUNGER, BENJAMIN MALTBIE & JOSEPH CRANE to set value on rest of qtr section; DAVID ordered to pay appaisal price of $8 per acre or convey land to father's estate. DAVID gave notice of appeal to Supreme Court. pp 190, 191, 192, 193, 194, 195, 196, 197, 198, 199

Case 17. JACOB SMITH vs JOSEPH FOUTZ & JENNY FOUTZ. JOSEPH & JENNY summoned to show cause why JACOB should not be granted guardianship of JAMES SMITH, JACOB SMITH & SARAH SMITH, minor heirs of PETER SMITH, dec. Case dism by plntf. p 213

Term of December, 1816

Case 34. Petition of GEORGE NEWCOM & JOSEPH H. CRANE, guardians of minor heirs of HUGH ANDREWS, dec, to sell 100 acres in Sec 15, T 2, R 8. Personal estate settled debts only. Money needed to maintain and educate NANCY, SAMUEL, ELIZA, JAMES & HUGH ANDREWS. Dism by Court. p 274

Case 38. JACOB KOOGLER & SAMUEL KOOGLER, adms of
ADAM KOOGLER, dec, petition to sell land. On 6
Nov, 1813, ADAM sold 50 acres in Sec 25, T 3, R 8
to WILLIAM HUGHEY, to convey deed when patent obtained. 19 Sept, 1814, HUGHEY conveyed 170 acres
in same S-T-R to ISRAEL HALE, later assigned in
1816 to JOHN COSTS. Patent now obtained, Court
granted permission. pp 277, 278

Case 39. Petition of JAMES WINGATE & DAVID HUS-
TON, execs of will of JOSEPH WILSON. Request
that court appt person to execute deeds on behalf
of heirs, fulfill contracts made on 22 July,
1813. JAMES McFADDEN and ELIZABETH MONTGOMERY to
purchase 130 acres in Sec 14, T 2, R 7. Court
empowered DAVID HUSTON to convey deeds. p 278

Term of May, 1817

Case 6. JAMES C. COTTOM & ELIZABETH, his wife vs
JAMES RIDDLE, surviving obligor of RIDDLE &
RICHARD GRAY, dec. On 12 Sept, 1814 $400 note to
ELIZABETH RIDDLE, now ELIZABETH COTHAM, to be
paid money collected from MARY RIDDLE. Dfnt refused to pay. Suit filed, $250 damage. Dfnt
refuted debt, to give evidence of plntfs' indebtedness. Disc. pp 283, 284, 285

Case 37. PETER ROUF vs DANIEL GRIPE. On 27
April, 1812, CRIPE to sell land in Sec 12, T 5, R
4 to PETER RUHF for DANIEL RUHF, ADAM ROUF and
FREDERICK PANDER. Certificate held by PETER;
DANIEL ROUF to return within year. If fail to
return, assign certificate to ADAM & FREDERICK.
1 May, 1812 agreement: PETER to sustitute for
DANIEL CRIPE JR, son of DANIEL, in militia duty.
Served 6 months, to be paid $200. 28 Apr, 1813,
DANIEL RUHF had not returned; CRIPE refused to
assign title as agreed. Suit filed, $500 damages.
Jury summoned: JACOB CAYLOR, JAMES CHATHAM,
PETER EAGLE, JAMES HANNA, MARTIN HOOBLER, DAVID
JOHN, PETER LEHMAN, ISAAC MILLER, CHARLES SMITH,
DAVID ULRICH, JOHN WAITMAN, TOBIAS WHITESEL.
Jury acquited CRIPE. Dfnt rcvr $24.81 costs. pp
322, 323, 324, 325

Case 53. NANCY IFERT (or IFORD) vs ABRAHAM BAR-
NET. Case heard in JP court for bastardy. NANCY
pregnant "since middle of June (1816)". Dfnt's
bail by HENRY CURTNER, SAMUEL WATTON. Suit disc,
dfnt pay costs. p 349

Term of October, 1817

Case 11. Petition for adms of CHRISTIAN FOGELGA-
SONG to convey land. Minor heirs, all under age
21: CATHERINE, GEORGE, JACOB & CHRISTIAN. Land
in Sec 13 & 24, T 4, R 4E. 26 Sept, 1804: FOGEL-
GASONG gave bond to JACOB SLEIFER of Hamilton Co
to convey deed for 200 acre in Sec 13, deed to be
made by Jan, 1808. On 6 March, 1806, agreemt to
convey additional 200 acre in Sec 24. Money now
paid, title conveyance authorized. pp 363, 364

Case 16. JOHN DEVOR & MARY GRAY, adms of RACHEL
ARMSTRONG, vs ROBERT GRAY JR. In 1807 or 1808,
ROBERT GRAY made verbal contract to convey land
in Sec 26 & 35, T 12, R 2 to RACHEL ARMSTRONG of
Darke Co. Ist paymt of $320 made Aug, 1808 &
land was assigned to RACHEL who was to make payts
on behalf of ROBERT & his brother RICHARD GRAY.
RACHEL later learned more interest had accrued on
land than she had been told; became basis of dispute between parties. RACHEL laid $38 for final
payt due on table. ROBERT refused to accept; not
enough to cover balance due & interest. Money
picked up by WILLIAM GRAY, brother of ROBERT JR.
RACHEL, trusting seller, had failed to obtain
recpts when making payt. After her death, ROBERT
filed $600 suit against adms. Deposition sworn
before DAVID BRIGGS, JP, Miami Co, Jan, 1816.
ROBERT admitted agreement, claimed RACHEL knew
she was to pay all money due on Sec 26, reimburse
him for $320 he previously paid on land. Deposi-
tion of JANE GRAY, Darke Co: She & husband RICH-
ARD, now dec, heard conversation at home of
ROBERT GRAY SR between RACHEL & ROBERT JR. He
refused $38 as insufficient. WILLIAM GRAY later
accepted money. Case dismissed by court. pp
372, 373, 374, 375, 376, 377

Case 17. ROBERT GRAY vs JOHN DEVOR, adm of
RACHEL ARMSTRONG. Recap above case. Agreement
entered 1 May, 1810 with RACHEL during her life &
widowhood. She owed debt of $320 on 1 March,
1811. Suit filed. Plntf rcvr $119.86, $12.63
costs. pp 378, 379, 380

Case 22. ALBERT STEIN, native of Prussia,
declared intent to become US citizen. p 385

II.   Common Pleas Probate Docket Books

"Probate" is synonomous with "wills" to many people. In the early days of Montgomery County, a variety of legal matters were recorded under the heading of "Probate", all useful to the genealogist. Docket books record the progess of each case as it comes before the court. The first entry is the appointment of an executor (or an administrator if the person died intestate, without having made a will). Guardianship of minor children and appraisal of personal property are recorded, followed by the public sale bill list. The last entry, the final settlement, may not be made for several years.

All of this can be a rich source of genealogical information. First, an approximate time of death is known. The person providing the security bond for an estate or guardianship is most likely a relative. Heirs may be named, especially valuable in administrations. Even when relationships are not clearly defined, a note due the estate or an auction buyer might suggest a missing brother or son. The final settlement can provide a clue if a notation was made that the balance of the estate was divided among "a widow and seven children". As always, the papers may have been recorded long after an event, resulting apparently in the names of deceased persons showing up as buyer at an auction, etc. Dates are included when they were given in the original record.

The final bills of an estate were often expenses associated with a death, not an indication of profligate indebtedness. Occupations of some early settlers can be learned from these notes: the carpenter who made the coffin, the auctioneer who "cryed" the sale, the distiller who made the whiskey served on sale day, undoubtedly contributing to profit!

The five docket books which have been abstracted here are found at the Probate Court office, Montgomery County Courts Building. Case numbers were added later. For those wishing to pursue a will or administration noted here, the first stop is the Probate office noted above. The will or administration case number must be obtained from the index. Copies of an original will may be obtained from the Probate clerk, currently at $1.00 per page. To see an original will book or administration packet, the researcher must take the index/case number to the County Records Office, sixth floor of the Reibold Building, where the items are stored. Copies may also be obtained there.

Term of November, 1803

Case 1. Adm of estate of THOMAS DAVIS, late of state of Delaware, granted to widow HANNAH DAVIS. Sec: OWEN HATFIELD, WILLIAM HATFIELD. p 1

Case 2. Adm of estate of JOSEPH BIGGER of Washington Twp, granted to ABIGAIL BIGGER & JAMES BIGGER. Sec: JAMES PETTICREW, JACOB LONG. p 1

Term of June, 1804

Inv and appr of estate of THOMAS DAVIS. Total worth $1176.10. Appr'd by AARON NUTT, JAMES SCOTT. pp 2,3

Inv and appr of estate of JOSEPH BIGGER, dated 5 Dec, 1803. Total worth $284.67. Appr'd by RICHARD MASON, JOHN DAY. WILLIAM GRIFFIN, clerk. pp 4, 5

Case 3. Adm of estate of WILLIAM MAULSBY, late of Dayton, granted to MARIA MAULSBY & GEORGE NEWCOM. Sec: DANIEL C. COOPER, DAVID SQUIER. p 5

Special session 13 August, 1804

Case 3.5. THOMAS COPPOCK appt'd "guardian to five orphan children under his care, namely" --, left blank, only JOHN COPPOCK later written in. p 6

Case 4. DANIEL C. COOPER appt'd guardian to THOMAS ADAMS & NANCY ADAMS, orphans, late under the care of RALPH FRENCH. p 6

Case 5. JOHN GERARD appt'd guardian to RICHARD COCHRAN alias SLOAN, orphan child now in his care. p 6

Case 6. WILLIAM SNODGRASS appt'd guardian to JOHN PALMER, an orphan under care of ANDREW LOCK, and SUSANNA DONAHOO, an orphan under care of WILLIAM ELLIS. p 6

Case 7. JOHN MILLER of Wolf Creek appt'd guardian to WILLIAM ELLIOTT, an orphan now in care of PAUL D. BUTLER. p 6

Case 8. Complaint dated 8 Aug, 1804, filed by JAMES MILLER & WILLIAM HAMER, Overseers of the Poor, Dayton Twp, against SAMUEL THOMSON. Under powers granted by "An act providing for appt of guardians to lunaticks and others", plntfs felt THOMSON was wasting estate, would bring his family to want, and should properly come under said act. Jury: JOHN BENNET, D.C. COOPER,

DAVID SQUIER, STEPHEN LUDLOW, JOHN FOLKERTH, JAMES MILLER Coroner, MATHEW NEWCOM, MATTHEW PATTON, JAMES GILLESPIE, RALPH FRENCH, HUGH McCOLLUM, GEORGE SMITH. Found THOMSON, through excessive drinking, idleness and debauchery, "will involve himself and family in distress, misery and ruin." GEORGE NEWCOM and WILLIAM VAN CLEVE appt'd guardians. pp 7, 8

Term of November, 1804

Case 9. Adm of estate of HENRY MOYER, late of German Twp, granted to ELIZABETH MOYER & CHRISTIAN MOYER. Sec: MICHAEL MOYER, JOHN MIKESELL. Appr: JOHN MILLER, LEONARD WOLF, DANIEL MILLER. p 8

Case 10. Adm of estate of DANIEL COX, late of Elizabeth Twp, granted to JOSEPH COE & ELIZABETH, his wife. Sec: JOHN GERARD, JEROM HOLT. p 9

Case 11. Adm of estate of GABRIEL SWINEHART, late of German Twp, granted to SALOME SWINEHART & ADAM SWINEHART. Sec: JACOB FOUTS, JESSE DAVENPORT. Appr: JOHN MILLER, LEONARD WOLF, DANIEL MILLER. p 9

Case 12. Adm of estate of PETER GEPHART, late of German Twp, granted to CATHERINE GEPHART & DANIEL MILLER. Sec: JOHN BOWMAN, ZACARIAH HOLE. Appr: JOHN QUICK, PETER BANTA, MICHAEL MYERS. p 9

Term of February, 1805

Case 13. Adm of estate of EDWARD MITCHEL, late of Washington Twp, granted to EDWARD MITCHEL & SARAH MITCHEL. Sec: BENJAMIN ROBINS, THOMPSON ENNES. Appr: AARON NUTT, JAMES SCOTT, JAMES RUPEL. p 10

Case 14. Col. ROBERT PATTERSON appt guardian to NELLY TAYLOR & LEWIS TAYLOR, orphans in care of GEORGE NEWCOM. p 10

Case 15. GEORGE NEWCOM appt guardian to ABRAHAM PAGE & JAMES MAULSTON, orphans in care of Col. ROBERT PATTERSON. p 10

Inv and appr of estate of GABRIEL SWINEHART. Total $1580.69. List of property kept by widow = $335.24. Public sale, buyers: JACOB BOWMAN, JOHN BOWMAN, WILLIAM BULLER, JACOB CRULL, JESSE DAVENPORT, WILLIAM HOLMES, JOHN HOWARD, REZIN HOWARD, CHARLES CARTROE*, GEORGE KUNS, GEORGE LESLIE, MURPHY LESLIE, GEORGE LOY, JACOB LOY, JOHN LUCAS, JOHN MILLER, JACOB MULLENDORE, JOHN MURPHY, JOHN MIKESELL, DANIEL OYLER,

ISAAC RICHARDSON, JACOB RICHARDSON, GEORGE SHIDLER, WATTY SIMPSON, EDWARD SULGROVE, ADAM SWINEHART, PETER SWINEHART, BOAZ THARP, JOHN WAGGONER. pp 10, 11, 12, 13, 14, 15 (* probably CHARLES KETTEROW)

Inv and appr of estate of HENRY MOYER, total $1648.26 Debts owed to estate of HENRY MOYER: bonds on JOHN SHUPERT, THOMAS KORR, JOHN WEIDMAN, MATTHIAS FRANTZ & accts owed by GEORGE KUNS, JACOB KUNS, HENRY BOWSER & ADAM SWINEHART, total $8140.26. MOYER appr's deposition dated 17 Nov, 1804. DANIEL BOWSER & DANIEL MILLER valued above goods, sworn before JOHN EWING, JP. JOHN MILLER appeared 5 Feb, 1805, agreed to valuation, sworn JOHN FOLKERTH, JP, Dayton Twp. Inv of goods kept by widow of HENRY MOYER, she being one of the adms, total $1006.36. Public sale on 20 Dec, 1804. Buyers: PETER BANTA, ABRAHAM BARNET, DANIEL BOWSER, DANIEL BOWSER SR, GEORGE BOWSER, PHILIP BOWSER, WILLIAM BROWNE, CHRISTIAN BROWER, JACOB HECK, DANIEL ILER, JOHN KOON, JOHN KAYLOR, JOSEPH KINGREY, MARTIN McCREA, JOHN MIKESELL, JAMES MILES, JACOB MILLER preacher, JOHN MILLER, AARON RICHARDSON, ABRAHAM RICHARDSON, SAMUEL RUDY, JOHN SIMMONS, JOHN WAGGONER, total $329.36. Remarks by adm CHRISTIAN MOYER: 1. HENRY MOYER'S widow purchased 100 acres from PHILIP BOWSER, sum not included in inventory as land is to be divided among heirs. 2. Bond on THOMAS KORR belongs to brothers and sister of MOYER, not his heirs. Bond was acquired from estate of MOYER's father. 3. JACOB BOWMAN, heir's husband, purchased bed at appr'd price of $10. 4. CHRISTIAN MOYER, adm, purchased clothing at appr'd price of $7.00. pp 15, 16, 17, 18, 19, 20, 21, 22, 23, 24

Filed 1 April, 1805. Inv and appr of estate of PETER GAPHART, total $867.42. Debts due estate: bonds on JOHN SHAFFER, JOHN BATTEICHER total $736.61. Apprs deposition dated 19 March, 1805 sworn before PHILIP GUNCKEL, JP, German Twp. List of property kept by widow of PETER GEPHART, total $183.30. Public sale, buyers: PETER BANTA, JOHN BARNET, JACOB BOWMAN, DANIEL BOWSER, GEORGE BOWSER, HENRY BOWSER, PHILIP BOWSER, CHRISTIAN BROWER, JOSEPH CORBILL, JOHN CRAIG, CHRISTOPHER EMRICK, DANIEL HOLE, ZACARIAH HOLE, DANIEL KRIPE, JACOB KRIPE, JOHN MIKESELL, JOSEPH MIKESELL DANIEL MILLER, JAMES MILLER, JAMES PANTIER, ADAM REPLOGEL, ANTHONY RICKET, AARON RICHARDSON, ABRAHAM RICHARDSON, JOSEPH RORER, ALEXANDER SCOTT, DAVID SCOTT, JOHN SHUPERT, HENRY TAYLOR, ROBERT TAYLOR, JAMES THOMSON, GEORGE ULRICH, JOHN VANARSDALE, CHRISTIAN WELDY, MICHAEL WISEMAN. Total $527.16. pp 24, 25, 26, 27, 28, 29

Filed 1 May, 1805. Inv and appr of estate of EDWARD
MITCHEL, total $527.16.   Debts owed to estate of
EDWARD MITCHEL.   "Money held at SAMUEL FINDLAY's" &
at SQUIRE McDONALDS.   JORDAN's note. Cash recv'd of
SAMUEL BECK, "of WILLIAM", of THOMSON ENNES.   By --
DILTS, by JOHN BECK, by JOHN McNIGHT, by SAMUEL
MARTIN, by N. TALBERT, by BENJAMIN & FRANCIS MOORE,
by WILLIAM WOOD, by PHILIP BALTIMORE, by JOHN SIMMON.
Total $509.93.   pp   29, 30, 31

Term of August, 1805

Case 16.   Adm of estate of WILLIAM TAYLOR, late of
the state of PA, granted to NATHANIEL LYON of German
Twp.   Sec: JAMES PORTER, ZACARIAH HOLE.   Appr: BENJA-
MIN SMITH, GEORGE WORTHINGTON, SAMUEL HAWKINS.   p 31

Case 17.   Adm of estate of JOHN BARNET, late of
Dayton Twp, granted to ELIZABETH BARNET & ABRAHAM
BARNET.   Sec: DAVID RIFFLE, ANDREW HAYS. Appr: JOHN
McCABE, JOHN MILLER, WILLIAM WESTFALL.   p 31

Case 18.   Adm of estate of JOSIAH SMITH, late of
German Twp, granted to LETTITIA SMITH.   Sec: ANDREW
THARP, BOAZ THARP.   Appr: JACOB FOUTS, JOHN MURPHY,
ROBERT HARDING.   p 32

Case 19.   Will of JANET VANARSDALE filed.   Exec JOHN
VANARSDALE. Witness: JAMES SNOWDEN, PETER SUNDERLAND
Appr: JAMES McGREW, JOHN McCABE, DAVID LAMME.   p 32

Adm of HENRY MOYER's estate filed assignment of dower
to widow ELIZABETH, dated 25 Aug, 1805.   100 acres
located Sec 26, Twp 3, Range 5, "east of JOHN WAGGON-
ER's line", adjoining tract in same S-T-R, both total
of 150 acre.   ELIZABETH takes as her 3d part of real
estate owned by HENRY MOYER.   Agreement signed DANI-
EL MILLER, JOHN MILLER.   Witness: JOHN MOYERS &
ABRAHAM MILLER.   pp 32, 33

Case 20.   Adm of estate of JOHN CULBERTSON, late of
Dayton Twp, granted to IGNATIUS ROP.   Sec: JEROM
HOLT, PAUL D. BUTLER. Appr: JAMES MILLER SR, WILLIAM
HAMER, JAMES GILLESPIE.   p 33

CASE 20.5.   DANIEL C. COOPER apptd guardian of POLLY
ABBOT, now in his care.   p 33

Filed 28 September, 1805.   Case 21.   Adm of estate of
THOMAS DAVIS, late of Dayton Twp, granted to MARY
DAVIS.   Sec: DAVID REID, DANIEL C. COOPER.   p 33

Term of December, 1805

Inv and appr of estate of JOSIAH SMITH, total $1751.10. Appr: ROBERT HARDING, JOHN (x) MURPHY, JACOB (x) FOUTS. Appr's deposition dated 23 Dec, 1805. pp 34, 35

Inv and appr of estate of JOHN CULBERTSON. Total $97.37. Appr: JAMES MILLER, WILLIAM HAMER, JAMES GILLESPIE. Public sale of property of JOHN CUL-BERTSON, undated. Buyers: JAMES GILLESPIE, WILLIAM ELLIS, JACOB SMITH, GEORGE NEWCOM, BAZIL WILLIAMS, MICHAEL HENDRICKS, RALPH FRENCH, ROBERT CULBERTSON, WILLIAM NEWCOM, GEORGE MAFFET, SMITH GREGG, PAUL D. BUTLER. Clerk: WILLIAM SNODGRASS. pp 35, 36

Inv of estate of JENNET VANORSDALE, dated 10 Sept, 1805. Notes held against WILLIAM VANARSDALE, JOHN VANARSDALE, FRANCIS DILTS, total $172.63. Appr: JAMES McGREW, JOHN McCABE, DAVID LAMME. Sworn before JOHN EWING, associate judge. pp 36, 37

Case 22. JOHN BROWER & CHRISTIAN BROWER appt'd guardians of JACOB MOYER, age 17, PETER MOYER, age 15, JOHN MOYER, age 18, DANIEL MOYER, age 13, ELIZABETH MOYER, age 10, MICHAEL MOYER, age 12, JOHN MOYER* age 6, heirs of HENRY MOYER, dec. Those over 14 chose guardians. Sec: JACOB MILLER, JOHN NOFFZINGER. p 37 *Youngest son named JONAS in other records.

Case 23. MARY DAVIS and JOHN McCABE appt'd guardians of MARY DAVIS, age 8, and ESTHER DAVIS, age 6, heirs of THOMAS DAVIS, dec. Sec: JAMES THOM. p 38

Case 24. SALOME SWINEHART and ADAM SWINEHART named guardians of ANNA SWINEHART, age 4, ELIZABETH SWINE-HART, age 2, & GABRIEL SWINEHART age 1, heirs of GABRIEL SWINEHART, dec. Sec: HENRY SHEIDLER, JONATHAN LEATHERMAN. p 38

Term of April, 1806

Case 25. Adm of estate of ABRAHAM BANTA, dec, granted to PETER BANTA. Sec: JACOB LONG, JOHN VAN-ARSDALE. p 38

Case 26. Will of LEVI BOWEN filed. Execs: JOSEPH HANCOCK, JAMES SCOTT. Witness: ROBERT SCOTT, BENJA-MIN WALLINGFORD. Appr: BENJAMIN ROBINS, OWEN HATFIELD, JOHN LUCE. p 39

Inv and appr of estate of THOMAS DAVIS, date 6 Oct, 1805. Total $797.28. pp 39, 40

Term of August, 1806

Case 27. Will of JOSEPH REEDER. Exec HANNAH REEDER. Witness: DANIEL REEDER, WILLIAM REEDER, THOMAS CASON. p 41

Court granted extention of time to settle estate of JOSIAH SMITH. p 41

Case 28. JOHN EDWARDS appt'd guardian of WILLIAM JACKSON, age 12, and GILES JACKSON, age 9, heirs of WILLIAM JACKSON, late of Warren Co, OH. Sec: DANIEL REEDER. p 41

Case 29. VALENTINE GEPHART and MATTHIAS RIGAL named guardians of ELIZABETH GEPHART, age 8, and JOHN GEPHART, age 5, heirs of PETER GEPHART, dec. Sec: DANIEL BOWSER SR, HENRY BOWSER. p 41

Case 30. JOHN McCABE named guardian of LEWIS DAVIS, age 18. Sec: JAMES THOMSON. p 42

Case 31. Adm of estate of MATTHEW NEWCOM, late of Dayton, granted to GEORGE NEWCOM. Sec: JOHN FOLKERTH & JEROM HOLT. p 42

Appr of estate of LEVI BOWEN, dated 14 May, 1806. Total $62.00. Appr: BENJAMIN ROBBINS, OWEN HATFIELD. Sworn before ABNER GARARD, JP, Washington Twp. p 42

Filed 27 Nov, 1806. Inv and appr of estate of WIL- LIAM TAYLOR, dated 17 Sept, 1805, total $249.34. Appr: SAMUEL HAWKINS, GEORGE WORTHINGTON, BENJAMIN SMITH. Public sale dated 23 Dec, 1805. Buyers: JOHN LOY, GEORGE LOY, NATHANIEL LYON, JAMES QUIN, JAMES LEESON, JOHN CHAMBERLAINE, JOHN POGUE, SAMUEL POGUE, SAMUEL HAWKINS, JAMES SEASON, JOHN WILCOX, JOSEPH COTERO*. Total $133.96. * probably should be JOSEPH KETTEROW. pp 43, 44

Inv and appr of estate of JOHN BARNET, dated 14 Sept, 1805. Total $361.71. pp 44, 45

Term of Dec, 1806

Case 32. Adm of estate of NATHANIEL KNOTTS, late of Washington Twp, granted LYDIA KNOTTS. Sec: AARON NUTT, JOHN PRICE. Appr: BENJAMIN ROBINS, JOHN LUCE, OWEN HATFIELD. p 46

Case 33. Adm of estate of JACOB OLWINES, dec of German Twp, granted to DANIEL KEMP. Sec: MARTIN SHUEY, CHRISTOPHER EMRICK. Appr: JOHN PAULY, WILLIAM EMRICK, LEONARD STUMP. p 46

Case 34. Adm of estate of JOHN AIKEN, late of Dayton Twp, granted to JOHN DRISCOL. Sec: JOHN GRIMES, GEORGE NEWCOM. Appr: DAVID REID, CALEB HUNT, ROBERT NEWCOM. p 46

Case 35. Adm of estate of WILLIAM HAY, late of Dayton Twp, granted to ANN HAY. Sec: JOHN HAY, ALEXANDER TELFORD. Appr: WILLIAM ROBINSON, ALEXANDER SNODGRASS, WILLIAM HAMER. p 47

Inv and appr of estate of ABRAHAM BANTA, 20 May, 1806, total $120.37. Appr: CONRAD KASTER, TOBIAS WHITESELL, HENRY STRADER. Debts due estate by ALEXANDER DEMOT, JACOB LONG, ALEXANDER WOODS, JOHN ROBINSON, JOHN KING, DANIEL ROBINSON (sec by WILLIAM MOORE & ARCHIBALD DOWDEN/ suit brought, not settled). Acct against JAMES PETTICREW in dispute. Total of $300.50. Accts owed by estate to JAMES PETTICREW, JOHN STARR, PETER BANTA. Public sale, undated. Buyers: PETER BANTA, JOHN STAR, THOMAS CLAWSON, JAMES McCASHEN, JOSEPH PARKS, JACOB LONG. Total $102.93. p 47, 48, 49

Filed 16 Jan, 1807. Inv and appr of estate of JOHN AIKEN, dated 26 Dec, 1806. Total $366.75. Appr: CALEB HUNT, DAVID REID, ROBERT NEWCOM. Public sale, 9 Jan 1807. Buyers: JOSEPH CARPENTER, JOSEPH CONNOR, ROBERT CULBERTSON, HENRY CURTNER, JOHN DRISCOL, DANIEL FERREL, CHRISTIAN FRITTZ, JOHN GULLION, JACOB HALL, NIMROD HADDIX, JOHN HARNER, DAVID HILL, ALEXANDER HOUSTON, JEROM HOLT, SAMUEL HOPKINS, JACOB KUGLER, DAVID SQUIER, PATRICK MANIVILLE, HENRY MARQUART, MARTIN MYERS, EDWARD PAGE, ANDREW REED, JOHN SHAVER, FRANCIS SHAVER, HEZEKIAH STOUT, RICHARD SUNDERLAND, JAMES THOMSON, SAMUEL THOMSON, BENJAMIN VAN CLEVE, JAMES WELSH, BAZIL WILLIAMS, ENOS WILLIAMS total $522.24. DAVID HALL recv'd women's apparel from estate since MRS. HALL was MRS. AIKEN's sister, in lieu of payment for services. Debts owed by ALEXANDER KERR, HENRY SIDERSTAKER total $110.00. pp 50, 51, 52, 53, 54

Filed 4 Feb, 1807. Case 36. Adm of estate of SAMUEL WOODS, late of Dayton, granted to RHODA WOODS & JOHN ROBB. Sec: DAVID SQUIER, ROBERT NEWCOM. Appr: JOHN PATTERSON, MATTHEW PATTON, JAMES BROWN. p 55

COMMON PLEAS (PROBATE) DOCKET BOOK A-1

Case 37. Adm of estate of JACOB YOST, granted to
CASPER YOUNG. Sec: STEPHEN JAY, GEORGE GROVE. Appr:
DAVID SQUIER, MAXFIELD LUDLOW, JOHN GRIMES. p 55

Case 38. Adm of estate of ELIHU SAUNDERS, late of
Elizabeth Twp, granted MARY SAUNDERS. Sec: HEZEKIAH
HUBBEL, JOSEPH WHITTEN. Appr: JOHN MANN, PETER
HARMON, JESSE JENKINS. p 55

Case 39. Will of JOHN WHITTEN admitted to Probate,
filed 2 March, 1807. p 56.

Inv and appr of property of WILLIAM HAY, 30 Dec,
1806. Total $563.75. Appr: WILLIAM ROBINSON, ALEX-
ANDER SNODGRASS, WILLIAM HAMER. Bond due estate of
WILLIAM HAY, held by JAMES LAPSLEY of Adair Co, KY on
JOHN WOOLFORD & GEORGE RANOLDS in the amount of $320.
Public sale, dated 9 Jan, 1807. Buyers: ANN HAY,
ISAAC ELIE, ISAAC SPINNING, DAVID WORMAN, PETER
LEHMAN, GARNER BOBO, WILLIAM TAYLOR, SAMUEL GIVENS.
Total $438.35. pp 56, 57

Filed 2 March, 1807. Inv and appr of estate of JACOB
OLWINES on 3 Jan, 1807, total $207.26. Appr: JOHN
PAULY, WILLIAM EMRICK, LEONARD STUMP. Public sale,
undated. Buyers: MICHAEL AUNSPAW, JOHN BOWER, JOHN
BOYER, GEORGE BOYER, ABRAHAM BROWER, CHRISTIAN
BROWER, HENRY CRIST, WILLIAM DIGBY, JOHN DULLY,
MICHAEL EMRICK, WILLIAM EMRICK, JOHN GERDIN, GEORGE
HALL, JONATHAN HIGGINS, DANIEL KEMP, JACOB KEMP, JOHN
KEMP, PHILIP KEMP, CATY KERNS, GEORGE KERNS, JOSEPH
KETROW, MARTIN McCREA, JOHN McNUTT, JOHN MILLER,
DANIEL MILLER, PETER NEAGALY, JOHN PAULEY, JOHN
POGUE, SAMUEL POKE, JOHN REEM, ANTHONY RIGART,
CHRISTOPHER ROOR, MATTHIAS SCHWARTZLEY, LEONARD
STUMP, SAMUEL WARD, MARTIN SHUEY, PHILIP SNIP, DANIEL
STORMS, GABRIEL THOMAS, JOHN WAGGONER, JACOB STIVER.
Total $190.94. pp 58, 59, 60, 61

Sale of property of JOHN WHITTEN, 13 Feb, 1807.
Buyers: JOSEPH WHITTEN*, AARON BELLE, ISAAC CLARK,
JOSEPH CLARK, ANDREW DYE, SAMUEL EARLS, JAMES FRAZER,
THOMAS HAMMIL, PETER HARMAN, JOHN HOLDERMAN, EPHRAIM
McKINNEY, JAMES McKINNEY, PATRICK LAFFERTY, WILLIAM
MADDAN, HENRY MULKENS, HENRY ROBINSON, JONATHAN
ROLLINS, JOHN SMITH, STEPHEN WHITTEN*, BENJAMIN VAN
CLEVE*, WILLIAM WINTERS, JOHN WILLIAMS. * Purchases:
STEPHEN WHITTEN, his legacy in part; BENJAMIN VAN
CLEVE, his son's legacy; JOSEPH WHITTEN his legacy in
part, total $1097.43. Debts due estate from JEROM
HOLT, JOHN WHISTLER, DANIEL LANGDON, CORNELIUS
VOORHEIS, HENRY ROBINSON, SETH CUTTER. Accts against

SYLVESTER WILSON, PETER WILSON, PETER FELIX, B. VAN
CLEVE, -CLINGANS, MORDECAI MENDENHALL. pp 61, 62, 63

Term of April 1807

Case 40. Adm of estate of ROBERT HUEY JR, late of
Dayton Twp, granted to JOHN FOLKERTH & ALBERT R.
HUEY. Sec: CHRISTOPHER CURTNER, JAMES MILLER. Appr:
JOHN MILLER, JOHN RICHEY, WILLIAM KING. p 64

Case 41. ROBERT EDGAR apptd guardian of JOSEPH KIRK-
WOOD, age 11 yrs, heir of DAVID KIRKWOOD, dec. p 64

Case 42. JOHN COPPOCK serving as Trustee to DAVID
LUCAS, insolvent debtor. Sec: WILLIAM MADDAN. p 64

Case 43. Will of WILLIAM HATFIELD, late of Washing-
ton Twp, admitted to probate. Exec: widow ELIZABETH
HATFIELD. Witness: JOHN PRICE, OWEN HATFIELD,
WHITELY HATFIELD. p 64

Special Court 12 May, 1897

Case 44. Adm of estate of CHRISTIAN FOGELSONG, late
of Jefferson Twp, granted BARBARA FOGELSONG & CHRIS-
TOPHER MASON. Sec: HENRY HEPNER, PETER WEAVER. Appr:
DAVID MOYER, CHRISTIAN MOYER, ULRICH SAILER. p 65

Filed 18 July, 1807. Case 45. Trustees of the Poor
of Dayton Twp claimed CHRISTIAN FRITTZ was "lunatic";
jury to conduct inquiry. Jurors: JAMES McGREW, JAMES
STEELE, JAMES HANNA, CHARLES TULL, WILLIAM HAMER,
JOHN COMPTON, DAVID DUNCAN, ROBERT CULBERTSON, JOHN
MILLER, JEROM HOLT, GEORGE SOURBRAY, JOHN DODSON.
Eleven jurors certified FRITTZ as insane, not able to
care for himself; WILLIAM HAMER dissented. Decision
had to be unanimous; guardian not apptd. pp 65,66

Term of August, 1807

Inv and appr of estate of WILLIAM HATFIELD, dec 27
May, 1807. Total $139.25. Appr: AARON NUTT, JOHN
LUCE, BENJAMIN ROBINS. Debts due estate by OWEN
HATFIELD, EDWARD DYER total $10.25. p 66

Inv and appr of goods of LYDIA KNOTTS, dated 25 Dec,
1806: total $208.69. Appr deposition sworn ABNER
GARARD, JP, Washington Twp, by B. ROBBINS, JAS LUCE,
OWEN HATFIELD. p 67

Inv and appr of estate of ELIHU SAUNDERS, dated 9 Jan

1807. Total $291.75. Appr deposition sworn 9 Feb, 1807, ABNER GARARD, JP, Washington Twp, signed JOHN MAN, PETER (P) HARMAN, JESSE JENKINS. pp 67, 68

Case 46. Adm of estate of JOHN GENTLE to to WILLIAM NEWMAN & HANNAH GENTLE. Sec: RICHARD COX, JOHN COX. Appr: JOHN QUILLING, DANIEL HOOVER JR, GEORGE SINKS SR. p 68

Case 47. Adm of estate of PHILEMON PLUMBER, late of Jefferson Twp, granted to SOPHIA PLUMBER & GEORGE SINKS JR. Sec: THOMAS NEWMAN, JACOB BYRKET. Appr: JOHN QUILLING, JONATHAN JUSTICE, JOHN WAYMIRE. pp 68, 69

Inv and appr of estate of CHRISTIAN FOGELSONG of Jefferson Twp, dated 20 May, 1807. Total $596.83. Money owed estate by ALEXANDER STINSON, JOHN KEMP & JACOB KEMP, JOHN WHITWORTH. Accts due estate for whiskey purchases: CHRISTIAN BROWER, JOHN MIKESELL, AMOS HIGGINS, -- LESLIE. pp 69,70, 71

Special session 7 September, 1807

Court notified by Overseers of the Poor for Dayton Twp that CHRISTIAN FRITTZ is mentally deranged. Jury to conduct inquiry. Jurors: JOHN DEVOR, JOHN FOL-KERTH, DANIEL C. COOPER, JAMES HANNA, JAMES WILSON, WILLIAM BOMBERGER JR, LUTHER BRUEN, DAVID DUNCAN, ABRAHAM DARST, CHARLES TULL, JOHN MILLER, DAVID REID. Jury unanimous in insanity verdict. DAVID SQUIER, JOHN MILLER appt'd as guardians for FRITTZ. Sec: ABRAHAM DARST, GEORGE NEWCOM. pp 71, 72

Filed 22 December, 1807. Inv and appr of estate of JOHN GENTLE, dated 31 Oct, 1807. (name appeared as JOHN GENTRY on p 73.) Notes held on RICHARD COX (2), JACOB CURTICE, REDWOOD EASTON, WILLIAM NEAL, URIAH JOHNSTON, JOSEPH ELLMORE, HANNAH GENTRY, JOHN GRIGGSBY, WILLIAM HOLLINGSWORTH, TOLBIT IDDINGS, JAMES INSCO (2), RICE INVALLIS, JOHN McCOOLE, THOMAS McCOOLE, MICHAEL McDORMAN, THOMAS NEWMAN, WILLIAM NEWMAN, ISAAC RAMSAY, CALEB REESE, WILLIAM REESE. Total $516.25. Note of DAVID HEDDIN, insolvent (no value given). Appr: D. HOOVER JR, JOHN QUILLING, GEORGE SINKS. pp 72, 73

Inv and appr of estate of PHILEMON PLUMBER. Total $313.87. Public sale, undated. Buyers: HENRY CO-ZATT, THOMAS NEWMAN, JOHN PLUMMER, SOPHIA PLUMMER, FREDERICK SUMY, GEORGE SINKS. Total $244.72. pp 73, 74

COMMON PLEAS (PROBATE) DOCKET BOOK A-1

Term of December, 1807

Case 49. Will of PHILIP GUNTLE, late of German Twp, admitted to probate. Exec: JULIANN GUNTLE, MATTHIAS SCHWARTZEL. Witness: MELCHIOR MILLER, JACOB HELL. Appr: JOHN VANCE, JACOB COLMAN, HENRY SHEIDLER. p 75

Special court of 26 Jan, 1808

Notice presented by HUGH McCOLLUM, Overseer of the Poor of Dayton Twp, that CHRISTIAN FRITTZ's reason is restored. Jury summoned: JOHN RITCHIE, CHRISTOPHER CURTNER, GEORGE GROVE, PAUL BUTLER, HENRY CURTNER, ROBERT CULBERTSON, HENRY MARQUART, JOHN DODSON, AARON BAKER, JAMES HANNA, JOHN PATTERSON, JOHN DEVOR. Jury found in favor of FRITTZ. Guardians given until next term to settle accts. pp 75, 76

Term of April, 1808

Case 51. WILLIAM McCLURE of Dayton appt'd guardian of ALEXANDER McCLURE ELLIOT, age 14, minor heir of ROBERT ELLIOT, dec. Sec: JAMES WELSH, ANTHONY LOGAN. p 76

Case 51.5. IGNATIUS ROP, adm of estate of JOHN CULBERTSON, found estate insufficient for debts. DAVID REID, WILLIAM McCLURE appt'd trustees to make distribution. p 76

Adms of estate of JOSEPH BIGGER apply for permission to sell land. Appr: ABNER GARARD, JAMES SCOTT, AARON NUTT. p 77

Case 52. Adm of estate of CHRISTIAN TRINE, late of Dayton Twp, granted to PETER SUMAN. Sec: GEORGE GROVE, FRANCIS DILTS. p 77

Adm of estate of ROBERT HUEY JR given time extension to produce settlement. p 77

Term of September, 1808

Case 53. Will of TURPIN RENTFROW, late of German Twp. Exec: SARAH RENTFROW, JACOB NEFF. Witness: SAMUEL BOLTIN, JOHN MIKESELL SR. Appr: ALEXANDER SCOTT, DANIEL MILLER, MICHAEL MOYER. p 77

Case 54. Adm of estate of JOHN STUART, late of Dayton Twp, granted to PEGGY STUART, JAMES MILLEGAN. Sec: JAMES PATTERSON, JOHN PATTERSON SR. Appr: JOHN DEVOR, JOSEPH WILSON, THOMAS JOHN. p 78

Case 55. Will of WILLIAM KING, late of Washington Twp, filed. Exec: JAMES KEY, CHARLES MORGAN, RACHEL KEY. Witness: THOMAS CASON, LUCY WEBB. Appr: JOHN BIGGER, ABRAHAM HOSIER, SAMUEL IRWIN. p 78

DAVID REID & WILLIAM McCLURE, trustees for insolvent estate of JOHN CULBERTSON, request time extension to make settlement. p 78

Estate of NATHANIEL KNOTTS: land in Sec 29, Twp 3, Range 5 to be sold. Acct'ing by adm LYDIA KNOTTS: debts paid to JOHN PRICE, OWEN HATFIELD, EDWARD DYER. Note showing support paid for 4 children - not named. Court divided estate residue among 5 children. p 79

DAVID SQUIER, JOHN MILLER, late guardians of CHRISTI-AN FRITTZ, presented accts: 16 weeks board and care by ANTHONY CHEVALIER & bill pd to JOHN OWINGS. Cash recvd from LEWIS CASLER, D. REID, B. VAN CLEVE. p 80

JOHN VANORSDALE, exec of will of JENNET VAN AUSDALLEN presented accts: cash paid to WILLIAM VANOSDALL, "legacies to DILTS's daughters". p 80, 81

Filed 20 October, 1808. Inv and appr of estate of TURPIN RENTFREW of German Twp made 30 Sept, 1808. Total $308.81. Appr's deposition sworn 11 Oct, 1808 signed DANIEL MILLER, MICHAEL MYER, ALEXANDER SCOTT. pp 81, 82

Inv and appr of estate of CHRISTIAN TRINE, total $69.36. Appr's deposition made 26 Oct, 1808 signed LEWIS LECHLIDER, JOHN CROY, DAVID LEHMAN. p 83

Appr report on land of JOSEPH BIGGER. Valued at $4.50 per acre on 6 Sept, 1808. Appr's deposition sworn before JOHN McCABE, JP for Washington Twp, signed ABNER GARARD, AARON NUTT, JAMES SCOTT. Adm note: ABIGAIL BIGGER & JAMES BIGGER sold land of JOSEPH BIGGER to WILLIAM GRIFFIN for $3.00 per acre, tract of 503 acres, dated 4 July, 1808. p 84

Filed 3 January, 1809. Inv and appr of estate of JOHN STUART of Dayton Twp, dated 8 Oct, 1808. Total $413.41. Appr's deposition sworn before JOSEPH REY-BURN, JP, Dayton Twp. Public sale, undated. Buyers: DANIEL BAXTER, JOHN DEVOR, WILLIAM DEVOR, ROBERT ELLIOT, GEORGE GROVE, PETER LEHMAN, ALEXANDER LOGAN, HENRY MARQUART, JAMES McCLEAN, JAMES MILLEGAN, CUL-BERTSON PATTERSON, JAMES PATTERSON, JOHN PATTERSON, JOSEPH REYBURN, JAMES RIDDLE, ISAAC SPINNING, PEGGY STUART, WILLIAM STUART, NATHAN TALBERT, JAMES WOODS.

COMMON PLEAS (PROBATE) DOCKET BOOK A-1

Total $250.52. Signed adm: PEGGY STEWART, JAMES
MILLEGAN, WILLIAM STEWART. pp 85, 86, 87

Term of January, 1809

Case 56. Adm of estate of Dr. WILLIAM MURPHY of
Dayton Twp granted to HENRY DISBROW. Sec: MATTHEW
PATTON, HENRY MARQUART. p 88

Case 57. Will of ANDREW ROBINSON, Dayton Twp. Exec:
ROBERT PARK; co-exec MARGARET ROBINSON relinquished.
Witness: ROBERT ROBINSON, JOSEPH WILSON. Apprs:
JOSEPH WILSON, ROBERT McCLEARY, SAMUEL BRIAR. p 88

Case 58. LYDIA HUEY & HENRY DISBROW apptd guardians
of NANCY HUEY & ROBERT HUEY, minor heirs of ROBERT
HUEY, dec. Adms JOHN FOLKERTH & ALBERT R. HUEY to
appear next court term to give accounting. p 89

Case 51.5. Trustees' report on insolvent estate of
JOHN CULBERTSON. Debts owed: judgement in favor of
JOHN ELLIOT & AARON THOMPSON as admrs of CALEB THOM-
SON estate, WILLIAM THOMAS, JOHN WHETSTONE, ROBERT
CULBERTSON, WILLIAM SNODGRASS, MICHAEL HENDRICKS,
signed DAVID REID, WILLIAM McCLURE. pp 89, 90

Inv and appr of estate of WILLIAM KEY, total $545.87,
by JOHN BIGGER, SAMUEL IRWIN, ABRAHAM HOSIER. pp 90,
91

Inv and appr of estate of Dr. WILLIAM MURPHY, total
$271.44, by WILLIAM McCLURE, JAMES STEELE, HORATIO G.
PHILLIPS. Sworn before CHRISTOPHER CURTNER, JP.
Debts due estate by AARON BAKER, GEORGE H. SMITH,
ISAAC G. BURNET, BENJAMIN VAN CLEVE, PAUL D. BUTLER,
JOHN DODSON, GEORGE F. TENNERY, -- KROLL, --HIMES,
HUGH McCOLLOM. Public sale, undated. Purchasers:
JACOB BRENSINGER, LUTHER BRUEN, ANTHONY CHEVALIER,
FRANCIS DILTS, HENRY DISBROW, JOHN ELLIOT, WILLIAM
GEORGE, CHARLES GREEN, JOHN GRIMES, WILLIAM McCLURE,
JOHN MILLER, JOSEPH PEIRCE, HORATIO G. PHILLIPS, JOHN
RIGGANS, DAVID STEEL, WILLIAM M. SMITH, GEORGE F.
TENNERY, JAMES THOMSON, B. VAN CLEVE, JAMES WARUM,
JAMES WELSH, JACOB WORMAN, . Signed WILLIAM M.
SMITH, clerk. pp 91, 92, 93

Term of May, 1809

Adms of CHRISTIAN FOGELSONG presented final settle-
ment. Cash paid to GEORGE FOGELSONG SR, DANIEL
MILLER, JOHN WHITWORTH, GEORGE HORNER, WILLIAM
BROWNE, B. VAN CLEVE, GABRIEL THOMAS, Dr. DUBOIS,

NICHOLAS ELSROAD, DAVID WIDENER, JACOB SLEIFER, DAVID MOYER, CHRISTIAN MOYER, ULRICH SAILER, HENRY HEPNER, DAVID BOWMAN. Accts recvd from: ALEXANDER STINSON, JOHN & JACOB KEMP, JOHN WHITWORTH & CO, JOHN MIKESELL CHRISTIAN BROWER, AMOS HIGGINS. Amount granted for maintaining 4 children at $15 each per annum from 12 May, 1807. p 94

Case 59. Adm of estate of Dr. JOHN ELLIOT, Dayton Twp, granted to HORATIO G. PHILLIPS. Sec: JOSEPH H. CRANE, ISAAC G. BURNET. Apprs: JAMES WELSH, WILLIAM GEORGE, JOHN GRIMES. p 95

Adms of ROBERT HUEY presented accounts. Cash paid to JACOB KRULL, JAMES BLUE, B. VAN CLEVE, JOHN RITCHIE, JONATHAN DONNEL, ETHAN STONE, ARTHUR ST. CLAIR, SAMUEL HUEY, WILLIAM ELLIS, NICHOLAS SMALL, JOSEPH H. CRANE, DAVID REID, ALBERT R. HUEY, JOHN FOLKERTH, Dr. JAMES WELSH. Balance of $166.02. p 96

Filed 27 June, 1809. Inv and appr of estate of ANDREW ROBINSON by JOSEPH WILSON, ROBERT McCLEARY & SAMUEL BRIAR, total $88.40. Public sale, undated. Buyers: ROBERT PARKS, MARGARET ROBISON, ELIZABETH ROBISON, JOSEPH KENNEDY, ROBERT McCLEARY JR, ROBERT ROBISON, JOHN McCLEARY, JOSEPH COOPER. p 96

Term of Sept, 1809.

DANIEL MILLER & CATHERINE GEPHART, wife of DAVID MILLER, adms of estate of PETER GEPHART, made partial settlement. Cash paid: PETER BANTA "for whiskey for day of sale", CHRISTIAN FOGELSONG "for whiskey for day of sale", A. CHEVALIER (auctioneer), WILLIAM BROWNE, JOHN FOLKERTH, LORIN BELCHER, Dr. JOHN ELLIOT W. C. SCHENCK, ARTHUR VANDEVEER, GEORGE MOYER, DAVID MILLER (for maintenance of minor heirs), DANIEL MIL- LER. Balance of $867.42 on 29 Aug, 1809. pp 97, 98

IGNATIUS ROP, adm of JOHN CULBERTSON, presented recpts of apportionment to creditors. Estate fully administered except $.52 due MICHAEL HENDRICKS. p 99

Special Session 28 Oct, 1809

Case 60. Adm of MATTHIAS SWARTZEL of German Twp granted to HENRY CRIST, JACOB COLMAN. Sec: PHILIP SWARTZEL, HENRY SHEIDLER. Appr: PHILIP NEAGLEY, MARTIN SHUEY, CHRISTOPHER EMRICK. p 99

Inv and appr of estate of ROBERT HUEY, plus accts against WILLIAM WILSON & JONAS LINLEY, total $281.80.

Signed WILLIAM KING, JOHN MILLER, JOHN RITCHIE, dated 1 Aug 1807. Public sale, undated. Buyers: JAMES ARCHER, ZACARIAH ARCHER, MOSES BARNET, MATTHEW CONNER, NICHOLAS CRAVISTON, ALBERT R. HUEY, ROBERT HUEY, LYDIA HUEY, SAMUEL THOMSON, WILLIAM ELLIS, ISAAC ELLIS, JAMES HANNA, WILLIAM KING, JACOB KROLL, DAVID RIFFLE, SAMUEL HAGAR, NICHOLAS SMALL, JACOB RODEHAMEL, JOHN FOLKERTH, ANDREW KREITZER, PETER WOLF, WILLIAM VAN CLEVE, BAZIL WILLIAMS. pp 100, 101

Filed 7 Jan, 1810. Public sale of estate of THOMAS DAVIS by MARY DAVIS on 6 Nov, 1805. Purchasers: BENJAMIN ARCHER, STEPHEN ARCHER, STEPHEN ARCHER JR, DANIEL BAXTER, OWEN DAVIS, MARY DAVIS, DANIEL FERREL, JOHN GULLION, SAMUEL HOPKINS, SHADRACH HUDSON, ALEXANDER HUSTON, THOMAS JOHN, JAMES McCLURE, JAMES MILES AARON NUTT, JOHN PATTERSON, DAVID SQUIER, ROBERT TAYLOR, GEORGE F. TENNERY, JAMES THOMSON, WILLIAM VANORSDALL, total $231.92. Acct of property kept by widow, total $559.16. pp 101, 102, 103

Term of January, 1810

Adm of estate of THOMAS DAVIS produced settlement. Cash paid to: ARCHIBALD GRAHAM, Dr. ELLIOT, JOHN PATTERSON, ABRAHAM HOSIER, ABSALOM WESTFALL, JOHN COMPTON, B. VAN CLEVE on OWEN DAVIS' order, MATHIAS PARSON (coffin), FREDERICK NUTTZ, JOHN EWING, JOHN CAVENDER, HENRY YOUNT, EDWARD NEWCOM "for whiskey for the sale", JOHN BRADFORD, B. ARCHER, leaving $256.52 to be divided among 5 children, less $102 for maintenance of ESTHER & MARY DAVIS. pp 104, 105

Case 54. Cash in hand of adms of estate of JOHN STUART insufficient to make land paymts due US Govt after paying debts. Land to be appr for sale by JOHN DEVOR, JOHN BRADFORD, GEORGE NEWCOM. p 105

Term of May, 1809

Case 61. Adm of estate of DANIEL BUCHER granted to SAMUEL BUCHER. Sec: PETER LEHMAN, JOHN BRADFORD. Appr: JOHN DEVOR, ROBERT WEAD, ROBERT EDGAR. p 106

Case 62. Adm of estate of ROBERT KIRKWOOD granted to ANNA KIRKWOOD & SAMUEL GRIMES. Sec: HUGH ANDREWS, JACOB LONG. Appr: JOHN AINSWORTH, JOHN D. CAMPBELL, PETER SUNDERLAND p 106

Case 54. Petition of adm of estate of JOHN STUART to sell land in Sec 26, T 2, R 7, valued at $6 by apprs. p 106, 107

COMMON PLEAS (PROBATE) DOCKET BOOK A-1

Case 63. Will of JOHN HECK of Jefferson Twp. Exec:
DAVID MOYER. Witness: GEORGE BOWSER, JACOB NAFE.
Appr: LEONARD WOLF, CHRISTIAN MOYER, JACOB MULLEN-
DORE. p 107, 108, 109, 110

Inv and appr of estate of MATTHIAS SCHWARTZEL dated 2
Nov, 1809, total $1132.85. Public sale of estate on
17 Nov, 1809. Purchasers: BENJAMIN BARCALOW, JOHN
BARCALOW, THOMAS BETH, HENRY BORNSHIRE, PETER BORN-
SHIRE, CHRISTIAN COE, JACOB COLEMAN, NICHOLAS COLEMAN
JOHN COMPTON, WALTER COX, HENRY CRIST, JOHN DAY, BEN-
JAMIN EAKINS, JOSEPH ELY, CHRISTOPHER EMRICH, WILLIAM
EMRICH, JOHN ENOCH, DANIEL FEASTER, ABRAHAM FEIGT,
DAVID FINLEY, JACOB FRIGH, GEORGE HALL, CASPER
HARSHMAN, JOHN HOUSER, HENRY HUBBLE, DAVID IMLEY,
JOHN JORDAN, JACOB KERAGER, GEORGE KUNS, GEORGE LOY,
PETER LOY, SAMUEL MAW, JOHN McCASHEN, JACOB MILLER,
JOHN MINGLE, DANIEL MONBECK, PETER NEGLEY, JOHN
PAULEY, ANTHONY REGAR, ASTON ROSS, JOHN ROSS, TIMOTHY
ROBBINS, ZADOC SAXTON, PETE SHAVER, FREDERICK
SHEWPERT, MARTIN SHOUP, MARTIN SHUEY SR, GEORGE
SINKS, CASPER STAVER JR, EDWARD SULGROVE, ABRAHAM
SCHWARTZEL, PHILIP SCHWARTZEL, HENRY SWARTZEL,
MATHIAS SWARTZEL, SUSANNA SWARTZEL, WILLIAM TAPSCOTT,
MICHAEL TEMPLE, THOMAS THOMPSON, MOSES VAIL,
FREDERICK WOLF, WILLIAM YOUNG. Total $845.79. pp
111, 112, 113, 114, 115

Inv and appr of estate of ROBERT KIRKWOOD + debts
due from: MARY GRIMES, HENRY BROWN, JACOB AUGHEY,
HENRY MULKINS (absconded), no total given. Signed
JOHN AINSWORTH, JOHN D. CAMPBELL, PETER (x) SUNDER-
LAND. Sworn JOHN FOLKERTH 4 Aug, 1810. p 116

Inv and appr of estate of DANIEL BUCHER, on 18 Aug,
1810, total $1866.38. Appr JOHN DEVOR, ROBERT WEAD,
ROBERT EDGAR. p 117

Term of September, 1810

Case 64. Will of ROBERT HOOD of Madison Twp. Exec:
ANDREW HOOD. Witness: WILLIAM WILSON, NEHEMIAH
THOMAS. Court reserved right of DAVID TORRENS, Scott
Co, KY, to join Probate as co-exec. p 118

Case 65. Will of VALENTINE GEPHART of Washington
Twp. Exec: widow CATHERINE, PHILIP GEPHART. Wit-
ness: JOHN KARCHER, MATTHIAS RIGAL. Appr: FREDERICK
NUTZ, JACOB BAUM, MATTHIAS RIGAL. p 118

Case 66. Will of JACOB MAST. Exec: DAVID HOOVER,
NANCY MAST & DAVID MAST. Certified under court seal

of Ashe County, NC where will was written. Appr:
JOHN QUILLING, DANIEL YOUNT, DANIEL HOOVER JR. p 118

Case 67. Adm of estate of GEORGE YOUNT SR of Ran-
dolph Twp granted to GEORGE YOUNT JR & ANDREW SINKS.
Sec: DANIEL HOOVER JR, THOMAS NEWMAN. Appr: DAVID
MAST, DAVID SHEETZ, JAMES INSCO. p 119

Case 68. Adm of estate of LEWIS DAVIS of Dayton Twp
granted to widow MARY DAVIS. Sec: JEROM HOLT, GEORGE
GROVE. Appr: ROBERT EDGAR, GEORGE NEWCOM, PETER
LEHMAN. p 119

Case 69. Adm of estate of JOHN MILLER of Jefferson
Twp granted to widow SUSANNA. Sec: DANIEL MILLER,
JOHN MIKESELL. Appr: CHRISTIAN BROWER, JACOB MULLEN-
DORE, JACOB NEFF. p 119

Filed 4 Sept, 1810. Inv and appr of estate of JOHN
HECK, taken under direction of exec DAVID MYER by
JACOB MULLENDORE, CHRISTIAN MOYER, JACOB WIRICK on 26
May, 1810. Total $172.18. Sworn before ABRAHAM
TROXEL, JP, 21 Aug, 1810. pp 119, 120

Filed 19 Nov, 1810. Inv and appr of estate of JACOB
MAST of Randolph Twp, total $509.50. Property sold
27 Sept, 1810 plus debts due estate totaled $628.04.
pp 121, 122, 123, 124

Filed 25 Dec, 1810. Inv and appr of estate of GEORGE
YOUNT, total $336.63. Public sale held 27 Oct, 1810
total $308.47 less $5 debt. Signed GEORGE YOUNT,
ANDREW SINKS. p 125, 126

Filed 2 Jan, 1811. Inv and appr of estate of VALEN-
TINE GEPHART. Cash of $189.38 plus debts owed to
estate by: JOHN BARLOT, JOHN BRACK, JOHN BUKART,
JACOB BURNET, CHARLES BURRIS, MICHAEL BURRIS, WILLIAM
CLARK, PETER CLAWSON, THOMAS CLAWSON JOHN CRAIG, JOHN
DODDS, JOSEPH DODDS, MILLER DODDS, WILLIAM DODDS,
JOSEPH FOUTS, CHRISTIAN GARBER, JOHN GEPHART, PHILIP
GEPHART, SAMUEL GEPHART, PHILIP GUNCKEL, JOHN HOLE,
WILLIAM HOLE, SILAS HUTCHINSON, JACOB CARGHER, DANIEL
LEARY, WILLIAM LEWIS, JACOB LONG, JESSE LONG, DAVID
MAXFIELD, THOMAS MAXFIELD, WILLIAM McCLURE, WILLIAM
McMULLEN, ISAAC MILLER, GEORGE NUTTZ, ADAM REPLOGEL,
MATTHIAS RIGAL, ROBERT ROBINSON, JOHN RUSSEL,
ALEXANDER SCOTT, BENJAMIN SCOTT, DAVID SCOTT, WILLIAM
SMITH, JAMES THOMSON, SIRUS TRAXTER, GEORGE WEAVER,
JOHN WESLER, MARTIN WIBRICHT, MICHAEL WISEMAN, ROBERT
WOOD, OUWE WYCOFF, ROBERT YOUNG, total $671.87. pp
126, 127, 128, 129

Inv and appr of estate of ROBERT HOOD of Madison Twp. Notes due estate by JAMES FINDLEY of KY, ANDREW HOOD plus property, total $290.73. Signed apprs ROBERT WILSON, ROBERT PARKS, JOHN MILLER. Sworn ARCHIBALD GRAHAM, JP, 15 Jan, 1811. Public sale, purchasers: ANDREW HOOD, ROBERT HOOD, total $91.50. p 130

Term of May, 1811

Case 70. Will of JACOB CRESS. Exec: ELIZABETH CRESS. Witness: JOSIAH LAMB, NICHOLAS COBLE SR. Co-exec JOHN CRESS declined service. Appr: DANIEL HOOVER SR, DAVID HOOVER, JOHN QUILLING. p 131

Case 71. Adm of estate of JONATHAN HATFIELD granted to widow AMEY & JOHN ARCHER. Sec: BENJAMIN ARCHER, EDWARD MITCHEL. Appr: JAMES RUSSEL, JAMES C. ANDER- SON, WILLIAM TURNBULL. p 131

Motion by LEVIN HATFIELD & wife SARAH, late DAVIS, heir of THOMAS DAVIS, requesting JOHN PRICE & wife HANNAH, late DAVIS, admr of estate, to show cause why estate should not be settled. p 131

Citation issued to HENRY DISBROW, adm, to show cause why estate of Dr. WILLIAM MURPHY is not settled. p131

Inv and appr of estate of DANIEL COX of Elizabeth Twp produced by adms JOSEPH COE and wife ELIZABETH, signed apprs JAMES BLUE, NATHANIEL GERARD, ABRAHAM HATHAWAY. Debts owed estate by DANIEL FLINN & THOMAS SHAW total $501.75. Cash paid to JOEL WILLIAMS, CORNELIUS VOORHEIS left bal of $261.67. Voucher to JAMES FLINN disallowed. pp 132, 133

Case 71.5. JAMES HANNA apptd guardian of JAMES L. ROGERS, under 14 yrs, minor heir of ALEXANDER ROGERS, dec, late of PA. p 133

Filed 3 June, 1811. Inv and appr of estate of JACOB CRESS. $984.42 total includes obligations due estate in the State of VA. p 134

Term of September, 1811

Case 72. Will of GEORGE SOURBRAY of Dayton. Exec: CHRISTOPHER CURTNER & JOHN PATTERSON. Witness: BEN- JAMIN VAN CLEVE, GEORGE GROVE, HENRY CURTNER. Appr: DAVID REID, DAVID DUNCAN, GEORGE NEWCOM. p 135

Case 73. Will of JOHN NEFF of Dayton Twp. Exec: DANIEL NEFF & HENRY NEFF. Witness: JOHN WOLF, JOHN

REED. Sec: CHRISTIAN NEFF, ABRAHAM NEFF. Appr: JOHN McCLEARY, LUDOWICK SPEECE, JOHN WOLF. p 135

Case 74. Adm of estate of LEONARD STUMP granted to JULIANNA STUMP & GEORGE STUMP. Sec: PHILIP GUNCKEL, WILLIAM EMRICK. Appr: CHRISTIAN EMRICK, JACOB BOWER, DANIEL GUNCKEL. p 135

ADAM SWINEHART, adm of estate of GABRIEL SWINEHART, pd $252.23 to land office, canceling bond given to DANIEL ROBBINS, original proprietor. p 135

Case 75. SUSANNA SWARTZEL, widow of MATTHIAS, apptd guardian of JOHN SWARTZEL, age 10, & FREDERICK SWART-ZEL, age 6. Sec: ABRAHAM BROWER, JOHN STIVER. p 136

Public sale of estate of JACOB CRESS on 31 Aug, 1811, totaled $139.29, signed ELIZABETH CRESS, exec. p 136

Inv and appr of estate of JONATHAN HATFIELD of "Centreville" on 13 May, 1811, total $415.39. (included wood and woodworking tools, probably a cabinetmaker or carpenter.) Debts due estate of $353.24. pp 136, 137

Special Session 9 Nov, 1811

Case 76. Adm of estate of JAMES McCANN of Dayton Twp granted to NANCY McCANN. Sec: JAMES HANNA, JAMES BAY Appr: DAVID SQUIER, GEORGE NEWCOM, JEROM HOLT. p 138

Filed 16 Nov, 1811. Case 77. Adm of WILLIAM WILSON of Dayton Twp granted to THOMAS RAMSAY & JOHN RITCHIE. Sec: DAVID REID, WILLIAM McCLURE. Appr: JOHN H. WILLIAMS, WILLIAM KING & JOHN MILLER. p 138

Inv and appr of estate of LEONARD STUMP of German Twp on 11 & 12 Sept, 1811, total $2891.17. p 139

Filed 28 Nov, 1811. Inv and appr of estate of GEORGE SOURBRAY on 5 Oct, 1811, total $1559.75. Public sale undated. Buyers: LARANCE ASBIE, JOHN DILLEY, GEORGE HANEY, JOHN M. GROVE, JOHN WOLF, WILLIAM SOURBRAY, GEORGE SOURBRAY, JACOB CRULL, HENRY MARQUART, JOHN DODSON, ADAM SMITH, JOHN MILLER. No total given, signed GEORGE GROVE. pp 139, 140, 141

Term of January, 1812

Case 78. Will of MARTIN COBLE. Exec: widow MARY COBLE. Witness: CHRISTOPHER MASON, DAVID BOWMAN. Sec: JOHN COBLE, WILLIAM BROMBAUGH. Appr:

CHRISTOPHER MASON, DAVID BOWMAN, ABRAHAM HOSIER. p 142

Case 79. DANIEL DAVIS, 18 yrs, minor heir of LEWIS DAVIS, dec, chose WILLIAM McCLURE as guardian. p 142

Case 80. WILLIAM EMRICK appted guardian of GEORGE STUMP, 11 yrs, heir of LEONARD STUMP, dec. p 142

Inv and appr of estate of WILLIAM WILSON on 27 Nov, 1811, total $474.62. Debts owed to IRA SMITH, JOHN KINZEY, MATTHEW PATTON, ROBERT CULBERSON, Blacksmith STEPHENS, GEORGE WICAEL, I. G. BURNET, ALBERT HUEY. Public sale buyers: DAVID ALSPAUGH, DAVID ANDREWS, ABRAHAM BARNET, ENOCH BOWEN, DAVID BROWER, DANIEL BURKET, CHARLES CHEVALIER, HENRY CLARK, THEOPHILUS EADINGS, JAMES ELLIOT, DANIEL FALTER, JOSEPH FOUTS, WILLIAM FRAIM, ARCHIBALD GRAHAM, JAMES HANNA, JAMES HENDERSON, JONAS HOOVER, ALBERT HUEY, DAVID JOHN, JOHN KAYLOR, PETER KELLER, DAVID KEISER, JOHN KEYSER, JOHN KINZEY, JAMES KYLE, WILLIAM LINCK, WILLIAM MASON, JOHN McBEE, AARON MILLER, JOHN MILLER, ADAM NEFF, EDMOND PARROT, GEORGE PARSON, JACOB PITSBURGER, JAMES RICHEY, DAVID RIFFLE, JOHN RITTER, WILLIAM SISSEL, NICHOLAS SMALL, IRA SMITH, ELIJAM SWAM, JOHN TROYER, JOB WESTFALL, JOHN H. WILLIAMS, BARTHOLOMEW WILLIAMS, PETER ZETRICK, JOHN ZUMMAMAN. No total. pp 143, 144, 145, 146

Case 81. DAVID LOWRY, 14 yrs, heir of ARCHIBALD LOWRY, dec, chose JAMES STEELE & HORATIO G. PHILLIPS as guardians. Sec: JOHN RIGANS. p 147

Case 82. Adm of the estate of SIMON MASON granted to DANIEL FETTERS. Sec: DANIEL MARTIN, ROBERT WOODS. Appr: DAVID HOOVER, JACOB SMITH, DAVID MILLER. p 147

Inv and appr of estate of JAMES McCANN on 17 Nov, 1811; note due on JONATHAN MILHOLLEN. Total $124.70. Public sale, buyers: JOHN McCANN, JOSEPH GILLESPIE, PETER LEHMAN, DAVID LEHMAN, JOHN READ. pp 147, 148

Case 83. JOHN LATHAM, 17 yr old minor, chose DAVID REID as guardian. p 148

Case 84. JOHN GRIMES, 14 yr old minor, chose CHRIS- TOPHER CURTNER as guardian. p 148

Case 85. WILLIAM SOURBRAY apptd guardian of ABIJAH FISHER, 10 yr old minor. p 148

Debts due estate of SIMON MASON from: JOHN VANEMAN,

ELIJAH WOODS, GEORGE KUNS, MICHAEL BURNS, JOHN GROPIUS, DANIEL FETTERS plus cash totaled $517.35. pp 148, 149

Filed 21 March, 1812. Case 86. Adm of estate of RICHARD GRAY of Dayton Twp granted to JANE GRAY. Sec: JOHN DEVOR, JEROM HOLT. Appr: GEORGE NEWCOM, JOHN BRADFORD, PETER LEHMAN. p 149

Case 87. Will of GEORGE FRIBERGER. Exec: PETER LEHMAN, GEORGE NEWCOM. Witness: VALENTINE EYLER, JACOB MILLER, HENRY LEHMAN. Appr: LUDWICK KEMP, ROBERT EDGAR, JAMES THOMSON. p 149

COMMON PLEAS (PROBATE) DOCKET BOOK B-1

Term of May, 1812

Case 88. ROBERT EDGAR apptd guardian of RACHEL GRAY, 4 yrs, & ROBERT GRAY, 1 yr, minor heirs of RICHARD GRAY, dec. p 1

Case 89. Adm of estate of WILLIAM COTTINGHAM of Dayton Twp granted to MARY COTTINGHAM. Sec: JOSEPH WILSON, JAMES COTTOM. Appr: ROBERT EDGAR, MATTHEW PATTON, JOHN PATTERSON. p 1

Inv and appr of estate of GEORGE FRYBERGER on 29 Apr, 1812. Total $814.14. Public sale on 1 May, 1812, purchasers: ISAAC AILY, DAVID ALSPACH, DANIEL BAXTER, JAMES BAXTER, JOHN BRADFORD, ABRAHAM BRANNERMAN, SAMUEL BUCHER, DAVID BURNS, HENRY BUTT, LEWIS CASLER, JOSIAH CLAWSON, JOHN CORY, WILLIAM COX, JOSEPH H. CRANE, ROBERT CULBERTSON, CHARLES DEPRAISE, FRANCIS DILTS, JOHN DODSON, VALENTINE EYLER, PETER FAVORITE, JACOB FRIBERGER, JAMES GILLESPIE, JOSEPH GILLESPIE, LEWIS GORDON, SAMUEL HAGAR, JONATHAN HERSHMAN, JOHN HUFFMAN, ALEXANDER HUSTON, DAVID HUSTON, JOHN HUSTON, SUSANNA IFERT, JACOB KEMP, JOSEPH KEMP, LUDWICK KEMP, LEWIS LECHLIDER, DAVID LEHMAN, HENRY LEHMAN, JACOB LEHMAN, PETER LEHMAN, HENRY MARQUART, ISAAC MILLER, JACOB MYERS, CHRISTIAN NEFF, GEORGE NEWCOM, JOHN NEWCOM, GEORGE PATTERSON, JOHN RENCH, JAMES RIDDEL, JACOB RODEHAMEL, JAMES SHAW, GEORGE SOURBRAY, BARN-HART SPECK, JOHN STRAUSBERGER, ABRAHAM TEAGARDEN, JAMES THOMSON, SAMUEL THOMSON, JAMES WILSON, GEORGE YOUNG. Total $720.55. pp 1, 2, 3, 4, 5, 6.

Inv and appr of estate of RICHARD GRAY signed GEORGE NEW, PETER LEHMAN (in german script) & JOHN BRADFORD, total $194.50. Public sale on 13 June, 1812, buyers: JAMES KEY, ANDREW STUART, JOSEPH WILSON, JAMES ARNOLD

SAMUEL HOLMES, SAMUEL EILER, DAVID JOHN, JOHN ENSEY, ROBERT EDGAR, JOHN BRADFORD, ADAM GERLACH. Total $90.85. pp 6, 7

Inv and appr of estate of SIMON MASON on 14 Feb, 1812, total $139.75. Signed JACOB SMITH, DAVID HOOVER & DAVID MILLER (german script). pp 7, 8

Case 90. Adm of estate of DANIEL RICHISON granted to HENRY BOWSER, agreeable to widow. Sec: PHILIP BOWSER & WILLIAM BOWSER. Appr: JAMES KYLE, PETER DETRICK, ADAM RODEBAUGH. p 8

Inv and appr of estate of WILLIAM COTTINGHAM on 3 Aug, 1812. Many tools included, probably a cabinet maker or carpenter. Total not given. Debt due from PETER MONFORT. pp 9, 10

Inv and appr of estate of DANIEL RICHISON on 6 July, 1812, total $93.27, signed by PETER DIETRICK & ADAM ROTEBAUGH. Public sale, purchasers: HENRY BOWSER, PHILIP BOWSER, GEORGE BOWSER, JACOB BITSONPANIES, GEORGE WASHINGTON DAVIS, JOHN FALKNER, JAMES FERGUSON JAMES GWINNE, HENRY HACKPENER, HENRY HUNTSING, JACOB KROLL, JOHN KROLL, JOHN MIKESELL, ABRAHAM MILLER, DANIEL MILLER, JOHN MILLER, TOBIAS TANNER, DAVID WAGNER, PETER WILAND, total $170.96. pp 11, 12

Term of September, 1812

Settlement of estate of JOHN GENTRY presented by WILLIAM NEWMAN & HANNAH GENTRY, adm. Cash paid to: DANIEL HOOVER, Dr. JOHN MOTE, HENRY PHOUTZ, WILLIAM FINCHER, JEREMIAH MOTE, WILLIAM NEWMAN. Insolvent debtors to estate: DAVID HEDDING, CALEB REESE, JOHN GRIGGSBY, URIAH JOHNSTON. Note held on WILLIAM REESE. Balance of $295.66 to be divided among five children. Allowance for keeping children: JOHN for 1 yr @ $15, MARGARET for 4 yr @ $60, ABIGAIL for 5 yr @ $75. Note inserted on page: Certified WILLIAM NEWMAN settled with estate of JOHN GENTRY on 23 Sept, 1812, signed HANNAH (x) GENTRY. Witness JONATHAN NEWMAN. pp 12,13

Case 91. Will of STEPHEN ARCHER JR, proven in Scott Co, KY. ZACARIAH ARCHER appted adm. Sec: SAMUEL ARCHER, JOHN MIKESELL SR. Appr: JOHN H. WILLIAMS, WILLIAM KING, NATHAN WORLEY p 14

Case 92. ELIZABETH STUMP, 14 yrs, chose PHILIP GUNCKEL as guardian. Sec: ABRAHAM BROWER. p 13

Case 93. EPHRAIM GENTRY, 15 yrs, minor heir of JOHN

GENTRY, dec, chose HANNAH GENTRY as guardian. Sec: RICHARD COX, HENRY WOODHOUSE p 13

Case 94. HANNAH GENTRY appted guardian of SAMUEL, age 13, JOHN, age 12, MARGARET, age 7 and ABIGAIL, age 5, minor heirs of JOHN GENTRY, dec. p 13

Case 95. Adm of estate of JOHN COMPTON of German Twp granted to LUCY COMPTON & BENJAMIN DUBOIS. Sec: JOSEPH COMPTON, JOSEPH VAN NOTE. Appr: GEORGE LANE, JOHN DENISE, JOHN VANTILBURGH. p 13

Term of January, 1813

Case 96. Will of JOHN BROWER. Execs: MARY BROWER, JOHN BROWER. Witness: WILLIAM BROWNE, JOHN STAVER. Appr: JOHN STAVER, HENRY BUHLER, JACOB BROWER SR. p14

Case 97. Will of SOLOMAN HARDMAN. Exec: ANNE MARY HARDMAN, SAMUEL NOFFSINGER. Witness: DAVID HARDMAN, HENRY LEEDES. Appr: ISAAC SHIVELY, CHRISTIAN MILLER, PHILIP WAGNER. p 14

Case 98. Will of CATHERINE DEETER. Exec: ABRAHAM DEETER. Witness: JOHN MILLER, JOHN DEETER. Sec: SAMUEL DIETER, EMANUEL FLORY. Appr: DAVID MILLER, JACOB BOWMAN, JOHN BYRKET. p 14

Case 77. Consent of MARTHA WILSON, widow of WILLIAM WILSON, to allow trustee JOHN RITCHIE to sell property. Appr: JOHN H. WILLIAMS, SAMUEL ARCHER, IRA SMITH. p 15

Case 99. SILAS RICE, 17 yrs, minor son of HERVEY RICE, dec, chose HENRY MARQUART as guardian. p 15

Case 100. Adm of estate of WILLIAM McCLURE granted to DAVID McCLURE & JAMES STEELE. Sec: JOHN RITCHIE, JOHN H. WILLIAMS. Appr: HORATIO G. PHILLIPS, G. W. SMITH, WILLIAM BOMBERGER. p 15

Case 101. Will of HENRY NEFF. Exec: MAGDALENE NEFF, JOHN KERR. Witness: JOHN WOLF & LUDWICK SPEECE. Sec: JOSEPH KENNEDY, JOHN S. RIGGS. Appr: JOHN RUDY, LUDWICK SPEECE, JOHN WOLF. pp 15, 16

Case 102. LEWIS NEFF, 19 yrs, DANIEL NEFF, 17 yrs, and POLLY NEFF, 13 yrs, minor heirs of HENRY NEFF, dec, chose JOHN KERR as guardian. p 16

Case 103. JOHN DAVIS, age 18, HANNAH DAVIS, age 14, LEVI DAVIS, age 12, heirs of THOMAS DAVIS, dec, chose

COMMON PLEAS (PROBATE) DOCKET BOOK B-1

LEVIN HATFIELD as guardian. Sec: OWEN HATFIELD. p 16

DANIEL FETTERS requested time extension to settle estate of SIMON MASON. p 16

JOHN PRICE & HANNAH PRICE, late HANNAH DAVIS, adm of estate of THOMAS DAVIS, produced settlement. Balance of $666.05 to be divided among 5 children. Bond held by ELIZABETH DAVIS: THOMAS DAVIS was to pay five pounds per year during her lifetime. p 16

Special Session, 20 January, 1813

Case 104. Adm of estate of CHRISTIAN NEFF granted to JESSE CLARK. Sec: GEORGE BEARDSHEAR, HENRY CLARK. Appr. JOHN REED, JOHN WOLF, JAMES LOWRY. p 17

Case 105. Will of DANIEL BOWSER JR. Exec: widow ANNE, HENRY BOWSER. (ANN declined service.) Witness: NATHANIEL STUTSMAN, WILLIAM BOWSER. Appr: SAMUEL BALDWIN, CHRISTIAN BROWER, DANIEL MILLER. p 17

Inv and appr of estate of JOHN COMPTON on 5 Nov, 1812, total of $773.52. Public sale, purchasers: HENRY ALLEN, JOHN ALLEN, VINCENT ANTONIDES, THOMAS BAISE, WILLIAM CHAMBERS, DAVID COMPTON, JOSEPH COMPTON, LUCY COMPTON widow, MOSES COMPTON, WILLIAM CONOVER, JOHN DENISE, DANIEL DUBOIS, MARTIN AIRHART, GEORGE HALL, DAVID IMLAY, ANDREW KADOCK, MICHAEL KEITOCK, GEORGE LOY, WILLIAM MARTIN, ELIJAH MILLS, SAMUEL RHOADES, ASTON ROSS, JOHN H. SCHENCK, JOSEPH SUTPHIN, WILLIAM TAPSCOTT, JOSEPH VANNOTE, JOHN VANTILBURGH, JAMES WHITFIELD, total $834.82. pp 17, 18, 19, 20

Special Session, 27 Febuary, 1813

Case 106. Adm of estate of GEORGE WASHINGTON DAVIS granted to DAVID JOHN & RACHEL DAVIS. Sec: DAVID BOWEN, JOSEPH JOHN. Appr: HENRY FLORY, DANIEL SHIVELY, JOHN OLINGER. p 20

Filed 23 March, 1813. Inv and appr of estate of HENRY NEFF on 13 Jan, 1813, total $808.86. Signed JOHN REID, JOHN WOLF. Public sale on 10 Feb, 1813, purchasers: DAVID ALSPACH, LAWRENCE ASHBY, GEORGE BEARDSHEAR, SAMUEL COSAD, WILLIAM COSAD, SAMUEL DILLE JAMES FERGUSON, JAMES GILLESPIE, MOSES HALL, JONATHAN HERSHMAN, ABNER HOBBS, THOMAS HAMER, JOSEPH KENNEDY, RUTH KERR, BENJAMIN KISER, DAVID LEHMAN, WILLIAM MASON, MARGARET McCLEARY, JOHN MILLER, WILLIAM MILLAR,

JONATHAN MORGAN, JAMES MORRIS MARTIN MYERS, ADAM NEFF, LEWIS NEFF, MAGDALENA NEFF, GEORGE PARSONS, HENRY REAL, JOHN S. RIGGS, JOHN ROBY, JOHN SETUR, DAVID SIMMONS, STEPHEN SPRAIG, BENJAMIN VAN CLEVE, JACOB WATTYES, CHRISTIAN YAZEAL, total of $881.67. List of goods kept by widow. Debts owed by HENRY CLARK, A. BRANNEMAN, STEPHEN SPRAGUE, DANIEL NEFF, J. COOK. pp 21, 22, 23, 24

Filed 27 March, 1813. Inv and appr of estate of DANIEL BOWSER (JR) total $1455.16, signed SAMUEL BOLTIN, DANIEL MILLER, CHRISTIAN BROWER. Portion owed from estate of HENRY MOYER, dec: bonds not yet due nor interest known. Public sale undated, buyers: ABRAHAM BARNET, GEORGE BOWSER, HENRY BOWSER, PHILIP BOWSER, WILLIAM FRAME, HENRY HUNTSINGER, JONATHAN MORGAN, GEORGE NUTT, CHRISTIAN SHUTER, CORNELIUS VAN-OSDAL, ROBERT WOOD, total $311.56. pp 25, 26

Inv and appr of estate of SOLOMAN HARDMAN totaled $121.33. Public sale on 16 Jan, 1813, purchasers: HENRY BOWSER, MICHAEL CRUMRINE, JOSEPH FOUTZ, BENJA-MIN HARDMAN, MARTIN HUBER, DAVID LASSLEY, AARON MILLER, DAVID MILLER, JACOB OLINGER, WILLIAM PRIDDY, GEORGE PUTERBAUGH, JOHN RITTER, ISAAC SHIVELY, JOHN ZIMMERMAN. Total $110.76. p 27

Filed 31 May, 1813. Inv and appr of estate of G. W. DAVIS, total $1055.87. Public sale, purchasers: DAVID DAVIS, ARCHIBALD GRAHAM, WILLIAM KING, ROBERT McCULHANEY, JOSEPH POWEL, JOHN SNIDER, HENRY SWISHER. Total $1081.98. pp 28, 29, 30

Term of May, 1813

Case 107. Adm of estate of ROBERT GILCHRIST granted to JOHN WILSON & JOHN R. PARKS. (widow relinquished right.) Sec: JOSEPH KENNEDY, JOHN GRIMES. p 30

Case 108. Adm of JAMES SHAW estate to MARY SHAW & SAMUEL McFADDON. Sec: GEORGE NEWCOM, CONKLIN MILLER. Appr: JAMES MILLER, JAMES BLACK, HENRY DEAM. p 30

Case 109. Adm of estate of WILLIAM NEWCOM granted to JAMES NOLAN. (widow relinquished right) Sec: HENRY CURTNER, GEORGE GROVE. Appr: GEORGE SOURBRAY, WIL-LIAM SOURBRAY, CHRISTOPHER CURTNER. p 30

Case 110. Adm of estate of DANIEL SUNDERLAND granted to MARY SUNDERLAND & JACOB PRILLEMAN. Sec: DAVID RIFFLE, ANDREW RUSSEL. Appr: LEVI JENNINGS, HENRY JENNINGS, ROBERT MILLER. pp 30, 31

Case 111. JOHN D. CAMPBELL appted guardian to SAMUEL SUNDERLAND, 1 yr old, minor heir of DANIEL SUNDERLAND p 31

Application of RACHEL GRAY, adm, for time extension to settle estate of RICHARD GRAY. p 31

Case 112. JOHN DAVIS, 17 yrs, minor heir of LEWIS DAVIS, dec, chose MARY DAVIS, his mother, as guardian Sec: WILLIAM VAN CLEVE. p 31

Case 113. JOHN WILSON, 16 yr old son of JOHN WILSON, chose CHRISTOPHER CURTNER as guardian. p 31

Settlement of estate of Dr. JOHN ELLIOT by adm. Public sale on 23 June, 1809, buyers: JAMES BECK, ANTHONY CHEVALIER, ROBERT CLARK, D. C. COOPER, JOSEPH H. CRANE, ROBERT CULBERTSON, CHRISTOPHER CURTNER, Dr. DAVIDSON, HENRY DISBROW, DANIEL H. FISHER, ISAAC GERARD, JOHN GRIMES, JEROM HOLT, MARTIN MYERS, JAMES NOLAN, WILLIAM PATTERSON, MATTHEW PATTON, HORATIO G. PHILLIPS, THOMAS REED, MR. SAYRE, SIMON SHOVER, DAVID SQUIER, BENJAMIN VAN CLEVE, Dr. WOOD, JAMES WELSH, total $204.62. Cash paid to: ANTHONY CHEVALIER (auctioneer), Col. GRIMES, WILLIAM McCLURE, MATTHEW PATTON (coffin), Dr. WELSH. Cash rcvd from: WILLIAM DODDS, ISAAC BURNET, ANDREW ROBINSON, JOHN CALHOUN. pp 31, 32, 33, 34

Case 114. Adm of estate of Dr. JOHN HOLE granted to MASSEE HOLE & JOHN EWING. Sec: JOHN ALLEN, JOSEPH COLMAN. Appr: MATTHEW PARSON, WILLIAM WAUGH, SAMUEL COLE. p 34

JACOB NEFF & SARAH MILES, late SARAH RENTFREW, execs of TURPIN RENTFREW, filed settlement. Cash paid to SAMUEL CALDWELL, Dr. B. DUBOIS, BARBARA CRIPE. p 34

CHRISTIAN MOYER, adm of HENRY MOYER, produced settlement. p 34

Case 115. FRANCIS INNES, 15 yrs, heir of FRANCIS INNES, chose NATHANIEL INNES of KY as guardian. p 35

Petition by adm of HENRY NEFF to authorize land sale contract with MARTIN HOUSER. p 35

Inv and appr of estate of WILLIAM McCLURE on 29 April, 1813, total $453.25. pp 35, 36

Inv and appr of estate of CHRISTIAN NEFF on 20 Feb, 1813, total $294.87. Public sale, purchasers: GEORGE

BEARDSHEAR, JOHN BOWSER, ABRAHAM BRANAMAN, JESSE CLARK, JOHN COX, WILLIAM COX, GEORGE FRIBACK, WILLIAM GILLESPIE, ABNER HOBBS, JOSEPH KENNEDY, BENJAMIN KISER, JAMES LOWRY, JONATHAN MAYHALL, JOHN McCLEARY, JOSEPH MEEKER, WILLIAM MILLAR, ABRAHAM NEFF, ADAM NEFF, DANIEL NEFF, LEWIS NEFF, MAGDALENE NEFF, JOHN S. RIGGS, LUDWICK SHAW, ADAM SHEPARD, JOHN SHEPARD, GEORGE SHOUP, BARNHART SPECK, JOHN STOKES, JOHN WOLF JOHN ZIDECKER, total $277.39. pp 37,38,39,40

Filed 28 June, 1813. Inv and appr of estate of ROBERT GILCHRIST, total $486.64, by EDMUND MUNGER & NICHOLAS HORNER. Sworn WILLIAM LONG, JP, 18 June, 1813. pp 40, 41

Inv and appr of estate of DANIEL SUNDERLAND, total $99.75. Note due estate by JAMES WILLIAMS on ANDREW RUSSEL. p 42

Filed 30 July, 1813. Public sale of estate of WIL-LIAM NEWCOM. Buyers: DANIEL BURKET, JAMES CHATHAM, JAMES CORY, ROBERT CULBERTSON, DANIEL H. FISHER, Capt. JAMES FLINN, JOHN FOLKERTH, JOHN LEHMAN, HENRY MARQUART, JOHN MILLER, JOHN NEWCOM, SAMUEL NEWCOM, JAMES NOLAN, GEORGE SOURBRAY, WILLIAM SOURBRAY, BENJAMIN VAN CLEVE. No total. pp 42, 43

Filed 12 Aug, 1813. Inv and appr of estate of JAMES SHAW, total $1010.62, signed JAMES MILLER, HENRY DEEM, JAMES BLACK. Public sale, buyers: ZACH ARCHER, JAMES BEY, JAMES BLACK, ELI COMPTON, WILLIAM DAUGHER-TY, JOHN GILE, LEVI JENNINGS, WILLIAM JOHNSTON, BEN-JAMIN KISER, JONATHAN KNIGHT, JAMES LOWRY, DAVID McCONNAUGHEY, PHILIP McCORMACK, JAMES McILWAIN, GEORGE NEWCOM, JOHN PETTICREW, JAMES RIDDLE, LUDWICK SHAW, PETER SLUSHAR, RICHARD SUNDERLAND, JOHN ZEDECKER, total $367.51. pp 43, 44

Inv and appr of estate of Dr. JOHN HOLE, total $156.89. Sworn before JP on 10 June, 1813. p 45

Filed 8 Dec, 1810 -- omitted in error. Inv and appr of estate of JOHN MILLER of Jefferson Twp on 11 & 12 Sept, 1810. List of property kept by widow. Notes due estate from DANIEL FETTERS, JAMES BARNET, HENRY RUSH, CHRISTIAN HUSSY, ABRAHAM STUDEBAKER's estate, DANIEL HOOVER JR, ABRAHAM MILLER, DANIEL STUTZMAN, MATHIAS RIGAL, --YOUNG (tanner), -- HOSLET (tanner), JAMES MILES. Total $1190.75. Public sale, buyers: DAVID ALSPACH, GEORGE BEARD, ENOCH BOWEN, JACOB BOWMAN, DANIEL BOWSER JR, GEORGE BOWSER, PHILIP BOWSER, JOHN BROWER, WILLIAM BROWNE, MICHAEL BURNS,

JOSEPH CONNOR, PETER CONNOR, NICHOLAS CREVISTON, ROBERT ELLIOT, DANIEL FETTERS, GEORGE GAPHART, JOHN GAPHART, JACOB GRIPE, CHRISTIAN HAUN, PETER HECK, PETER KAYLOR, JACOB KRULL, CONRAD LIGHTY, JOHN MIKESELL, DANIEL MILLER, DAVID MILLER, MOSES MILLER, SUSANNA MILLER, GEORGE MORNINGSTAR, DAVID MOYER, JOHN MOYER, MICHAEL MOYER, JACOB MULLENDORE, JAMES B. OLIVER, ABRAHAM PONTIUS, WILLIAM PRINGLE, DANIEL REPP HENRY ROYER, JOSEPH RYANS, JOHN SHEIDLER, JACOB SHUPERT, JACOB SINK, JACOB SMITH, PETER SMITH, DAVID SNIDER, MICHAEL SNIDER, JAMES THOMSON, JOSEPH WAGGON-ER, CHRISTIAN WELDY, JACOB WIRICK, PETER WOLF, ELIJAH WOOD, ROBERT WOOD, total $623.11. pp 45, 46, 47, 48, 49, 50, 51

Filed 20 Aug, 1813. Inv and appr of estate of LEWIS DAVIS on 15 Sept, 1810, total of $478.25. Property kept by widow = $205.36. Public sale on 25 Aug, 1813, purchasers: DAVID ALSPACH, AARON BAKER, JOHN BAKER, LEWIS DAVIS, DANIEL H. FISHER, HENRY T. GILLESPIE, THOMAS HENDERSON, JEROM HOLT, ALEXANDER HUSTON, JACOB KUHN, JOHN LEHMAN, FRANCIS LETOINO, BENJAMIN LLOYD, HENRY MARQUART, JOHN McCLEAN, JONATHAN MORGAN, PETER MUSSELMAN, JOHN NEWCOM, JAMES NOLAN, JOSEPH PREVOST, SAMUEL RAMSAY, LAURENCE SHELL, GEORGE SHRIVER, GEORGE SOURBRAY, BARNHART SPECK, TIMOTHY SQUIER, SAMUEL THOMSON, BENJAMIN VAN CLEVE, JAMES WILLIAMSON, JAMES YOUART total $353.77. pp 53, 54, 55

Term of September, 1813.

Case 116. Adm of estate of HENRY WEAVER granted to MARY WEAVER, JOHN BROWER & RHINEHART SNEP. Sec: DANIEL SNEP, JOHN WEAVER. Appr: GEORGE ADAMS, JOHN McCABE, JOHN ELZROTH. p 55

Case 117. Adm of estate of JACOB YOUNT granted to ESTHER YOUNT. Sec: FREDERICK NUTTZ, HENRY STETLER. Appr: MATTHIAS RIGGAL, CASPER STAVER, DANIEL GUNCKEL. p 55

Case 118. HENRY WORMAN, 16 yrs, minor heir of GEORGE WORMAN, chose HENRY WORMAN as guardian. p 56

Case 119. CHARLOTTE NEWCOM apptd guardian of MARY, age 4 yrs, and ROBERT, age 1 yr, minor heirs of WILLIAM NEWCOM, dec. p 56

Case 120. JACOB MILLER, 16 yrs, minor heir of JOHN MILLER chose WILLIAM BROWNE as guardian. p 56

Case 121. Will of MARTHA McCLURE. Exec: Dr. JOHN STEELE. Witness: ALEXANDER LOGAN. p 56

Case 122. Petition of guardian of heirs of RICHARD GRAY for partition of lands co-owned with ROBERT GRAY. Land divided by: GEORGE NEWCOM, JAMES GILLESPIE & SAMUEL ARCHER. p 56

Admr of JOHN MILLER produced settlement. Cash paid to DAVID HOOVER, WILLIAM BROWNE, JACOB MULLENDORE, J. SHEIDLER, Dr. DUBOIS, C. BROWER, JACOB NEFF, J. PROTZMAN. $508.49 balance to be divided among children. pp 56, 57

Admr of SIMON MASON produced settlement. Money owed estate by JOHN VANNIMAN, JOHN CRIPE. Balance of $16.20 due estate. p 57

Case 123. WILLIAM BROWNE appted guardian of JACOB MILLER. Sec: DANIEL FETTER. p 58

Will of MARTHA McCLURE proven by witness JAMES McCLURE on 9 Sept, 1813. p 58

Admr of JOHN ELLIOT produced settlement. Acct rcvd from WILLIAM DODDS. Cash paid to A. SHEVALIER, WILLIAM McCLURE, M. PATTON, Dr. J. WELSH. Debts due estate from ANTHONY SHEVALIER, HUGH McCOLLOM, BENJA-MIN LEHMAN, ALEXANDER GUY, MATTHEW PATTON. p 58

Case 101. Admrs of HENRY NEFF petition to enact contract with MARTIN HOUSER. p 58

Admr of MATHIAS SWARTZEL produced settlement. Cash paid to ABRAHAM BROWER, NICHOLAS COLEMAN, Dr. B. DUBOIS, JACOB KULLMAN JR, JACOB KULLMAN SR, PHILIP SWARTZEL, WILLIAM STETLER, CHRISTOPHER SHUPERT, JOHN VANTILBURGH, GEORGE LOY (auctioneer), HENRY SHEIDLER, HENRY CRIST (blacksmith). Amount due children total $911.82. p 58, 59

Adm of DANIEL RICHISON produced settlement. Cash paid to JOHN BOWMAN, ISAAC BURNET, HENRY CRULL, TOBIAS DONNER (auctioneer), JOSEPH FOUTS, JACOB KRULL, JAMES KYLE, WILLIAM PURTY, JOHN RITCHIE, ADAM RODEBAUGH, PETER TETRICK, Dr. TREON, ABRAHAM TROXEL, DANIEL WAGNER. p 59

RICHARD MASON, JOHN ALLEN & JOHN TAYLOR to set off widow's portion of estate of Dr. JOHN HOLE. Personal estate insufficient to settle debt; land in Sec 3, T 1, R 6 to be sold. p 60

COMMON PLEAS (PROBATE) DOCKET BOOK B-1

Adm of G. W. DAVIS to sell land in Sec 31, T 4, R 5E.
p 60

Filed 24 Nov, 1813. Inv and appr of estate of HENRY
WEAVER, total $1139.07. Public sale, buyers: GEORGE
ADAMS, LUKE BRYAN, JOHN BURNS, PETER CALOR, ROBERT
CAMPBELL, ZACARIAH CECIL, ISAAC CLARK, JESSE CLARK,
GARRET CLAWSON, PETER CLAWSON, CORNELIUS DILTS,
FRANCIS DILTS, JAMES DODDS, WILLIAM DODDS, WILLIAM
ELLET, ROBERT ELLIOT, MICHAEL HAGAR, JOHN HUSTON,
JOHN JORDAN, JOSEPH KELLER, PETER KELLER, JOHN KISAR,
PETER LASLEY, DOMINICK McGRATH, JOHN McGREW, PHILIP
MIKESELL, JOHN MILLER, ANDREW PARK, BENJAMIN SCOTT,
JAMES SCOTT, PHILIP SNAP, RHYNEHART SNAP, BARNHART
SPECK, JACOB WEAVER, JOHN WEAVER, ABSOLEM WESTFALL.
Total $474.93. pp 60, 61, 62

Term of January, 1814

Adm of Dr. JOHN HOLE withdrew previous application
for land sale. Court ordered land in Sec 2 & 3, T 1,
R 6 to be sold. p 63

Case 125. Adm of estate of MICHAEL SMITH granted to
CATHERINE SMITH & HENRY DEAM JR. Sec: JOHN FRIBACK,
JOHN HOLDERMAN. Appr: WILLIAM COMPTON, LEWIS BRENNER.
p 63

Case 126. Will of DANIEL COURTNER. Exec: widow
CATHERINE COURTNER & JOHN COURTNER. Witness:
ANTHONY COBLE, DANIEL WAYMIRE. Sec: ANTHONY COBAL &
ANDREW WAYMIRE. pp 63, 64

Case 127. Will of VALENTINE EYLER. Exec: SUSANNAH
EYLER. Witness: JOHN FOLKERTH, JAMES McFADDEN.
Appr: JOSEPH WILSON, JOHN DEVOR, PETER LEHMAN. p 64

Case 128. Adm of estate of JOHN HIMES granted to
SAMUEL HIMES. (Widow relinquished right.) Sec:
HENRY CREGAR, JOSEPH COLMAN. Appr: JOHN EWING,
DAVID McCLURE, CHRISTIAN CREAGAR. p 64

Case 122. Guardian for heirs of RICHARD GRAY found
personal property insufficient to pay debts, requested sale of land in Sec 26, T 2, R 7. Appr by JAMES
GILLESPIE, JOHN BRADFORD, ROBERT WEAD. pp 64, 65

Case 129. Adm of estate of DAVID JOHN granted to
JOSEPH JOHN & JACOB JOHN. Sec: ENOCH BOWEN, BENJAMIN
JOHN. Appr: ABRAHAM NEFF, JOHN OBLINGER, HENRY
FLORY. p 65

Case 130. Adm of estate of JOHN VANOSDALL granted to CORNELIUS VANOSDALE & GEORGE ADAMS. Sec: JOHN EWING, AARON BAKER. Appr: WILLIAM DODDS, JACOB BAUM, JOHN SHAFFER. p 65

Case 114 & 124. Admr of Dr. JOHN HOLE gave bond with JOHN ALLEN as Sec for discharge of duty. Apprs given further time to assign dower lands. p 65

Inv and appr of estate of JACOB YOUNT, total $233.36, by MATHIAS RIGAL, DANIEL STETLER, JACOB SHUPERT. Note: "CATY HOOVER got of her mother 1 mare..." p 65, 66

Appr's report: land of Dr. JOHN HOLE valued at $6 per acre. Sworn before JAMES RUSSEL, JP, 4 Jan, 1814. p 66, 67

Case 131. ABNER GERARD produced JP commission signed by Gov'r, dated 5 Feb, 1814. Sworn into office. p 67

Case 132. Adm of estate of ANDREW LOCK granted to DAVID LOCK. Sec: GEORGE NEWCOM, JOHN GRIMES. Appr: WILLIAM VANDERSLICE, AARON BAKER, DAVID LUID. p 67

Case 133. Adm of estate of NATHAN TALBERT granted to OLIVER TALBERT & JOHN EWING. (HENRY CREAGER filed petition; widow declined adminstration.) Sec: GEORGE NEWCOM, HENRY CREAGER. Appr: JOHN ALLEN, ANTHONY LOGAN, CHRISTIAN CREAGAR. p 67, 68

(no cases 134 or 135; error by clerk)

Filed 26 Feb, 1814. Case 136. Adm of estate of JAMES MORRIS granted to NANCY MORRIS. Sec: ADAM SHEPHARD, MARTIN HOUSER. Appr: JACOB REPLOGEL, JACOB BREN--(page torn), THOMAS SHAW. pp 167, 168

Case 137. Adm of estate of DAVID SQUIER granted to SARAH SQUIER & JOSEPH H. CRANE. Sec: ARON BAKER, DAVID LINDSLEY. Appr: JOHN PATTERSON, MATTHEW PATTON LUTHER BRUEN. pp 68, 69

Case 138. Adm of estate of FRANCIS LETURNA granted to DAVID WORMAN. Sec: FRANCIS DILTS, ROBERT PATTER-SON. Appr: OWEN DAVIS, ADAM COBLENTZ, JACOB SHROYER. p 69

Case 139. Will of ALEXANDER HUSTON. Adm by GEORGE NEWCOM & JOHN EWING. (widow relinquished right.) Witness: WILLIAM PATTERSON, JOHN BRADFORD. Sec: GEORGE BRADFORD, JAMES RIDDLE. Appr: JOHN DEVOR,

COMMON PLEAS (PROBATE) DOCKET BOOK B-1

ROBERT EDGAR, CHRISTIAN CREAGAR. p 69

Inv and appr of estate of LEONARD STUMP, total
$1172.73. pp 70, 71, 72, 73

Filed 14 March, 1814. Case 140. Adm of estate of
WILLIAM SCHENCK granted to WILLIAM B. SCHENCK &
JOSEPH TAPSCOTT. (widow relinquished right.) Sec:
JOHN H. SCHENCK, WILLIAM CONOVER. Appr: NICHOLAS
HORNER, JOSEPH CRAIN, JONATHAN ROBBINS. p 73

Case 141. Adm of estate of JOHN MIKESELL granted to
PHILIP MIKESELL. (widow relinquished right.) Sec:
PETER HECK, SAMUEL NOFFZINGER. Appr: JACOB MULLEN-
DORE, DANIEL MILLER, CHRISTIAN BROWER. p 74

Case 142. Adm of estate of SAMUEL ARNOLD granted to
CHRISTIAN ARNOLD. Sec: JOHN ARNOLD, SAMUEL HARBETS.
Appr: JACOB LEATHERMAN, CHRISTIAN LEATHERMAN, FREDE-
RICK HOLSAPPLE. p 74

Inv and appr of estate of DAVID JOHN total $490.37.
Sworn before CHRISTIAN MILLER, JP, 12 Jan, 1814.
Public sale on 2 March, 1814, Madison Twp; buyers:
ENOCH BOWEN, DANIEL BURKET, LUKE CONNOR, JOSEPH L.
COWEN, DAVID DAVIS, RACHEL DAVIS, BENJAMIN JOHN,
DAVID P. JOHN, ELEANOR JOHN, JACOB JOHN, REBECCA
JOHN, SAMUEL McMONNEN, JOHN OLINGER, JOSEPH POWEL,
JOHN SNIDER, DANIEL STUTZMAN, SAMUEL ULERY. p 77

Inv and appr of estate of ANDREW LOCK, total
$1183.50. pp 78, 79

Filed 28 March, 1814. Inv and appr of estate of JOHN
HIMES, total $812.57. Sworn by JP on 31 Jan, 1804.
Public sale, no buyers names given. Total $591.74.
pp 80, 81, 82, 83

Inv and appr of estate of MICHAEL SMITH total
$287.50. p 84

Filed 1 April, 1814. Public sale of estate of MICHAEL
SMITH undated. Buyers: ZACARIAH ARCHER, JACOB BLACK,
LEWIS BRANER, ADAM DEAM, HENRY DEAM, ISAAC DARST,
HENRY ENOCH, JAMES FINCH, JOHN FREEMAN, GEORGE FRY-
BACK, WILLIAM GESEMAN, JOHN HAINES, THOMAS HANDY,
SIMON HENSLEY, JOHN HOLDERMAN, PETER KISER, ROBERT
McKINNEY, MOSES MILLER, PHILIP MILLER, ROBERT MILLER,
MARTIN NICELY, JACOB REPLOGEL, JOHN RIGGS, LUDWICK
SHAW, PETER SLUSER, CATHERINE SMITH, BARNHART SPECK,
JACOB STAKER, JOHN RIGHT, CASPER YOUNG, JOHN ZEDIKER,
total $289.33. pp 85, 86

Filed 15 Aug, 1814. Inv and appr of estate of FRANCIS LETURNA, total $187.50. Public sale, buyers: SAMUEL BUKER, DAVID BURNS, SHEM CARNEY, OWEN DAVIS, J. ELLIOT, JAMES GIVIN, GEORGE HAINES, JAMES HENDERSON, DAVID LEHMAN, JAMES McKAIG, AARON NUTT, BENJAMIN SCOTT, GEORGE SROYER, JACOB SROYER, GEORGE SHRIVER, CHARLES SMITH, PETER SUMAN, DAVID WORMAN. Total $212.07. pp 86, 87

Filed 29 April, 1814. Public sale of estate of ANDREW LOCK undated. Purchasers: PHILIP BARNET, DAVID BARNS, JAMES BARNS, JAMES BAY, OBADIAH CONOVER, CHRISTIAN FREDERIC, WILLIAM GEORGE, JOHN GRIMES, THOMAS HENDERSON, JOSEPH KENNEDY, DAVID LEHMAN, WILLIAM MASON, R. McCLEARY, JOSEPH MEEKER, GEORGE NEWCOM, JAMES NOLAN, R. PATTERSON, JOHN REID, DAVID RIFFLE, J. SLOAN, WILLIAM M. SMITH, GEORGE SNYDER, BARNHART SPECK, TIMOTHY SQUIER, NEIL THOMSON, SAMUEL THOMSON, JAMES WILLIAMSON, JONAS WOODS, ROBERT WOODS. Total $520.41. pp 88, 89

Filed 30 April, 1814. Inv and appr of estate of JOHN VANOSDALL on 12 Jan, 1814, total $262.18 signed JACOB BOWMAN, WILLIAM DODDS, GEORGE SLIFER. Public sale, no buyers names given. Total $332.11. pp 89, 90, 91

Memo of sale of land held by G. W. DAVIS in Sec 30 & 31, T 4, R 5. Sold by RACHEL DAVIS at house of DAVID JOHN on 27 Nov, 1813. Purchased by DAVID P. JOHN. Signed by BENJAMIN JOHN, clerk. p 91

Term of May, 1814

Inv and appr of estate of ALEXANDER HUSTON, total $574.22. Sworn CHARLES SMITH, JP, on 11 March, 1814. pp 92, 93

Case 143. Will of CHRISTIAN HOSTETLER. Exec: BARBARA HOSTETLER & DAVID KRIDER. Witness: AMOS EDWARDS, CHRISTIAN ARNOLD. Appr: CHRISTIAN ARNOLD, JOHN ARNOLD & MICHAEL BAKER. p 93

Case 144. Adm of estate of ROBERT PARK granted to JOHN CLARK. Sec: WILLIAM KING, GEORGE NEWCOM. Appr: JOSEPH KENNEDY, SAMUEL BRIAR, JOHN KERR. pp 93, 94

Case 145. Adm of estate of MARGARET ROBERTS granted to ROBERT ROBERTSON. Sec: WILLIAM KING, GEORGE NEWCOM. Appr: JOHN KERR, JOHN REED, ROBERT McCLEARY. p 94

Case 146. Adm of estate of ABRAHAM SHOWERS granted

to ANNA SHOWER & JOHN ROHRER. Sec: DAVID HOOVER, JOHN RAZOR. Appr: JOSEPH ROHRER, JACOB MICHAEL, JOHN WAITMAN. p 94

Filed 2 May, 1814. Case 114. Widow's dower, estate of Dr. JOHN HOLE: 119 acre tract in Sec 3, T 2, R 6. Sworn before JP on 15 March, 1814. p 94, 95

Case 147. Adm of estate of ALBERT BOWMAN granted to SARAH BOWMAN. Sec: ISAAC WOODWARD, DANIEL McNEIL. Appr: AARON NUTT, BENJAMIN ROBBINS, JOHN BECK. p 96

Case 122. Land belonging to RICHARD GRAY's estate valued at $6/acre, sold on 3 May, 1814 to EDWARD NEWCOM, the highest bidder, for $5.70/acre. p 96

Adm MARY ANN HARDMAN & SAMUEL NOFFSINGER produced estate settlement of SOLOMON HARDMAN. Cash paid to DAVID HARDMAN, SAMUEL RUDY, ISAAC SHIVELY, HENRY LEEDES, JOHN WAGGONER, JACOB MILLER. Balance of $59.57. pp 96, 97

Case 148. Adm of estate of JOHN WOODEMAN granted to JOHN FOLKERTH. Sec: JAMES STEELE, WILLIAM M. SMITH. Appr: AARON BAKER, GEORGE GROVE, MATTHEW PATTON. p 97

Case 129. Heirs of DAVID JOHN petition for completion of pay'ts due on land purchase Sec 22, T 7, R 5. Court to allow adm to convey deed to above land to ENOCH BOWERS. pp 97,98

Case 149. Will of THOMAS RAMSAY produced by witness JOHN FOLKERTH. p 98

Case 114. Petition by DAVID HOLE for partition of land of Dr. JOHN HOLE. Court ordered apprs to set of each heir's portion, certify value. p 98

Case 150. JOHN HOLE, 15 yrs, MATILDA HOLE, 14 yrs, & PHEBE HOLE, 12 yrs, minor heirs of Dr. JOHN HOLE, chose RICHARD MASON as guardian. p 98

Case 151. JAMES I. NESBIT granted adm of estate of SYLVANUS LOVELESS. Sec: HORATIO G. PHILLIPS. p 98

MARY DAVIS, admr of THOMAS DAVIS, produced settlement Cash paid included taxes on lots in Eaton (Preble Co), debts to DAVID DUNCAN, JOHN MILLER, AARON NUTT, JEROM HOLT, ALBERT BANTA, JACOB SHARTLE. p 99

Admr of LEONARD STUMP produced settlement, "widow's third and 3 children". Cash paid to WILLIAM EMRICK,

GEORGE LOY (auctioneer), JOHN PROTSMAN, CHRISTOPHER EMRICK, DANIEL GUNCKEL, JACOB BOWER, HENRY ZELLER, CONRAD EMRICK, JACOB SWANK, JOHN H. SCHENCK, ABRAHAM BROWN, GEORGE HORNER, GEORGE KESTER, JULIANNA STUMP, JOHN SHAWLEY, MICHAEL EMRICK, DANIEL MANNBECK, NICHO-LAS BOCKS. Each child to have $651.05. pp 100, 101

Report that real estate belonging to estate of Dr. JOHN HOLE has been sold. p 101

Special session 4 June, 1814

Case 152. Adm of estate of GEORGE WOODS* granted to PHILIP ROADS & JACOB ROADS. (widow relinquished right.) Sec: ABRAHAM TROXEL, CHRISTIAN MILLER. Appr: ABRAHAM HILDERBRAND, JACOB WEAVER & PETER RACHER. p 101 *Believe this to be clerical error; should be GEORGE RHOADS.

Filed 19 May, 1814. Inv and appr of estate of JOSEPH DODDS JR, total $48.25 + $46 cash. Signed JOHN TAY-LOR, JOHN ALLEN. Sworn before JP, 18 May, 1814. p102

Filed 24 May, 1814. Inv and appr of estate of CHRIS-TIAN HOSTETLER. Accts due from DAVID CRIDER, JOHN PEPINGER, JACOB BROMBAUGH, JOHN ARNOLD. Total $448.59. pp 103, 104

Inv and appr of estate of NATHANIEL TALBERT total $730.97. Sworn before JP 2 Apr, 1814. pp 105, 106, 107

Filed 14 June, 1814. Inv and appr of estate of JOHN MIKESELL on 21 March 1814. Total $172.55. Debts due from ZACHARIAS CRUMM, PHILIP RAYRIGH. pp 107, 108

Filed 20 June, 1814. Inv and appr of estate of GIL-BERT BOWMAN. Notes due from JOHN ARCHER, JOHN ARCHER JR, PHILIP BALTIMORE, HENRY BROOM, JOSIAH CLAWSON, JACOB CONSOLVER, THOMAS DAVIS, JACOB GEPHART, ABNER GERARD, DANIEL McNEAL, AARON NUTT, LEVI NUTT, JAMES RUSSEL, THOMAS SHANKS, DANIEL SMALL, THOMAS WELCH, ASHBURY WOOD, ISAAC WOODARD; money due for military duty at Greenville by BOMAN under Capt. WILLIAM LUCE; total of $170.79. Sworn before JP on 17 May, 1814. pp 108, 109 (see Case 147. ALBERT BOWMAN)

Case 153. Adm of estate of STILES PARKER granted to WILLIAM AUSTIN. Sec: JOHN BAKER, AARON BAKER. Appr: JOHN AINSWORTH, THOMAS PATTERSON, ROBERT YOUNG. p 109

Public sale of property of NATHAN TOLBURT on 8 April,

1814. Buyers: THOMAS BRADLEY, PATRICK BRISON, CHRIS-
TIAN CREAGER, HENRY CREAGER, PETER CREAGER, FRANCIS
DILTZ, JOHN DODDS, WILLIAM DODDS, ROBERT ELLIOT, JOHN
EWING, GEORGE GROVE, JOSEPH GILLESPIE, MARIANN
HOUSTON, DAVID LEHMAN, ALEXANDER LOGAN, ANTHONY
LOGAN, HENRY MARQUART, JACOB MULFORD, AARON NUTT,
MATTHIAS PARSON, JAMES PETTICREW, ROBERT PETTICREW,
THOMAS RUE, RICHARD SHAW, JOHN SHROYER, ADAM SMITH,
ISAIAH THOMAS, JANE TOLBURT, MARY TOLBURT, OLIVER
TOLBURT, RUTH TOLBURT, JOHN WADE. pp 110, 111, 112

Inv and appr of estate of JOHN WODEMAN, total
$110.25. p 113

Filed 15 July, 1814. Public sale of estate of JOHN
WODEMAN. Buyers: JAMES BROWN, CHRISTOPHER CURTNER,
HENRY CURTNER, CHARLES ESTE, DAVID LEHMAN, JOHN LEH-
MAN, BENJ. LLOYD, CONKLIN MILLER, ELIJAH MONTAWNIE,
SIMPSON McCARTER, JAMES NOLAN, JAMES RITCHIE, GEORGE
SNIDER, GEORGE SOURBRAY. Total $43.62. p 114

Inv and appr of estate of ABRAHAM SHOWER on 14 May,
1814. Total $339.71. Appr: JOSEPH B. ROHRER, JACOB
(x) MICHAEL, JOHN WEIDMAN*. Clerk AMOS EDWARDS. pp
115, 116 (*see Case 146)

Filed 16 Aug, 1814. Inv and appr of estate of MARGE-
RET ROBERTSON, total $149.37. Public sale, buyers:
JAMES BRIER, SAMUEL BRIER, SAMUEL BROWN, JOHN COX,
DANIEL H. FISHER, JOHN GRIMES, JOSEPH KENNEDY, JOHN
KERR, WILLIAM MASON, JONATHAN MAYHALL, ROBERT McCLEA-
RY, ALEX McNIGHT, DAVID MILLER, WILLIAM MILLER, ADAM
NEFF, EPHRAIM OWENS, JOHN REID, JOHN RIGGS, ROBERT
ROBINSON. Total $195.51. (See Case 145). pp 117, 118

Inv and appr of estate of WILLIAM SCHENCK, total
$265.12. Debts due from JOHN ROSSMAN, ELISHA SHUPERT
EDEN BURROWS, DANIEL SCHENCK, BARNS SHUPERT. Debts
owed to JOHN ROSSMAN, JOHN C. DEARTH, JOHN N. C.
SCHENCK, WILLIAM TAPSCOTT, ISAIAH ANDERSON, JAMES
PIPER, JOHN MOUNT, MARTIN EARHART, DAVID LABAW, WIL-
LIAM FOX, ALEXANDER NEER, JOSEPH TAPSCOTT, JOHN H.
SCHENCK, ARTHUR VANDEVEER. Public sale held, buyers:
ISAIAH ANDERSON, VINCENT ANTONIDES, DERRICK BARKALOW,
JOHN BARKALOW, WILLIAM P. BARKALOW, DAVID COMPTON,
JOHN COMPTON, WILLIAM CONOVER, JAMES DEARTH, JOHN C.
DEARTH, WILLIAM DEHAIS, PHILIP EVERMORE, DANIEL FEAS-
TER, GEORGE GILLESPIE, THOMAS GOODWIN, GEORGE HALL,
CHARLES HARDY, WILLIAM HARRISON, NICHOLAS HORNER,
JOHN KELLOW, GEORGE LOY, LYCUM MARSH, WILLIAM MARTIN,
WILLIAM MARTINHART, JAMES PETTICREW, JOSEPH PITMAN,
THOMAS RAY, THOMAS ROBINS, JOHN ROSSMAN, ADAM RUNSER

CRINEYANCE SCHENCK, DAVID SCHENCK, JOHN SCHENCK, JOHN N. C. SCHENCK, PARRET SCHENCK, WILLIAM B. SCHENCK, JACOB SHUPERT, GEORGE SNELL, HENRY STAREL, JOSEPH TAPSCOTT, WILLIAM TAPSCOTT, DANIEL TROYER, DANIEL UNGARY, DANIEL ULERY, THOMAS VANNOTE, REUBEN WOODWARD. Total $365.08. pp 119, 120, 121, 122, 123

Filed 20 Aug, 1814. Inv and appr of estate of ROBERT PARKS on 3 May, 1814, total $753.00. Public sale, buyers: DAVID ALSPAUGH, JAMES BENTLEY, JACOB BOWMAN, HENRY BOWSER, ANDREW BRIER, JAMES BRIER, SAMUEL BRIER DANIEL BROMBAUGH, SAMUEL BROWN, MICHAEL BURNS, JOHN CLARK, ROBERT CLARK, JER. COLLINS, JAMES CONNOR, O.B. CONOVER, JOHN COX, H. CRULL, JOHN DODDS, DAVID DUNCAN, WILLIAM FARMER, GEORGE HARRIS, JOSEPH HOLLINGSWORTH, DANIEL JONES, RICHARD JONES, JOSEPH KELLER, JAMES KELLY, JOSEPH KENNEDY, THOMAS KING, JOHN KIRBY, WILLIAM LITTLE, HENRY MARQUART, WILLIAM MASON, JONATHAN MAYHALL, EDWARD McDONOUGH, JAMES McELWAIN, ELIAS McGUIRE, JOHN McLEARY, ROBERT McLEARY, ALEX McNIGHT, ROBERT McSHONEY, JOSEPH MEEKER, CONKLIN MILLER, DAVID MILLER, JOHN MILLER, ADAM NEFF, JAMES NOLAN, BENJAMIN OWENS, JOSEPH PARK, PEGGY PARKS, WILLIAM PREDY, JAMES REED, JOHN REED, ROBERT ROBERTSON, ADAM RUDEBAUGH, HENRY SWISHER, JAMES WELSH, THOMAS WILLIAMS, PETER WINELAND, JOHN WOLF, ROBERT WOOD, ISAAC WORE, CALEB WORLEY, JOHN WRIGHT. Total $1026.73. pp 123, 124

Inv and appr of estate of GEORGE RHOADS, total of $2047.25, signed PETER RACHER, JACOB WEAVER. pp 127, 128 (See case 152)

Term of September, 1814

Case 154. Will of BENJAMIN JOHN. Exec: not named, widow mentioned. Witness: JOSEPH JOHN, REBECCA JOHN. p 128

Case 155. Will of JOHN ENSY. Exec: ELIZABETH ENSY, ABRAHAM ENSY. Witness: JACOB LECHLIDER, JOHN FOLKERTH. Appr: ABRAHAM HOSIER, JOHN BRADFORD, JACOB LECHLIDER. p 128

Case 156. PHILIP WAGNER & JOSEPH ROHRER apptd guardians to DAVID MILLER, 11 yrs, JOHN MILLER, 9 yrs, & ABRAHAM MILLER, 6 yrs, minor heirs of JOHN MILLER, dec. Sec: PHILIP HARTZEL, JACOB NEFF. p 129

Case 157. SAMUEL THRALL, 13 yrs, minor heir of JOSEPH THRALL, dec, chose JOSEPH BROWN as guardian. p 129

Case 158. ENOS MILES apptd guardian to ISAAC RENT-
FREW, 11 yrs, JACOB RENTFREW, 9 yrs, JOHN RENTFREW, 6
yrs, minor heirs of TURPIN RENTFREW, dec. Sec:
PHILIP WAGNER. p 129

Public sale of estate of GEORGE RHOADS, buyers: JACOB
HAY, SEBASTIAN HEIDER, DANIEL HESTAND, ABRAHAM HILDE-
BRAND, H. KNEE, JACOB MULLENDORE, MICHAEL RACHER,
HENRY RHOADS, JACOB RHOADS, JAMES RHOADS, PHIL
RHOADES, DANIEL SHIDLER. Total $56.09. pp 129, 130

Estate of MICHAEL SMITH insufficient to complete
payts on land in Sec 29, T 2, R 8. Admr ask permission to sell land. p 130

Case 159. JAMES RENTFREW, 14 yrs, chose ENOS MILES
as guardian. p 130

Case 160. Adm of estate of DANIEL BAXTER granted to
JAMES BAXTER (widow relinquished right). Sec: GEORGE
NEWCOM, ROBERT GRAY. Appr: JAMES RIDDLE, JOHN
BRADFORD, JOHN DEVOR. p 130

Case 161. Will of DANIEL RHUFF (proven last term, 3
May, 1814) proven by witness REBECCA PAINTER. p 130

Case 162. Will of JOHN GRIPE. Exec: JOHN GRIPE,
JOSEPH GRIPE. Witness: JOHN FOLKERTH, JONATHAN
HERSHMAN. Appr: JACOB WAGNER, JOHN WAGNER, JOHN
OLINGER. p 130

Case 163. Will of DANIEL HOOVER JR. Exec: JOHN
WAGGONER, MARY HOOVER. Witness: JOHN FOLKERTH, DAVID
HOOVER, JOHN WERTZ. Appr: --BUCHANON, ANDREW HOOVER,
GEORGE SINK. p 131

Case 164. JOHN SCHENCK appted guardian to DANIEL
SCHENCK, 13 yrs, minor heir of WILLIAM SCHENCK, dec.
Sec: DAVID SCHENCK. p 131

Case 165. Adm of estate of NICHOLAS SMALL JR granted
to NICHOLAS SMALL. Sec: SAMUEL ARCHER, ISAAC G.
BURNET. p 131

Case 166. JEREMIAH WOOD, age 17, heir of SAMUEL WOOD
dec, chose JONAS WOOD as guardian. p 131

Admr of estate of GEORGE YOUNT produced settlement.
Cash paid to H. HOOVER, DANIEL RAZOR, GEORGE YOUNT,
ANDREW SINK, widow. Balance of $297.48. p 131

Case 114. Land partition of Dr. JOHN HOLE ordered

recorded. p 132

Case 167. Estate of WILLIAM SCHENCK insufficient to
pay debts. Admrs request permission to sell land.
Appr: JOSEPH CRANE, FREDERICK NUTTZ, JOHN H. SCHENCK
p 132

Admr of JOHN COMPTON produced settlement. Cash paid
to: widow's third of estate, TOBIAS BARKALOW, ARCHI-
BALD CAMPBELL, JOHN DENISE, SIDNEY DENISE, BENJAMIN
DUBOIS, JOHN FRANCIS, PHILIP GUNCKEL, GEORGE HALL,
DAVID LABAN, GEORGE LANE, JAMES LANIER, LEARING MARSH
THOMAS ROBINS, JOHN H. SCHENCK, JOHN N. C. SCHENCK,
GEORGE STUMP, PHILIP SWARTZLEY, TUNIS VANDEVEER, JOHN
VANTILBURGH, THOMAS VANNOTE, WILLIAM WHITFIELD. Total
$322.(page torn). p 132

Inv and appr of estate of STILES PARKER. Debt due
from WILLIAM WILLIAMSON, THOMAS LUSK, JOHN AINSWORTH,
for total of $107.98. Margin note: Adm pd settlement
in full to DANIEL W. BANESTER, rep of the heirs, on
16 Sept, 1829. p 133

Public sale of estate of R. GILCHRIST on 17 Aug,
1813. No buyers names or total given. pp 133, 134

Special session 8 Oct, 1814

Case 168. Will of JOSEPH WILSON. Exec: JAMES
WINGATE, DAVID HUSTON. Witness: WILLIAM OWENS,
SAMUEL HOLMES. Appr: JOHN DEVOR, GEORGE NEWCOM,
LEWIS KEMP. p 135

Special session 17 Nov, 1814

Case 169. Adm of estate of CONRAD CASTER granted to
ELIZABETH CASTER. Sec: JOHN S. RIGGS, JOHN ENOCH.
Appr: WILLIAM JAMES, JOHN WOLF, ABRAHAM BRANNERMAN.
p 135

Case 170. Adm of estate of JOHN STRAIN granted to
ROBERT STRAIN JR (widow relinquished right). Sec:
JOHN RIGGANS, DAVID REID. Appr: H. G. PHILLIPS,
GEORGE W. SMITH, JAMES STEELE. p 135

Inv and appr of estate of JOSEPH WILSON, total
$981.00 by apprs LUDWICK KEMP, GEORGE NEWCOM, H.G.
PHILLIPS. Public sale on 11 Nov, 1814, buyers:
GEORGE ALEXANDER, DAVID ALSPACH, HENRY AMMERMAN,
NATHANIEL BLOOMFIELD, SAMUEL BLOOMFIELD, JAMES BUCHA-
NON, JOHN BUCHANON, JOHN DEVOR, JOE ELLFRITTS, JOHN
ELLFRITTS, JOHN ENSEY, JOHN GARRAT, ARCHIBALD GRAHAM,

SAMUEL HOLMES, DAVID HUSTON, JAMES JAMISON, DAVID
JOHN, THOMAS JOHN, JOHN KERR, HENRY LEHMAN, JACOB
LEHMAN, JAMES LEHMAN, SAMUEL LEONARD, ALEXANDER
LOGAN, JAMES LOWRY, NATHANIEL LYON, JAMES MACKEY,
JOHN MACKEY, JOHN McBRIDE, JAMES McLEAN, JOSHUA
MORGAN, SAMUEL MORGAN, JOHN MUSSELMAN, GEORGE NEWCOM,
WILLIAM OWENS, WILLIAM RAMSAY, JOSEPH REDIFER, JOHN
RIKE, SAMUEL SAWRIGHT, LAWRENCE SHELL, JOHN SHROYER,
RICHARD STEPHENS, JOHN WEAD, GEORGE WHITEMAN, JEREMI-
AH WILSON, ROBERT WILSON, CALEB WINGATE, JACOB WIN-
GATE, JAMES WINGATE, REUBEN WINGATE, JONAS WOODS,
JACOB WORMAN, total of $684.28. Debts due estate by
HENRY LEHMAN & ROBERT WILSON. Signed JAMES WINGATE,
DAVID HUSTON. pp 136, 137, 138, 139, 140, 141

Inv and appr of estate of DANIEL HOOVER made 26 Sept,
1814, total $410.05 by GEORGE SINK, ANDREW HOOVER,
GEORGE BUCHANON. Public sale held 7 & 8 Oct, 1814,
total of $377.14 plus notes due estate from DANIEL
DETER, JOSEPH PEARSON, ADAM ELLER, PHILIP RAZOR,
WILLIAM RITTENHOUSE, JOHN WESTFALL, JOSEPH MIKESELL,
JOHN CONNER, SAMUEL MARTINDALE, Widow NEEK, ANDREW
HOOVER JR, JACOB HOOVER JR, PHILLIP YOUN, FREDERICH
DITMER, JOHN WILLIAMS, MICHAEL WILLIAMS, HENRY ROGER,
JAMES NOLL, DAVID MILLER, VALENTINE WAYMIRE, SOLOMON
BIRKET, BETSEY SHEETS, RICHARD ROBINS, HENRY CROWEL,
DAVID SHEARER, MARY TUCKER, THOMAS NEWMAN. Total
$581.33. Kept by widow = $37.25. pp 141, 142, 143

Inv and appr of estate of DANIEL BAXTER total $251.37
Public sale on 4 Oct, 1814, buyers: JOHN BRADFORD,
JOHN BUCHANON, DAVID BURNS, CHARLES DEPRIEST, JOHN
EMRICK, JOHN ENSY, ARCHIBALD GRAHAM, ARCHIBALD GRIMES
SAMUEL HOLMES, MARY HUSTON, JOHN LOW, ELIAS MACKEY,
HENRY MARQUART, DOM. McGRATH, GEORGE NEWCOM, JOHN
NIGHT, WILLIAM OWENS, FRANCIS PATTON, THOMAS QUINN,
JAMES RIDDLE, DAVID RIFFLE, LAWRENCE SHELL, TIM
SQUIER, WILLIAM WILFOR, WILLIAM WILSON total $225.03.
pp 143, 144

Inv and appr of estate of CONRAD CASTOR made 26 Dec,
1814, total $736.57. Appr's note: left livestock for
support of widow & family. p 145

Term of January, 1815

Estate of PHILEMON PLUMMER insufficient to complete
land payts. Adms request permission to sell land in
Sec 13, T 5, R 5E to DANIEL WAYMIRE. p 146

Case 171. JOSEPH BUCHER, 17 yrs, heir of MATHIAS
BAKER, dec, chose PETER LEHMAN as guardian. p 146

Apprs recorded value of land of RICHARD GRAY. p 146

Case 172. Will of JOSEPH PEARSON. Exec: MELIA PEAR-
SON & WILLIAM HOLD. Witness: JOHN WERTZ, BENJAMIN
PEARSON & WILLIAM NOLL. Appr: JAMES NOLL, ABEL INSCO,
JOSEPH PEARSON. p 146

Petition by admr of CHRISTIAN FOGELSONG to convey
deed to PETER SOWDER. p 146

Case 173. Will of JESSE MOTE, proven by witness
FRANCIS JONES. p 146

SAMUEL HIMES, admr of JOHN HIMES, applied for time
extension to settle estate. p 146

Case 174. PETER YOUNT, 19 yrs, heir of JACOB YOUNT,
dec, chose FREDERICK NUTTZ as guardian. p 147

Case 175. Estate of WILLIAM McCLURE insufficient to
pay debts. Adm request permission to sell Dayton lot
86. p 147

Admr of MATHIAS SWARTZLEY found recpts for $80.30 not
accounted for in final settlement; paid cash over to
heirs. p 147

Petition by admrs of WILLIAM SCHENCK dated 26 Dec,
1814, to sell 132 acres in Sec 28, T 2, R 5, valued
at $18 per acre. p 147

Value of RICHARD GRAY's land set at $8.50 per acre by
JAMES GILLESPIE, ROBERT WEAD & JOHN BRADFORD SR. Adm
produced settlement. Cash paid to JANE GRAY, ROBERT
EDGAR, HORATIO G. PHILLIPS, EPHRAIM ARNOLD, LUTHER
BRUEN, ANDREW PARK, ROBERT WEAD, Dr. BENJ. DUBOIS,
JOSEPH H. CRANE, JOHN BRADFORD, JOSEPH BURROWS, JAMES
PETTICREW, WILLIAM VANDERSLICE, EDWARD NEWCOM, JAMES
BAXTER, DANIEL C. COOPER, JOHN FOLKERTH, RICHARD
STEPHENS (auctioneer) total $210.87. p 148

Value of WILLIAM McCLURE's lot set at $1800 on 5 Jan,
1815. p 148

Inv and appr of estate of CONRAD CASTER total $160.
Public sale held, total $253.62. p 149, 150

Inv and appr of estate of JOHN STRAIN on 6 Jan, 1815,
total $426.64. Public sale held 7 Jan, 1815, buyers:
POMPEY ALLEN, JOHN ANDERSON, JAMES BROWN, JAMES CLARK
WILLIAM COHOON, WILLIAM COX, GEORGE DAVIS, WILLIAM
GILLESPIE, JOHN HARRY, Capt. KEHLER, PET LAYTON,

COMMON PLEAS (PROBATE) DOCKET BOOK B-1

GEORGE MANCER, HENRY MARQUART, JOHN McCLEARY, H. G.
PHILLIPS, DANIEL REPP, JOHN RIGGANS, WILLIAM ROACH,
JOHN SHROYER, G. W. SMITH, WILLIAM SMITH, JOHN
STAKER, JAMES STEELE, R. STRAIN JR, JACOB SWANER
total $361.02 plus notes due from N. S. PETTIT,
DAVID REID, PETER MIKESELL, WILLIAM ENOCH, EDWIN
SMITH, JOHN GATH, JAMES NOLAN, DAVID DUNCAN, JOHN
BODLEY. Total $592.86. pp 150, 151, 152

Special session 2 March, 1815

Case 176. Adm of estate of HUGH McCOLLOM granted to
DANIEL LANDON & WILLIAM P. DAVIS. Sec: GEORGE
NEWCOM, GEORGE GROVE. Appr: H. G. PHILLIPS, JOHN
GRIMES, CHRISTOPHER CURTNER. p 152

Case 177. DAVID SIMMONS appted guardian of SCOTT
SHAW, 10 yrs, heir of FREEMAN SHAW. p 152.

End of Volume B-1

COMMON PLEAS (PROBATE) DOCKET BOOK C-1

Filed 5 Apr, 1815. Inv and appr of estate of HUGH
McCOLLOM on 6 March, 1815, total $583.06. (McCOLLOM,
an innkeeper, held a great deal of public business at
his "house"; auctions, court sessions, etc. Since
the note amounts are generally small, most are proba-
bly for a meal eaten while at a trial or on other
business.) Notes due estate: JOHN ALSPAUGH, VINCENT
ANTONIDES, SAMUEL ARCHER, STEPHEN ARCHER, EPHRAIM
ARNOLD, JAMES ARNOLD, LAWRENCE ASBY, HENRY BACON,
AARON BAKER, SAMUEL BALDWIN, JAMES BARNET, JOHN
BENNET, JAMES BLACK, THOMAS BLAIR, SAMUEL BOWEN,
ELIJAH BRANNON, JAMES BROWDER, JOHN BROWN, JOSEPH
BRYAN, LUKE BRYAN, WILLIAM BUTCHER, JOHN CAMPBELL,
PATRICK CAMPBELL, ANTHONY CHEVALIER WILLIAM CLARK,
THOMAS CLAWSON, JOHN COLE, DANIEL C. COOPER, JOSEPH
CONNER, PETER CONNER MATTHEW CRANE, JOHN CREIGH, JOHN
CRIDER, ROBERT CULBERTSON, JAMES CURRY, WILLIAM
CUTRIGHT, JACOB DAVIS, OWEN DAVIS, WILLIAM P. DAVIS,
MICHAEL DEARMONT, HENRY DEAM, AARON DEEN, WALTER DIL-
LON, CORNELIUS DILTZ, FRANCIS DILTZ, WILLIAM DILTZ,
JOSEPH DODDS, WILLIAM DODDS, DAVID DUNCAN, WILLIAM
ELLIS, JESSE ENNIS, JOHN ENOCH, ALEX EWING, JACOB
FAASNAUGHT, DANIEL FERREL, JOHN FOLKERTH, young
WILLIAM FOX, WILLIAM FREEMAN, CHRISTIAN FREDERICK,
ABNER GARARD, WILLIAM GARDNER, JOSEPH GILLESPIE,
WILLIAM GILLESPIE, GIDEON GOODSTEAD, JOHN GORDON,
RICHARD GORDON, TIMOTHY GREEN, SMITH GREGG, ARCHIBALD
GRIMES, GEORGE GROVE, SOLOMON HAMER, SAMUEL HAWKINS,
JAMES HENDERSON, ABRAHAM HILDEBRAND, JERRY HOLE,

JEROM HOLT, SHADRACH HUDSON, LYDIA HUEY, ROBERT HUEY, THOMAS JONSTON, JOHN JUDY, JAMES KELLY, JOHN KINZEY, JACOB KUHN, PATRICK LAFFERTY, GEORGE LONG, JESSE LONG, NICHOLAS LONGWORTH, JOHN LOWE, JERRY LUDLOW, HENRY MARQUART, ELY MARTIN, DUNCAN McARTHUR, WILLIAM McCANN, ARCHIBALD McCLAIN, JOHN McCLEARY, JOSEPH McCLEARY, THOMAS McCLEARY, ROBERT McCLEARY, WILLIAM McCORMICK, PETER McCREA, DANIEL McDONNEL, THOMAS McNUTT, FERGUS MICKEL, CONKLIN MILLER, JACOB MILLER, MATHEW MINTON, GODFREY MONG, JAMES MURPHY, MARTIN MIRES, DAVID MUSSELMAN, JOHN MUSSELMAN, JOHN NEWCOM, JAMES NOLAN, ANDREW PARK, JOSEPH PARKS, JOHN PATTERSON, THOMAS PATTERSON, JAMES PETTICREW, HORATIO G. PHILLIPS, SAMUEL RAMSAY, MICHAEL RAZER, JOHN REDICK, HENRY REEL, JOSEPH REISE, Capt. JAMES RHEA, JAMES RICHEY, JAMES RIDDLE, JOHN RIDDLE, DAVID RIFFLE, JAMES ROBISON, ROBERT ROBISON, JOHN ROBY, MATTHEW RUHFF, JESSE RUSH, ALEX SCOTT, BENJAMIN SCOTT, JAMES SHAVER, SAMUEL SHOUP, DAVID SIMMONS, SAMUEL SIMONTON, CHARLES SMITH, BARNHART SPECK, TIMOTHY SQUIER, JOHN STAKER, Dr. JOHN STEELE, JACOB SUMAN, PETER SUMAN, FRANCIS SUMMERS, ALEX TENNANT, WALTER THOMAS, JAMES THOMPSON, MOSES THOMSON, WILLIAM THOMPSON, NATHANIEL THROLL, JOHN TODD, BENJ VAN CLEVE, WILLIAM VAN CLEVE, AARON VANSCOYK, JOHN WAGNER, RUBIN WAGNER, WILLIAM WALLACE, SAMUEL WALTON, WILLIAM WATTON, JAMES WELSH, ISAAC WESTFALL, JOB WESTFALL, JOEL WESTFALL, MATHEW WIGHBRIGHT, GEORGE WILSON, DAVID WOOD, ELIJAH WOODS, JOHN WOODERMAN, HENRY WERTS, MICHAEL RIGHT, CASPER YOUNG. Total $1079.07. pp 1, 2, 3, 4, 5

Term of May, 1815

Case 178. Will of FREDERICK WOLF proven by witness ANDREW ZELLER. p 6

Case 179. Will of ELIZABETH WOLF. Exec: FREDERICK KIMMERLING, ABRAHAM PAULUS. Witness: FREDERICK WOLF, GEORGE WOLF. p 6

Case 180. Will of GEORGE STETLER. Exec: DANIEL STETLER, GEORGE STETLER. Witness: MATHIAS RIGGAL, JOSIAH GUSHWA. Appr: GEORGE LANE, SYDNEY DENISE, WILLIAM DENISE. p 6

Case 181. Will of GEORGE GEPHART. Exec: JOHN GEPHART, JACOB GEPHART. Witness: MATTHIAS RIGGAL, EMANUEL GEPHART. Appr: PETER BANTA, FREDERICK NUTTZ, JAMES CAROTHERS. p 6

Case 173. Will of JESSE MOTE proven January term before ZACARIAH LINDLY, JP, Washington Co, Indiana

Territory. Exec: JAMES PATTY, reserving the right of DAVID PATTY to serve as exec. Appr: JOHN McCLIN-TOCK, DANIEL HOOVER, DAVID MAST. pp 6, 7

Case 182. Will of MARGERY PARKS. Exec: JOSEPH MEEKER. Witness: DANIEL NEFF, ROBERT McCLEARY JR. Appr: JOSEPH KENNEDY, JOHN WOLF, DANIEL WOLF. p 7.

Case 183. JOSEPH PARKS JR, 18 yrs old, minor heir of ROBERT PARKS, dec, chose JOSEPH PARKS as guardian. Sec: JOHN KERR. p 7

Case 184. Will of JOHN BICKEL, proven by witness MARIA BICKEL. p 7

Case 185. Adm of estate of JACOB STONER granted to JOHN C. NEGLEY. Sec: PETER NECK, MARY STONER. Appr: HENRY OLDFATHER, ABRAHAM STUTSMAN, JOHN KINZEY. p 7

Case 186. JOSEPH PARK appted guardian of ELIZABETH D. PARK, 3 yrs, minor heir of ROBERT PARK, dec. Sec: SAMUEL BRIER. p 7

Case 187. JAMES PARK appted guardian of THOMAS B. PARK, 8 yrs, minor heir of ROBERT PARK. p 7

Case 188. WILLIAM KING appted guardian of ANDREW PARK, 10 yrs, and ISABELLA PARK, 6 yrs minor heirs of ROBERT PARK, dec. Sec: WILLIAM MASON. p 8

Case 189. SALLY SQUIER appted guardian of PHEBE SQUIER, 8 yrs, ELIZA SQUIER, 6 yrs, JULIET SQUIER, 4 yrs, and REBECCA SQUIER, 9 months, minor heirs of DAVID SQUIER. Sec: TIMOTHY SQUIER. p 8

Admr of JACOB YOUNT produced settlement. Balance of $179.89 remaining. p 8

Case 190. WILLIAM WILSON, 18 yrs, minor heir of JOSEPH WILSON, chose H. G. PHILLIPS as guardian. p 8

Case 170. Petition of admr of JOHN STRAIN to exchange 1/2 Dayton lot #182 for ROBERT STRAIN SR's 1/2 Dayton lot #206. Permission granted. p 8

Case 191. Admr of WILLIAM McCLURE to sell half lot. Sale ordered recorded. p 9

Case 192. JAMES MORROW, 16 yrs, minor heir of JAMES MORROW, dec, chose JEROM HOLT as guardian. p 9

Admr of FRANCIS LETORNO produced settlement. Balance

COMMON PLEAS (PROBATE) DOCKET BOOK C-1

of $70.13 remains. p 9

JOHN STAVER produced paper, swore it to be will of
JOHN BICKEL. Court ordered this will plus previous
statement by MARIA BICKEL be recorded. p 9 (see
Case 184)

Admr of WILLIAM McCLURE made settlement. Balance of
$1178.61 remains. p 9

Case 193. Adm of will of JOHN BICKEL. Exec: SIMON
BICKLE. Sec: FREDERICK WOLF, SAMUEL BOWER. Appr:
JOHN STAVER, JOHN ZELLER, GEORGE KULLMAN. p 9

Admr of JACOB MAST made settlement. Balance of
$172.52 remains. p 10

Admr of Dr. JOHN HOLE made settlement. Balance of
$1501.87 remains. p 10

Inv and appr of estate of GEORGE GEPHART of Washing-
ton Twp made 15 May, 1815. Notes due estate: JOHN
WARRICK, JOHN GEBHART. Total $1709.99. Public sale
on 26 May, 1815; buyers: VINCENT ANTONIDES, PETER
BANTA, JACOB BOAS, JOSEPH COOPER, WILLIAM EMRICK,
SAMUEL GASTON, ANTHONY GEBHART, DANIEL GEBHART, EMAN-
NUEL GEPHART, GEORGE GEPHART, JACOB GEPHART, JOHN
GEPHART, JOHN GEPHART SR, MARGARET GEPHART, ROBERT
GRAY, JAMES GREADE, WILLIAM HANSON, WILLIAM HARRISON
JOHN HENKER, JOHN KERCHER, JACOB LEIGHTY, MICHAEL
LEIGHTY, GEORGE LONG, JACOB LONG, WILLIAM LONG, ISAAC
McFEALA, BARBARY MICHAEL, JACOB MILLER, LEONARD
MINNICK, FREDERICK NUTTZ, PETER PENROD, JAMES PETTI-
CREW, PHILIP PROSIUS, POLLY PROSIUS, AARON ROCKEN-
FIELD, PETER SHAFFER, JOHN TREON, MICHAEL TREON,
PETER TREON, MICHAEL UNGARY, JACOB WEAVER, CHRISTIAN
WELDY, HENRY WHITESELL, TOBIAS WHITESELL, total
$109.67 + $77.70 + $98.10 (page totals) p 11, 12,
13, 14, 15

Admr of JACOB YOUNT made settlement. "widow's third".
Cash paid to DANIEL STETLER, MATHIAS RIGAL, GEORGE
LOY, JAMES SHEPARD, FREDERIC WOLF, BENJAMIN VAN CLEVE
JOSEPH H. CRANE. Balance of $179.89 remains. p 16

Admr of FRANCIS LATURNAS produced settlement. Cash
paid to HORATIO G. PHILLIPS, MARY DAVIS, PETER SUMAN,
WILLIAM HUFFMAN, B. VAN CLEVE, AARON NUTT, Dr. JOHN
STEELE, CHARLES SMITH, ADAM COBLENTZ, OWEN DAVIS,
SHEM CARNEY, PHEBE SHAW, DOMINICK McGRATH, ADDISON
SMITH, DANIEL C. COOPER. Balance of $70.13 remains.
p 16

COMMON PLEAS (PROBATE) DOCKET BOOK C-1

Term of May, 1815 continued

Admr of WILLIAM McCLURE produced settlement. Cash paid to JOHN REGANS, JACOB BURNET, B. VAN CLEVE, JAMES WELSH, JAMES ELLIOTT, PIERSON SPINNING, JOHN RITCHIE, ANTHONY LOGAN, IRA SMITH, WILLIAM KING, JOHN FOLKERTH, JOHN KING, JAMES STEELE, WILLIAM WATTON, GEORGE GROVE, HENRY MARQUART, LUTHER BRUEN, JAMES HEATON, MARTHA McCLURE. Cash recvd from JAMES McCLURE, GEORGE DRUMMOND, JOHN EWEN, WILLIAM SHAFER, JEROM HOLT, DAVID McCLURE. Balance of $1178.60 remains. p 17

Admr of JACOB MAST produced settlement. Cash paid to JOHN McLINTOCK, THOMAS NEWMAN, JAMES HALZELOW, ANDREW HOOVER, RICHARD ROBINS, DAVID FOUT. Balance of $172.52. p 18

Admr of Dr. JOHN HOLE produced settlement. Cash paid to BENJAMIN ARCHER, JOHN ARCHER, ELIZABETH CRAIG, M. S. PETTIT, JAMES FINLEY, DAVID HOLE, HENRY CREAGER, FRANCIS DILTS, OWEN HATFIELD, WHITLEY HATFIELD, JEAN MULFORD THOMAS BRADLEY, BENJAMIN ROBINS, PETER BANTA, HENRY BROWN, ANTHONY LOGAN, WILLIAM LONG, JAMES McGREW, Dr JOHN TREON, RUNNALS WRIGHT, RICHARD SHAW, AARON BAKER. Debts due from EDMUND MUNGER, ROBERT GRAHAM. Balance of $991.81 remained. pp 18, 19

Public sale of estate of ALEXANDER HUSTON. Buyers: JOHN BRADFORD, THOMAS BRADLEY, PETER BREWER, JAMES BUCHANON, SAMUEL BUCHER, WILLIAM CONCANNON, HENRY CREAGER, THOMAS CREAGER, FRANCIS DILTS, MATTHEW M. DODDS, SAMUEL EILER, ROBERT ELLIOT, DENNIS ENSY, EDWARD HUSTON, JOHN HUSTON, MARY ANN HUSTON, SAMUEL HUSTON, SUSANNA IFORD, DAVID JOHN, ROBERT JOHNSON, JOSEPH KEMP, JOHN KEY, RACHEL KEY, DANIEL LECHLIDER, GEORGE LECHLIDER, JACOB LEHMAN, DOMINICK McGRATH, JEREMIAH MILLS, MATHEW MINTON, JACOB MULFORD, GEORGE NEWCOM, JOHN NEWCOM, JAMES NOLAN, FRANCIS PATTERSON, GEORGE PATTERSON, NICHOLAS PLOTTER, JOHN RICE, JAMES RIDDLE, JOHN ROBY, JACOB RODEHAMEL, THOMAS RUE, LAWRENCE SCHELL, RHINEHART SNEPP, JAMES STACKHOUSE, EVAN STEPHENS, ANDREW STUART, PETER SUMAN, JACOB SWEADNOR, JEREMIAH WILSON, JOHN WOLF. Total $553.26. pp 19, 20, 21

Inv and appr of estate of JOHN BICKEL total $8271.93. "SIMON BICKEL's land valued at price given by his father"; "HENRY BICKEL's land valued at price given by father". p 21

Additional public sale list for estate of CONRAD

CASTER. Buyers: ABRAHAM BRANNON, JOHN CRIDER,
ELIZABETH CASTER, JAMES STACKHOUSE, CONRAD CASTER,
ABNER HOBBS. Total $124.69. p 21

Term of September, 1815

Case 194. Adm of estate of THOMAS JOHNSON granted to
JOHN JOHNSON. Sec: JOSEPH COLMAN, PETER COBLENTZ.
Appr: CHRISTIAN CREAGER, HENRY CREAGER, JOHN EWING.
p 23

Case 195. Adm of estate of THOMAS DAVIS granted to
SARAH DAVIS. Sec: CALEB BARRET, BENJAMIN ARCHER.
Appr: PETER SUNDERLAND, JOHN DUNCAN, DANIEL WILSON.
p 23

Case 196. Will of THOMAS JAY. Exec: WALTER D. JAY,
JAMES JAY. Witness: JOHN JAY, JOHN JAY JR. Appr:
JOHN NORTH, GEORGE SINKS, JAMES MACEY. p 23

Case 197. JACOB HOOVER, age 18 yrs, heir of DANIEL
HOOVER, dec, chose ANDREW HOOVER as guardian. p 23

Case 198. FREDERICK HOOVER, age 16, heir of DANIEL
HOOVER, dec, chose DANIEL YOUNT as guardian. Sec:
DAVID HOOVER. p 23

Case 199. EDWARD FORD, age 16, heir of STEPHEN FORD,
chose JAMES WHITFIELD as guardian. p 23

Case 200. JAMES COTTINGHAM, age 15, heir of WILLIAM
COTTINGHAM, dec, chose THOMAS COTTOM as guardian. p
23

Case 201. NATHANIEL TAYLOR, age 17, heir of WILLIAM
TAYLOR, dec, chose SALLY WILSON as guardian. p 24

Case 202.   SALLY WILSON appted guardian of RICHARD
TAYLOR, age 13, WILLIAM TAYLOR, age 12, heirs of
WILLIAM TAYLOR, and to JANE WILSON, age 2, heir of
JOSEPH WILSON. Sec: NATHANIEL LYON. p 24

Petition of adms of JONAS HATFIELD to convey land in
Sec 20, T 3, R 4E to PHILIP GUNCKEL.   Permission
granted by court. p 24

Case 203. Adm of estate of CHRISTIAN KOCK granted to
MARGARET KOCK & JOHN ZELLER. Sec: PHILIP GUNCKEL,
FREDERIC WOLF. Appr: ULRICH SAILOR, PHILIP STAVER,
JACOB RUBY. p 24

Case 104. Petition of MARTIN HOUSER, requesting adm

of CHRISTIAN NEFF to convey deed to land in Sec 15, T 2, R 6. Granted. p 24

Will of FREDERICK WOLF. Exec: FREDERIC WOLF, PHILIP WOLF. Proven by witness ADAM CONRAD. Proven at previous court term by witness ANDREW ZELLER. Appr: JOSIAH GUSHWA, GEORGE MOYER, ABRAHAM PAULUS. pp 24, 25

Case 204. POWELL JOHN, 20 yrs, BOWEN JOHN, 18 yrs, MARY JOHN, 16 yrs, SAMUEL JOHN, 14 yrs, and ANNA JOHN, 12 yrs, minor heirs of DAVID JOHN, chose ELEANOR JOHN as guardian; ELEANOR also appted as guardian to DANIEL, 10 yrs, SALLY, 8 yrs, ELEANOR, 5 yrs, minor heirs of DAVID JOHN. p 25

Case 205. Petition by adm of JOHN STRAIN to sell real estate: Dayton 1/2 lots #206, #182. Appr by OBADIAH B. CONOVER, JOHN ANDERSON, AARON BAKER. p 25

Case 206. SARAH MAST, age 12, heir of JACOB MAST, dec, chose LEONARD ELLER as guardian; ELLER also appted as guardian of REBECCA MAST, age 10, heir of JACOB MAST, dec. p 25

Case 207. JOHN WAGGONER appted guardian to SUSANNA MAST, age 8, and NANCY MAST, age 6, minor heirs of JACOB MAST, dec. p 25

Admr of ABRAHAM SHOWER request permission to convey title. 130 acres in Sec 24, T 6, R 4 sold to PETER WILL. Request granted. p 26

Case 205. Sale of JOHN STRAIN land. p 26

Case 208. JOHN RIGGANS appted guardian to CHLOE LETURNO, 5 yrs, minor heir of FRANCIS LETURNO. p 26

Admr of WILLIAM COTTINGHAM produced settlement. Cash paid to PHILIP SOWERS, ROBERT WEAD, DAVID JOHN, SAMUEL HENDERSON. Balance of $19.61 each for six heirs. p 26

Admr of GEORGE FRIBERGER produced settlement. Cash paid to SAMUEL ARCHER, JOHN MILLER, JOHN LEHMAN, JAMES WILSON, JOHN ALEXANDER, SOLOMON SHOUP, JOHN HOLDERMAN, ADAM COBLENTZ, VALENTINE WEAVER, HENRY BUTT, SUSANNAH IFORD, DAVID RIDDLE, JOHN REGANS, DANIEL TRYER, JACOB MILLER, IRA SMITH, JOSEPH COLMAN, DAVID STERKER, AARON NUTTS, PATRICK BRYSON, PETER LEHMAN, JACOB FAASNICH. Debts due from GEORGE SHOUP, PHILIP SOWERS, PETER MUSSELMAN, JOHN HOLDERMAN,

JOSEPH WILSON, VALENTINE WEAVER, ANDREW HAYES, SAMUEL SHOUP, SUSANNAH IFORD, JOHN COX, DAVID KERCHER. Balance of $2170.60 remains. pp 27, 28

Case 209. Guardians of minor heirs of HUGH ANDREW petition to sell 100 acres in Sec 15, T 2, R 8. Appr: BENJAMIN VAN CLEVE, JAMES SETTLE, JOHN AINSWORTH. p 28

Admr of DAVID JOHN produced settlement. Debts due from JAMES FINLEY, HENRY SWISHER, ABRAM HESS, JACOB STUTSMAN, ENOCH BOWEN, Dr. JOSEPH POWELL, RACHEL DAVIS, DAVID P. JOHN. Estate paid for admr's trip to Chambersburgh, PA. Balance of $155.71 remains. pp 28, 29

Inv and appr of estate of JOSEPH PEARSON. Total $115.876, by ABEL INSCO, JOSEPH PEARSON, JAMES HALL. Public sale, buyers: WILLIAM COMPTON, ABRAHAM CRESS, JOHN CRESS, GEORGE FENTERS, JOHN FOLAND, NOAH HOOVER, ABEL INSCO, THOMAS JAY, DAVID LUCAS, HANNAH PEARSON, JOSEPH PEARSON, WILLIAM PEARSON, GEORGE SINK SR, MARTIN STALEY, JOHN YOUNT. Total $111.00. pp 29, 30

Inv and appr of estate of CONRAD CASTER made 10 June, 1815. Total $45.25. Public sale, undated, total $126.40. p 30

Case 210. Adm of the estate of JAMES NOLAN granted to MARY NOLAN & JOSEPH H. CRANE. Sec: JOHN PATTERSON, WILLIAM PATTERSON. Appr: CHRISTOPHER CURTNER, JOHN MILLER, DAVID REID. p 31

Special session 9 Oct, 1815

Case 211. Will of HENRY GEPHART. Exec: PHILIP GEP-HART, DANIEL BOWSER & MICHAEL HOOBLER. Appr: ABRAHAM TROXELL, DANIEL BOWSER & MICHAEL HOOBLER. p 31

Case 212. Adm of estate of ABRAHAM HILDEBRAND granted to HENRY BOWSER. Sec: DANIEL STUTZMAN, JACOB LEHER. Appr: ADAM RUDEBAUGH, DAVID MILLER, DANIEL MILLER. p 32

Inv and appr of estate of CHRISTIAN KOOCK on 4 Oct, 1815. Sworn before SAMUEL KINNAMON, JP. Total $672.02. pp 32, 33

Special session 13 Oct, 1815

Case 213. JOHN McCOLLOM, age 14, and PATTY McCOLLOM, age 13, heirs of HUGH McCOLLOM, chose GEORGE NEWCOM as guardian. p 34

Case 214.   RACHEL McCOLLOM apptd guardian of MARIA
McCOLLOM, age 11, LUCINDA McCOLLOM, age 6 and ETHAN
McCOLLOM, age 4, heirs of HUGH McCOLLOM. p 34

Case 215.   Adm of estate of GEORGE SHIDLER granted
to MARY SHIDLER & GEORGE SHIDLER. Sec: PHILIP
MIKESELL, CHRISTIAN BROWER. Appr: ABRAHAM TROXELL,
JACOB WEAVER, JACOB MULLENDORE. p 34

Case 216.   Adm of estate of JOHN SHIDLER granted to
MARY SHIDLER & GEORGE SHIDLER. Sec: PHILIP MIKESELL,
CHRISTIAN BROWER.   Appr: ABRAHAM TROXELL, JACOB
WEAVER, JACOB MULLENDORE. p 34

Special session 18 November, 1815

Case 217.   Adm of estate of SAMUEL CROWEL granted to
ELIZABETH CROWEL & DAVID LINDSLEY. Sec: AARON
BAKER, JOSEPH PIERCE. Appr: JOHN BRADFORD, ROBERT
EDGAR, JEREMIAH MILLS. p 35

Case 218.   Adm of estate of MARTIN SHOUB granted to
MATHIAS RIGAL & JACOB SHUPERT. Sec: HENRY STETLER,
JACOB CRULL.   Appr: JOSIAH GUSHWA, CHRISTOPHER
SHUPERT & GEORGE MOYER. p 35

Case 219.   JOHN SHOUB, 17 yrs, heir of MARTIN SHOUB,
dec, chose DANIEL STETLER as guardian. p 35

Case 220.   BARBARA SHOUB, age 15, heir of MARTIN
SHOUB, dec, chose WILLIAM STETLER as guardian. p 35

Case 221.   MARTIN SHUEY appted guardian of MARTIN,
age 12, HENRY, age 13, & LYDIA (no age given), heirs
of MARTIN SHOUB, dec. p 35

Case 222.   DANIEL STETLER appted guardian to CATHER-
INE, age 8, and ELIZABETH, age 6, minor heirs of
MARTIN SHOUB, dec. p 35

Case 223.   Adm of estate of ADAM KUCKLER granted to
SAMUEL KUCKLER & JACOB KUCKLER. Sec: GEORGE HENRY,
CONRAD BATES. Appr: SAMUEL DILLE, BENJAMIN WAGGONER,
VALENTINE SHERER. p 36 (See Case 228)

Filed 6 Dec, 1815. Inv and appr of estate of JOHN
GRIPE on 16 Sept, 1814. Total $949.39. "Cash paid
the same JOHN GRIPE in his lifetime as part of the
portion to SAMUEL ULRICH & wife." List of property
kept by widow. Public sale, buyers: JACOB GRIPE,

JOHN GRIPE, JOSEPH GRIPE, JOSIAH GRIPE, GEORGE
KINSEY, GEORGE KUNS, CHRISTIAN SHIVELY, DAVID
SHIVELY, ISAAC ULERY, JOSEPH ULERY, SAMUEL ULERY.
Total $378. pp 36, 37, 38, 39

Inv and appr of estate of THOMAS JOHNSON of Washing-
ton Twp, total $408.23, signed JOHN JOHNSON, adm.
Note due estate by THOMAS JOHNSON JR. List of prop-
erty kept by widow. Public sale on 16 Oct, 1815;
buyers: DAVID ALSPAF, PETER BANTA, DAVID BOWAR, SOLO-
MON BOWAR, DAVID BROWN, GARRAT CLOSSON, JOHN COLE,
JOSEPH COLEMAN, ABRAHAM COVAULT, WILLIAM DODDS, FRAN-
CIS DILCE, WILLIAM DILCE, ROBERT GRAHAM, JOHN HALL,
WILLIAM HILE, JEROM HOLT, JOHN HUSTON, JOHN JOHNSON,
ROBERT JOHNSON, ARON NUTT, ROBERT RIDDLE, BENJAMIN
SCOTT, JOHN SHROYER, CHARLES SMITH, ISRAEL TAYLOR,
JOHN TAYLOR, WILLIAM THARP, REUBEN WAGGONER, DAVID
WORMAN, GEORGE YOUNG. Total $311.39. pp 39, 40, 41,
42, 43

Inv and appr of estate of HENRY GEPHART, held 14 Oct,
1815. Total $3148.61. p 44

Inv and appr of estate of ABRAHAM HILDERBRAND on 14
Nov, 1815. Total $174.55. List of property kept by
widow. Public sale, buyers: JACOB BOWMAN, HENRY
BOWSER, PHILIP BOWSER, GEORGE CONNER, JACOB HOKE,
MARY HILDERBRAND, MATHIAS HUNTSINGER, GEORGE KUNTZ,
PHILIP MIKESELL, DANIEL MILLER, DAVID MILLER, PETER
RODABAUGH, DAVID SNIDER, DANIEL STUTSMAN, ARON
VANCOYK, JACOB WESINGER, ELIJAH WOOD. Total $194.85.
pp 45, 46, 47

Term of January, 1816

Case 224. Will of HENRY WARNER. Exec: JACOB WARNER,
SAMUEL FOLKERTH. Witness: JACOB PUTERBAUGH, JOHN
WORTZ. Appr: JACOB PUTERBAUGH, DAVID MILLER, WILLIAM
HART. p 48

Case 225. HENRY SHOUP, age 14, son of MARTIN SHOUP,
dec, chose MARTIN SHUEY JR as guardian. Sec: JOHN
DENNIS. p 48

Case 226. Will of JAMES SULGROVE. Exec: CATHERINE
SULGROVE, JOHN SULGROVE. Witness: JOSEPH HARTER,
JOHN BROWER JR. Appr: JOSIAH HARTER, JOHN BROWER JR,
HENRY OLDFATHER. p 48

Case 227. Adm of estate of WILLIAM SNIDER granted to
JACOB WARNER & SAMUEL FOLKERTH. Sec: THOMAS NEWMAN,
DAVID HOOVER. Appr: DAVID MILLER, WILLIAM HART,

COMMON PLEAS (PROBATE) DOCKET BOOK C-1

JACOB PUTERBAUGH.   p 48

Case 228.   MARY COGLER, age 17, daughter of ADAM
COGLER, chose ANDREW REID as guardian.   Sec: ARON
BAKER.   p 49   (See Case 223)

Case 229.   Adm of previously unadmininstered estate
of WILLIAM NEWCOM granted to JOHN BAKER.   Sec: ARON
BAKER, JOHN DODSON.   p 49

Case 229.5.   DAVID WHETON, age about 14 yrs, minor of
JOHN WHETON, chose ROBERT PATTERSON as guardian.   p 49

Admr of JOHN GRIPE produced settlement.   Cash paid to
BARBARA RENCH, JOSIAH SHIVELY (blacksmith), PHILIP
HARTZEL (tax collector), CHRISTIAN SHIVELY (coffin).
Balance of $857.01 remained.   p 49

Case 230.   On application of JACOB ROARER: MICHAEL
MYERS & ARON MILLER were granted guardianship of JOHN
ROARER, age 7, CATHERINE age 5, JACOB JR, age 4,
MARY, age 2, minors of JACOB ROARER.   p 50

Case 231.   Admr of ADAM COOGLER granted permission to
sell land in Sec 5, T 1, R 11E.   p 50

Inv and appr of estate of ADAM COOGLER on 19 Dec,
1815, total $381.42.   Notes due estate by ISRAEL
HOLE, ROSS WALLACE.   pp 50, 50a, 50b.

no page numbered 51

Public sale of estate of ADAM COOGELER on 19 Dec,
1815.   Buyers: SHEM CARNEY,   JOSIAH CLAWSON,
JACOB COOGLER, MARGARET COOGLER, SAMUEL COOGLER,
SARAH COOGLER, WILLIAM GESEMIN, PETE GRINDLE, GEORGE
HARRY, GEORGE HAYNEY, JOHN HAYNEY, WILLIAM HUGHEY,
OWEN JONES, DANIEL KISER, ARON LAMBERT, GEORGE LOW,
EDWARD McDERMED, HENRY MERCER, JOHN MILES, MATHEW
MINTURN, CORNELIUS OGDEN, JOHN PROCTOR, JOHN
REPLOGEL, RHYNEHART REPLOGEL, THOMAS SHAW, GEORGE
SIMMERMAN, JACOB STAKER, JOHN STAKER, JOHN TENNEY,
JOHN ZETAKER.   Total $415.23.   pp 52, 53

Land belonging to JESSE MOTE appr at $12 per acre/ 60
acres.   Inv and appr of estate of JESSE MOTE by JOHN
STOTE, JOHN WAGGONER & CALEB MERDSHALL, total
$129.46.   p 54

Filed 16 Feb, 1816. Inv and appr of estate of SAMUEL
CROWEL on 23 Nov, 1815. Total $355.50.   Public sale
on 30 Dec, 1815; buyers: JOHN BRADFORD, JAMES

COMMON PLEAS (PROBATE) DOCKET BOOK C-1

BUCHANON, DAVID BURNS, ELIZABETH G. CROWEL, JOSEPHUS
GARD, JEROM HOLT, DAVID LINDSLEY, JAMES WILSON,
SAMUEL YOUNG. Total $226.70. Property kept by widow
total $110.75. Notes due estate from JONATHAN MILLER
ENOCH FAIRCHILD & DAVID LINDSLEY. pp 55, 56, 57, 58

Inv and appr of estate of JAMES SULGROVE, total
$190.25. Sworn before JP on 26 Feb, 1816. p 59

Inv and appr of estate of GEORGE SHEIDLER on 9 Nov,
1815. No total given. pp 60, 61

Inv and appr of estate of JOHN SHIDLER on 9 Nov,
1815. Total $114. p 61

Public sale of estate of GEORGE SHEIDLER. Buyers:
SAMUEL ANDREW, JOHN ARNOLD, ABRAHAM BARNET, JACOB
BILMAN, BENJAMIN BOWMAN, GEORGE BOWSER, HENRY BOWSER,
CHRISTIAN BROWER, JOHN CASPER, CONRAD COFFMAN, JACOB
CROLL, JOHN CROLL, HENRY CROW, PHILIP EMOT, ANDREW
EMRICH, JAMES FERGUSON, JOEL FOUTS, JOHN GARBER,
DANIEL GEPHART, GEORGE GEPHART, DAVID HARKER, JOHN
HARTMAN, JOHN HEETER, JACOB KEISTER, DAVID HOOVER,
ELI HOOVER, MICHAEL HUBLER, GEORGE KEISTER, JOHN
KETTNER, HENRY KLINGER, ABRAHAM LASLY, PETER LASLY,
ABRAHAM ZOOK, ENOS MILES, ADAM MILLMAN, JACOB MULLEN-
DORE, DAVID MYERS, JOHN M. MYERS, MICHAEL MYERS,
WILLIAM NICHOLAS, DANIEL OSWALT, GEORGE PUTERBAUGH,
FREDERICK PURKY, PHILIP RARIGH, HENRY RODES, JOSEPH
RYANS, DAVID SCOTT, BARBARY SHEIDLER, DANIEL SHEIDLER
MARY SHEIDLER, SOLOMON SHEIDLER, ABRAHAM SHOCK, JACOB
SHOCK, JACOB SINKS, HENRY SKINIMERMAN, ADAM SWINEHART
MICHAEL TREON, ABRAHAM TROXELL, CHRISTIAN WELDY,
FREDERICK WOOLF. No total given. pp 62,63,64, 65,66

Public sale of estate of JOHN SHEIDLER. Purchasers:
JOHN ARNOLD, GEORGE EIGENBRIGHT, GEORGE EMRICK, VAL-
ENTINE B. MIKESELL, JOHN MYERS, PETER RAKER, DANIEL
SHEIDLER, DAVID SHEIDLER, SOLOMON SHEIDLER, DAVID
SHOWERS, PETER SOUDER, ABRAHAM TROXELL. No total
given. pp 66,67

Filed 16 April, 1816. Inv and appr of estate of
HENRY GEPHART on 14 Oct, 1815. No total given.
Public sale, buyers: GEORGE AIGENBRIGHT, JACOB
BILMAN, PETER BOLABAUGH, ISAAC BOUGHMAN, DANIEL
BOWSER, GEORGE BOWSER, HENRY BOWSER, JOHN BROWER,
CONRAD COFFMAN, JOSEPH COOPER, JACOB CREAGER, JACOB
CROLL, EDWARD DOLLY, BURREL EAKERS, JACOB GARBER,
JOHN GARBER, DANIEL GEPHART, EMANUEL GEPHART, HENRY
GEPHART, GEORGE GEPHART, MAGDALENE GEPHART, PHILIP
GEPHART, JACOB HARRY, ADAM HARTSEL, JACOB HAY, DAVID

167

HEISTAND, MICHAEL HUBLER, MICHAEL KETTNER, SAMUEL KETTNER, ABRAHAM LEES, THOMAS LIBECAP, MICHAEL LYDY, GEORGE LYE, JACOB MIKESELL, PHILIP MIKESELL, ABRAHAM MILLER, ABRAHAM MOLLENDORE, JACOB MULLENDORE, ISAAC MYER, PETER MYERS, MICHAEL MYERS, JOHN NAGALY, GEORGE NANGLE, GEORGE PERSON, JAMES PETTIT, MICHAEL RAGER, PHILIP RARIGH, PHILIP REPLOGEL, ARON ROCKENFIELD, ALEXANDER SCOTT, JOHN SHAFER, DANIEL SHEIDLER, DAVID SHOCK, CHRISTOPHER SHUPERT, JACOB SHOOPERT, PETER SHEWPERT, PETER TREON, JACOB TROXELL, WILLIAM TURN-BARGER, GEORGE WARNER, JACOB WEAVER, PETER WEAVER, CHRISTIAN WELDY, PHILIP WOLF, JOHN YAZEL, total $2298.15. Notes due estate by HENRY BEAGLER, ANDREW GEPHART, JOHN WERTZ, MATTHIAS RIGAL, JOHN SCHNEP, ADAM SWINEHART, DANIEL ISELEY, WILLIAM BROMBAUGH, JACOB GEPHART, MICHAEL KETTNER, ABRAHAM ZOOK, PETER BOLLABAUGH. pp 68, 69, 70, 71, 72, 73, 74, 75, 76

Filed 18 April, 1816. Inv and appr of estate of THOMAS JAY. No total or date given. Sworn before HENRY HOOVER, JP, 28 Sept, 1815. Notes due from MICHAEL BRICKER, THOMAS BROWN, JACOB BYRKIT, LEONARD FINCHER, JESSE FRIEND, DAVID HOOVER, MARYDA HUTCHIN, JAMES INSCO, JAMES JAY, JOHN JAY, JON JONES, STEPHEN JONES, THOMAS JONES, THOMAS MACY, ISAAC R. MARSH, JOHN McMULLEN, SOLOMON MIKEL, JACOB MILLER, JOHN MOTE, THOMAS NEWMAN, WILLIAM NORTH, WILLIAM PERSON, POWEL PERSON, JAMES PERSON, PHILIP RODES, DAVID SHEARER, ANDREW SINKS, ELIJAH SPENCER, ANDREW WAYMIRE, JOSEPH WILLIAMS, JACOB YOUNT. No total given. Accounts due estate, written by execrs on 7 April, 1816: MARY HOOVER, FRANCIS MILLION, JAMES PERSON, RICHARD ROBBINS, JOHN NORTH, ANDREW HOOVER, ADAM ELLER, GEORGE NOLE, WILLIAM NORTH, JOHN WERTZ, LEONARD ELLER, JAMES INSCO, FRANCIS NORTH, JAMES EMBREE, JOHN JEFFRIES, TALBOT IDDINGS, THOMAS WALKER. pp 76,77, 78,79, 80

Filed 20 April, 1816. Inv and appr of estate of MARTIN SHOUP on 2 Dec, 1815. Included 6 year lease on land with BENJAMIN BARKALOW. No total given. pp 81, 82

Term of April, 1816

Case 232. Will of JAMES SCOTT. Exec: THOMAS SCOTT, WILLIAM KELLEY. Witness: DAVID WATKINS, WILLIAM MAJORS. Appr: OWEN HATFIELD, DAVID WATKINS, EDWARD MITCHEL. p 83

Case 233. Adm of estate of DAVID COMPTON granted to JOHN H. SCHENCK. (widow relinquished right.) Sec:

JOSEPH VANNOTE, DANIEL STETLER. Appr: JONATHAN
ROBBINS, JOHN DENISE, SIDNEY DENISE. p 83

Case 234. Adm of estate of JACOB MILLER granted to
ARON MILLER. (widow relinquished right.) Sec:
DANIEL MILLER, DAVID MILLER. Appr: ISAAC SHIVELY,
SAMUEL NOFFZINGER, JOHN RITTER. p 83

Case 235. Adm of estate of MARTIN SHEETZ granted to
DAVID SHEETZ. (widow relinquished right.) Sec:
DAVID HOOVER, DANIEL YOUNT. Appr: GEORGE FINTRESS,
DANIEL RAZOR, JAMES EWING. pp 83, 84

Case 236. JOSEPH FOUTS & JENNY FOUTS granted guardianship of JAMES SMITH, age 9, and SARAH SMITH, age
6, minor heirs of PETER SMITH. p 84

Case 237. SAMUEL CARVER, 16 yrs, minor heir of JOHN
CARVER, dec, chose JOHN RITTER as guardian. Sec:
DAVID MILLER. p 84

Case 238. JOHN WILSON, 16 yrs, minor heir of JOSEPH
WILSON, dec, chose JOSEPH PEIRCE as guardian. p 84

Admr of GILBERT BOWMAN produced settlement. Cash
paid to ISAAC WOODWARD, OWEN HATFIELD. Balance of
$43.36 remains. p 84

Case 181. Execrs of GEORGE GEPHART produced settlement. "written in Dutch... not well understood by
Court" Appeared to be 7 heirs plus widow. Her share
= $436.87; each child's share = $228.29. p 85

Case 137. Petition of admr of DAVID SQUIER to sell
land; personal estate insufficient to settle debts.
Appr: ANDREW HOOD, SAMUEL WILLIAMS, GARRET RITTEN-
HOUSE. p 85

Filed 8 June, 1816. Inv and appr of estate of JAMES
SCOTT. Included 2 notes due from THOMAS SCOTT. No
total given. pp 85, 86

Filed 5 July, 1816. Inv and appr of estate of DAVID
COMPTON of German Twp made 11 June, 1816. Total
$239.91. Appr: JOHN DENISE, SIDNEY DENISE. p 87

Filed 20 July, 1816. Inv and appr of estate of
MARTIN SHEETZ on 3 May, 1816. Public sale held 24
May, 1816; buyers: DAVID BIRKET, DANIEL BOMGARDNER,
MICHAEL BRICKER, THOMAS CLARK, JOHN COFFY, JOSEPH
CONNER, JOSHUA COX, JACOB CURTIS, DANIEL DEETER, AMOS
EDWARDS, GEORGE FETTERS, HENRY HART, WILLIAM HART,

DAVID HOOVER, NOAH HOOVER, TALBERT IDDINGS, ABEL INSCO, ISAAC R. MARSH, DAVID MAST, JOHN MAST, JOHN MULLON, THOMAS NEWMAN, GEORGE NOCK, JAMES NORTH, FREDERICK SHANK, DAVID SHEETS, JACOB SHEETS, JOHN SHEETS, MARTIN SHEETS, ANDREW SINKS, ELIJAH SPENCER, ANDREW TREASE, CHRIELLY YOUNG, CHRISTIAN YOUNG. Total $197.48. pp 88, 89, 90, 91

Filed 27 July, 1816. Inv and appr of estate of JACOB MILLER on 24 May, 1816, included property kept by widow; no total given. Notes due by JOHN FEES, JOHN HART, ARON MILLER, DAVID MILLER, JOHN (illeg), MARTIN HOOVER, BENJAMIN HARTMAN, JOHN RITTER, JOHN MILLER. Public sale, buyers: ZACARIAH ALBAUGH, MICHAEL EMRY, DAVID FEES, JOHN FEES, WILLIAM FRAIM, SAMUEL GRIPE, JOSHUA HARDMAN, GEORGE HUFFMAN, DANIEL KAYLOR, DAVID KAYLOR, JACOB KAYLOR, PETER KAYLOR, ULRICH KESSLER, ABRAHAM KINSEY, JOHN KINSEY, PHILIP MIKESELL, DANIEL MILLER, ARON MILLER, DAVID MILLER, JOHN MILLER, TOBIAS MILLER, PROSPER NICHOLAS, SAMUEL NOFFSINGER, JOHN RITTER, DANIEL SHIVELY, ISAAC SHIVELY, JOHN SNELE, RICHARD THRALL, GEORGE WARNER Total $212.13. p 92, 93, 94, 95, 96

Admr of GEORGE GEPHART produced settlement. Widow's third = $291.99. Children's part = $584, divided by 7 for $83.42 each. Land value to be added. p 96

Inv and appr of estate of GEORGE STETLER. No total given. Original written in German by apprs. p 97

Term of August, 1816

Case 239. Will of BENJAMIN RICHARDS. Exec: MASSY RICHARDS & BENJAMIN RICHARDS. Witness: CHARLES HARDY, FREDERICK FOX. Appr: NICHOLAS HORNER, JAMES PETTICREW, WILLIAM BROWN. p 98

Case 240. Adm of estate of JACOB YAZEL granted to JOHN YAZEL. Sec: PETER BANTA, GEORGE PARSONS. Appr: JACOB BAUM, TOBIAS WHITESEL, ISAAC MYERS. p 98

Case 241. BETSEY GEPHART, 16 yrs, & JOHN GEPHART, 15 yrs, minor heirs of PETER GEPHART dec, chose PETER BANTA as guardian. Sec: GEORGE PARSONS, JAMES CHATHAM. p 98

Case 242. MARGARET KOCK, age 15, & BETSEY KOCK, age 13, heirs of CHRISTIAN KOCK, chose FREDERICK STAVER as guardian. Sec: ULRICH SAILOR. p 98

Case 243. HENRY KOCK, 14 yrs, heir of CHRISTIAN

KOCK, chose ULRICH SAILOR as guardian. p 98

Case 244.   CASPER STAVER appted guardian of POLLY
KOCK, 10 yrs, & FREDERICK KOCK, 8 yrs, heirs of
CHRISTIAN KOCK. Sec: LEWIS SHUEY. p 99

Case 245.   PHILIP GUNCKEL appted guardian of SALLY
KOCK, age 6, CHRISTIAN KOCK, age 4, & MICHAEL KOCK,
age 2, minor heirs of CHRISTIAN KOCK. p 99

Case 246.   SAMUEL HEARN appted guardian to ISABELLA
DODDS, age 8, & WILLIAM DODDS, age 5, minor heirs of
JOSEPH DODDS JR. Sec: CHRISTIAN CREAGER. p 99

Admr of GILBERT BOWMAN showed money received after
settlement. p 99

Case 247. Adm of estate of GEORGE PHILLIPS granted to
ELIZABETH PHILLIPS & JACOB HARSHBARGER. Sec: HENRY
HARSHBARGER, RALPH WILSON. Appr: HENRY SWISHER,
HENRY BOWSER, HENRY CRULL. p 99

Petition of TAMER JAY, widow of THOMAS JAY, to make
election and claim dower per state laws in preference
to allowance by will. p 99

Case 248.   Admr of DAVID SQUIER petitioned to sell
land. Permission granted. p 99

Case 249.   Admr of HUGH McCOLLOM petitioned to sell
land. Permission granted. p 100

Admr of HENRY MOYER produced settlement. After cash
recvd from THOMAS KORRS, JACOB KLEIN, total estate
$8572.68. Cash paid to DAVID MYERS, JACOB MILLER,
JOHN BROWN, JOHN HUNSINGER, CHRISTIAN SHEIDLER, total
$3980.47 pp 100, 101

HUGH McCOLLOM's land, Dayton lot 109, appraised value
of $1200 on 28 Aug, 1816. p 101

DAVID SQUIER's land, Dayton lot 17 apprsed @ $433 &
lot 6 @ $75, both unimproved. p 102

Case 178. Inv and appr of estate of FREDERICK WOLF of
German Twp on 18 Nov, 1815. 120 acres valued at $4.50
per acre. Sworn before HENRY DUCKWALL, JP, 18 Nov,
1815. p 102

Filed 8 Oct, 1816. Inv and appr of estate of GEORGE
PHILLIPS on 17 Sept, 1816. Total of $44.85, appr by
HENRY BOWSER & HENRY KRULL. p 103

COMMON PLEAS (PROBATE) DOCKET BOOK C-1

Special session 12 Oct, 1816.

Will of JONATHAN POWEL. Exec: CONRAD ROBERTS who
relinquished right. Widow BARBARA POWEL & ARON BAKER
granted exec. Witness: JOHN FOLKERTH, WILLIAM HUFF-
MAN. Sec: JOHN DODSON, MOSES SIMPSON. Appr: WILLI-
AM HUFFMAN, JOHN PATTERSON, SAMUEL WATTON. p 104

Admr of ABRAHAM HILDEBRAND presented evidence of
insolvent estate. p 104

Special session 13 November, 1816

Case 251. Will of JOHN CRAIG. Exec: ELIZABETH
TERRY, late widow ELIZABETH CRAIG. Witness: HENRY
ATCHISON who testified to doubt that testator was in
right mind at time of making will. Court ruled will
should not be recorded. Adm granted to ENOS TERRY &
wife ELIZABETH. Sec: DANIEL RICHARDSON, JAMES
THOMSON. Appr: PETER BANTA, FREDERICK NUTTZ, JACOB
KERCHER. p 105

Case 252. Adm of estate of PETER WINELAND granted to
PETER DIETRICK (widow relinquished right). Sec:
ADAM RODEBAUGH, DAVID MILLER. Appr: JACOB BOWMAN,
HENRY SWISHER, JAMES BRIER. p 105

Inv and appr of estate of JACOB YEAZEL total $332.11.
Public sale on 14 Dec, 1816; buyers PETER BANTA,
JACOB BAUM, ANDREW BROCK, JAMES CRAIG, HENRY EAGLE,
DANIEL GEPHART, JOHN KELGNER, JOHN KERCHER, JOHN
KERTNER, JOHN LAROSE, GEORGE NUTTZ, ALEXANDER SCOTT,
DAVID SCOTT, PETER SHAFER, DANIEL SHEARER, DANIEL
SMALL, JOHN SMITH, CHRISTIAN WELDY, HENRY WHITESEL,
BETSEY YEAZEL, JOHN YEAZEL. Total $233.50. pp 106,
107

Inv and appr of estate of JONATHON POWELL of Dayton
Twp total $167.00. Public sale held on 23 Oct, 1816;
buyers: AARON BAKER, WILLIAM CLARK, WILLIAM COX,
GEORGE C. DAVIS, LEWIS DAVIS, JOHN DODSON, CHARLES
ESTE, MOSES FOSTER, F. GOSNEY, GEORGE GROVE, AARON
HENDRICKS, GEORGE KIRKENDALL, JACOB KIRKENDALL, JACOB
LEHMAN, JOHN LEHMAN, BENJAMIN LLOYD, HENRY MARQUART,
JOSHUA McINTOSH, C. OBLINGER, BARBARA POWELL, AARON
RICHARDSON, SAMUEL ROADS, CONRAD ROBERTS, SAMUEL
ROBERTS, AARON SIMPSON, ALEXANDER SIMPSON, JOHN
SNIDER, SIMON STONESEIFER, DAVID SWANK, BENJAMIN VAN
CLEVE, total $183.89. (Chattels included lasts,
awls, skins, probably a cobbler.) $13 in property
kept by widow BARBARA POWELL. Debts due from DAVID
BEAN, MARY DAVIS, JOHN DAVIS, NANCY DIFFENDAPHER,

JOSEPH DODDS, JOHN DODSON, CHARLES ESTE, Dr. JOHN
FAULK, NIMROD HADDIX, SAMUEL HADDIX, GEORGE KIRKEN-
DALL, DAVID LEHMAN, HENRY MARQUART, HENRY RIDGELY,
JOSEPH RODEFFER, WILLIAM M. SMITH, JACOB SWADENER,
ROBERT TANNER, JAMES THOMSON, JOSEPH WOODWARD. Total
$105.92. pp 107, 108 109, 110, 111, 112

Admr of GILBERT BOWMAN presented recpt for $40, rcvd
14 Sept, 1816, for 6 month tour of duty with U. S.
military served by BOWMAN. p 112

Inv and appr of estate of WILLIAM SNIDER on 16 Jan,
1816 by apprs WILLIAM HART, DAVID MILLER, JACOB
PUTERBAUGH. No total given. pp 112, 113, 114.

Term of December, 1816

Case 253. JOHN HUSTON appted guardian of MARY
BAXTER, age 11, PEGGY BAXTER, age 8, ANNA BAXTER, age
5, & DANIEL BAXTER, age 3, minor heirs of DANIEL
BAXTER, dec. Sec: HORATIO G. PHILLIPS. p 115

Case 168. Exec of JOSEPH WILSON petitioned to convey
deed to 130 acres in Sec 14, T 2, R 7, to JAMES
McFADDON & ELIZABETH MONTGOMERY. DAVID HUSTON
empowered to convey. p 115

Case 254. GEORGE FOGELSONG, 15 yrs, & JACOB FOGEL-
SONG, 14 yrs, minor heirs of CHRISTIAN FOGELSONG,
dec, chose JOHN HIZER as guardian. HIZER also appted
guardian of CHRISTIAN FOGELSONG, 13 yrs, minor heir
as above. p 115

Case 255. Will of ARCHIBALD WISELY produced by NEIL
McNEIL. Witness: JOHN COLE, SAMUEL COLE, JEREMIAH
ALLEN. p 115

Case 256. DAVID JOHNSON, 16 yrs, & POLLY JOHNSON, 14
yrs, minor heirs of DAVID JOHNSON dec, chose JOHN
JOHNSON as guardian. Sec: JESSE JOHNSON, HENRY
MARQUART. p 115

Case 257. ISAAC MIDDLETON, 14 yr old orphan, chose
AARON NUTT JR as guardian. p 116

Case 258. Will of PHILIP MILLER. Exec: JOHN
ZIDECKER (widow relinquished right). Witness: JOHN
FOLKERTH, JAMES STEELE. Sec: JACOB REPLOGEL, JOSEPH
KELLER. Appr: LEWIS BRENNER, JOHN BUCHER, VALENTINE
SHERER. p 116

Case 259. Will of GEORGE HANEY. Exec: JACOB CRULL

(widow relinquished right). Witness: OWEN JONES, ELEAZER GRIFFITH, SAMUEL ARCHER. Sec: SAMUEL KUGLER, JOHN HANEY. Appr: MARTIN HOUSER, JAMES GRIMES, SAMUEL McFADDON. p 116

Case 260. Adm of estate of PETER LEHMAN granted to WILLIAM WAUGH. Sec: JAMES THOMSON, ELEAZER GRIFFITH. Appr: ROBERT JOHNSON, JAMES McGREW, DAVID LAMME. p116

Case 261. RUSSEL RICE, 18 yrs, chose JOHN LEHMAN as guardian. p 116

Case 255. Adm of estate of ARCHIBALD WISELY granted to NEIL McNEIL. Sec: JOHN DUNCAN, JOHN FARNHAM. Appr: PATRICK BRYSON, BENJAMIN LUCE, TITUS H. IVES. p 116

JACOB & SAMUEL KUGLER, admrs, petition to convey land of ADAM KUGLER, dec. Permission granted. p 117

Admr of JOHN B. MIKESELL produced settlement. Rcpts included payt to ABRAHAM TROXEL, Dr. DUBOIS. Balance of $19.54 remained. p 117

Filed 28 Jan, 1817. Inv and appr of estate of PETER WINELAND total $262.12. Debts owed by JAMES BANKER, PHILIP BOWSER, DANIEL BRUMBAUGH, JOSEPH HOLLINGSWORTH HENRY BOUEN, JACOB PITTSENBERGER, HENRY SWISHER total $43.55. Public sale, buyers: JOHN ARRITON, JACOB BOWMAN, PHILIP BOWSER, DANIEL BROMBAUGH, HENRY BURN, JOSEPH CONNOR, LUKE CONNOR, JONATHAN COX, SOLOMON DANNER, PETER DIETRICK, ENOCH FARMER, GEORGE FETTER, JOHN FOLK, JAMES GORDON, ARCHIBALD GRAHAM, JOHN GREER, JOSHUA GREER, JACOB GRIPE, JOHN HELMICK, DANIEL JACOBS, THOMAS KING, HENRY KRULL, JAMES KYLE, ABRAHAM LASLEY, SAMUEL McCORMICK, DAVID MILLER, JACOB MILLER, JOHN MILLER, DANIEL OX, GEORGE PLAYSINGER, ELIAS RATLIFF, WILLIAM RITTENHOUSE, ADAM RODEBAUGH, DAVID RODEBAUGH, GEORGE SANDS, JOHN SMITH, ANN STUDE-BAKER, DANIEL STUDEBAKER, JACOB STUDEBAKER, PHILIP STUDEBAKER, VALENTINE WHITEHEAD, ELIZABETH WILAND, JOHN WILAND. Total $314.17. pp 117, 118, 119, 120

Special Session 1 Feb, 1817

Case 262. Adm of estate of CHARLES ESTE granted to MARY D. ESTE & WARREN MUNGER. Sec: GEORGE GROVE, JOSEPH BROWN. Appr: Dr. JOHN STEELE, JAMES STEELE, MATTHEW PATTON. p 120

Case 263. Adm of estate of JOHN B. RITTENHOUSE granted to RACHEL RITTENHOUSE & ELISHA BRABHAM. Sec:

COMMON PLEAS (PROBATE) DOCKET BOOK C-1

DAVID DUNCAN, DAVID GRIFFIN.   Appr: HENRY BROWN,
GEORGE W. SMITH, DAVID REID.   pp 120

Inv and appr of estate of JOHN CRAIG on 15 Nov, 1816,
total $326.12.   Public sale, buyers: VINCENT ANTONI-
DES, JOHN BERLOT, JOHN CARINGER, WILLIAM CONOVER,
ELIZABETH CRAIG, JAMES CRAIG, NANCY CRAIG, SEYMOUR
CRAIG, JACOB GAVER, DANIEL GEPHART, JOHN KERCHER,
ARCHIBALD McGREW, HENRY SHEWEY, TIMOTHY SQUIER,
CHRISTOPHER VISE, CHRISTIAN WELDY, GEORGE WIMER,
JACOB WOLF, CALEB WORLEY, DAVID YEAZEL.   Total
$293.12. List of property kept by widow total
$46.50. pp 120, 121, 122

Inv and appr of estate of PHILIP MILLER total of
$112. p 123

Special session 7 Feb, 1817

Case 264.   Adm of estate of JOHN GEPHART granted to
GEORGE GEPHART (widow relinquished right).   Sec:
HENRY GEPHART, DANIEL GEPHART. Appr: ABRAHAM TROXEL,
JACOB WEAVER, JOHN SCHNEP. p 123

Special session 3 March, 1817

Case 265.   Adm of estate of ANDREW EMRICK granted to
BETSEY EMRICK & GEORGE EMRICK. Sec: MICHAEL EMRICK,
PETER EMRICK.   Appr: CHRISTOPHER EMRICK, GEORGE
STUMP, JOHN RISINGER. p 124

Case 262.   Inv and appr of estate of Dr. CHARLES
ESTE on 7 Feb, 1817.   "After allowing widow her
year's maintenance", total was $378.37. (Majority of
estate was medical supplies.) pp 124, 125

Case 264. Inv and appr of estate of JOHN GEBHARD of
Jefferson Twp on 15 Feb, 1817, total $78.00.   Debt
due estate: portion of estate of his father, HENRY
GEPHART. Public sale on 1 March, 1817; purchasers:
DANIEL GEPHART, JACOB LICHTY, MICHAEL LICHTY, total
$42.26. Widow allowed $150.50 in property for maintenance. Sworn before JOHN M. SINGER, JP, on 15 Feb,
1817. p 126

Inv and appr of estate of JOHN RITTENHOUSE on 17 Feb,
1817. After setting off widow's provision", total of
$182.05. Accts due from JOHN FREEMAN, JOHN THOMPSON,
EKANA GUSTIN, JONATHAN MAYHALL, JOSEPH RYAN, ALEXAN-
DER BROWN, PETER WEAVER. Total $174.90. p 127

Case 260.   Inv and appr of estate of PETER LEHMAN on

30 Jan, 1817. Total $126.37. Appr: ROBERT JOHNSON, JAMES McGREW, DAVID LAMME. p 128 (See Case 260)

Inv and appr of estate of BENJAMIN RICHARDSON of Washington Twp on 7 Sept, 1816. Total of $22.50. Appr: JAMES PETTICREW, WILLIAM BROWN, NICHOLAS HORNER. p 128

Filed 11 April, 1817. Inv and appr of estate of ARCHIBALD WISELY. Total $17.50. p 128

Inv and appr of estate of GEORGE HANEY of Wayne Twp. Total $497.25. Sworn before JAMES MILLER, JP, on 24 Jan, 1817. Public sale, buyers: SAMUEL BARNARD, WILLIAM BERRYMAN, JOHN BODLEY, JOHN BUCHER, JOSEPH CAMP, JOSIAH CLAWSON, HENRY ENOCH, ELEAZER GRIFFITH, JAMES GRIMES, JOHN HANEY, ABRAHAM HARRY, JOHN HARRY, JOHN JOHNSON, OWEN JONES, JOSEPH KELLER, JACOB KOOGLER, SAMUEL KOOGLER, WILLIAM MASON, EDWARD MESSER, ROBERT MILLER, CORNELIUS OGDEN, DAVID PUTERBAUGH, GEORGE PUTERBAUGH, JOHN REEL, JACOB REPLOGEL, ABRAHAM RITCHARDSON, ROBERT SHARER, THOMAS SHAW, ELIJAH SLIDER, JOHN SLOAN, PETER SLUSSER, THOMAS SNODGRASS, JOHN STOKES, PHILIP SWAGERT, JOHN TULLIS, WILLIAM VAN CLEVE, ALEXANDER WEAD, JOHN WOLF, JACOB WORMAN. Total $266.65. pp 129, 130, 131

Term of May, 1817

Case 266. JAMES CRAIG, 17 yrs, minor heir of JOHN CRAIG, dec, chose SEYMOUR CRAIG as guardian. Sec: EMANUEL GEPHART. p 132

Case 267. NANCY CRAIG, 17 yrs, & JEREMIAH CRAIG, 15 yrs, minor heirs of JOHN CRAIG, dec, chose SEYMOUR CRAIG as guardian. Sec: EMANUEL GEPHART. p 132

Case 268. ENOS TERRY apptd guardian of ALEXANDER CRAIG, 12 yrs, DAVID CRAIG, 12 yrs, & PHEBE CRAIG, 10 yrs, minor heirs of JOHN CRAIG, dec. Sec: GEORGE PARSONS. p 132

Case 269. STEPHEN JONES, 15 yrs, minor heir of MOSES JONES, chose JOHN HUSTON as guardian. Sec: EBENEZER WEAD. p 132

Case 270. NATHANIEL BLOOMFIELD appted guardian to ALEXANDER WILSON (no age given), minor heir of JOSEPH WILSON, dec. Sec: OBADIAH B. CONOVER, JAMES WINGET. p 132

Case 271. DANIEL GEPHART, 16 yrs, minor heir of JOHN

GEPHART, dec, chose HENRY GEPHART as guardian. Sec:
GEORGE GEPHART. p 132

Case 272. Adm of estate of ABRAHAM TEAGARDEN granted
to REBECKAH TEAGARDEN. Sec: JOHN D. CAMPBELL,
HENRY ENOCH. Appr: MARTIN HOUSER, BENJAMIN WAGNER,
JAMES AIGHER. p 132

Case 273. Will of MARTIN HOOVER. Exec: AARON MILLER
(co-exec ABRAHAM TROXEL relinquished right). Witness:
JOHN KEPLER, JOHN CRULL, WILLIAM NICHOLAS. Appr:
JACOB CRULL, JACOB ROHRER, PETER KREITZER. pp 132,133

Case 274. Will of ANTHONY LOGAN. Exec: JANE LOGAN,
ALEXANDER LOGAN (co-exec WILLIAM KING relinquished
right). Witness: RALPH EWING, WILLIAM IRWIN. Appr:
JOHN TAYLOR, JOSEPH EWING, JOHN DUNCAN. p 133

Case 275. Will of JOHN TUCKER. Exec: widow MARGARET
TUCKER. Witness: DAVID JOHNS, GEORGE SHRIVER.
Appr: GEORGE SHRIVER, ADAM COBLENTZ. p 133

Case 276. MOSES CARR, 16 yrs, minor heir of JOHN
CARR, dec, chose HENRY CLARK as guardian. p 133

Case 277. JACOB HERSHBERGER appted guardian of
ELIZABETH PHILLIPS, age 6, & WILLIAM PHILLIPS, age 7,
minor heirs of GEORGE PHILLIPS, dec. Sec: ROBERT
McLEARY. p 133

Case 278. Admr of estate of JOHN B. RITTENHOUSE
petitioned to sell real estate. Appr GEORGE W.
SMITH, LUTHER BRUEN, WILLIAM VAN CLEVE apptd to set
value. p 133

Case 279. JACOB YOUNT, age 17, minor heir of JACOB
YOUNT, dec, chose FREDERICK NUTTZ as guardian. Sec:
JAMES PETTICREW. p 133

Case 280. Admr of CONRAD CASTER petition to sell 110
acres in Sec 1 & 2, T 2, R 6. JAMES LOWRY, WILLIAM
E. LOWRY & GEORGE SHOUP to set value. pp 133, 134

Case 281. Petition of WILLIAM & MARTHA THOMPSON for
partition of land of JOHN CRAIG. Writ of partition
granted. JACOB KERCHER. EMANUEL GEPHART & FREDERICK
NUTTZ appted to divide land. p 134

Special session 30 May, 1817

Admr of WILLIAM SCHENCK made settlement. Cash rcvd
from EDEN BURROWS, JOSEPH DOWNS, JOHN ROSSMAN,

DANIEL SCHENCK, BARNS SHUPARD, E. SHUPARD; land
sold to GEORGE NUTTS. Cash paid to widow, ISAIAH
ANDERSON, WILLIAM BOMBERGER, SAMUEL CALDWELL, JAMES
CLARK, THOMAS CONOVER, WILLIAM CONOVER, WILLIAM
CONOVER JR, WILLIAM COX, JOSEPH CRAIN, JOHN C.
DEARTH, SYDNEY DENISE, BENJAMIN DUBOIS, DANIEL DUBOIS
MARTIN EARHART, NICHOLAS HORNER, JOHN KING, DAVID
LABAN, JAMES LODGE, THOMAS MAXWELL, JOHN ROSSMAN,
JAMES RUSSEL, JOHN H. SCHENCK, JOHN N. C. SCHENCK,
BARNS SHUPARD, JACOB SHUPARD, ADDISON SMITH, DANIEL
STOVER, JOSEPH TAPSCOTT, WILLIAM TAPSCOTT, THOMAS
THOMSON, BENJAMIN VAN CLEVE, ARTHUR VANDERVEER, JOHN
WOODS, MARY McDONALD YOUNG. Total $800. 21. Common
Pleas court, term of August, 1816: Heirs of WILLIAM
SCHENCK vs DANIEL SCHENCK. Dfnt to pay $395 + int
and additional $312 for disputed 39 acres. Judgement
unpaid. pp 134, 135

Admr of ABRAHAM HILDERBRAND produced settlement.
Entry x'd out. p 135

Admr of JOHN HIMES produced settlement. Balance of
$340.93 remains; widow kept $285.25 of property. Cash
paid to EPHRAIM ARNOLD, THOMAS BRADLEY, DAVID G.
BURNET, PETER CLAWSON, JOHN COMPTON, CHRISTIAN
CREAGER, HENRY CREAGER, HENRY DICKENSHEETS, FRANCIS
DILTS, HUGH DININ, JOHN EWING, FIELDING GOSNEY,
GEORGE GROVE, LEVIN HATFIELD, OWEN HATFIELD, JACOB
HUFFARD, LEWIS KEMP, JOHN KING, HENRY MARQUART, JOHN
McCLURE, JAMES NOLAN, AARON NUTT SR, JOHN PRICE,
GEORGE SOURBRAY, JOHN STRAUSBURGER, JAMES STEELE,
JACOB SWEADNER, JOHN TREON, JOHN TROYER, WILLIAM VAN
CLEVE, JAMES WEBB. pp 135, 136

Admr of ABRAHAM HILDERBRAND made final settlement.
Creditors paid: JOHN A. MIKESELL, AMOS THORNBRIGHT &
HILDERBRAND's note to E. WOOD, JACOB WEAVER, WILLIAM
BROWNE, CHRISTOPHER SHUPERT, MICHAEL LYDY, JOHN GEP-
HART, admr of -- VANOSDALL, PETER BECHER, JACOB STOV-
ER, GEORGE CONNOR, MATHIAS RIGAL, ABRAHAM TROXEL,
GEORGE SHIDELER, HENRY SWISHER, ISAAC SHIVELY,
CHRISTIAN MILLER, HENRY LEEDES. pp 137, 138

Admr of HENRY MOYER presented recpts from DANIEL
BOWSER & JOHN MOYER. p 138

JOHN BROWER & MARY WESTFALL, admrs of HENRY WEAVER,
produced settlement with $489.99 balance. Cash paid
to Dr. DUBOIS, JOHN ELSROTH, WILLIAM VAN CLEVE,
RHINEHART SNEP, SAMUEL ARCHER, JOSEPH GILLESPIE
(clerk at sale), PHILIP MIKESELL (auctioneer), HENRY
WATSON. Widow kept $33.25 of property. p 138, 139

Admr of HENRY NEFF produced settlement. Cash paid
to JOHN KING (land taxes), JOHN REED, JOHN W.
CAMPBELL, JOHN HOUSER, IRA SMITH, BENJAMIN KISER,
JOSEPH KENNEDY, WILLIAM KENNEDY, B. COX SR, BENJAMIN
COX JR, JOHN KERR, -- MAYHALL, JOHN WILLIAMS, G.
SHOUP, JOHN REGANS. Total $159.75. p 139

Apprs report land of JOHN B. RITTENHOUSE, Dayton
outlot 9, valued at $1200. p 140

Public sale of estate of PETER LEHMAN; purchasers:
SOLOMON BOWEN, PETER CLAWSON, GARRET CLAWSON, FRANCIS
DILTS, JOHN HUSTON, JOHN LEHMAN, JAMES McGREW, JOSEPH
MILLER, WILLIAM WAUGH. Total $117.91. p 140

Inv and appr of estate of ANDREW EMRICK included debt
owed by JOSEPH BANKER, accounts left in Columbiana
County; total $737.25. Public sale undated, buyers:
JAMES BROWN, CHARLES BUXTON, PETER CATROW, ANDREW
COX, WALTER COX, BENJAMIN EAKINS, CHRISTOPHER EMRICK
JR, GEORGE EMRICK, JACOB EMRICK, JOHN EMRICK, PETER
EMRICK, JOHN GOOD, JOHN GUNCKEL, PHILIP GUNCKEL,
Widow HENDERSON, GEORGE HORNER, JOSEPH HEFFNER, JOHN
JUDY, PETER KASTER, JAMES KELLY, JOHN KITZER, JOHN
KOON, JACOB LOY, JOHN LOY, PHILIP MANSEL, MARTIN
McCREA, JACOB MILLER, THOMAS MORGAN, JOHN REAM,
CHARLES SELBY, MIDDLETON SELBY, JACOB TERNBILL, JOHN
THOMAS, FREDERICK WOLF, GEORGE WOLF. Total $598.7.
pp 140, 141, 142

Filed 19 Aug. 1817. Inv and appr of estate of ABRA-
HAM TEAGARDEN. Total $187.87. Widow kept $64.88 of
property. Public sale, total $122.99. pp 143, 144

Filed 13 Sept. 1817. Adm of estate of JOHN GILE
granted to NANCY GILE & JAMES MILLER. Sec: OBADIAH
B. CONOVER, SAMUEL ARCHER. Appr: JAMES McFADDON,
JAMES MILLER SR, LEWIS BRANER. p 144

Land of JOHN STRAIN sold at auction. WILLIAM PORTER
bought lots 206 & 7. ROBERT STRAIN bought 9 ft of
lot 182. NATHANIEL WILSON bought 40 ft of lot 182.
Total of sales $1190. p 144

Filed 4 Oct. 1817. Inv and appr of estate of ANTHONY
LOGAN on 20 June, 1817; no total given. Memo of
property set aside for support of family. Public
sale on 24 June, 1817; buyers: JOHN BECK, WILLIAM
CODDINGTON, JOSEPH DODDS JR, JOSEPH EWING, ADAM
GARLOUGH, SAMUEL HEARN, DAVID HUSTON, DANIEL JORDAN,
ALEXANDER LOGAN, JANE LOGAN, MARGARET LOGAN, WILLIAM
McCANLESS, JAMES McCLURE, JAMES MITCHEL, JOHN NEWTON,

AARON NUTT SR, JOSHUA NUTT, GEORGE PATTERSON, EPHRAIM
PETTIT, WILLIAM SOURBRAY, PETER SUNDERLAND, JOSEPH
WHITE. No total given. pp 144, 145, 146, 147, 148,
149, 150

Term of October, 1817

HENRY GEPHART's exec request time extension to settle
estate. p 150

Case 282. ROBERT BYARS vs WILLIAM BYARS & other
heirs of JAMES BYARS, dec. Court ordered land
partition to be made by GEORGE NEWCOM & EDMUND
MUNGER. pp 150, 151

Case 283. ALEXANDER BRANDON & MARGARET BRANDON vs
JOSEPH PARKS & minor heirs of ROBERT PARKS. Court
ordered land partition to be made by SAMUEL BRIER,
JACOB GOODLANDER, JOHN KERR. p 151

Case 284. Adm of estate of JOSEPH HARDMAN granted to
ELIZABETH HARDMAN & SOLOMON HARDMAN. Sec: CHRISTIAN
WELDY, ALEXANDER SCOTT SR. Appr: AARON MILLER,
NICHOLAS STUTSMAN, ISAAC SHIVELY. p 151

Case 285. Adm of estate of THOMAS SHANKS granted to
JOSEPH SHANKS SR. Sec: SAMUEL ARCHER, JACOB BENNER.
Appr: TOBIAS WHITESELL, PETER EAGLE, HENRY STRADER.
p 151

Case 286. Will of HENRY BURKHARD. Exec: JOHN BURK-
HARD, JOHN KESSLER. Witness: ABRAHAM HESS, JOHN
MILLER. Appr: JOHN OBLINGER, JOHN MURRAY, JACOB
BOWMAN. p 151

Case 287. Will of EDWARD GALAHAN. Exec: ELIZABETH
GALAHAN, ISAAC MAHONIN. Witness: WILLIAM GALAHAN,
EZAKIEL BALDWIN, SETH MAHONIN. Appr: SAMUEL MARTIN-
DALE, WILLIAM PEARSON, SAMUEL REED. pp 151, 152

Case 288. Admrs of CHRISTIAN FOGELSONG petition to
convey deed for 200 acres in Sec 13 & 24, T 4, R 4E
to JACOB SLIFER. Permission granted. p 152

Admr of JACOB YAZEL request time extension to settle
estate. p 152

Case 289. Adm of estate of DANIEL H. FISHER granted
to CHRISTOPHER CURTNER. Sec: JOHN COMPTON JR,
GEORGE GROVE. Appr: HENRY CURTNER, GEORGE SOURBRAY,
WILLIAM WATTON. p 152

Case 290. Adm of estate of JOHN EWING granted to JOSEPH & SAMUEL EWING (widow relinquished right). Sec: JOHN DODDS, DAVID LAMME. Appr: HENRY CURTNER, GEORGE SOURBRAY, WILLIAM WATTON. p 153

Admr of JOHN B. RITTENHOUSE petitioned to sell real estate. Permisson given. p 153

Admr of GEORGE FRYBERGER credited $180.32 for property kept by widow. p 156

Exec of GEORGE STETLER produced acquittance from legatee, widow EVE STETLER for $148 share. Witness: GEORGE ERGENBRIGHT. p 156

Case 294. SAMUEL MARTINDALE apptd guardian to INSCO JAY, 4 yrs, & JOANNA JAY, 2 yrs, minor heirs of THOMAS JAY. Sec: WILLIAM HALL. p 157

Case 294.5. GEORGE GEPHART appted guardian to JACOB GEBHART, 11 yrs, & ABRAHAM GEBHART, 2 yrs; MICHAEL HOOBLER appted guardian to CATHERINE GEBHART, 9 yrs, BARBARA GEBHART, 7 yrs, & MARGARET GEBHART, 4 yrs, all being minor heirs of JOHN GEBHART, dec. p 157

Admr of MARTIN SHOUB produced settlement. Cash paid to JOHN DENISE (coffin), JOSIAH GUSHWA, GEORGE MYER, CHRISTOPHER SHUPPERT, MARTIN SHUEY, JOHN H. SCHENCK (whiskey), GEORGE LOY (auctioneer), BENJAMIN BARKA-LOW, HENRY KING (taxes), PHILIP LONG, EPHRAIM HARRIS, Dr. JOHN LEOPOLD, JACOB KELLER, JAMES LANIER. Total $50.31. p 157

Dower of widow of THOMAS JAY to be set apart by DAVID HOOVER, ANDREW WAYMIRE & GEORGE BUCHANON. p 158

Inv and appr of estate of MARGERY PARKS made 13 Oct, 1817. Total $10.25. p 158

Inv and appr of estate of HENRY BURKHARD of Madison Twp on 18 Oct, 1817. Notes due estate from DAVID LEONARD, VALENTINE LEONARD left with ISAAC FOUTS of Rowan County, NC; notes on ELIJAH RINKER & WILLIAM STEWART & PETER WHARTON left with MARTIN FRANHAM in NC; JACOB ADIR, LEONARD AYRE, SAMUEL BARNICASTLE, SAMUEL BIRD, GEORGE BOTTFRIED, JOHN BRINKLEY, STEPHEN BRINKLY, WILLIAM CARVELL SR, DANIEL COOPER, ANDREW CRAVER, JOHN CRAVER, MICHAEL CRAVER, MARK CRUMP, CUTBIRTH DANIEL, ELISHA DANIEL, DAVID ELLER, CHARLES GREENE, VALENTINE HAGE, BENJAMIN HENKEL, GASPER HENKLEY, NICHOLAS JAMES, DAVID LEONARD, VALENTINE LEONARD, HENRY LONG, HENRY LOUIS, WILLIAM McRARY,

JOHN MICHAEL, GEORGE NOTHING, FREDERICK RAKER, CHRISTIAN SIMMERMAN, DANIEL SIMMERMAN, JOHN SNIDER, DANIEL STUDABAKER, AREHART SYTHELOVE, CHRISTOPHER VOGLER, DANIEL WAGGONER, JOSHUA WILSON total $4320.62. Balance on hand 18 Oct, 1817 of $2163.81. pp 158, 159, 160, 161

Special session of 28 October, 1817

Heirs of JOHN CRAIG consented to WILLIAM THOMSON relinquishing his election to purchase land at appraisal price. Court ordered land to be sold by Sheriff. p 162

Special session of 14 November, 1817

Case 295. Will of PETER BECKER. Exec: widow ELIZABETH BECKER, CHRISTIAN WINEBREINER. Witness: FREDERICK GRUMDNER, JACOB OBLINGER. Appr: CHRISTIAN MILLER, AARON MILLER, PETER KREITZER. p 162

Filed 5 Dec, 1817. Inv and appr of estate of JOSEPH HARDMAN. Included note due from GEORGE GEPHART. Total $1064.25. p 162, 163

Inv and appr of estate of JOHN GUILE of Wayne Twp. Total $188.25. Public sale on 9 Oct, 1817; buyers: JAMES ARTHUR, JACOB CARVER, JAME FRENCH, GEORGE FRIBACK, JOSEPH HALL, JOHN HARVEY, WILLIAM MASON, JOHN REED, RHINEHART REPLOGEL, JACOB STOKER, JOHN WEAVER, JOSEPH YOUNG. Total $219.73. pp 163, 164, 165, 166

Filed 18 Jan, 1818. Public sale of estate of WILLIAM SNIDER on 26 Jan, 1818. Purchasers: JOHN ALLBACH, HENRY ALLEN, JACOB ALLBACK, DAVID BAKER, HENRY BAKER, JOHN BAKER, MICHAEL BAKER, JOHN BAUCHER, JAMES BENKER, NICHOLAS BIESECKER, GEORGE BOCHMAN, JOHN BOOGHER, JOHN BOWER, HENRY BROMBACH, JACOB BROMBACH, JOHN BROMBACH, JOHN COFFEY, GEORGE CONNER, JACOB CRIPE, JOHN CRULL, PAUL DEAL, DANIEL DEETER, THOMAS EDMONDS, AMOS EDWARDS, DANIEL EILER, ABNER ELLER, HENRY ELLER, JACOB EWING, JAMES EWING, JOSHUA FALKNER, LEVI FALKNER, DANIEL FETTER, PETTER FETTER, SAMUEL FOLKERTH, ANDREW FOUTZ, HENRY FOUTZ, JESSE FRIEND, SAMUEL GRIPE, HENRY HART, DANIEL HOOVER, NOAH HOOVER, SUSANNA HOOVER, ISAAC MAST, JOHN MAST, JOHN McINTIRE, ABRAHAM MILES, ABRAHAM MILLER, DANIEL MILLER, DAVID MILLER, SAMUEL MILLER, FRANCIS MILLION, HENRY MINER, JOHN MOTE, JOHN OVERHOLSER, FREDERICK PAINTER, JOHN PIPPINGER, JACOB PUTERBAUGH, JOHN RAZOR DANIEL ROHRER, JOHN ROHRER, HENRY ROYER, JOHN SLAYTE,

FREDERICK SMITH, DAVID SNIDER, JACOB SPITLER, JOHN STOUDER, DAVID STUTSMAN, JACOB STUTSMAN, SAMUEL STUTSMAN, STEPHEN STUTSMAN, JOHN TIPNER, NOAH WAGGONER, CHARLES WELBAUM, ANDREW WERNER, DAVID WERNER, JACOB WERNER, Widow WERNER, GEORGE WITMAN, ELIJAH WOOD, MARTIN WYBRIGHT, ADAM YOUNG, CHARITY YOUNG, PHILIP YOUNG. Total $1010.38. pp 165, 166, 167, 168, 169, 170, 171, 172

Case 296. Will of HENRY WEBB. Exec: PHILIP BARRET. Witness: AUSTIN WEBB, MICHAEL KINGERY. Appr: CHAR-LES MORGAN, GEORGE PATTERSON, DAVID JOHN. p 172

Case 297. Adm of estate of GEORGE LANE granted to JOHN N. C. SCHENCK & JOSEPH VANDEVEER. Sec: WILLIAM DODDS, H. G. PHILLIPS. Appr: WILLIAM D. CRAIG, JAMES VANKIRK, SIDNEY DENISE. p 172

Case 298. JOHN C. LANE, 18 yrs, minor heir of GEORGE LANE, dec, chose SIDNEY DENISE as guardian. Sec: JOHN H. SCHENCK. p 172

Term of January, 1818

Case 299. NANCY HARDMAN, 16 yrs, & ELIZABETH HARDMAN 13 yrs, minor heirs of JOSEPH HARDMAN, dec, chose ELIZABETH HARDMAN & SOLOMON HARDMAN as guardians. Both also apptd guardians of SARAH HARDMAN 10 yrs, SUSAN HARDMAN 8 yrs, MARY HARDMAN 6 yrs, JOSEPH HARDMAN 4 yrs & WILLIAM HARDMAN, 2 yrs. Sec: SAMUEL NOFFSINGER, ALEXANDER SCOTT. p 173

Case 300. JACOB RUBY appted guardian of JACOB HAY, 8 yrs, GEORGE HAY, 6 yrs, MICHAEL HAY, 2 yrs, minor heirs of JACOB HAY ("dec" lined out). Sec: PHILIP RHODES. p 173

Case 301. JOHN CULBERTSON, age 16, & ACENITH CUL-BERTSON, 14 yrs, minor heirs of JOHN CULBERTSON, dec, chose ROBERT CULBERTSON as guardian. Sec: WARREN MUNGER. p 173

Case 302. NATHAN BAYLESS, 14 yrs, minor heir of SAMUEL BAYLESS, dec, chose BENJAMIN BAYLESS as guardian. p 173

Case 303. GEORGE PARSONS appted guardian of AARON TOFF, 6 yrs, minor heir of ABRAHAM TOFF, dec. Sec: JOHN COMPTON. p 173

Case 304. JESSE BRACKEN, 14 yrs, minor heir of JESSE BRACKEN, dec, chose ALEXANDER HUGHEY as guardian.

Sec: NATHAN SHARP, JOHN DENISE. p 174

Admr of HUGH McCOLLOM petitioned to sell real estate. p 174

Case 305. Admr of CONRAD CASTER petitioned to sell real estate. p 174

Filed 2 Feb, 1818. Admr of EDWARD MITCHEL produced settlement. After setting aside widow's dower, balance of $247.07 remained.. Cash paid to BENJAMIN ARCHER, JOHN McINTOSH, for "WILLIAM MITCHEL dead infant of Intestate". pp 174, 175

Exec of HENRY GEPHART produced final settlement. Widow's third = $1712.05; each of 8 heirs rcve $428.01. Cash paid to DANIEL BROWER, MICHAEL HUBLER, MATTHIAS KYLE, BENJAMIN H. LODGE, GEORGE LOY (auctioneer), PHILIP MIKESELL, JOHN H. SCHENCK, JACOB SHAVER (whiskey for estate sale), HENRY STODDARD, WILLIAM TROXELL, JOHN WERTZ total $410.32. Public sale, total $2298.15. Property kept by widow MAGDALENE GEPHART = $8.25. Notes due from PETER BALLABAUGH, HENRY BRACKLER, WILLIAM BROMBACH, DANIEL FEIBY, ANDREW GEPHART, HENRY GEPHART, JACOB GEPHART, MICHAEL KETTNER, JOHN SHUPP (taken as part of wife's share), ANDREW SWINEHART, JOHN WERTZ. pp 175, 176

Exec of JOSEPH WILSON made final settlement. Balance of $451.50. "Amount willed to the widow", amount "bequeathed to EASTHER WILSON", clothing distributed among 3 eldest boys, leather rcvd of RALPH & N. WILSON since sale. Cash paid to GEORGE ALEXANDER, ANDREW D. BRIER, PATRICK BRYSON, DANIEL DEARDORFF, JOHN DEVOR, SAMUEL EILER, JOHN McBRIDE, JAMES McFADDEN, GEORGE NEWCOM, AARON NUTT (auctioneer), HENRY ROBERTSON, Dr. CIMMERMAN, JACOB SMITH, ROBERT WEAD, RALPH WILSON total $689.73. pp 176, 177, 178

Exec of JESSE MOTE made final settlement. Cash paid to DAVID EDWARDS, FRANCIS JONES, JOHN JONES, "to WALLICE JONES for keeping children of the deceased, RHODA & JESSE 9 months & 17 days", SAMUEL JONES, DAVID MOTE, JOHN MOTE, WILLIAM MOTE, ISAAC THOMPSON, total $278.29. Public sale total $151.33. Land sold to RACHEL DEVORS, JOHN MOTE. Balance $601.47. pp 178, 179

Adm of GEORGE PHILLIPS made final settlement. $32.50 in property kept by widow. Cash paid to HENRY BOWSER HENRY KRULL, JOS. LODGE, JAMES KYLE. p 179

Heirs of JOHN CRAIG and widow, now wife of ENOS
TERRY, made agreement: Widow to rcve & have interest
free use of $292.75 from land sale, return to heirs
at end of 4 yrs. Widow relinquished dower claim.
Land sale cash balance to be distributed among heirs.
DANIEL RICHARDSON & ENOS TERRY gave bond for agreement. Land sold to EMANUEL GEPHART. p 180

Special session 19 Feb, 1818.

Case 306. Adm of estate of BENJAMIN BARKALOW granted
to ZEBULON BARKALOW & LEWIS DAVIS. Sec: JOHN H.
SCHENCK, JOHN DENISE. Appr: TUNIS VANDEVEER, JAMES
WHITFIELD, JAMES VANKIRK. pp 180, 181

Inv and appr of estate of PETER BECKER held 6 Dec,
1817. Blacksmith tools listed. Property kept by
widow = $433.00. Notes due from LOAMI ASHLEY, SIMON
BRYAN, JACOB FRIEND, JOHN GARBER, HENRY GASAWAY, JOHN
GREEN, WILLIAM HARRISON, ADAM HARTMAN, JOSHUA HARTMAN
JOHN HELMICK, MICHAEL HOOBLER, JOSEPH KEPLER, GEORGE
KERNS, JOHN KESSINGER, JOHN KINSEY, GEORGE KNEE,
ABRAHAM LEES, CHRISTOPHER LEES, JACOB LONG, JOHN A.
MIKESELL, ADAM MILMAN, JOHN MYERS, CHRISTIAN NOLLER,
JACOB OLINGER, GEORGE PUTERBAUGH, PHILIP RARIGH,
MATTHIAS RIGLE, DAVID SHOCK, JACOB SHOCK, ALEXANDER
SMITH, JOHN SMITH, HENRY WEAVER, CHRISTIAN WELDY,
ISRAEL WILLIAMS, JAMES WILLIAMS, JAMES WILLSON,
ABRAHAM ZOOCK. Total $2412.09. Public sale, buyers:
PETER ADAM, HENRY ARNOLD, ELIZABETH BECKER, GEORGE
BOWSER, GEORGE CONNER, JOHN CONNOR, NICHOLAS CRAVAS-
TON, THOMAS CRITZER, DANIEL CRULL, JACOB CRULL, JOHN
CRULL, DANIEL DENISH, ADAM HARTZEL, HENRY HEETER,
SEBASTIAN HEETER, PETER HEISTAND, JAMES HILDERBRAND,
JACOB HOKE, JOHN HOLLOWAY, FREDERICK HOLDERMAN, JACOB
HOLDERMAN, ELI HOOVER, JOSHUA HOOVER, DAVID KAYLOR,
JOHN KAYLOR, JOSEPH KEPLER, JOHN KESLER, JOHN KITSER,
HENRY KLINGER, PHILIP KNEE, GEORGE KUNSE, FREDERICK
LATCH, ADAM METSKER, ANDREW MIKESELL, ENOS MILES,
AARON MILLER, JONAS MILLER, JOHN MUSSELMAN, LEWIS
MUSSELMAN, WILLIAM NICHOLAS, ABRAHAM PUTERBAUGH,
JACOB PUTERBAUGH, MICHAEL RAGER, JACOB RARICK, JOHN
REASON, MOSES RENTFREW, FREDERICK RIGHLY, THOMAS
ROBINSON, JACOB RORER, GEORGE ROWDENBUSH, JOHN
SCHNEPP, PETER SHAFFER, WILLIAM SHANEFELT, ADAM
SHOCK, JACOB SHOCK, MICHAEL WEAVER, CHRISTIAN WINE-
BREINER, JACOB WIRICK, ELIJAH WOOD, ABRAHAM ZOOCK.
Total $996.94. pp 181, 182, 183, 184, 185, 186, 187

Special session 25 Febuary, 1818

Case 307. Adm of estate of JOSEPH BLICKENSTAFF

granted to DAVID ULRICH & LEONARD WOLF JR (widow relinquished right). Sec: JOHN ULRICH, SAMUEL WISE. Appr: CHRISTIAN SHIVELY, JOHN SHIVELY, ISAAC ULRICH. p 188

Case 262. Omitted in proper place. Public sale of property of CHARLES ESTE on 8 March, 1817. Buyers: ELI ANDERSON, SAMUEL ARCHER, JOSEPH BROWN, ASA COLEMAN, DANIEL C. COOPER, GEORGE DAVIS, JOHN DODSON, HENRY DISBROW, JOHN DUNN, FIELDING GOSNEY, ELEAZER GRIFFITH, JOHN GRIMES, GEORGE GROVE, JOB HAINES, JAMES HARVEY, ISAAC HENDERSHOT, GEORGE HOLLISON, GEORGE S. HUSTON, DAVID LEHMAN, HENRY MARQUART, WARREN MUNGER, GEORGE PIERSON, THOMAS ROBISON, ROBERT J. SKINNER, GEORGE W. SMITH, JOHN STEELE, EBENEZER STEBBINS, BENJAMIN VAN CLEVE, JAMES WELSH. Total $316.30. Accounts due estate from NANCY ANDREWS, ALEXANDER ARMSTRONG, JOHN BAKER, MARY BALDWIN, ABRAHAM BARNET, JOHN BARNHART, BENJAMIN BAYLISS, JOHN BELL, WILLIAM BOMBERGER, ELISHA BRABHAM, JOHN BRADFORD, JOHN BRANDENBURGH, GABRIEL BRISTER, JAMES BROWN, JOSEPH BROWN, LUTHER BRUEN, JOHN BURNS, WILLIAM CALHOUN, JESSE CLARK, WILLIAM CLARK, JACOB CLAWSON, CHRISTOPHER COON, D. C. COOPER, AARON COZAD, BENJAMIN CRAIG, JOHN CRANE, CHRISTOPHER & HENRY CURTNER, ABRAHAM DARST, GEORGE C. DAVIS, JOHN DAVIS, LEWIS DAVIS, OWEN DAVIS, WILLIAM P. DAVIS, HENRY DISBROW, DAVID DUNCAN, SIMEON DUNN, ABRAHAM EDWARDS, JOHN EMRICK, HENRY ENOCH, JOHN ENOCH, ISAAC ENOCH, ENOCH FAIRCHILD, DANIEL H. FISHER, JOSEPH FLOYD, JOHN FLUKE, JOHN FOLKERTH, EDWARD GALLAHAN, ABNER GARARD, JOHN GILLESPIE, WILLIAM GILLESPIE, GIDEON GOODSPEED, FIELDING GOSNEY, Widow JANE GRAY, CHARLES R. GREENE, DAVID GRIFFIN, ALEXANDER GRIMES, JOHN GRIMES, JAMES HADLEY, DAVID HALE, GEORGE HANEY, MOSES HATFIELD, Widow HARE, GEORGE HARRIS, DAVID HILL, JEROM HOLT, JOSEPH HOUGH, JOSEPH HUET, EDWARD HUSTON, GEORGE HUSTON, THOMAS JAMES, THOMAS JOHNSTON, DAVID JOICE, THOMAS KING, ANTHONY KOZAD, MICHAEL KECHVEN, JOHN LANDEMAN, HENRY LEATHERMAN, JOHN LEHMAN, PETER LEHMAN DAVID LINDLEY, GEORGE LOGAN, JAMES LONG, WILLIAM MACKEY, HENRY MARQUART, JAMES McCANN, JOHN McCLEAN, JAMES McCLURE, HUGH McCOLLOM, JAMES McCORMICK, SAMUEL McCORMICK, WILLIAM McCORMICK, ARCHIBALD McDONALD, EDWARD McDONAUGH, DOMINICK McGRAW, JOHN MIKESELL, CONKLIN MILLER, DANIEL MORRISON, WARREN MUNGER, WILLIAM MURPHY, WILLIAM NEILY, EDWARD NEWCOM, JOHN NEWCOM JAMES NOLAND, CHRISTOPHER OBLINGER, ASA OWENS, WILLIAM OWENS, FRANCIS PATTERSON, MATTHEW PATTON, ANDREW PARKS, WILLIAM PECK, HORATIO G. PHILLIPS, JOSEPH PIERCE, SAMUEL RAMSAY, WILLIAM RAMSAY, JOHN REGANS, JAMES RHEA, WILLIAM RHODES, JAMES RIDDLE,

(Debts due estate of CHARLES ESTE, continued)
AARON RICHARDSON, Widow RICHARDSON, JAMES RICHEY,
JOHN RUBY, JOSEPH RYAN, ELISHA SEARLS, THOMAS SHAW,
DAVID SIMMONS, MOSES SIMPSON, PETER SLUSHER, CHARLES
SMITH, GEORGE W. SMITH, WILLIAM M. SMITH, GEORGE
SNIDER, WILLIAM SOURBRAY, TIMOTHY SQUIER, BLACKALL
STEPHENS, ROBERT STRAIN, D. & JONATHAN STUTSMAN,
RICHARD SUNDERLAND, ABRAHAM TEAGARDEN, JAMES
THOMPSON, BENJAMIN VAN CLEVE, WILLIAM VAN CLEVE,
SAMUEL & WILLIAM WATTON, JOS. WATZ, JOHN WEAVER,
THOMAS WHELING, BENJAMIN WILLSON, ROBERT WILLSON,
WILLIAM WOOD, JOHN WOODERMAN, ELIJAH WOODROUGH,
CHRISTIAN YAZEL, GEORGE YOUNG total $1808.20.
Debts against estate of Dr. CHARLES ESTE to JOSEPH
BROWN, O. B. CONOVER, GEORGE P. DAVIS, MOSES HAT-
FIELD, H. G. PHILLIPS, LUDWIG SPEECE total $1429.68.
List of property kept by widow = $22.75.   pp 188,
189,190, 191,192,193

Inv and appr of estate of BENJAMIN B. BARCALOW of
German Twp on 25 Feb, 1818.   Total $824.65.   Debts
owed estate from JACOB HARKRADER, DAVID LABOW, LEWIS
LAFORD, JAMES W. LANIER, CATHERINE PENROD, PETER
PENROD, SAMUEL POTTS, JACOB REPLOGEL, PHILIP
REPLOGEL. Public sale on 6 March, 1818; buyers:
GEORGE AIGENBRIGHT, SAMUEL ANDREW, JACOB BAIRD, ZEB-
ULON BAIRD JR, ZEBULON BARCALOW, DAVID BRANDON, PETER
BULLINSBAUGH, JOHN COMPTON, MOSES COMPTON, JACOB
DEARDORFF, JOHN DENISE, CHRISTOPHER EMRICK, JOHN
ETTER, HENRY GEESY, WILLIAM HALE, JACOB HARKRADER,
JACOB HARP, LEWIS HASSLEMAN, GEORGE HEFNER, JOSEPH
IVANS, GEORGE KEARN, JOHN KELLY, JAMES KERRY, CHAR-
LES KETROW, JOHN KITCHEN, ISAAC LANE, CHRISTOPHER
LONGSTREET, STEPHEN LONGSTREET, GEORGE LOY, JOHN
MARSH, COONROD MARSHAL, JAMES McEWING, GEORGE McKEAN,
JONATHAN MORRIS, HENRY OILER, JOSEPH PITMAN, JACOB
ROOF, MIDDLETON SELVEY, JOHN SHALBY, JACOB SHOUPARD,
JOSEPH TAPSCOTT, WILLIAM VAIL, DAVID VANDEVEER, ROB-
ERT WHITE, JOHN C WINANS, DANIEL WOLF, GEORGE WOLF.
Total $825.71.   pp 193, 194, 195, 196

Filed 21 April, 1818.   Inv and appr of estate of
JOSEPH BLICKENSTAFF on 19 March, 1818. Total $530.55.
Public sale, buyers: ELISHA ASHLEY, JAMES BANKERD,
GEORGE BOWSER, HENRY BOWSER, PHILIP BOWSER, DANIEL
BRUMBAUGH, WILLIAM BRUMBAUGH, DANIEL CALER, JOHN
CLARK, HENRY CRULL, SOLOMON DANNER, PETER DETRICK,
JOHN DIXSON, JOEL FOUTZ, SOLOMON HAMER, SEBASTIAN
HEETER, JACOB HOLDERMAN, JONAS HOOVER, BAZZEL HUNT,
THOMAS HUNT, ISAAC JUSTER, SHEM KERNEY, JAMES
KYLE, ROBERT McCONNEL, WILLIAM McCONNEL, ELIAS
McGUIRE, ANDREW METZKER, DAVID MILLER, MICHAEL MYER,

JOHN OBLINGER, DANIEL OXE, JOSEPH PARKS, GEORGE PLESINGER, JACOB PLESINGER, JONATHAN PRIMSLEY, JOHN REED, DAVID RODEBAUGH, ISRAEL WILLIAMS, JACOB WOLF, LEONARD WOLF SR. Total $503.90. pp 197, 198, 199

Inv and appr of estate of EDWARD GALLAHAN total $122.12. Public sale, buyers: LUCAS BALDWIN, DAVID BANKET, ABRAHAM BLICKENSTAFF, JACOB BLICKENSTAFF, MATTHEW BOWLISS, ROBERT CAMPBELL, ELI COMPTON, JOHN FREEMAN, JONAS GALLAHAN, WILLIAM GALLAHAN, SAMUEL MARTINDALE, JOHN McMAHAN, JAMES L. MILLER, WILLIAM MOONEY, ISAAC REED, JACOB REED, JOHN RITTENHOUSE, RICHARD SUNDERLAND, JOHN SWALLOW. Total $130.45. pp 199, 200

Term of April, 1818

Case 308. Adm of estate of JOHN REGANS granted to HENRY BROWN (widow relinquished right). Sec: OBADIAH B. CONOVER, CHARLES TULL. Appr: JAMES STEELE, DAVID GRIFFIN, DAVID HENDERSON. p 201

Case 309. Adm of estate of DANIEL SHIVELY granted to CHRISTIAN SHIVELY JR & ISAAC ULRICH (widow relinquished right). Sec: SAMUEL ULRICH, STEPHEN ULRICH. Appr: JACOB CRIPE, JACOB SHIVELY, JOHN VANNIMAN. p201

Case 310. Will of ISAAC MILLER. Exec: ABRAHAM MILLER & ABRAHAM HORNER. Witness: JACOB DIEHL, HENRY LEEDES. Appr: PHILIP WAGNER, JACOB RUBY, ANDREW MIKESELL. p 201

Case 311. Will of JOHN ULRICH. Exec: SAMUEL ULRICH, ISAAC ULRICH. Witness: CHRISTIAN SHIVELY, LEONARD WOLF. Appr: JOHN VANNIMAN, CHRISTIAN SHIVELY, STEPHEN ULRICH. p 201

Case 312. Will of JACOB OVERHOLSER. Exec: NANCY OVERHOLSER, DANIEL GRIPE. Witness: JACOB DIEHL, STEPHEN ULRICH. Appr: JOSEPH GRIPE, HENRY WEAVER, JOHN MUSSELMAN. p 201

Case 313. Will of JOHN GRIPE. Exec: CATHERINE GRIPE, widow, & HENRY MEDSKER. Witness: STEPHEN ULRICH, CHRISTIAN SHIVELY, ISAAC ULRICH. Appr: STEPHEN ULRICH, SAMUEL ULRICH, ANDREW MEDSKER. p 202

Case 314. JOHN EWING, 16 yrs, minor heir of JOHN EWING, dec, chose WILLIAM GARDNER EWING as guardian. Sec: ALEXANDER LOGAN. p 202

Case 315. DANIEL HEISTAND appted guardian of JACOB

HAY, 9 yrs, GEORGE HAY, 6 yrs, MICHAEL HAY, 2 yrs, children of JACOB HAY who agreed to the appointment. Sec: ANDREW MEDSKER. p 202

Case 316.   ELIZABETH BECKER appted guardian of BARBARY, 11 yrs, ELIZA, 8 yrs & 5 mo, JOHN 6 yrs, & PETER, 3 months, minor heirs of PETER BECKER. Sec: JOHN OBLINGER, FREDERICK GROUNDIRER. p 202

Case 317.   Petition of JOHN H. SCHENCK, SARAH SCHENCK, JOHN DENISE, MARY DENISE, ANN BARCALOW and ABITTAH LANE & JOHN LANE by guardian SIDNEY DENISE (heirs of GEORGE LANE) for partition of land of GEORGE LANE, dec.   Court apptd BENJAMIN MALTBIE, EDWARD MUNGER & WILLIAM DODDS to divide land after setting off widow's dower land. p 202

Admr of Dr. CHARLES ESTE granted time extension to settle estate. p 202

Case 318.   TERRIS SIMPSON, 13 yrs, chose WILLIAM BOMBERGER as guardian. p 203

Case 319. Adm of estate of GEORGE ZELLER granted to widow REBECCA ZELLER & JOHN ZELLER. Sec: MARTIN SHUEY, PHILIP GUNCKEL.   Appr: MARTIN SHUEY JR, JOHN C. HEGLEY, GEORGE COLEMAN. p 203

Case 320.   ELIZABETH GALAHAN apptd guardian of JOHN GALLAHAN, 8 yrs, POLLY GALLAHAN, 5 yrs, ELIZA GAL-LAHAN, 8 months, minor heirs of EDWARD GALLAHAN. Sec: ELI COMPTON. p 203

Admr of PETER LEHMAN produced settlement. Cash paid to Dr. JOHN STEELE, ISAAC BANTA, SOLOMON BOWEN, DAVID P. JOHN, JOHN SROYER, DAVID HOLE, ISRAEL TAYLOR, JAMES AKINS, JOHN FARNHAM total $92.43. p 203

Case 321. Petition of ALEXANDER M. ELLIOT & his wife requesting partition of land of JOHN EWING, dec. Court apptd JAMES RUSSELL, AMOS EWING & JOHN TAYLOR to divide land. p 204

Case 322. Petition of admr of JAMES NOLAN, request-ing sale of part of Dayton lot 38 to satisfy debts. GEORGE S. HUSTON, JOHN GRIMES & DAVID REID apptd to set value. p 204

Case 323. Admr of JOHN CRAIG petition to convey deed to PETER TREON. Permission granted. p 204

Case 324. Admr of JOHN EWING petition to convey deed

to ANTHONY LOGAN. p 205

Admr of JOHN STRAIN reported $145.17 to be added to estate. Cash paid to IRA SMITH (auctioneer), ADDISON SMITH, ROBERT PORTER, WILLIAM SHORT, widow MARGARET STRAIN. Balance of $1389.35 remained. p 205, 206

Case 322. Admr of JAMES NOLAN granted order to sell land. p 206, 207

Case 325. JAMES REEDER appted guardian of CAMPBELL BOWMAN, 6 yrs, minor heir of GILBERT BOWMAN. Sec: DANIEL REEDER, ISAAC WOODWARD. p 207

Admr of JOHN GEPHART made final settlement. Widow's half = $147.26; each of 10 heirs rcve $7.36. p 207

Case 326. Admr of CONRAD CASTER permitted to sell 110 acres to ABRAHAM KINSEY and JACOB WAGGONER. p 207

Case 327. Admr of JOHN B. RITTENHOUSE petitioned to sell real estate to settle debts. p 208

Filed 6 May, 1818. Inv and appr of estate of JOHN ULRICH. Total $439.50. p 209

Filed 20 May, 1818. Inv and appr of estate of DANIEL SHIVELY. Total $689.55. Public sale, buyers: ELISHA ASHLY, LOAMI ASHLEY, GEORGE BEAM, DAVID BRUMBAUGH, JOSEPH CONNER, LUKE CONNER, JACOB CRULL, JOHN CRULL, SOLOMON DANNER, JACOB DEAL, JOHN DICKSON, CALEB FAGER WILLIAM FRAME, JOHN HEEDER, DANIEL HEISTAND, JAMES HILDERBRAND, JACOB HOLDERMAN, JAMES HUNT, DAVID KAYLOR, GEORGE KUNS, DAVID LEHMAN, CHRISTIAN MILLER, WARREN PEACE, JOHN REED, PETER REID, WILLIAM RITTEN-HOUSE, SUSANNA SHIVELY, MICHAEL SMITH, ISAAC ULRICH, CHRISTIAN WELBAUM, ISRAEL WILLIAMS, ELIJAH WOOD, CHRISTOPHER ZWENER. Total $251.48. pp 210, 211, 212

Inv and appr of estate of JOHN CRIPE on 25 April, 1818. Total $542.62. p 213

Filed 12 June, 1818. Public sale of ISAAC MILLER on 1 May, 1818. Purchasers: PETER ADAMS, DAVID ANDRESS, SAMUEL ANDREW, GEORGE BOWSER, PETER CRITZER, JACOB CROLL, JAMES CROSS, JOHN DEAL, JACOB FRIEND, JOHN HEETER, GEORGE HEPNER, JAMES HILDERBRAND, GEORGE HOL-LER, JACOB HOLLER, ABRAHAM HORNER, ALEXANDER HORNER, SAMUEL KINNAMON, HENRY KLINGER, FREDERICK LEATCH, JACOB MARTIN, JOHN MASON, ABRAHAM MILLER, ISAAC MILLER, JOHN MILLER, JONAS MILLER, MOSES MILLER,

ABRAHAM MINER, CHRISTIAN MISENER, MICHAEL NAVE, AMOS
OBLINGER, JACOB RUBY, DAVID SHEPLEY, DANIEL SHIDLER,
DAVID SHOCK, ROBERT SKELTON, DAVID SNIDER, PETER
SOWDER, PHILIP WAGGONER, JACOB WEAVER, JOHN WIRIGH,
ELIJAH WOOD. Total $383.42. Inv & appr of estate of
ISAAC MILLER on 29 April, 1818. Debts due from JACOB
CROLL, GABRIEL LASTY, HENRY LEATCH, JOHN MIKESELL SR,
JOHN MILLER, MOSES MILLER, HENRY RARIGH, JOHN RUBY,
JOSEPH STOUDER, HENRY WEAVER, pp 214, 215, 216, 217,
218, 219

Inv and appr of estate of MARTIN HOOVER of Jefferson
Twp by JACOB CRULL, PETER KRITZER & JACOB RORER,
total $173.75. Notes due from DAVID HOOVER, JACOB
KRULL, CHRISTIAN HOOVER. pp 219, 220

Filed 9 July, 1818. Inv and appr of estate of JACOB
OVERHOLSER on 24 April, 1818. Included debts due
from HENRY HUNTSINGER, DAVID WAGGONER, STEPHEN
ULRICH. Total $476.95. p 221

Special session 3 May, 1818.

Case 328. Will of HENRY SEILER. Exec: PETER SEILER,
ULRICH SEILER. Witness: JACOB RUBY, SAMUEL RODE-
HAFFER. Appr: PHILIP SCHLEIFER, JACOB RUBY, LEWIS
FOUST. p 222

Case 329. Will of MATTHIAS PAINTER. Exec: PHILIP
SLIVER. Witness: JACOB RUBY, JOHN PENCE. Appr:
JACOB RUBY, JOHN PENCE, SAMUEL RODEHAFFER. p 222

Case 330. Will of JOHN WAGNER. Exec: DAVID WAGNER,
DANIEL WAGNER. Witness: CHRISTIAN SHIEBELI JR,
LEONARD WOLF JR. Appr: CHRISTIAN SHIEBLI JR, DAVID
SCHEIBELI, PHILIP WAGNER. p 222 (See Docket Book D,
page 1)

Case 331. Will of SAMUEL KINNAMAN proven by witness
HUGH MOORE. p 222

Case 332. Adm of estate of JACOB STUTSMAN granted to
JONATHAN STUTSMAN & JACOB BOWMAN (widow relinquished
right). Sec: JOHN LEHMAN, DAVID MILLER. Appr: PET-
ER DIETRICK, DANIEL STUTSMAN, JOHN KREIB. pp 222, 223

Case 333. Adm of estate of MARTIN RUSE granted to
JOHN RUSE & GEORGE SHANK (widow relinquished right).
Sec: DAVID WAGNER, DANIEL WAGNER. Appr: JOHN
WERTS, EMANUEL FLORRA, JOSEPH MIKESELL. p 223

Filed 17 Dec, 1817. omitted in proper place. Inv

and appr of estate of JOHN EWING on 31 Oct, 1817. No total given. pp 223, 224

Special session 3 October, 1818

Case 334. Adm of estate of Rev. BACHUS WILBUR granted to MARY W. WILBUR. Sec: JAMES STEELE, H. G. PHILLIPS. Appr: MATTHEW PATTON, JOSEPH PEIRCE, B. VAN CLEVE. p 225

Case 335. Adm of estate of PETER LEHMAN granted to JOHN LEHMAN (widow relinquished right). Sec: DAVID LEHMAN, MOSES HATFIELD. Appr: GEORGE NEWCOM, AARON BAKER, JOHN BRANDENBURGH. p 225

COMMON PLEAS (PROBATE) DOCKET BOOK D-1

Filed 1 Aug, 1818. (Case 330) Inv & appr of estate of JOHN WAGGONER on 13 June, 1818 by PHILIP WAGGONER, CHRISTIAN SHIVELY, DAVID SHIVELY. Total $1192.55. Notes due from JOHN MIKESELL, JOHN MYER, CONRAD KNISS. p 1

Term of August, 1818

Will of SAMUEL KINNAMON proven by witness WALTER KINNAMON. Exec: JOHN T. KINNEMAN, RICHARD KINNEMAN. Appr: JACOB WIRICK, JACOB RUBY, LUDWIG FOUST. p 2

Case 336. Will of DAVID ARCHIBALD. Exec: ROBERT ARCHIBALD. Witness: ELIAS MATTHEWS, ROBERT MILLER. Appr: ROBERT MILLER, DAVID MARTIN, ELIAS MATTHEWS. p2

Case 337. Adm of estate of RICHARD THRALLS granted to ANNA THRALLS. Sec: JACOB KELLER, JOSEPH BROWN. Appr: SAMUEL NOFFZINGER, MICHAEL MILLER, HENRY LEEDES. p 2

Case 338. Adm of estate of JACOB BAKER granted to CATHERINE BAKER. Sec: PETER ALBAUGH, FREDERICK REGLEY. Appr: JACOB RUBY, ABRAHAM SWARTZLEY, JOHN MILLER. pp 2, 3

Case 339. Adm of estate of JACOB WIRICK granted to JACOB WIRICK & JOHN T. KINNAMAN (widow relinquished right). Sec: WALTER KINNAMAN, JOHN HISER. Appr: PHILIP SLIFER, JACOB RUBY, LUDWIG FOUST. p 3

Case 340. JACOB SHEIDLER, 19 yrs, ELIAS SHEIDLER, 16 yrs, & SARAH SHEIDLER, 13 yrs, minor heirs of GEORGE SHEIDLER, dec, chose mother MARY SHEIDLER as guardian. Sec: PHILIP MIKESELL. p 3

Case 341. GEORGE WASHINGTON CASSADY, 15 yrs, heir of PETER CASSADY, chose JOHN CASSADY as guardian. p 3.

Inv and appr of estate of MATTHIAS PAINTER on 25 June, 1818. After setting aside widow's share, total of $294.50. Public sale, no buyers' names given, total $292.93. pp 3,4,5

Case 342. Will of DANIEL C. COOPER. Exec: SOPHIA COOPER, JAMES STEELE, H.G. PHILLIPS. Witness: JOSEPH H. CRANE, JOSEPH PEIRCE, JOB HAINES. Appr: JOSEPH PEIRCE, HENRY BACON, DAVID REID. p 6

Case 343. Will of JAMES THARP. Exec: CHARLES THARP. Witness: THOMAS THARP & JAMES THARP. Sec: THOMAS THARP, JAMES THARP. Appr: ROBERT HARDING, JACOB SWINEHART, ADAM BUTT. p 6

SOPHIA COOPER, widow of DANIEL C. COOPER, claimed dower right in estate in lieu of legacy as given in will. p 6

Case 344. Will of RUBEN WAGGONER. Exec: JOSEPH EWING, JACOB MULFORD. Witness: JOHN TAYLOR, ALLEN TALLMAN. Appr: JOHN TAYLOR, JAMES CHATHAM, WILLIAM DODDS JR. pp 6, 7

Admr of CHARLES ESTE found estate was insolvent, requested time extension to settle. p 7

Case 345. Adm of estate of PHILIP BRANER granted to JACOB BRANER. Sec: LEWIS BRANER, PETER STUTSMAN. Appr: JACOB MATTHEWS, JACOB REPLOGEL, ANDREW WESTFALL. p 7

Exec of BENJAMIN RICHARDS produced settlement accts, total $422.50. p 7

Admr of CHRISTIAN NEFF produced settlement. Cash paid to GEORGE BARDSHIRE, ABRAHAM BRENNEMAN, WILLIAM BOMBERGER, DAVID BRIGGS, ISAAC G. BURNET, DOLLY CLARK JOHN COMPTON JR, JOHN GIEL, JOHN HOUSER, MARTIN HOUSER, JOHN KERR, JACOB KUHN, PETER LEHMAN, WILLIAM MASON, HUGH McCOLLOM, JOHN MILLER, GEORGE NEWCOM, ADAM NEFF, MARY M. NEFF, DANIEL NEFF, JAMES NOLAN, H. G. PHILLIPS, JOHN REED, GEORGE SHOUP, JOSEPH WAGGON-ER, CONRAD WOLF, JOHN WOLF total $288.20. Cash rcvd from WILLIAM COX, JOHN GIEL, MARTIN HOOVER, STEPHEN MACEY, CONKLIN MILLER, ADAM NEFF, THOMAS QUEEN, ADAM SHEPHERD. Public sale, no names or total given. Balance of $40.68 remains. pp 8, 9

Admr of THOMAS JOHNSON produced settlement. Widow kept $131,81 in property. Cash paid to AARON BAKER, DAVID BOWEN, JOSEPH COLEMAN, FRANCIS DILTS, CHARLES ESTE, JOHN HUSTON, SOLOMON ISAVAGLE, JOHN SHROYER, Dr. JOHN TREON. Balance of $479.20. pp 10, 11

AARON BAKER, admr of estate of JONATHAN POWEL, produced settlement. Widow kept $13.00 in property. Cash paid: to MARY DAVIS for PETER BURKEY, to MARY DAVIS for maintaining SUSAN POWEL, JOHN DODSON, Dr. CHARLES ESTE, Dr. FALKS, MOSES FOSTER, WILLIAM HUFFMAN, HENRY MARQUART, MATTHEW PATTON (coffin), HENRY RIDGELY, CONRAD ROBERTS, Dr. JOHN STEELE. pp 11, 12

WILLIAM P. DAVIS, admr of HUGH McCOLLOM, produced settlement. Cash paid to SAMUEL ARCHER, ABRAHAM BARNET, JAMES BRYAN, GEORGE C. DAVIS, WILLIAM DOUGHERTY, JOHN FOLKERTH, WILLIAM FREEMAN, DAVID GRIFFIN, JOHN HOLT, JACOB HOSIER, DANIEL LANDON, JOHN MILLER, HORATIO G. PHILLIPS, SAMUEL RAMSAY, ROBERT ROBERTSON, THOMAS SKILLMAN, JOSEPH SLOAN, ADDISON SMITH, DAVID STEELE, JOHN VAN ESNMONS, JOHN WAGGONER, RUBEN WAGGONER. Balance of $1732.85 remains. pp 12, 13, 14

Admr of PETER WINELAND produced settlement. Cash paid to JAMES BINKERD, JACOB BOWMAN, PHILIP BOWSER, JAMES BRIER (auctioneer), DANIEL BRUMBAUGH, HENRY BURN, JOHN FOLCK, JOHN FOLKERTH, JACOB GRIPE, SAMUEL HAGER, PHILIP KNEE, DAVID MILLER, JOSEPH POWEL, ADAM RODEBAUGH, DANIEL STUDEBAKER, HENRY SWISHER, RALPH WILSON, ABRAHAM ZOOCK, total $180.91 plus $300.30. pp 14, 15

Inv and appr of estate of NICHOLAS ROOS of Madison Twp total $328.71. Included note from NICHOLAS CRAVISTON. Sworn before C. ARNOLD, JP, on 9 June, 1818. pp 16, 17, 18

Inv and appr of estate of GEORGE ZELLER on 11 July, 1818, total $924.31. Sworn before GEORGE W. MILLER, JP. pp 19, 20

Inv and appr of estate of HENRY SILER. Widow kept $525.37 in property. Public sale on 9 July, 1818, total $107.25. pp 21, 22

Inv and appr of estate of JACOB STUTSMAN, total $157.50. Debts due from JONATHAN BRIMLEY, DANIEL GRIBE; total $10.31. Public sale, undated. Buyers: JACOB FETTERS, JACOB HARTLE, JOSEPH ROHRER, CATHERINE STUTSMAN, JONATHAN STUTSMAN, total $180.67. pp 22, 23

Inv and appr of estate of JACOB BAKER of Jackson Twp, total $96.25. Sworn before JOHN HOLMES, JP. Widow kept $38.25 in property. Public sale on 22 Aug, no year given. Buyers: PETER ALLBAUGH, JOHN ANDRESS, PETER BOOMERSHINE, NICHOLAS BUCK, GEORGE CLENCY, JOHN FEAGLER, JOSHUA D. IZOR, JACOB MILLER, JOHN I. MILLER, GEORGE PETERFISH, FREDERICK RIGLEY, THOMAS SNIDER, ADAM STAVER, MATHIAS SWARTZEL, PETER WOLF, total $125.72. pp 24, 25

Inv and appr of estate of Rev. BACHUS WILBUR on 5 Oct, 1818, total $1767.50. Public sale on 19 Oct, 1818. Buyers: SAMUEL ARCHER, RICHARD BACON, AARON BAKER, ELISHA BRABHAM, JOHN BRADFORD, J.W.BRIER, JOSIAH BROADWELL, SILAS BROADWELL, HENRY BROWN, LUTHER BRUEN, JOHN BURNS, H. CARPENTER, J. H. CRANE, HENRY CURTNER, J.W. FOLKERTH, AUGUSTUS GEORGE, WILLIAM GEORGE JR, WILLIAM GILLESPIE, LEWIS GORDON, FIELDING GOSNEY, C.R. GREENE, JAMES HANNA, GEORGE HARRIS, NAT. HUNT, G.S. HUSTON, WILLIAM KING, JACOB LEHMAN, HENRY MARQUART, JOHN MILLER, GEORGE NEWCOM, C. OBLINGER, WILLIAM PATTERSON, MATT PATTON, H.G. PHILLIPS, DANIEL PIERSON, WILLIAM RHOADS, DAVID SIMMONS, ROBT. J. SKINNER, G.W. SMITH, GEORGE SNIDER, KETTY SOURBRAY, EBENEZER STEBBINS, JAMES STEELE, JA. THOMSON, B. VAN CLEVE, RICHARD WEAKLEY, total $1035.68. pp 25, 26, 27, 28, 29, 30, 31, 32, 33

Inv and appr of estate of SAMUEL J. KINNAMON, total $104.25, signed Exec's JOHN T. KINNAMON, RICHARD KIN-NAMON. Widow kept $212.37 in property. Debts due from JOHN ANDRESS, SAMUEL HOWARD, RICHARD KINNAMON, NATHANIEL POPES, JACOB WAUY, JOHN B. WILLIAMS total $873.93. Public sale on 9 Oct, 1818. Buyers: GEORGE CLENZY, JACOB HARKRADER, WILLIAM HOLMES, JOHN A. MIKESELL, SAMUEL RODEHAFFER, JOHN SAILER, PETER SELER, JACOB WIRICK, total $133.93. pp 33, 34, 35

Filed 23 Oct, 1818. Inv and appr of estate of JACOB WIRICK. Total $190.27. Widow kept $106.87 in proper-ty. Public sale on 21 Aug, 1818. Buyers: HENRY BUTT, GEORGE CLENZY, JAMES CROSS, ANDREW LESSLEY, JOHN A. MIKESELL, JACOB MILLER, JAMES I. NESBIT, GEORGE SHADER, JACOB WARRY, ROBERT N. WILLIAMS, DAVID WIRICK, JOHN WIRICK, total $103.70. Notes due from JOHN ANDRESS, SAMUEL BECTELL, EMANUEL GLYMPSE, WILLIAM HOLMES, VALENTINE HUFFMAN, JOHN KELSON, JOHN T. KINNAMON, JOHN PEIRCE, ADAM RUMBARGER, GEORGE RUMBARGER, DAVID SHEPLEY, GEORGE TITTLE, JOHN B. WILLIAMS, DAVID WIRICK, JACOB WIRICK, WILLIAM WIRICK total $191.18. pp 36, 37, 38

Term of November, 1818

Case 346. Adm of estate of ABRAHAM ZESS granted to ELIZABETH ZESS. Sec: ADAM SHOCK, HENRY HIPPLE. Appr: WILLIAM NICHOLAS, CHRISTIAN WINEBRANER, JACOB OBLINGER. p 39

Admr of estate of THOMAS W. SHANKS requested time extension to settle. p 39

Case 347. GEORGE HIMES, 19 yrs, MARTIN HIMES, 17 yrs, FRANCIS HIMES, 15 yrs, & NANCY HIMES, 13 yrs, minor heirs of JOHN HIMES, dec, chose JOSEPH COLEMAN as guardian. COLEMAN also appted guardian of THOMAS HIMES, 11 yrs, and RACHEL HIMES, 4 yrs. Sec: HENRY CREAGER, GEORGE GROVE. p 39

Case 348. Adm of estate of JAMES JAMESON granted to REBECCA JAMISON & JOHN MILLER. Sec: SMITH GREGG, BENJAMIN KIZER. Appr: JOHN KERR, JOSEPH KENNEDY, JOHN McKNIGHT. pp 39, 40

Case 349. JOHN H. SCHENCK & SIDNEY DENISE appted guardians of ZEBULON BARCALOW, 7 yrs, GEORGE BARCALOW 6 yrs, DERRICK BARCALOW 5 yrs, ELEANOR BARCALOW 3 yrs JOHN BARCALOW 1 yr, & ANN, 4 months, minor heirs of BENJAMIN BARCALOW, dec. Sec: OBADIAH B. CONOVER, MARTIN SHUEY JR. p 40

Case 350. CATHERINE SHOUP, 12 yrs, minor heir of MARTIN SHOUP, chose ABRAHAM PONTIUS as guardian. Sec: JACOB HARKRADER. p 40

Admr of HENRY BURKHARD request time extension to settle estate. p 40

Case 351. Petition of JACOB DEHL & JOHN HEISTAND for apptmt of guardian for PETER HEISTAND, "a lunatic". Jury summoned: JAMES BLACK, LUTHER BRUEN, JOHN DICKENSHEETS, DAVID GRIFFIN, THOMAS KING, DAVID KINSEY, JOSHUA McINTOSH, GEORGE MILLER, JAMES B. OLIVER, SAMUEL WILLIAMSON, RALPH WILSON. Found petition to be truthful. Sec: SAMUEL HEISTAND. pp 40, 41

Case 352. JACOB DIEHL appted guardian of PETER HEISTAND. p 41

Case 353. JOHN MILLER, 14 yrs, minor heir of JOHN MILLER, dec, chose JOEL FOUTS as guardian. Sec: JOHN WAGGONER. p 41

Case 354. ABRAHAM TROXEL appointed guardian to

ELIZABETH ARNOLD, 10 yrs, MARY 9 yrs, SARAH 7 yrs, JACOB 6 yrs, CATHERINE 3 yrs, children of CHRISTIAN ARNOLD, to care for estate left by grandfather GEORGE SHEIDLER & JOHN SHEIDLER, dec. Sec: JOHN MIKESELL, HENRY LEEDES. p 41

Case 355. Admr of CHARLES ESTE request sale of Dayton outlot to settle debts. Appr: SAMUEL ARCHER, JOHN GRIMES, OBADIAH B. CONOVER. p 41

Admr of HUGH McCOLLOM request sale of real estate. JAMES STEELE, AARON BAKER & CHARLES R. GREENE to appr lot 109, including buildings, located at SW corner of Main & Second Sts. Valued at $3500; terms of sale set by court. pp 42, 43

Inv and appr of estate of CHARLES ESTE on 11 Nov, 1818. Total $175.00. Since admr found estate insolvent, court ordered sale of Dayton lot 8 (10 acres in Sec 5, T 1, R 7). Admr empowered to convey deed. pp 43, 44

Admr of GEORGE SHEIDLER produced settlement. Widow's dower of $196.17. Balance of $392.34 to distribute to other heirs. pp 44, 45

Admr of JOHN SHEIDLER produced settlement. Balance of $95.33 remains. pp 45, 46

Admr of CHARLES ESTE requested time extension to settle estate. p 46

Admr of JACOB MAST presented tax recpts. p 46

Adm of estate of PETER LEHMAN presented settlement. Cash paid to AARON NUTT (auctioneer), HENRY CRYER, JAMES CHATHAM, GEORGE YOUNG, JO. JOHN, ISAAC WOODWARD ISAAC RICHARDSON, WILLIAM WAUGH. pp 46, 47

Admr of ABRAHAM SHOWERS produced settlememt. Cash paid to DANIEL RASOR, CHRISTIAN YARS, JOSEPH ROHRER, JACOB SMITH, AMOS EDWARDS, JOSEPH SHAW, WILLIAM M. SMITH. Balance of $13.64. pp 47, 48

Case 357. Will of DANIEL RAZOR. Exec: DAVID HOOVER. Witness: JOSEPH ROHRER, JOSEPH ROHRER JR, JOHN SPITLER. Appr: JOSEPH ROHRER, DAVID KREIDER, JOHN WERTS. p 48

Admr of JAMES NOLAN reported land sale to AARON BAKER. pp 48, 49

Case 358. Will of ABRAHAM HOSIER. Proven by witness JOSEPH C. SILVER. p 49

Case 359. Adm of estate of NATHAN SILVER SR granted to JOSEPH C. SILVER (widow relinquished right). Sec: CHARLES TULL, ELLIS BALDWIN. Appr: DANIEL WILSON, BENJAMIN ARCHER, THOMAS HORNER. p 49

Inv and appr of estate of PETER HEISTAND, imbecile, ordered made on 11 Oct, 1818. Included note due from DAVID SHEPLEY, JACOB DIEHL, HENRY WEAVER, total $353.94. Appr: PETER CRITZER, ANDREW MIKESELL, HENRY WEAVER. pp 49, 50

Filed 17 Oct, 1818 Inv and appr of estate of RICHARD THRALLS on 8 Aug, 1818. Sworn before PHILIP MIKESELL JP. List of property kept by widow, total $125. Inv included tools indicating may have been a blacksmith and/or a harness maker. Debts due from JOHN APPLE, BENJAMIN BOWMAN, DAVID BYERLY, JACOB CAYLOR, SAMUEL CAYLOR, WILLIAM PHRAIM, JOHN HUNTSINGER, PHILIP KEEN, JOHN KINZEY, GEORGE KNEE, PETER LASLEY, PHILIP MIKE- SELL, DAVID MILLER, MICHAEL MILLER, DANIEL MYERS, MICHAEL MYERS, JOHN NOFFSINGER, SAMUEL NOFFSINGER, DANIEL REPP, JOHN RITTER, NICHOLAS STUTSMAN, ABRAHAM WESTFALL, ISAAC WESTFALL, JACOB WESTFALL, JACOB WOLF, total $101.60. Public sale on 22 Aug, 1818; buyers: ADAM BOLLIN, DAVID CAYLOR, JACOB CAYLOR, PETER CAY- LOR, SAMUEL CAYLOR, DAVID DUNCAN, WILLIAM FRAME, JOHN HEATER, JOHN JOKEY, JOHN KINSEY, PHILIP KNEE, PHILIP MIKESELL, DANIEL NOFFSINGER, MICHAEL RAGER, DANIEL REPP, JOHN RITTER, MICHAEL RITTER, ISAAC SHIVELY, AMIA THRALLS, JOSEPH WALTERS, GEORGE WERNER, BARTHOL- OMEW WILLIAMS, JACOB WORMAN, total $191.73. pp 51, 52, 53, 54, 55

Filed 11 Dec, 1818. Inv and appr of DANIEL C. COOPER on 17 Aug, 1818. Widow allowed $1000 for year's maintenance; estate total $3626.00. Public sale on 28 Sept, 1818; buyers: STEPHEN C. AYRES, HENRY BACON, JOHN BRADFORD, SAMUEL BRINGHAM, EPHRAIM BROADWELL, WILLIAM COX, LAYTON DICK, FIELDING GOSNEY, WILLIAM W. GREEN, JOHN GRIMES, FREDERICK HAMMER, GEORGE HAMMER, DAVID HUSTON, NOAH JOHNSON, WILLIAM KING, JACOB LEHMAN, HENRY MARQUART, THOMAS MORRISON, WILLIAM OWENS, JOSEPH PEIRCE, HORATIO G. PHILLIPS, DANIEL PIERSON, ABRAHAM RICHARDSON, JOSEPH RODEFER, ISAAC SPINNING, EBENEZER STEBBINS, BENJAMIN VAN CLEVE, total $769.18. pp 55, 56, 57, 58

Filed 29 Dec, 1818. Inv and appr of estate of PETER LEHMAN on 23 Dec, 1818. Total $229.00. Public sale

on 24 Oct, 1818. Buyers: JOHN BELL, JOHN BRANDEN-
BURGH, PETER BREWER, SAMUEL BURGHER, DAVID BURNS,
NICHOLAS HALL, DAVID LEHMAN, JACOB LEHMAN, JOHN LEH-
MAN, HENRY MARQUART, WARREN MUNGER, FREDERICK OCKS,
ALEXANDER SIMPSON, DANIEL STUTSMAN, RICHARD WHEATLEY,
total $226.66. pp 58, 59, 60, 61

Filed 26 Jan, 1819. Inv and appr of estate of NATHAN
SILVER SR on 21 Nov, 1818. Total $201.92. Debt due
from LUCENDA EDWARDS. pp 61, 62

Inv and appr of estate of JAMES JAMISON on 8 Dec,
1818. Total $156. Widow kept $87.00 in property.
Public sale on 1 Jan, 1819; buyers: THOMAS BELL, JOHN
BUCHANON, JEREMIAH COLLINS, JOSEPH KENNEDY, CHARLES
W. LIONS, JOSEPH MEKER, JOHN MILLER, JOHN PORTER,
JOHN REED, total $72.63. pp 62, 63, 64

Inv and appr of estate of ABRAHAM ZESS or HESS on 14
Nov, 1818. Total $164.54 included judgement due from
WILLIAM ROBINSON. Widow ELIZABETH ZESS/HESS allowed
$164.50 for year's maintenance. pp 64, 65, 66

Filed 15 March, 1819. Inv and appr of estate of
PHILLIP BRENNER by apprs JACOB MATTHEWS, JACOB REPLO-
GEL, no total given. Public sale on 18 Nov, 1818.
Accounts due estate from MICHAEL BOYER, GEORGE BREN-
NER, JACOB BRENNER, LEWIS BRENNER, PHILIP BRENNER,
SIMON BRENNER HENRY DEAM, HENRY FRY, JACOB REPLOGEL,
FREDERICK SHANKS, PETER SCHLOSSER, GEORGE SHANKS,
JOHN ZIDIKE, plus 2 notes due on persons formerly in
VA, JOHN P. ROACH & NATHAN TUMMELSTOUS. Total
estate $4299.63. pp 66, 67, 68

Filed 21 April, 1819. Inv and appr of estate of
REUBEN WAGGONER on 29 Jan, 1819, total $89.00. p 68

Special session 13 Feb, 1819

Case 360. Will of WILLIAM WAUGH. Witness: WILLIAM
KING, MICHAEL SHANK, GEORGE P. SAVAGE. Exec: JANE
WAUGH & SAMUEL ARCHER. Appr: DAVID LAMME, JAMES
McGREW, MICHAEL SHENCK. p 69

Case 361. Adm of estate of DANIEL HOOVER granted to
ANDREW HOOVER, MARTIN SHEETS. Sec: SOLOMON BYRKET,
ANDREW FOUTS. Appr: JOSEPH KESSLER, DANIEL RAZOR,
ANDREW LINKS. p 69

Term of April, 1819

Case 362. Will of GEORGE LINKS or SINKS. Exec:

MARY LINKS/SINKS, GEORGE LINKS/SINKS, ANDREW LINKS/
SINKS. Witness: DAVID HOOVER, JOHN WERTZ. Appr:
DANIEL YOUNT, JAMES INSCO, DANIEL RAZOR. p 70

Case 363. Adm of estate of HENRY CLARK JR granted to
JESSE CLARK & ANDREW CLARK (widow relinquished right)
Sec: GEORGE C. DAVIS, DAVID P. JOHN. Appr: WILLIAM
DODDS JR, ALBERT R. HUEY, JOHN HIZER. p 70

JOHN WAGGONER, exec of estate of DANIEL HOOVER JR,
relinquished guardianship of heirs. p 70

Case 364. WILLIAM MANLOW, 17 yrs, son of WILLIAM MAN-
LOW, dec, chose ALEXANDER McCONNEL as guardian. p 71

Case 365. NIMROD HADDIX, 14 yrs, son of NIMROD
HADDIX, dec, chose JOHN HADDIX as guardian. p 71

Case 366. LEMUEL JAMES EDWARDS, 14 yrs, son of JOHN
EDWARDS, dec, chose WILLIAM DODDS SR as guardian. p
71

Case 367. Heirs of WILLIAM SNIDER, dec: SUSANNAH
SNIDER, 15 yrs, chose HENRY BROMBAUGH as guardian.
Sec: JOHN BAKER, JACOB WARNER. p 71

Case 368. SAMUEL FOLKERTH appted guardian of HENRY
SNIDER, 13 yrs, JACOB, 11 yrs, CATHERINE 9 yrs,
DANIEL 7 yrs, all minor heirs of WILLIAM SNIDER, dec.
Sec: HENRY BROMBAUGH, JACOB WERNER. p 71

Heirs of JACOB STONER, dec:
Case 369. FANNY STONER, 17 yrs, chose GEORGE STUMP
as guardian. Court appted STUMP guardian of JOHN,
13 yrs, POLLY 11 yrs, ANNA 9 yrs, JACOB 5 yrs, all
heirs of JACOB STONER, dec. Sec: SAMUEL LARRICK.
pp 71, 72

MARTIN HOOVER's heirs:
Case 370. MARTIN HOOVER, 16 yrs, chose JONAS HOOVER
as guardian. Court apptd JONAS guardian of PEGGY
HOOVER, 8 yrs. Sec: ROBERT McCONNEL. p 72

Case 371. DANIEL HEISTAND appted guardian of ABRAHAM
HOOVER, 12 yrs, & ESTHER HOOVER, 10 yrs. Sec: GEORGE
PUTERBAUGH. p 72

CATHERINE HOOVER, widow of MARTIN, relinquished right
to be apptd guardian. p 72

Case 372. Admr of JACOB BAKER petitioned to sell
land. p 72

Case 373. Adm of estate of WILLIAM CURTZ granted to GEORGE BRUNER. Sec: CHRISTOPHER TAYLOR, LEWIS SHUEY. Appr: FREDERICK HAFFNER, GEORGE HAFFNER, GEORGE RAW. p 73

Heirs of ANDREW EMRICK, dec:
Case 374. CATHERINE EMRICK, 15 yrs, chose CHRISTO-PHER EMRICK as guardian. Sec: JOHN STUMP. p 73

Case 375. ELIZABETH EMRICK, 14 yrs, chose CHRISTO-PHER TAYLOR as guardian. Court appted TAYLOR as guardian of SAMUEL EMRICK, 11 yrs. Sec: GEORGE BRUNER. p 73

Case 376. GEORGE EMRICK apptd guardian to JOHN EMRICK, 9 yrs, & POLLY EMRICK, 6 yrs. Sec: CHRISTO-PHER TAYLOR. p 73

Case 377. LEWIS SHUEY appted guardian of PETER EMRICK, 4 yrs, & ANDREW EMRICK, 1 yr. Sec: PHILIP GUNCKEL. p 73

Case 378. JAMES HANNA appted guardian of AMOS THOMPSON HANNA, 8 yrs, & HARRIET NEWELL HANNA, 2 yrs, children of said JAMES, who are entitled to share of estate of dec mother & under will of grandfather JOHN McLEAN, dec. Sec: OBADIAH B. CONOVER. p 74

Case 379. JOHN WILLIAMS appted guardian to his children, to receive legacy from grandfather (not named). Children: JOHN 12 yrs, NATHANIEL 10 yrs, WILLIAM 9 yrs, MATILDA 5 yrs, ELIAS 3 yrs. Sec: ABRAHAM DARST. p 74

Case 380. JOHN GIEL, 17 yrs, minor heir of JOHN GIEL, dec, chose SAMUEL ARCHER as guardian. Sec: WARREN MUNGER. p 74

Case 381. Adm of estate of ABNER GARARD granted to JONATHAN GARARD & WILLIAM BUCKELS (widow relinquished right). Sec: WILLIAM LUCE, EDWARD MITCHEL. Appr: BENJAMIN ARCHER, BENJAMIN MALTBIE, SAMUEL BROADAWAY. pp 74, 75

Case 382. Will of ELIZABETH EWING. Witness: JOHN STEELE who attested to signature of other witness, WILLIAM WAUGH, dec. Exec: SAMUEL EWING. p 75

Case 383. Admr (JAMES FERGUS & MARGARET MILLER, late MARGARET ARCHER) of estate of ZACARIAH ARCHER peti-tion to allow deed conveyance to JOHN STOKER SR. p 75

Admr of WILLIAM SNIDER requested authority to make land paymts to U.S. to procure patent. p 75

Case 384. Admrs (JOSEPH H. CRANE, AARON BAKER & MARY BAKER, late MARY NOLAND) of JAMES NOLAND petition to sell Dayton lot 38. JAMES STEELE, JOHN M. GROVE, LUTHER BRUEN appted to appr. Value set at $500. Court set terms of sale. pp 75, 76

Case 385. BENJAMIN ARCHER, trustee of property of JOSEPH C. SILVER, an insolvent debtor, produced accounts. Balance of $35.37 remains. p 76, 77

Admr of GEORGE SHEIDLER & JOHN SHEIDLER filed heirs' receipts: SOLOMON SHEIDLER, GEORGE SHEIDLER, DANIEL SHEIDLER, BENJAMIN BOWMAN, DAVID SHEIDLER, ABRAHAM TROXELL, BARBARA GRIPE. p 77

Exec of HENRY GEPHART filed heirs' receipts: HENRY GEPHART, GEORGE GEPHART, JOHN SHAW, GEORGE GEPHART as admr of estate of JOHN GEPHART, HENRY APPLE, JACOB WEAVER. pp 77, 78

Exec of JACOB OVERHOLSER produced settlement. Balance of $18.04. Cash paid to JOHN A. MIKESELL, LEONARD WOLF (coffin), PHILIP MIKESELL, HENRY GOODLANDER. Accts rcvd from JOHN MUSSELMAN, DAVID WAGGONER. pp 78, 79

Admr of JAMES NOLAND produced accounts while NOLAND was acting as admr of estate of WILLIAM NEWCOM. Cash paid to ISAAC G. BURNET, D.C. COOPER, JOHN GRIMES, HUGH McCOLLOM, JANE NEWCOM, JOHN NEWCOM, widow CATHERINE NEWCOM, now wife of JOHN BAKER. NEWCOM estate turned over to BAKER who produced settlement. Cash paid to JOHN DODSON (taxes), JOHN KING (taxes), HENRY MARQUART, JOHN REGANS (taxes), IRA SMITH (taxes). Widow's third rcvd by "CHARLOTTE, wife of said BAKER, widow of said WILLIAM." pp 79, 80, 81

HENRY BOWSER, admr of DANIEL BOWSER, produced settlement. Cash paid to CHRISTIAN ARNOLD, SAMUEL BOLTIN, ANN BOWSER, CHRISTIAN BROWER, ISAAC G. BURNET, PETER CAYLOR, CHARLES R. GREEN, JACOB GROW, DANIEL HECK, PETER HECK, DAVID HOOVER, JOHN HUNTZINGER, PHILIP MIKESELL, DANIEL MILLER, JACOB MYERS, JOSEPH RYAN, NATHANIEL STUTSMAN, Dr. PETER TREON, HENRY WERTZ, total $183.80. Cash paid to JOHN EMRICK for bringing money from PA. Balance of $99.39. pp 82, 83

JOHN R. PARKS, admr of estate of ROBERT GILCHRIST, produced settlement. Widow's third = $329.93, to other heirs = $659.87. pp 83, 84

Admr of WILLIAM SCHENCK produced settlement. Balance
of $2398.75 remained. pp 84, 85

Admr of SAMUEL CROWELL produced settlement. Cash
paid to JOHN BAKER, BENJAMIN BAYLESS, GEORGE G. BRAD-
FORD, JAMES G. BRADFORD, JOHN BRADFORD, HENRY BROWN,
O.B. CONOVER, JOHN ENSEY, Dr. CHARLES ESTE, ENOCH
FAIRCHILD, ROBERT GRAY, JEROM HOLT, SMITH LANE, JOHN
MILLER, JOHN STEELE, ALEX WEAD, ROBERT WEAD. Balance
of $379.11. pp 85, 86

Admr of GEORGE HANEY produced settlement. Cash paid
to ABRAHAM BRANNAMAN, SAMUEL DILLE, ROBERT J. SKIN-
NER, JACOB KOOGLER, SAMUEL KOOGLER, PETER MIKESELL,
JAMES MILLER, H.G. PHILLIPS, total $83.77. pp 86, 87

Admr of ANDREW EMRICK produced settlement. Widow's
third = $202.86, due $101.01; 7 other heirs to divide
$405.73. Cash paid to JOSEPH BANKER, GEORGE BOYER,
CHARLES BUXTON, HENRY CHRIST, ADAM DROLLINGER, CHRIS-
TOPHER EMRICK, GEORGE EMRICK, JOHN GUNCKEL, JOHN
KELLER, GEORGE LOY, JACOB OVERHOLSER, GEORGE SHEIDLER
MARY SHEIDLER, LEWIS SHUEY, ROBERT J. SKINNER (print-
ing ads), JOHN STIVER GEORGE STUMP, MICHAEL TEMPLE,
THOMAS WINTERS. Cash rcvd from SARAH MARSH. pp 87,
88, 89

Admr of GEORGE SOURBRAY produced settlement. Each of
5 heirs to rcve $70.98. Debts owed estate by SAMUEL
ARCHER, ABRAHAM BARNET, JAMES BARNET, JAMES BECK,
WILLIAM BOMBERGER, GEORGE CROFT, CHRISTOPHER CURTNER,
HENRY CURTNER, FRANCIS DILTS, DAVID DUNCAN, ABRAHAM
EDWARDS, WILLIAM GEORGE, GEORGE GROVE, GEORGE HARRIS,
JEROM HOLT, JOHN LEHMAN, HENRY MARQUART, JAMES
McCANN's heirs, SIMPSON McCARTER, JOHN McCLEARY (pd
$2.50 for digging widow's grave), AARON MILLER, JAMES
MILLER, JOHN MILLER, PETER MONFORT, GEORGE NEWCOM,
JAMES NOLAN, H.G. PHILLIPS, JOSEPH PREVO, GEORGE W.
SMITH, WILLIAM M. SMITH, BARNHART SPECK, WILLIAM VAN
CLEVE, WILLIAM VANDERSLICE, PHILIP WAGGONER, SAMUEL
WATTON, WILLIAM WATTON, JAMES WELSH, JOHN WODERMAN,
PETER WOOD. pp 89, 90, 91

Admr of CHARLES ESTE reported land did not sell (lack
of bids). Request time extension to settle estate.
pp 91, 92

Admr of JAMES NOLAN produced settlement. Debts owed
to estate by JOHN BAKER, JOHN BRADFORD, JOSEPH BROWN,
ISAAC DAVIS, JOHN DAVIS, MARY DAVIS, CHARLES ESTE,

WILLIAM P. FINDLEY, JACOB FISHER, DAVID HARTMAN, MOSES HATFIELD, G. J. HUSTON, WILLIAM IRVIN, DAVID LINDSLEY, JAMES LODGE, HENRY MARQUART, JOHN MILLER, E.K. MUNGER, WILLIAM MURPHY, PETER MUSSELMAN, SAMUEL NEWCOM, AA. NUTT, MATT PETTON, H.G. PHILLIPS, DAVID SIMMONS, WILLIAM TYLER, JAMES WELSH, MARTIN WEYBRIGHT ROBERT WILSON, total $309.37. Notes due estate from JOS. BROWN, THOMAS COTTOM, THOMAS HAMER, WILLIAM PATTERSON. Balance of $333.84. pp 92, 93, 94

Inv and appr of estate of DANIEL RAZOR on 14 Jan, 1819. Total $570.81. Debts due from DANIEL RAZOR JR, JACOB ARNOLD, JOHN OBLINGER, JOHN WAITMAN, JOHN ARNOLD, total $965.48. pp 94, 95, 96, 97

Public sale of estate of JAMES NOLAN on 11 Nov, 1815. Buyers: JOHN ANDERSON, JAMES BARTLOW, HENRY BOWSER, JOHN BRADFORD, JOSEPH BROWN, ROBERT CAMPBELL, WILLIAM CLARK, JOHN COX, WILLIAM COX, J.H. CRANE, CHARLES ESTE, FIELDING GOSNEY, GEORGE GROVE, GEORGE HUFFMAN, JACOB KUHN, WILLIAM LANE, DAVID LEHMAN, PETER LEHMAN, THOMAS LENNON, BENJAMIN LONG, JAMES MORGAN, MOSES MORRISON, HARRY NOMAN, JOHN PATTERSON, DANIEL PIERSON NATHANIEL RHOADS, IRA SMITH, WILLIAM M. SMITH, GEORGE SNIDER, JOHN SNIDER, DAVID STEELE, JACOB STEPHENS, JACOB STEPHENSON, JAMES THOMSON, MOSES THOMSON, ROBERT WILSON, total $207.76. Inv and appr of estate of JAMES NOLAN, total $307.37. Allowance of $100 for support of widow, child. pp 97, 98, 99, 100, 101, 102, 103

Filed 12 May, 1819. Inv and appr of estate of DANIEL HOOVER on 1 March, 1819. Total of $789.78. Debts owed by PETER HOOVER, JOSEPH RORER, ANDREW WAYMIRE, DANIEL YOUNT total $201.30. Public sale on 5 March, 1819; buyers: CHRISTIAN BURKET, DANIEL BURKET, JACOB BURKET ABRAHAM COBLE, SUSANNA COBLE, JOHN COX, JOHN CURTIS, EPHRAIM ELKERS, ANDREW FOUTS, JOHN FOUTS, JAMES HALL, ANDREW HOOVER, DANIEL HOOVER, DAVID HOOVER, HENRY HOOVER, JONAS HOOVER, MICHAEL HOOVER, NANCY HOOVER, MARTIN HOW, BENJAMIN HUTCHINS, BENJAMIN IDDINGS, ABEL INSCO, DRURY JONES, STEPHEN KENNEDY, JOHN MAN, JOHN McCLINTOCK, ABRAHAM McINTOSH, JOHN MOTE, JOSEPH NEWMAN, THOMAS NEWMAN, JOHN NORTH, CORNELIUS PIPPINGER, PHILIP RASOR, JOHN RITTENHOUSE, WILLIAM RITTENHOUSE, MARTIN SHEETS, ANDREW SINKS, DANIEL SMITH, JACOB SMITH, LEVI STALEY, MARTIN STALEY, JOHN STARE, ANDREW WAYMIRE, JACOB ZOOK. Total $797.47. pp 103, 104, 105, 106, 107, 108, 109, 110

Filed 20 April, 1819. Inv and appr of estate of JOHN REGANS on 19 Apr, 1819. Included allowance set off for widow & family. Accts owed by WILLIAM BOMBERGER, AARON BAKER, ELIAS BALDWIN, DAVID HILDRETH (absconded), JEROM HOLT, JAMES LOUGH, PETER MIKESELL, DAVID REID, ISAAC SPINNING, WILLIAM TAYLOR total $525.78. Cash paid to DAVID REID, ALEX GRIMES, HENRY BROWN, DAVID WORMAN. Balance of $180.98. pp 111, 112

Filed 8 June, 1819. Public sale of estate of JAMES SCOTT, undated. Buyers: JOSEPH BACON, DAVID BEER, THOMAS BEER, MOSES CODINGTON, JACOB CROWELL, GEORGE DILL, JOHN FURMAN, JOSEPH GILLESPIE, JOB KEYS, EDWARD MITCHEL, DAVID MAJOR, JAMES MOYER, WILLIAM NEATH, WILLIAM REEDER, ROBERT SCOTT, ROBERT SWIFT, DANIEL WATKINS, GEORGE WATKINS, ISAAC WOODWARD, total $160.40. pp 112, 113, 114

Inv and appr of estate of ABNER GARARD on 19 May, 1819. Total $793.45. Public sale on 20 May, 1819; buyers: DAVID ARCHER, JOHN BOWEN, DANIEL BRELSFORD, ALEXANDER BRICE, DANIEL BROADSTREET, WILLIAM BUCKLES, JACOB CANE, SAMUEL CAVENDER, ABRAHAM CHAMBERLIN, GOLDSMITH CHANDLER, THOMAS CLAWSON, ISAAC COON, MAHLON DAVIS, AARON FERGUSON, JOSEPH FISK, WILLIAM FULLERTON, BENJAMIN FRASURE, JOHN GARARD, JONATHAN GARARD, JOHN JAMES, JEREMIAH HATFIELD, JOHN HATFIELD, WILLIAM LUCE, JOHN LUNKEN, BENJAMIN MALTBIE, CHARLES MILLER, EDWARD MITCHEL, AARON NUTT, MOSES NUTT, GEORGE PERSON, JOHN ROBERT, ROBERT SILVERS, HENRY STANSEL, ABEDNIGO STEPHENS, MICHAEL SWIGART, ABIJAH TAYLOR, JACOB WILTRE, ASHBERRY WOOD, ABEL WRIGHT. Total $841.75. Debts owed estate by SOLOMON BLUE, JACOB CONSOLER, ABRAHAM CRAMER, HENRY DAMPIER, JOHN GARARD, JACOB GATES, BENJAMIN HILLMAN, ALLEN JAMES, DAVID JONES, WILLIAM McNEAL, ISAIAH NOLAND, JAMES PARKER, JOHN PETTIT, THOMAS SHEETS, JACOB TRANT total $123.66. pp 114, 115, 116, 117, 118, 119, 120, 121

Filed 2 July, 1819. Inv and appr of estate of GEORGE SINKS on 27 May, 1819. Total $532.81. Debts due from JOSEPH BURKET, JOSHUA COX, JOHN FOLAND, PETER HOOVER, THOMAS NEWMAN, DANIEL RAZOR, JACOB SHEETS, GEORGE SINKS JR, MARTIN STALEY, JOHN WAGGONER, FREDERICK WAYMIRE, JOHN WERTZ, DANIEL YOUNT, JOHN YOUNT total $841.96. pp 121, 122, 123

Inv and appr of estate of WILLIAM WAUGH on 17 Feb, 1819. Total $1083.50. pp 124, 125, 126

Special session 29 July, 1819

Case 386. Adm of estate of DAVID P. JOHN granted to MARY JOHN. Sec: HENRY MARQUART, GEORGE C. DAVIS.

Appr: GEORGE GROVE, GEORGE NEWCOM, JOHN FOLKERTH. p127

Filed 2 Aug. 1819. Inv and appr of estate of HENRY CLARK JR. Total $253.67. Debts due from NELSON R. BROWN, BENNET CARTER, ANDREW CLARK, HENRY CLARK, JESSE CLARK, JOHN DODDS, MATTHEW DODDS, WILLIAM DODDS, SAMUEL HAGAR, ALBERT HUEY, EDMUND PARROTT total $241.15. pp 127, 128

Filed 5 July, 1819. Public sale of estate of WILLIAM WAUGH on 13 March, 1819. Buyers: JOHN BRANDENBURGH, JAMES CHATHAM, PETER CLAWSON, THOMAS CLAWSON, ROBERT COLEMAN, SAMUEL DILLE, WILLIAM DILS, MOSES IRWIN, DANIEL LICHLIDER, LEWIS LICHLIDER, SAMUEL LONGSTREATH ARCHIBALD McGREW, JAMES MORRISON, AARON NUTT, MATHIAS PARSON, JACOB REESE, JOHN RIKE, BENJAMIN SCOTT, JOHN SHROYER, JACOB SWADNER, JAMES THOMSON. Total $267.39. Debts owed by JOHN COLE, WILLIAM DAY, WILLIAM DODDS, JACOB EATON, GIDEON GOODSPEED, TAYLOR HALL, JOHN NEIBLE, GEORGE P. SAVAGE, HENRY SIMMERMAN, ISRAEL TAYLOR, B. VAN CLEVE total $240.62. pp 129, 130, 131

Term of August, 1819

Case 387. Will of GEORGE YOUNT. Witness: DANIEL YOUNT, JOHN YOUNT. Exec: Widow MARY YOUNT & FREDE-RICK YOUNT. Appr: DANIEL YOUNT, SAMUEL MARTINDALE, DAVID HOOVER. p 131

Case 388. Will of MARY BICKEL. Witness: HENRY SHUEY, ANDREW ETZLER. Exec: GEORGE SHAFFER. Appr: MARTIN SHUEY, WILLIAM DODDS, JACOB BANN. p 132

Case 389. Will of HENRY CLARK. Witness: NATHAN WORLEY, GEORGE RENNICK. Exec: AMOS CLARK & ANDREW CLARK. Appr: JOHN M. WILLIAMS, WILLIAM KING, ROBERT WILSON. p 132

Case 390. Will of EBENEZER WEADE. Witness: JOHN CRABS, BENJAMIN CRABS. Exec: DAVID HUSTON. Appr: JOHN CRABS, BENJAMIN CRABS, ABRAHAM NOUER. p 132

Case 391. Adm of estate of HENRY ROYER granted to GEORGE ROYER (widow relinquished right). Sec: JOHN MIKESELL, NICHOLAS CREVISTON. Appr: MARTIN WIBRIGHT, PETER SWANK, ISAAC THOMSON. pp 132, 133

Case 392. Adm of estate of SETH KELLOGG granted to ETHEL KELLOGG & ELIHU KELLOGG (widow EUNICE KELLOGG relinquished right). Sec: JOHN ARCHER, ISAAC WOOD-WARD. Appr: BENJAMIN MALTBIE, HENRY STANSEL, JOHN HARRIS. p 133

Case 393. JOSEPH EVANS, 16 yrs, heir of LEWIS EVANS, dec, chose MARTIN SPRAGUE as guardian. p 133

Admr of JACOB WIRICK requested time extension to settle estate. p 133

Case 394. Adm of estate of STEPHEN ARCHER SR granted to JAMES MILLER. Sec: SAMUEL ARCHER, ISAAC GRIFFITH. Appr: JACOB ARNOLD, JOHN KNIGHT, SIMON BRANER. p 134

Case 395. DANIEL RUSE, 16 yrs, minor heir of NICHO-LAS RUSE chose NATHANIEL STUTSMAN as guardian. Sec: ADAM MILMAN. p 134

PETER HEISTAND restored to reason; guardianship to be dissolved. p 134

Case 396. Adm of estate of THOMAS KELSEY granted to DANIEL KELSEY, WILLIAM KELSEY (widow relinquished right). Sec: ISAAC WOODWARD, ISAAC COON. Appr: SAM-UEL BROADAWAY, BENJAMIN MALTBIE, BENJAMIN ARCHER. p 135

Admr of CHARLES ESTE reported land sale. p 135

Admr of JAMES NOLAN reported land sale. p 135

Admr of JACOB BAKER reported land sale. pp 135, 136

JULIANNA CLARK, widow of HENRY CLARK, made election to take her dower, relinquishing legacy of the will. p 136

Case 397. Admr of estate of THOMAS JAY petitioned to convey deed to WALTER D. JAY for 60 acres in Sec 6, T 3, R 6. Permission granted. p 136

Admr of CHARLES ESTE requested time extension. p 136

Case 398. PETER CASTOR, 19 yrs, heir of CONRAD CAS-TOR, chose SAMUEL BRINGHAM as guardian. Sec: ABRAHAM DARST. pp 136, 137

Case 399. THOMAS CASTOR, 18 yrs, & JOHN CASTOR, 16 yrs, heirs of CONRAD CASTOR, chose BENJAMIN WAGGONER as guardian. Sec: GEORGE BEARDSHIRE. p 137

Case 400. JAMES JOHNSON appted guardian of ELIZABETH CASTOR, 10 yrs, BARSHEBA CASTOR, 7 yrs, REBECCA CAS-TOR, 5 yrs. Sec: EDWARD McDERMOTT. p 137

Case 401. Widow of HENRY CLARK relinquished right to

be appted guardian. MICHAEL RAGER appted guardian of JOHN CLARK, 6 yrs, & REBECCA CLARK, 3 yrs, minor heirs of HENRY CLARK, dec. Sec: ABRAHAM BARNET. p 137

JOHN ZIDECKER, exec of estate of PHILIP MILLER, made settlement. Whole estate ($100) paid to widow. p 137

Admr of estate of JACOB STONER produced settlement. $180.10 to be paid 1/2 to widow, balance to heirs. Cash paid to HENRY ZELLER, JAMES McBRIDE. Notes due from JOHN KINZEY, ADAM SWINEHART, ROBERT SILVER an insolvent debtor, WILLIAM MILLER ("who is dead or gone to parts unknown"), and a judgement against JAMES QUINN. p 138

Admr of SAMUEL KINNAMON produced settlement. Cash paid to JOHN HOLMES, ADAM MILMAN, JOHN OLDFATHER, ROBERT J. SKINNER (printing ads), ADAM STIVER, HENRY WEAVER, JOHN WEAVER. Balance of $255.91. Widow's half = $127.95. p 139

Admr of JAMES NOLAN requested time extension to settle estate. p 140

Special session 25 Aug, 1819

Case 402. Adm of estate of MARY MAGDALENE GEPHART granted to HENRY GEPHART & GEORGE GEPHART. Sec: JACOB WEAVER, JOHN SNEP. Appr: ABRAHAM TROXELL, PETER RACHER, MATTHIAS RIGAL. p 140

Special session 11 Sept, 1819

Case 403. Adm of estate of ENOCH BOWEN granted to NATHANIEL WILSON (widow relinquished right). Sec: RALPH WILSON, DAVID HENDERSON. Appr: THOMAS KING, JOHN MURRAY, GEORGE NEWCOM. p 141

Case 404. Will of MARY DAVIS. Witness: BENJAMIN VAN CLEVE, CATHERINE ETTER & ELEANOR RICHARDSON. Exec: LEWIS DAVIS & DANIEL DAVIS. Appr: GEORGE GROVE, JAMES HANNA, ISAAC CONOVER. p 141

Public sale of estate of THOMAS JAY, no date given. Buyers: MICHAEL BRICKER, THOMAS BROWN, JACOB BURKET, ABRAHAM CRESS, JOHN CRESS, HENRY ELLER, LEMUEL FINCH-ER, JESSE FRIEND, DAVID HOOVER, HENRY HOOVER, MERLIE HUTCHINS, MERRIDA HUTCHINS, ABEL INSCO, JAMES INSCO, JAMES JAY, SAMUEL JAY, TAMER JAY, WILLIAM JAY, STEPHEN JONES, JAMES NIGHT, THOMAS MACY, ISAAC R. MARSH, SOLOMON MICHAEL, JOHN MOTE, JONATHAN NEWMAN,

WILLIAM NORTH, CHARLES PATTY, JAMES PEARSON, POWEL
PEARSON, WILLIAM PEARSON, PHILIP RATER, JOHN ROHRER,
DAVID SHEARER, ANDREW SINKS, GEORGE SINKS, ELIJAH
SPENCER, JUDITH SWEET, GEORGE WALKER, ANDREW WAYMIRE,
JOSEPH WILLIAMS, JAMES WRIGHT, JOHN YOUNT. Total
$372.69. pp 142, 143, 144, 145

Admr of SAMUEL CROWELL produced heirs' recpts: LINESY
JOHNSON, ELLIS BALDWIN, widow ELIZABETH CROWELL for
herself and as guardian of CHARITY, PHEBE & MARY
CROWELL. p 146

Filed 21 Sept, 1819. Inv and appr of estate of MAG-
DALENE GEPHART of Jefferson Twp. Included notes due
from JOHN CASPER DILL, PHILIP GEPHART, ABRAHAM TROX-
ELL, JOHN VERTS. Total $2095.51. pp 146, 147, 148

Special session 20 Sept, 1819

Case 405. Adm of estate of TALLMAN HALL granted to
CHARLES SMITH & FRANCIS DILTS. Sec: H.G. PHILLIPS,
HENRY MARQUART. Appr: DAVID LAMME, JAMES McGREW,
HENRY DIEHL. pp 148, 149

Special session 2 Oct, 1819

Case 406. Adm of estate of ISAAC WOODWARD granted to
JEMIMA WOODWARD & JAMES WOODWARD. Sec: JOHN BECK,
JOHN C. MURPHY. Appr: BENJAMIN ROBBINS, AARON NUTT,
LEVI NUTT. p 149

Special session 7 Oct, 1819

Case 407. Adm of estate of JOSHUA WHITE granted to
NANCY WHITE. Sec: JOSEPH BROWN, JAMES WATTS. Appr:
JONATHAN HARSHMAN, ALEXANDER SNODGRASS, HENRY ROBIN-
SON. p 149

Filed 22 Oct, 1819. Inv and appr of estate of HENRY
ROYER, made by apprs PETER SWANK, MARTIN WIBRICHT,
ISAAC THOMSON. Widow kept $46.80 in property. Pub-
lic sale, no date given. Buyers: ISAAC ARNOLD, JONA-
THAN BRIMLEY, JANE BROWN, NICHOLAS CRAVISTON, DAVID
HECK, BASTIAN HEETER, GEORGE HEETER, JOHN HEETER, F.
HOLTZAPPLE, HENRY HUNTSINGER, GEORGE KEPLER, DANIEL
MUNDHENK, JACOB RARICK, JOHN RARICK, MICHAEL ROGER,
HENRY ROOF, PETER ROOF, GEORGE ROYER, DANIEL SWANK,
PETER SWANK. Total $121.30. pp 150, 151, 152

Public sale, estate of MAGDALEN GEPHART, 1 Oct, 1819.
Buyers: JOHN BOLENBAUGH, PETER BOLENBAUGH, BENJAMIN
BOWMAN, DANIEL BOWSER, JOHN GARVER, THOMAS CRITSER,

GEORGE EIKENBRIGHT, JOHN EIKENBRIGHT, EBENEZER EMMONS
JACOB EMRICK, DANIEL GEBHART, GEORGE GEBHART, HENRY
GEBHART JR, HENRY GEBHART SR, JACOB GEBHART, JOHN
GEBHART's widow, PHILIP GEBHART, JOHN GETTER, DAVID
GUSHWA, DAVID HOOVER, GEORGE KOONS, CHRISTOPHER
LEATHY, JOHN LEIPCAP, MICHAEL LITEY, GEORGE LOY,
ENOCH MILES, ABRAHAM MULLENDORE, JACOB MULLENDORE,
FREDERICK NEWHART, JOHN NINE, JOSEPH ROCKENFIELD,
MICHAEL ROGER, HENRY RUNNELS, ABRAHAM SCOOK, DANIEL
SHEIDLER, JACOB SHEPHERD, JACOB SHOCK, JOHN SHOOTER,
JOHN SNEP, BENJAMIN STIVER, SUSANNA STUDEBAKER, JOHN
TREON, ABRAHAM TROXELL, STEPHEN ULRICH, JACOB WEAVER,
JACOB WEAVER JR, MICHAEL WEAVER, GEORGE WEIMER,
CHRISTIAN WELDY, DANIEL WOLF, JACOB WOLF, JOHN YEAZEL
Total $404.02.   pp 152, 153

Inv and appr of estate of EBENEZER WEAD JR of Dayton
Twp on 16 Aug, 1819. Total $128.00. pp 153, 154

Filed 8 Nov, 1819. Inv and appr of estate of GEORGE
YOUNT of Butler Twp on 16 Oct, 1819.   Total $769.43.
pp 154, 155

Inv and appr of estate of ENOCH BOWEN on 18 Sept,
1819. Total $689.25. p 156

Inv and appr of estate of THOMAS KELSEY on 9 Sept,
1819. Totl $676.25. Public sale on 11 Sept, 1819.
Buyers not named; total $599.68.   pp 157, 158, 159,
160

Inv and appr of estate of SETH KELLOGG on 17 Sept,
1819. Total $271.81. Public sale on 18 Sept, 1819;
buyers: NATHAN BALLARD, ROBERT BRANNUM, THOMAS BROWN,
PETER CARRINGTON, THOMAS CLAWSON, ISAAC COON, BENJA-
MIN FRAZER, JONATHAN GARARD, THOMAS HALL, TITUS H.
IVES, ELIHU KELLOGG, ETHEL KELLOGG, EUNICE KELLOGG,
DANIEL KELSEY, WILLIAM LUCE, BENJAMIN MALTBIE, DANIEL
McNEAL, JOHN McNEAL, GEORGE MEDARD, SIMON MORGAN,
EDMUND MUNGER, JONATHAN MUNGER, JOHN ROBERTS, JAMES
SMITH, JACOB SMOOT, ASHER TIBBALS, NOAH TIBBALS,
HOWELL WATSON, JACOB WILLSEY, JAMES WONDERLY.   pp
161, 162, 163, 164

Term of November, 1819

Case 408. Heirs of DANIEL SHIVELY: DANIEL SHIVELY,
19 yrs, chose SUSANNAH SHIVELY, widow of DANIEL, as
guardian. She relinquished right of guardianship of
all other heirs. Sec: DAVID ULRICH. p 165

Case 409. DAVID SHIVELY, 17 yrs, chose DAVID SHIVELY

as guardian. Sec: JACOB SHIVELY. p 165

Case 410. JOHN SHIVELY, 15 yrs, chose JACOB SHIVELY as guardian. Sec: DAVID SHIVELY. p 165

Admr of BENJAMIN BARKALOW produced settlement. Widow's half = $149.96. Notes due from JACOB HARKRIDER, JAMES W. LANIER, CATHERINE PENROD, SAMUEL POTTS. Cash paid to ZEBULON BARKALOW, JAMES CARR, THOMAS CORWINE, WILLIAM D. CRAIG, MICHAEL CRIST, GEORGE W. DALLEY, JOHN DENISE, SIDNEY DENISE, BENJAMIN DUBOIS, PHILIP GUNCKLE JR, GEORGE HALL, JACOB HARKRIDER, WILLIAM HARRISON, ISAAC HUTCHON, JOHN KELLY, DAVID D. LABOW, JAMES W. LANIER, GEORGE LOY, JAMES MORLATT, PETER PENROD, JOSEPH PITMAN, ABRAHAM PONTIUS, JACOB REPLOGEL, PHILIP REPLOGEL, JOHN ROBBINS, JOHN ROBERTSON, TIMOTHY ROBBINS, JOHN H. SCHENCK, JOHN N.C. SCHENCK, WILLIAM C. SCHENCK, MIDDLETON SELBY, EMANUEL SMITH, SUSANNA SWARTZEL, ANN TAPSCOTT, JOSEPH TAPSCOTT, PETER TREON, TOBIAS VANSCOYK, AUKEY WIKOFF, BENJAMIN WOODBRIDGE, JOHN WORLAND, ADAM ZELLER total $693.83. Debts due estate from LEWIS LEFORD, PHILIP REPLOGEL, DANIEL D. LABOW, PETER PENROD. pp 165, 166, 167

Filed 22 Nov, 1819. Exec of THOMAS JAY produced settlement. Cash paid to MICHAEL BRICKER, GEORGE BUCHANON (coffin), HENRY CROWELL, LEONARD ELLER, WILLIAM HALL, HENRY HOOVER, MARY HOOVER, ABEL INSCO, JAMES JAY, JESSE JAY, JOHN JAY, SAMUEL JAY, THOMAS MACY, SAMUEL MARTINDALE, WILLIAM McWASSON, JOHN MOTE, JONATHAN NEWMAN, JOHN NORTH SR, AMELIA PEARSON, PHILIP RADER, DAVID SINKINS, GEORGE SINKS SR, JOHN STEELE, JOHN WAGGONER, GEORGE WALKER, JOHN WERTZ, MARY YOUNT total $365.46. pp 168, 169, 170

Admr of THOMAS SHANKS of Washington Twp produced settlement. Appr by PETER EAGLE, TOBIAS WHITESEL, HENRY STRADER. Total $5.62. Balance of 97 cents on 19 Sept, 1818. p 171

Admr of NATHAN TALBERT produced settlement. Cash paid to ROBERT EWING, JOHN McCLURE, AARON NUTT, JAMES RUSSELL, RICHARD SHAW, JOHN SROYER, JACOB SWEADNOR. Balance of $529.23 after widow kept $296.42 in property. p 172

Admr of JAMES JAMISON requested time extension to settle estate. p 173

Admr of NATHAN SILVER requested time extension to settle estate. MARY SILVER, widow of NATHAN. p 173

Case 411. Adm of estate of JAMES RHEA granted to
HORATIO G. PHILLIPS. Sec: HENRY BACON, WILLIAM
HUFFMAN. Appr: CHARLES R. GREEN, WILLIAM EAKER,
ABRAHAM DARST. p 173

Case 412. Will of JOHN KINSEY. Witness: ADAM SWINE-
HART, JOHN ETTER, GEORGE ROUDEBUSH. Adm granted to
JACOB MULLENDORE (widow relinquished right). Sec:
PHILIP GUNCKEL, JOHN ETTER. Appr: JACOB SINK, ADAM
SWINEHART, Rev. JOHN BROWER. pp 173, 174

Filed 30 Dec, 1819. Inv and appr of estate of HENRY
CLARK on 28 Dec, 1819. Total $703.87. pp 174, 175

Inv and appr of estate of ISAAC WOODWARD on 27 Oct,
1819. Total $1157.76. List included hats and hat-
making supplies, most likely worked as a hatter. Pub-
lic sale on 29 Oct, 1819. Buyers: JESSE AMONS, DAV-
ID ARCHER, JOHN ARCHER, NATHAN BALLARD, JOHN BECK,
HENRY BECK, JOHN BENHAM, RICHARD BENHAM, JAMES CAMP-
BELL, JOHN CARR, JOHN CASTER, EDWARD DYER, JOHN FARN-
HAM, JOSEPH FISK, BENJAMIN FRAZER, JOHN HATFIELD,
JACOB HORNER, ELISHA JONES, SAMUEL McLUCAS, DANIEL
McNEIL, JOHN McNEIL, JOHN C. MURPHY, AARON NUTT SR,
JAMES READ, GEORGE REEDER, WILLIAM REEDER, AARON ROB-
BINS, LEVI ROBBINS, ABRAHAM RUSSELL, JAMES RUSSELL,
JOHN RUSSEL, PETER SHAFFER, JOHN SOWARD, PETER SUND-
ERLAND, ELNATHAN WERTZ, JAMES WOODWARD, JEMIMA WOOD-
WARD, SAMUEL WOODWARD. pp 176, 177,178, 179,180, 181

Inv and appr of estate of TALLMAN HALL on 14 Oct,
1819. Total $129.37. pp 181, 182

Special session 31 January, 1820

Case 413. Adm of estate of JOHN MURRAY granted to
widow ELIZABETH MURRAY. Sec: CHARLES WELBAUM, JOHN
MILLER. Appr: JACOB STUDEBAKER, HENRY FLORY, JACOB
PLESSINGER. p 182

Filed 16 Feb, 1820. Inv and appr of estate of JOSHUA
WHITE. No date given. Total $1452.69. Widow allow-
ed $200 for year's maintenance. Public sale, no date
given. Buyers: NELSON BROWN, WILLIAM COX, HENRY
ENOCH JR, HENRY ENOCH SR, WILLIAM HODGE, JACOB KEMP,
ABRAHAM B. LAWTON, DANIEL LECHLIDER, DAVID LEMON,
MICHAEL MARLEY, HENRY McGREW, WILLIAM McKEGG, JOSEPH
McREYNOLDS, ABRAHAM MORGAN, SAMUEL PREATHER, HENRY
ROBISON, HENRY ROTHAMEL, JACOB ROTHAMEL, JACOB SHEMP,
ROBERT SKINNER, PETER SLOOSER, THOMAS SNODGRASS,
THOMAS SULLIVAN, JOHN TULLIS, HENRY WHITE, NANCY
WHITE. Total $536.06. pp 183, 184, 185, 186, 187

Special session 11 Febuary, 1820

Case 414. Adm of estate of CONRAD LIGHTY granted to JACOB LIGHTY & CHRISTOPHER LIGHTY (widow SUSANNAH LIGHTY relinquished right). Sec: GEORGE GEPHART, DANIEL MYERS. Appr: PETER HECK, MICHAEL MYERS, GEORGE GEPHART of Jefferson Twp. p 187

Filed 25 Feb, 1820. Public sale of the estate of GEORGE LANE, no date given. Property kept by widow. Buyers: VINCENT ANTONIDES, JOHN BARKALOW, HENDRICK BREWER, GEORGE CONOVER, JOHN COX, WALTER COX, LEWIS DAVIS, JOHN DEN, JOHN DENISE, SIDNEY DENISE, ANDREW GEPHART, DANIEL GEPHART, HUGH HOUSEMAN, GILBERT LANE, JOHN LANE, GILBERT LAW, ISAAC LAW, JOHN LIGHTCAP, STEPHEN (STOPHEL) LONGSTREET, GEORGE LOY, HENRY MAR-SHALL, JOHN H. SCHENCK, J.N.C. SCHENCK, E.T. SMITH, ADAM SPITLER, JOSEPH VANDERVEER. Total $643.54. pp 187, 188, 189, 190

Inv and appr of estate of JOHN KINSEY total $1143.75. pp 191, 192

Term of March, 1820

Case 415. Adm of estate of CHRISTIAN WELDY granted to JACOB GROH & PHILIP MIKESELL (widow relinquished right). Sec: ABRAHAM TROXEL, NICHOLAS STUTSMAN. Appr: JACOB WEAVER, JOHN RANK, MICHAEL HOOBLER. p 192

Case 416. Will of JOHN McCABE. Witness: POLLY GONDY & BASIL SILER. Exec: JOHN McCABE, HEZEKIAH ROBINSON. Appr: HENRY ROBINSON, ROBERT McREYNOLDS, JOHN TULLIS. pp 192, 193

Case 417. SUSANNAH SHEIBLY appted guardian of CHRIS-TOPHER SHEIBLY, 13 yrs, & SUSANNAAH SHEIBLY, 9 yrs, heirs of DANIEL SHEIBLY, dec. Sec: DAVID SHEIBLY, PETER REPLOGEL. p 193

Case 418. FREDERICK HOLSAPLE appted guardian of JACOB RUSE 13 yrs, NANCY RUSE 9 yrs, MARY RUSE 6 yrs, GEORGE RUSE 4 yrs, & PHILIP RUSE, 1 yr, heirs of NICHOLAS RUSE. Sec: JOHN WERTZ. p 193

Case 419. WILSON CLARK, 15 yrs, heir of HENRY CLARK, dec, chose SOLOMON CLARK as guardian. Sec: AMOS CLARK. p 193

Case 420. Adm of estate of MATHIAS SWARTSELL granted to ABRAHAM SWARTSEL (widow relinquished right). Sec: PHILIP GUNCKEL, MARTIN SHUEY. Appr: JOHN MYERS,

ADAM BUTT, JOHN COLEMAN. pp 193, 194

Admr of estate of DANIEL SHIVELY produced settlement.
Widow's third = $229.52. Cash paid to DANIEL GRIPE,
CHRISTIAN MILLER, ROBERT J SKINNER, IRA SMITH (taxes)
JOHN M. SINGER, ASHER TIBBALS, GEORGE WEIMER total
$362.48. pp 194, 195

Exec of PETER BECKER made settlement. Cash paid to
LOAMI ASHLY, HENRY BACON, J. BROADWELL, HENRY DEBLIN,
PETER GRISTNER, THOMAS GRITZNER, FREDERICK GRUENTNER,
CHRISTIAN HALLER, PHILIP KNEE, GEORGE LOY, ENOS MILES
AARON MILLER, CHRISTIAN MILLER, GEORGE NAGLE, JACOB
OLLINGER, GEORGE PUTERBAUGH, CHRISTIAN SCHLETY,
CHRISTOPHER SEVIS, JOHN SHEPLER, GEORGE SHIDLER,
ISAAC SHIVELY, JACOB SHOCK, GEORGE SIMMERMAN, MICHAEL
WEAVER, SAMUEL WISE. pp 195, 196, 197

Admr of NICHOLAS RUSE made settlement. Cash paid to
JOHN ARNOLD, ADAM MILMAN, HENRY RUSE, JACOB RUSE,
MARTIN SHEETS, JAMES STEELE, JOHN WERTZ total $97.83.
pp 197, 198

Case 421. AARON BAKER appted guardian to MARY NEW-
KIRK, 8 yrs, child of CATHERINE REED, wife of ABRAHAM
REED. p 198

Admr of ADAM KOOGLER produced settlement. Money rcvd
from sale of land in Miami Co. Cash paid to GEORGE
ALEXANDER, DAVID BOWERSOCK, TOBIAS BRITNEY, LUTHER
BRUEN, THOMAS BULLY, ROBERT CLERK, JAMES CLENSY,
MOSES COLLIER, GEORGE COONS, SAMUEL DILLEY, WILLIAM
GORDON, ISRAEL HALE, JACOB HANES, JACOB HERRING,
GEORGE HORNER SR, MARTIN HOUSER, WILLIAM HUFFMAN,
JACOB KOOGLER, MATHIAS KOOGLER, WILLIAM LAW, ANDREW
REED as exec of JONATHAN MERCER, dec, GEORGE NEWCOM,
SAMUEL PELHAM, WILLIAM SHEARER, GEORGE SIMMERMAN,
ANDREW SMELSER, MATTHIAS SMITH, WILLIAM M. SMITH,
ALEXANDER SNODGRASS, JOHN TENNEY, BENJAMIN WAGGONER,
RALPH WILSON, JACOB WORMAN, total $769.10. pp 198,
199, 200

JAMES JOHNSON & ELIZABETH, his wife, late ELIZABETH
CASTOR, admr of estate of CONRAD CASTER, produced
settlement. Cash paid to ABRAHAM BRANEMAN, DANIEL C.
COOPER, WILLIAM GEORGE, admr of ROBERT GILCHRIST,
SOLOMON HAMER, VICTOR KING (taxes), SAMUEL KUGLER,
WILLIAM LONG for SAMUEL LONG, JOHN McCLURE, EDMUND
PURDY, RICHARD SHAW, IRA SMITH, ABRAHAM SUTHERLAND.
Balance due admr of $104.29. pp 201, 202

Case 422. ELIZABETH BURKHARD appted guardian of

ISAAC BERKHARD 17 yrs, who is deaf & dume, ANNA BERK-
HARD 10 yrs, MARTIN BERKHARD 8 yrs, BARBARA BERKHARD
5 yrs, minor heirs of HENRY BERKHARD. Sec: HENRY
FLOY, LEONARD HIER. p 202

Case 423. ALEXANDER CRAIG & DAVID CRAIG, 16 yrs,
heirs of JOHN CRAIG, chose SEYMOUR CRAIG as guardian.
Sec: ABRAHAM BARNET, EMANUEL GEPHART. pp 202, 203

Admr of JOHN JAMISON produced settlement. Cash paid
to GEORGE BEARDSHEER, LUTHER BRUEN, BENJAMIN COFFIN,
DAVID HUSTON, JOSEPH KENNEDY, JAMES MILLER, JOHN REED
JOHN S. REGGS, JOSEPH RENNED, DANIEL YOUNT total
$95.48. Cash rcvd from ROBERT LONG. Balance of
$112.01 remained. pp 203, 204

Case 424. Adm of estate of JONATHAN HILDREATH grant-
ed to HENRY STODDARD. Sec: SAMUEL ARCHER, WARREN
MUNGER. Appr: JAMES GRIMES, RALPH WILSON, DAVID
HENDERSON. p 204

Admr of HUGH McCOLLOM produced settlement. House and
Dayton lot 109 sold for $3030. Cash paid to AARON
BAKER, JOSEPH CANARDY, WILLIAM CLARK, JOHN COMPTON,
ANDREW CRITZER, CHRISTOPHER CURTNER, WARREN MUNGER as
admr of CHARLES ESTE, JACOB HOSIER, JOHN HUNT, NATHA-
NIEL HUNT, DAVID LINDLEY, JOSEPH PIERCE, WILLIAM M.
SMITH, GEORGE SNIDER (auctioneer), total $1904.35.
pp 204, 205

Filed 25 Feb, 1820. Inv and appr of estate of GEORGE
LANE on 2 March, 1818. Included notes due from VIN-
CENT ANTONIDES, LEWIS BASTEDO, JOHN COMPTON, PETER
CONOVER, JOHN DENISE, SAMUEL DENISE, HENDRICK LANE,
Widow PENROD, GEORGE SMOCK, ADAM SPITLER, MOSES VAIL,
EZEKIEL VANNOTE, RACHEL VANNOTE, JOHN VANTILBURGH, A.
WYKOFF, total $3502.90. pp 206, 207

Filed 11 March, 1820. Inv and estate of STEPHEN
ARCHER SR of Wayne Twp total $38.92. Sworn before
ELIAS MATTHEWS, JP, on 7 Sept, 1819. p 208

Special session 25 March, 1820.

Case 425. Adm of estate of JOHN BRADFORD granted to
GEORGE G. BRADFORD & ROBERT CHARLTON (widow relinquished right). Sec: JAMES GILLESPIE, SAMUEL BUCHER
Appr: ROBERT EDGAR, GEORGE NEWCOM, DAVID LEHMAN. p
209

Inv and appr of estate of JONATHAN HILDRETH, total
$149.75. pp 209, 210

Filed 15 April, 1820. Inv and appr of estate of JOHN MURRAY of Madison Twp on 11 Feb, 1820, total $449.63. Debts due from NATHANIEL ALLEN, JOHN ERLIN, WILLIAM FARMER, DANIEL OCKS, NICHOLAS SMALL, SAMUEL ULRICH, NATHANIEL WILSON, total $36.36. pp 210, 211, 212

Public sale of estate of JOHN WAGGONER of Madison Twp Buyers: MICHAEL BEAKLY, JOHN BURKET, JOHN COFFEE, SOLOMON DANER, ANDREW FOUTS, JACOB GRIPE, JOHN GRIPE, GEORGE HAMMER, JOHN HARSHALL, BOSTON HETER, JACOB HOLDERMAN, JAMES HOOVER, JONAS HOOVER, BASIL HUNT, JAMES HUNT, THOMAS HUNT, DAVID HUSTON, HENRY KESLER, JOHN KINSEY, ROBERT McCONNEL, WILLIAM McCONNEL, JOHN MILLER, JONAS MILLER, FREDERIC PORTER, JOHN READ, JOHN REICK, HENRY SLAGHT, JACOB SMITH, MICHAEL SMITH, DANIEL WAGGONER, DAVID WAGGONER, JOSEPH WALKER, JOSEPH WALTER, DAVID WESTON, CHRISTIAN WINEBRENER, JOHN YORKEY, total $308.55. pp 213, 214, 215

Public sale of estate of JOHN MURRAY on 11 Feb, 1820. Buyers: JACOB ALBAUGH, DANIEL BURKERD, NICHOLAS CREVISTON, DAVID DAVIS, JOHN DICKSON, JOSEPH FLORA, JACOB GOSSBRENNER, ARCHIBALD GRAHAM, JACOB GRIPE, JACOB KUNS, RENOLD McCLURE, JOHN MIKESELL, JOSEPH MIKESELL, DANIEL RORER, JAMES STILLWELL, DAVID STUDEBAKER, JACOB STUDEBAKER, DANIEL SWANK, HENRY WELBAUM, CHARLEY WELLBAUM, DAVID WELLBAUM, FREDERICK WEIGHBRIGHT, total illegible. pp 215, 216, 217

Filed 1 May, 1820. Inv and appr of estate of CHRIS- TIAN WELDY on 21 March, 1820. Total $419.75. Prop- erty kept by widow = $304.37. Debts due from DANIEL GEPHART, GEORGE GEPHART, PHILIP GEPHART, HENRY GROW, JOHN HANDLEBURG, SOLOMON HARDMAN, DAVID HOOVER, PHIL- IP HUET, JACOB KERGHER, MICHAEL LYDY, JOSEPH MULLEN- DORE, JACOB SHADE, JACOB SHOCK, DAVID SHOWER, JOHN STUMP, ABRAHAM TROXEL, total $1235.26. pp 218, 219, 220, 221

Inv and appr of estate of MATTHIAS SWARTZEL of Jack- son Twp. Total $150.46. Property kept by widow = $36.37. Sworn before JOHN HOLMES, JP, on 4 March, 1820. pp 222, 223

Admr of BENJAMIN BARCALOW filed recpts dated 24 Nov, 1819. Widow ANN BARCALOW rcvd her dower of $149.96; guardians rcvd heirs' portions of estate totaling $149.96. p 224

Admr of DANIEL RICHISON filed recpts; NANCY RICHISON, dated 11 Sept, 1813, for full amount of estate. p 224

Filed 27 May, 1820. Public sale of estate of MATHIAS
SWARTZEL. Buyers: PETER ALSBAUGH, FREDERICK AULT,
CHARLES BARNECK, THOMAS BECK, JACOB BONNER, HENRY
BOOMERSHINE, PETER BOOMERSHINE, JACOB BOWMAN, JOHN
BUTT, HENRY CLINE, GEORGE COOPER, JOHN T. EINGE, JOHN
GARGER, JACOB HAWK, MELKY MILLER, JACOB MINGLE, JOHN
MINGLE, PETER PENROD, SAMUEL PENROD, FREDERICK REAGLY
PETER SOUDER, ABRAHAM STUTSMAN, HENRY SWARTSEL, JESSE
TAYLOR, PHILIP TELKERD, EMANUEL VANTRESS, WILLIAM
YOUNG, total $165.84. Note for $50 due from GEORGE
SNIDER, dec. pp 224, 225

Filed 21 June, 1820. Inv and appr of estate of JOHN
BRADFORD on 30 March, 1820. Total $1307.87. Public
sale on 12 & 13 April, 1820. Buyers: SQUIER BALDWIN,
DAVID BOWEN, GEORGE G. BRADFORD, JAMES G. BRADFORD,
JOHN BRADFORD, MARGARET BRADFORD, MARY BRADFORD, SAM-
UEL D. BRADFORD, WILLIAM BRADFORD, JOHN BRANDENBURGH,
SILAS BROADWELL, NELSON BROWN, DAVID BURNS, ROBERT
CHARLTON, JOSIAH CLAWSON, JOSEPH COLEMAN, PETER COY,
PETER CURGUS, JACOB DARST, ALEXANDER DEEN, DAVID
DIEL, DENNIS ENSEY, BARTON FAIRCHILD, JOHN GILLESPIE,
JOSEPH GILLESPIE, ELEAZER GRIFFITH, ISAAC HARRISON,
HENRY HILT, CHRISTOPHER JONES, JOSEPH KEMP, JAMES C.
KINNAMON, ABRAHAM KISER, GEORGE KISER, CONRAD LECHLI-
DER, DANIEL LECHLIDER, DAVID LEHMAN, JACOB LEHMAN,
SOLOMON LEHMAN, JOHN LINDLEY, WILLIAM MANNING, HENRY
MARQUART, JOSEPH McREYNOLDS, JACOB MINTUN, MATTHEW
MINTUN, JOHN MORGAN, JOHN MUNDAY, SAMUEL OILER, JOHN
PRUGH, MOSES A. REID, ROBERT RIDDLE, JOHN RIKE,
TAYLOR SNODGRASS, BARNHART SPECK, NICHOLAS STEPHENS,
ISAAC STOKER, JOHN STONEBERGER, RICHARD SWAN, MRS.
VAN FLEE, JAMES WADE, JAMES WEAD, ALETHON WORT, ASA
WRIGHT. Total $1367.14. pp 225, 226, 227, 228, 229,
230, 231

Filed 3 July, 1820. Public sale of estate of CHRIS-
TIAN WELDY on 24 March, 1820. Buyers: JAMES BLACK-
BURN, PETER BOLENBAUGH, JACOB BUTT, JAMES CHAMBERLAIN
JESSE CLARK, GEORGE CLENCY, JOHN DENISE, JOSEPH DODDS
CHRISTOPHER EMRICK, JOHN GARVER, JOSEPH GILLESPIE,
HENRY GROW, JACOB GROW, DANIEL HECK, MICHAEL HILLEGAS
PHILIP HUET, JAMES HUNTSINGER, JOSEPH IVENS, JACOB
IFORD, JACOB KAYLOR, JOHN KELLER, JOHN KROLL, ROBERT
LAMME, JACOB LIGHTY, GEORGE LOY, MICHAEL LYDY, JOHN
MARCH, FREDERICK METTARD, HENRY MICHAEL, JACOB B.
MIKESELL, PHILIP MIKESELL, DANIEL MILLER, JACOB MULL-
ENDORE, JOSEPH MULLENDORE, FREDERICK NUTTZ, MICHAEL
RAGER, ABRAHAM RARIGH, JOHN RIGAL, WILLIAM ROCKHILL,
PETER SHAFFER, ELISHA SHEPHERD, JACOB SHEPHERD, JACOB
SHOCK, JACOB SHUPERD, MICHAEL TREON, FREDERICK WALTZ,
PETER WALTZ, GEORGE WIMER, JOHN WISE, JOHN YAZEL,

total 594.29. pp 231, 232, 233

Term of July, 1820

Case 426. JULIA ANN NOLAN, 12 yrs, heir of JAMES NOLAN, dec, chose WILLIAM PATTERSON as guardian. Sec: JOHN PATTERSON. p 234

Case 427. ROSANNA BENNET, 15 yrs, heir of THOMAS BENNET, dec, chose JACOB OVERHOLSER as guardian. Sec: JOHN OVERHOLSER. p 234

Case 428. JOHN SHIVELY appted guardian to heirs of JOSEPH BLICKENSTAFFER: CATHERINE age 10, LEONARD age 9, ELIZABETH age 8, HANNAH age 6, JACOB age 4, JOSEPH age 2. Sec: LEONARD WOLF. p 234

Case 429. Will of SOLOMON HOLLINGSWORTH. Witness: THOMAS HORNER, DAVID HORNER, SOLOMON MILLER. Exec: SARAH HOLLINGSWORTH & ROBERT SCOTT. Appr: ABIJAH TAYLOR, THOMAS HORNER, GOLDSMITH CHANDLER. p 234

Case 430. Adm of estate of GEORGE PUTERBAUGH granted to CATHERINE PUTERBAUGH & JACOB OLINGER. Sec: JOHN OLINGER & DANIEL HIESTAND. Appr: JAMES B. OLIVER, PHILIP WAGNER, DAVID HARDMAN. pp 234, 235

Admr of ABNER GARARD requested time extension to settle estate. p 235

Case 431. Admr of ABNER GARARD petition to convey deed to BENJAMIN HILLMAN for 60 acres. Permission granted. p 235

Case 432. Admr of JOHN BRADFORD petitioned to convey deed to JOHN WILSON. p 235

Exec of ISAAC MILLER requested time extension to settle estate. p 235

Case 433. GEORGE LIGHTY, 17 yrs, heir of CONRAD LIGHTY, chose WILLIAM LONG as guardian. Sec: WARREN MUNGER. p 235, 236

Case 434. Will of ISAAC HYER. Witness: JOSEPH POWELL & ALEXANDER NEIPMAN. Exec: BARBARA HYER, WESLEY HYER. Appr: JOSEPH POWELL, ABRAHAM NEIPMAN, JOSHUA GREER. p 236

Case 435. JAMES CHATHAM appted guardian of JOHN H. WAGGONER, 11 yrs, & FARIBA WAGGONER, 9 yrs, heirs of REUBEN WAGGONER, dec. Sec: WILLIAM LONG. p 236

Admr of GEORGE HANEY produced settlement. Balance of $566.05 after widow kept $410.49 in property. p 236

Admr of ADAM KUGLER presented account; reciept from MATTHIAS KUGLER was lost. p 236

Exec of PETER BECKER produced settlement. Notes held on nsolvent debtors JOHN MYERS & JOSEPH KEPLER. p 237

Admr of JOSEPH BLICKENSTAFFER produced settlement. Widow's allowance = $82. Cash paid to JOSEPH BROWN, HENRY DAVILBASS, JOHN DITCH, JACOB GOODLANDER, FRED GRUNDNER, ELI HOOVER, WILLIAM HUFFMAN, DAVID P. JOHN, JOHN McDONALD, HENRY MEDSKER, JACOB MULLENDORE, PETER RODEBAUGH, GEORGE CIMMERMAN, JOHN M. SINGER, LEVI SMOKER, HENRY SWISHER, JOHN TREON, JOHN WAGGONER, LEONARD WOLF SR, total $267.63 plus $78.83. p 237

Admr of DANIEL HOOVER produced settlement. Cash paid to JOHN McCLINTOCK (auctioneer), DANIEL YOUNT. Balance of $919.22 remains. p 238

Inv and appr of estate of JONATHAN HILDRETH. p 238

Admr of CHARLES ESTE produced settlement, ordered by court to pay 20 cents on the dollar. pp 238, 239

1 August, 1820. Exec of DANIEL C. COOPER produced settlement. Cash paid to SAMUEL ARCHER, HENRY BACON, AARON BAKER, THOMAS BOYER, ELISHA BRABHAM, RICHARD S. BRITTON, LUTHER BRUEN, JOHN BURNS, THOMAS COTTOM, GEORGE C. DAVIS, LAYTON DICK, ELI ELDERS, WILLIAM GAHAGAN, JOHN GRIMES, JAMES HANNA, GEORGE HARRIS, JOHN HOLDERMAN, THOMAS S. HINDE, WILLIAM HUFFMAN, ISAAC JOHNSON, DAVID LATHAM, ISAAC MORGAN, GEORGE NASHEE, CHRISTIAN OBLINGER, JAMES PATTERSON, WILLIAM PATTERSON, JOHN H. PIATT, estate of JOHN REGANS, JOHN RITTER, JOSEPH RODEFFER, ROBERT J. SKINNER (printing ads), ALEXANDER SIMPSON, GEORGE SNIDER (auctioneer), BENJAMIN R. SPINNING, JOHN STEELE, JONATHAN STUTSMAN, ISRAEL TAYLOR, STEPHEN WHEELER, JAMES WELSH. Total $6970.29. pp 239, 240

Filed 28 July, 1820. Inv and appr of estate of CONRAD LIGHTY on 28 Feb, 1820. Total $823.31. List of property kept by widow = $316.75. Debts owed by JACOB SICKFOIL in PA, CHRISTIAN BROWER, JOHN BROWER, JACOB HATTEL, MICHAEL HUBLER, GEORGE WARNER. Public sale, buyers: VINCENT ANTONIDES, GEORGE ARGENBRIGHT, DANIEL BOWSER, HENRY BOWSER, GEORGE P. COFFY, HENRY DAVILISS, JACOB GARVER, JOHN GARVER, JOHN GARVER JR, GEORGE GEBHART, PHILIP GEBHART, JOHN HACK, PETER HACK

HENRY HEWETT, MICHAEL HUBLER, JOHN HUNTSINGER, JACOB
KIMMEL, JOSEPH IVENS, THOMAS KASSEL, SAMUEL LANEY,
SAMUEL LARN, JOHN LIGHTCAP, BENJAMIN LIGHTY, CHRISTO-
PHER LIGHTY, JACOB LIGHTY, SAMUEL LIGHTY, Widow
LIGHTY, WILLIAM LONG, SAMUEL LOREY, GEORGE LOY, ALEX-
ANDER MILLER, ROBERT MUBROOM, PETER MYER, ABRAHAM
PONTIUS, JOSEPH RICHARDSON, ABRAHAM SHUE, JACOB SHU-
PERD, HAZEL SPECKS, JOHN TREON, JOHN TREVOR, GEORGE
VARNER, PETER WALTZ, PETER WALYS, GEORGE WARNER,
PETER WATER. Total $572.65 pp 240, 241, 242, 243,
244, 245

Filed 31 July, 1820. Inv and appr of estate of JOHN
McCABE. Total of $149.72. Public sale on 3 June,
1820; buyers: SALLY BARNS, NELSON BROWN, JOSEPH CLY-
MER, ROBERT GIBSON, JOHN GILLESPIE, OWEN JONES, JESSE
KILER, MICHAEL MARLEY, DAVID PARROT, JOHN RENCH,
HEZEKIAH ROBINSON, JOHN TULLIS, ROBERT WEAD, RICHARD
WHEATLEY total $82.36. pp 245, 246, 247

Public sale of estate of JONATHAN HILDRETH on 26
July, 1820; buyers: ELISHA BRABHAM, OBADIAH CONOVER,
ELIJAH CONVERSE, JAMES COY, WILLIAM GILLESPIE, PETER
W. GRAHAM, DAVID GRIFFIN, JOB HAINES, D. HILDRETH,
JO. HOLLINGSWORTH, HENRY MARQUART, WARREN MUNGER,
JOHN SNIDER (GEORGE SNIDER SR), EBENEZER STEBBINS, R.
STRAIN, JOHN VAN CLEVE, NAT WILSON, JAC. WORMAN total
$173.18. pp 248, 249

Special session 16 September, 1820

Case 436. Will of CHARLES MORGAN. Witness: DAVID
HUSTON, JACOB DARST. Exec: ASA JOHN (reserved right
of JOHN MORGAN, other named Exec, to serve). Appr:
DAVID JOHN, RICHARD STEPHENS, GEORGE PATTERSON. p 249

Inv and appr of estate of ISAAC HYERS on 18 Aug, 1820
total of $569.25. Notes due from FREDERICK CLASON,
FREDERICK SMITH, ROBERT HOOD. Memo that BARBARA HIRE
purchased cutting box @ $2.00. pp 250, 251

Inv and appr of estate of GEORGE PUTERBAUGH of Jeff-
erson Twp on 19 Aug, 1820. Total of $198.22. Debts
owed estate by JOHN KINZEY, DAVID OLINGER. Listing of
property kept by widow CATHERINE PUTTERBAUGH. Public
sale on 22 Aug, 1820; buyers: RALPH BRADDOCK, JAMES
CUNNINGHAM, SOLOMON DANNER, ROBERT GIBSON, DANIEL
HEISTAND, ADAM HARTZEL, JACOB HOLDERMAN, ELI HOOVER,
JONAS HOOVER, JAMES HUNT, THOMAS HUNT, ROBERT
KENDALL, ABRAM KINZEY, ELIAS McGUIRE, JACOB METSKER,
ANDREW MIKESELL, MARTIN MIKESELL, PHILIP MIKESELL,
ABRAHAM MILLER, CHRISTIAN MOON, JOHN OBLINGER JR,

DAVID OLINGER, JACOB OLINGER, SOLOMON SANFORD, WIL-
LIAM SHENEFELT, JOHN WAGGONER, ELIZABETH WILAND,
ROBERT WILLIAMS, JOHN YOCKEY, JOHN ZIMMERMAN total
$188.93. pp 251, 252, 253

Filed 21 Oct, 1820. Inv and appr of estate of SOLO-
MON HOLLINGSWORTH on 19 Aug, 1820. Total $740.87.
pp 254, 255

Term of October, 1820

Admr of TALLMAN HALL requested time extension to
settle estate. p 256

Admr of ISAAC WOODWARD requested time extension to
settle estate. p 256

Case 437. Adm of estate of MICHAEL EMRICK granted to
WILLIAM EMRICK, JOHN STUMP (widow relinquished right)
Sec: PHILIP GUNCKEL, CHRISTOPHER EMRICK. Appr:
MICHAEL GUNCKEL, DANIEL GUNCKEL, HENRY BEECHLER. p256

Case 438. Adm of estate of JOHN STIVER granted to
ADAM STIVER (widow relinquished right). Sec: ABRAHAM
TROXELL, ABRAHAM SWARTZLY. Appr: JACOB SINKS, HENRY
SHEIDLER, ABRAHAM SWINEHART. p 256

Case 439. Adm of estate of JOSEPH C. SILVER granted
to JESSE CLARK (widow relinquished right). Sec:
GEORGE PARSONS, JOHN BROWER. Appr: JOHN MILLER on
Wolf Creek, JACOB JOHN, JACOB PLESINGER. p 256

Case 440. GEORGE YOUNG, 15 yrs, minor heir of GEORGE
YOUNG, dec, chose GEORGE WOLLASTON as guardian. p 256

Case 441. Will of MARGERY BEATON. Witness: WILLIAM
MORRISON, WILLIAM YOUNG. Exec: JAMES DEFREES, JOSEPH
DEFREES. Appr: JAMES RUSSEL, ALEXANDER LOGAN, GARD-
NER EWING. p 257

Case 442. WILLIAM HATFIELD, 20 yrs, & BENJAMIN HAT-
FIELD, 16 yrs, minor heirs of WILLIAM HATFIELD, dec,
chose JOHN BOWEN as guardian. Sec: JOHN HATFIELD. p
257

Case 443. MARY HATFIELD, 18 yrs, heir of WILLIAM
HATFIELD, dec, chose JONATHAN HATFIELD as guardian.
Sec: OWEN HATFIELD. p 257

Case 444. HENRY DEAL, 20 yrs, heir of PHILIP DEAL,
dec, chose JOHN STONEBERGER as guardian. p 257

Case 445. Adm of estate of JOHN MARTIN granted to
MARTHA MARTIN & WILLIAM MORRISON. Sec: WILLIAM
YOUNG, ROBERT BINGHAM. Appr: JAMES RUSSEL, ALEXAN-
DER LOGAN, ANTHONY JONES. p 257

Filed 1 November, 1820. Admr of estate of HENRY MOY-
ER produced settlement & receipts of Widow ELIZABETH,
NICHOLAS STUTSMAN as spouse of ANNA MOYER, JACOB BOW-
MAN as spouse of CHRISTIANNA MOYER, both daughters of
HENRY MOYER, and from MICHAEL MOYER, PETER MOYER,
JONATHAN MOYER, ELIZABETH MOYER, JOHN MOYER, JACOB
MOYER, DANIEL MOYER, also heirs of HENRY MOYER. (Some
heirs spelled family name MYERS.) pp 257, 258, 259

Case 446. Adm of estate of GARRET CONOVER granted to
OBADIAH B. CONOVER (widow relinquished right). Sec:
SAMUEL ARCHER, ABRAHAM BARNET. Appr: JOHN GROVE, H.
G. PHILLIPS, DAVID LINDSLEY. p 259

Admr of THOMAS KELSEY requested time extension to
settle estate. p 259

Admr of DANIEL C. COOPER requested time extension to
settle estate. p 259

Case 447. Adm of estate of THOMAS MAXWELL granted to
RACHEL MAXWELL. Sec: FLETCHER EMLEY, ANDREW SMALL SR
Appr: JAMES CARUTHERS, SAMUEL JACKSON, JONATHAN MUN-
GER. p 259

Exec of WILLIAM WAUGH produced settlement. Cash paid
to JACOB SWODENER, JACOB IFERT, W. J. LODGE, FRANCIS
DILTS, AARON NUTTS, JAMES RUSSELL, ELIJAH McGREW, H.
STODDARD, DAVID LAMME, ISAAC HARRISON, Dr. JOHN
STEELE. pp 259, 260

Admr of RICHARD THRALLS produced settlement. Cash
paid to DEWALT CROWELL, GEORGE KNEE, WILLIAM FRAME,
DAVID KAYLOR, JOHN KAYLOR, JOHN HUNTZINGER, HENRY
LEEDES, SAMUEL NOFFZINGER, DANIEL RUDY; total $37.08.
p 260

6 Nov, 1820. Admr of estate of JACOB BAKER produced
final settlement. Cash paid for land in Sec 15, T 4,
R 4E. Widow's third = $108.92; other heirs rcve
$217.85. p 261

Admr of estate of GEORGE ZELLER produced final set-
tlement. Cash paid to NICK BOOT, JOHN STONER, JOHN
GENGER, GEORGE LOY, HENRY SHUEY, ADAM ZELLER, JOHN
ZELLERS total $119.12. Widow kept $200 in property.
Public sale on 20 Aug, 1818; buyers: JACOB ARNOT,

TOBIAS BICKLE, JACOB BOWMAN, SAMUEL BOWER, THOMAS
CATROW, DANIEL CLARK, WALTER COX, GEORGE F. DECHANT,
MATHEW M. DODDS, BENJAMIN EAKINS, GEORGE EMRICK,
GEORGE ERGENBRIGHT, JACOB FOUTS, JACOB GARST, GEORGE
GEPHART, LEWIS HASSELMAN, CHRISTIAN HAWN, JOHN HEND-
ERSON, GEORGE HETZEL SR, NICHOLAS HOLLAR, CONRAD
ISELY, JOHN KADERMAN, MICHAEL KEARNEY, GEORGE KISTER,
JOHN KITSON, DAVID LANDIS, JESSE LANDIS, GEORGE LOY,
DANIEL MILLER, JACOB MILLER, JOSEPH MILLER, STEPHEN
MILLER, DANIEL MONBEEK, GEORGE RENKER, PHILIP REPLO-
GEL, JACOB ROOF, LEONARD SELVY, GEORGE SHAFFER, JOHN
C. SHAFFER, HENRY SHUEY, MARTIN SHUEY, JACOB SHUPERT,
GEORGE SOWERS, GEORGE STONER, GEORGE STUMP, ELI SUL-
GROVE, GABRIEL THOMAS, JACOB TITTLE, DANIEL TROYER,
PHILIP WOLF, SAMUEL WRIGHT, PHILIP ZERING, ANDREW
ZELLER, JOHN ZELLER, MARGARET ZELLER, MICHAEL ZELLER,
total $172.46.   pp 261, 262, 263

GEORGE BRUNER, admr of estate of WILLIAM CURTZ, produced final settlement.   p 264

Case 448. JOSEPH SHOLLEY, 16 yrs, minor heir of JOHN
SHOLLEY, chose said JOHN SHOLLEY as guardian.   Sec:
GODFREY KOUCHER.   p 264

Admr of estate of WILLIAM HAY filed heirs' release
dated 1 Nov, 1820. Deceased left 6 children: JAMES,
JOHN, WILLIAM & JOSEPH HAY, JANE married MOSES
WALLACE & POLLY married JOHN R. SEWELL. POLLY & JOHN
SEWELL both deceased. Receipts signed by JAMES HAY,
JOHN A. HAY, WILLIAM HAY, JOSEPH HAY, MOSES WALLACE.
p 264, 265

Filed 1 Dec, 1820. Public sale of estate of STEPHEN
ARCHER SR on 3 Nov, 1820. Buyers: SOLOMON DAVIS,
JOHN HAINES, JOSEPH HAINES, SAMUEL HOLMES, JOHN LOW,
JAMES PETTICREW, JOHN SHAFFER, WILLIAM WRIGHT. Total
$10.95.   p 265

Special session 9 December, 1820

Case 449.   Adm of estate of HENRY HART granted to
JOHN BAKER (widow relinquished right).   Sec: JACOB
WARNER, DAVID BAKER.   Appr: DAVID SHEETS, ABRAHAM
McCLINTOCK, HENRY KEPLER.   p 265

Adm of goods yet to be administered from estate of
HUGH McCOLLOM granted to ELISHA BRABHAM.   Sec: HENRY
MARQUART, GEORGE C. DAVIS.   pp 266

Case 450.   Adm of estate of THOMAS HAMER granted to
WILLIAM HAMER.   Sec: AARON BAKER, JOHN YOUNG.   Appr:

COMMON PLEAS (PROBATE) DOCKET BOOK D-1

HENRY ROBINSON, JOHN TULLIS, BENJAMIN WAGGONER. p 266

Special session 20 December, 1820

Case 451. Adm of estate of LUCEANNA ZIEGLER granted
to JOSEPH PEIRCE & JAMES STEELE. Sec: DAVID LINDSLEY
WILLIAM EAKER, OBADIAH B. CONOVER. Appr: HORATIO G.
PHILLIPS, GEORGE W. SMITH, GEORGE S. HUSTON. p 266

Inv and appr of estate of CHARLES MORGAN on 19 Sept &
15 Dec, 1820. Total $1539.97. pp 266, 267, 268, 269

Filed 19 Jan, 1821. Inv and appr of estate of MICH-
AEL EMRICK on 19 Jan, 1821. Total $1605.30. pp 269,
270, 271, 272, 273

Inv and appr of estate of JOHN STIVER of Jackson Twp
on 21 Nov, 1820. Total $698.29. Sworn before HENRY
SHEIDLER, JP. Property kept by widow = $96.05; recpt
signed MARGARET (x) STIVER. Public sale on 23 Nov &
5 Dec, 1820; buyers: JOHN ALT, JACOB BUTT, GEORGE
CLENCY, WILLIAM DIBERT, SAMUEL DRAYER, JACOB GARVER,
JAMES M. GRIMES, JOEL GRIMES, JOHN GUNDLE, PETER
GUNDLE, ROBERT S. HAGEN, PHILIP IZOR, JOHN KETZER,
GEORGE LOY, JOHN MENGLE, JOHN MINNICK, JOHN PIERCE,
ANTHONY RICHARDS, PETER SEILER, DAVID SHEIDLER, HENRY
SHEIDLER, LEWIS SHEIDLER, JOHN SNABLY, ADAM STIVER,
ADAM STIVER JR, HENRY STIVER, JACOB STIVER, VALENTINE
STIVER, SAMUEL TRAGER, ADAM SWINEHART, MICHAEL VANCE,
JACOB WIRICK, total $710.73. pp 273, 274, 275, 276,
277

Inv and appr of estate of MARY DAVIS on 20 Sept, 1819
total $500.62. Public sale, buyers: DAVID ALSPACH,
JOHN ANDERSON, WILLIAM AUSTIN, JOHN BAKER, WILLIAM
BOTKIN, DAVID BURNS, ISAAC CONOVER, JOHN COX, WILLIAM
COX, JACOB DAVIS, LEWIS DAVIS, CATHERINE ETTER, ROB-
ERT GIBSON, JAMES GUY, HENRY HALL, JOHN HOLLINSWORTH,
JOHN IMMICK, JOHN KELLER, JACOB KEMP, DAVID LEHMAN,
JOHN LEHMAN, HENRY MARQUART, SAMUEL MILLER, THOMAS
MORRISON, ADAM NEFF, SAMUEL NEWCOM, SAMUEL NICHOLAS,
WILLIAM OWENS, DANIEL OX, FREDERICK OX, W. PATTERSON,
AARON RICHARDSON, JOHN RIGGS, HENRY ROTHAMEL, SAMUEL
STITES, ALEX WHITE, JOHNSON WHITE, JOHN WILSON total
$699.96. pp 278, 279, 280, 281, 282

Inv and appr of estate of JOHN MARTIN on 22 Dec,
1820. Total $107.12. pp 282, 283

Special session 8 Febuary, 1821

Case 452. Will of WILLIAM VANDERSLICE. Witness:

JOHN FOLKERTH, WILLIAM ROTH, JOHN MILLER. Exec: GEORGE NEWCOM. Appr: GEORGE HARRIS, GEORGE GROVE, WILLIAM EAKER. p 283

Inv and appr of estate of GARRET CONOVER on 6 Nov, 1820. List included hat blocks, furs, findings -- most likely a hatter. Total $540.20. Accounts due from AARON BAKER, JAMES BROWN, JOSEPH BROWN, DAVID HAWTHORN, WILLIAM HUEY, ISAAC JESTER, JOSEPH KELLER, DAVID KINZEY, WILLIAM MILLER, JOHN MONDAY, JOHN NEW-COM, SAMUEL SHOUB, HENRY SLACK, JAMES SLACK, GEORGE W. SMITH, DANIEL WOLF, JACOB WORMAN total $53.43. Public sale on 13 Dec, 1820; buyers: JACOB ALEY, DAVID ALSPACH, HENRY BASTWICK, WILLIAM BUMBARGER, SILAS BROADWELL, RICHARD S. BUTTON, JOHN BIMON, O.B. CONOVER, ELIJAH CONVERSE, HENRY CURTNER, LEWIS DAVIS, SAMUEL DILL, DAVID EDWARDS, BARTON FARECHILD, GEORGE D. FENIMORE, PETER GRAHAM, JOHN GREEN, JAMES HARRIS, JOSEPH HOLLINGSWORTH, JOHN LINDSLEY, WILLIAM MILLER, JACOB MILMAN, JOHN MONDAY, SAMUEL MOON, WILLIAM PATTERSON, DANIEL PIERSON, STEPHEN S. RHODES, SAMUEL SHOUP, WILLIAM SHROYER, R.J. SKINNER, HENRY SLACK, DANIEL SMALL, JOHN SMALL, CHRISTOPHER TAYLOR, JOHN TULLIS, PHILIP WAGNER, JACOB WORMAN, total $399.42. pp 284, 285, 286, 287, 288

Inv and appr of estate of HENRY HART of Randolph Twp on 14 Dec, 1820, no total given. Public sale held 16 Dec, 1820; buyers: DAVID BAKER, PHILIP BARTMESS, ANDREW BECKER, DAVID BECKER, JOHN BECKER JR, JOHN BECKER SR, JOHN BOWER, HENRY BRUMBAUGH, JACOB CARROL, JAMES CATTIN, JAMES CLARK, ABRAHAM COBLE, JOHN COFFERS, GEORGE CONFER, BENJAMIN COLEMAN, PAUL DEIL, WILLIAM DOTSON, AMOS EDWARDS, ELIZABETH EDWARDS, ABRAHAM ELLER, LEVI FALKNOR, PETER FETTERS, JOSEPH GARBER, JACOB GLOSSBRENNER, JOHN GREABILL, ELIZABETH HART, JOSEPH HAUVER, MARTIN HOW, JOHN HEAGEN, HENRY HESTER, ABRAHAM HISSONG, JOHN HISSONG, DANIEL HOOVER, DAVID HOOVER, ENOS HOOVER, JOSEPH HOOVER, JOHN F. JAY, HENRY KESLER, DANIEL LANDAS, FELIX LANDAS, DANIEL LEEDY, DAVID LEEDY, DANIEL MARKER, ABRAHAM McCLINTOCK, SAMUEL MILLER, HENRY MOYER, JAMES PATTIN, DAVID SHEETS, MARTIN SHEETS, GEORGE SMITH, ANDREW WARNER, DANIEL WARREN, total $651.55. pp 288, 289, 290, 291, 292, 293, 294

Term of March, 1821

Case 453. Adm of estate of ABRAHAM REED granted to AARON BAKER (widow relinquished right). Sec: WILLIAM HAMER, WILLIAM TAYLOR. Appr: THOMAS COTTOM, JAMES HANNA, JOHN PATTERSON. p 294

Case 454. Adm of estate of CONRAD LECHLIDER granted to DAVID HUSTON (widow relinquished right). Sec: GEORGE NEWCOM, DAVID JOHN. Appr: JOHN BONNER, JOHN NEWCOM, EDWARD NEWCOM. p 295

Case 455. RUHAMAH LECHLIDER appted guardian to MARY ANN LECHLIDER, 3 yrs, & ADAM LECHLIDER, 11 mo, minor heirs of CONRAD LECHLIDER, dec. Sec: JACOB LECHLIDER. p 295

Case 456. Will of HANNAH <u>LEARN.</u> Proven by witness ABRAHAM STUTSMAN. p 295

Admr of CONRAD LICHTY granted time extension to settle estate. p 295

JOHN MORGAN, an exec of estate of CHARLES MORGAN, was sworn. p 295

JOHN LEHMAN, admr of estate of PETER LEHMAN, directed to show cause why estate is not settled, on order of Mr. STODDARD. p 295

(Case 456.) Will of HANNAH <u>LEARR</u> proven by second witness, ABRAHAM STONER. Ordered recorded. p 295

Case 457. Will of DANIEL HEISTAND. Witness: REUBEN LONG, JACOB OLINGER. Exec: MAGDALENA HEISTAND & JACOB HEISTAND. Appr: ISAAC SHIVELY, JACOB OLINGER, JONAS HOOVER. p 296

Case 458. DAVID D. BRADFORD, 15 yrs, chose JAMES G. BRADFORD as guardian. Sec: JOHN BRADFORD. p 296

Case 459. JOHN BRADFORD appted guardian of ALLEN BRADFORD, 8 yrs, heir of JOHN BRADFORD, dec. Sec: JAMES BRADFORD. p 296

Case 460. "Court appointed JOHN BONNER guardian to EBENEZER WEAD...BONNER a minor 8 yrs old, heir of the JOHN BONNER who gave a bond with DAVID JOHN..." p 296

Exec of WILLIAM WAUGH produced vouchers. p 296

Case 461. Will of STEPHEN C. AYRES. Witness: DANIEL PIERSON, MATTHEW PATTON, JOSEPH HOLLINGSWORTH. Exec: COMFORT AYRES. Appr: DANIEL PIERSON, MATTHEW PATTEN, JOSEPH HOLLINGSWORTH. pp 296, 297

Case 462. JOSEPH REED, 14 yrs, heir of ABRAHAM REED, dec, chose GEORGE S. HUSTON as guardian. p 297

Case 463. SARAH REED, 13 yrs, heir of ABRAHAM REED, dec, chose JAMES HANNA as guardian. HANNA was also appted guardian of HAGET M. REED 8 yrs, ELIZABETH REED 6 yrs, MATILDA REED 3 yrs, & ABRAHAM REED, 1 yr. Sec: JOHN HISER. p 297

Case 464. CATHERINE BOWSER 14 yrs & SARAH BOWSER 12 yrs, minor heirs of DANIEL BOWSER, dec, chose HENRY BOWSER as guardian. HENRY also appted guardian of HENRY 11 yrs, DAVID 9 yrs, DANIEL 7 yrs, minor heirs of DANIEL BOWSER, dec. Sec: PHILIP BOWSER. p 297

Admr of estate of ISAAC WOODWARD requested time extension to settle estate. p 297

Admr of estate of DANIEL C. COOPER requested time extension to settle estate. p 297

Admr of estate of JOHN McCABE requested time extension to settle estate. p 297

Admr of PETER LEHMAN produced vouchers. Cash paid to WILLIAM BOMBARGER, SAMUEL BOOHGER, GEORGE C. BRADFORD HENRY BUTT, JOHN COLLINS, JOHN COMPTON, OBADIAH B. CONOVER, ABRAHAM DARST, AUGUSTUS GEORGE, CHARLES R. GREENE, ALEXANDER GRIMES, JONATHAN HARSHMAN, MOSES HATFIELD, JACOB LEHMAN, JOHN LEHMAN, E.K. MUNGER, JAMES I. NESBIT, MATTHEW PATTON, JACOB SHARTEL, ALEXANDER SIMPSON, WILLIAM M. SMITH, GEORGE SNIDER, GEORGE SOURBRAY, JOHN STEELE, JOHN SYPHERS total $526.50. Cash recved from AARON BAKER, ALEXANDER GRIMES, JOHN GRIMES, MOSES HATFIELD, HENRY MARQUART, SAMUEL RAMSAY, JAMES WOODS total $431.54. pp 298, 299

Admr of JOHN B. RITTENHOUSE produced settlement. Cash paid to ENOCH BOWEN, JOSEPH BROWN, DAVID BREWER, WILLIAM CLARK, JOSIAH CLAWSON, ISAAC CONOVER, WILLIAM COX, HENRY CURTNER, WILLIAM P. DAVIS, JOHN DODSON, JOHN DUNN, JOHN FREEMAN, WILLIAM GILLESPIE, JOSEPH HOLLINGSWORTH, JACOB HOSIER, JACOB LEHMAN, JOSEPH McCLEARY, JOHN McCORMACK, ISAAC MORGAN, H.G. PHILLIPS JAMES RIDDLE, ROBT. J. SKINNER, JAMES SLOUGHT, GEORGE SNIDER, WILLIAM SOURBRAY, TIMOTHY SQUIER, EBENEZER STIBBINS, JAMES THOMSON, WILLIAM VANDERSLICE total $1431.80. Balance of $1520.90. pp 300, 301, 302

Case 396. Admr of THOMAS KELSEY requested permission to convey 4 acres in Sec 29, T 3, R 5 to JOHN C. MURPHY. Permission granted. p 302

Admr of JONATHAN HILDRETH produced public sale bill, total of $173.18. Creditors due $606.94; estate found insolvent. Admr ordered by court to pay 21.5 cents on the dollar to O.B. CONOVER, JOHN DODSON, GEORGE GROVE, JOB HAINES, MICAH HILDRETH, NOAH JOHNSON, JOSHUA McINTOSH, H.G. PHILLIPS, JOHN STEELE, EL. STILKINS, ROBT STRAIN. pp 302, 303, 304

Admr of estate of JOHN ULRICH produced rcpt from widow for personal property appr at $439.50. p 304

HENRY METSKER, exec of JOHN GRIPE, produced rcpt of widow CATHERINE GRIPE for personal goods. p 304

Exec of ISAAC MILLER produced vouchers, paying EDEN BURROWS, JACOB CROWL, JACOB CRULL, JOHN HARDMAN (auctioneer), SAMUEL HEISTAND, HENRY LEEDES, ANDREW MIKESELL, PHILIP MIKESELL, CATY MILLER, JOHN J. MILLER, JACOB RUBY, ADAM SHOCK, PHILIP WAGGONER, JACOB WEAVER total $114.69. pp 304, 305

Case 465. CHRISTIAN SHIVELY appted guardian of JACOB HAY 12 yrs, GEORGE HAY 9 yrs, MICHAEL HAY 5 yrs, minor heirs of JACOB HAY. Sec: ANDREW METTSKER. p 306

Case 466. ANDREW SHAW, 15 yrs, heir of FREEMAN SHAW, dec, chose ABRAHAM DARST as guardian. p 306

Special session 7 May, 1821

Case 467. Adm of estate of JOHN YATES granted to HENRY ARNOLD. Sec: FREDRICH SHAFFER, JACOB FOUTS. Appr: CHRISTIAN JUDY, HENRY ZELLER, HENRY MOYER. p306

Special session 2 July, 1821

Case 468. Adm of estate of WILLIAM LUCE granted to BENJAMIN ARCHER & JUDITH LUCE. Sec: THOMAS CLAWSON, EDWARD MITCHEL. Appr: PETER SUNDERLAND, HENRY STANCEL, BENJAMIN MALTBIE. pp 306, 307

Filed 14 March, 1820. Inv and appr of estate of THOMAS MAXWELL, total $424.50. List of property kept by widow = $116.50. Public sale on 9 Dec, 1820; buyers: JAS. Y. BACON, JOHN COOK, ANDREW CROCKET, JOHN DENNICE, SAMUEL JACKSON, DAVID MAXWELL, SAMUEL MAXWELL, JOHN MILLER, LEONARD MINNEIGH, JAMES MULLIN, JOB ROBBARTS, WILLIAM SCHENCK, JOHN SCOTT, ANDREW SMALL, DANIEL SMALL, JOHN SMALL, JOHN UPDEGRAF, ABRAHAM VOORHES, DANIEL H. WEAL, JOHN WYKOFF. pp 307, 308, 309, 310

Filed 16 March, 1821. Inv and appr of estate of LUCEANNA ZEIGLER on 9 Feb, 1821. Total of $14067.77.

Notes due estate from GRIFFIN YEATMAN, GRIFFITH FOSS. Noles held by Judge LEFFORD HAND total $10700.00. pp 311, 312, 313, 314, 315, 316, 317

Filed 24 March, 1821. Inv and appr of estate of THOMAS HAMER of Dayton Twp, total $513.10. p 318

Appr of estate of STEPHEN AYRES found, after setting aside allotment for widow and children, there was no estate remaining. Notes due from LEWIS MILLS & JACOB MILLS of Morristown, NJ, JOHN CROWDER, JACOB MUSGROVE JAS. THOMSON, JOHN H. REED. pp 319, 320

Filed 21 April, 1821. Inv and appr of estate of ABRAHAM REED on 10 March, 1821; total $350.52. Widow kept $62.10 in property. Public sale, no date given; buyers: DAVID ALSPACH, AARON BAKER, JOHN BELL, ADAM BOLENDER, LEVIN COTTOM, THOMAS COTTOM JR, LEWIS DAVIS NATHANIEL DAWSON, GEORGE D. FENNIMOR, WILLIAM P. GEORGE, ROBERT GIBSON, ROBERT HADLEY, JAMES HANNAH, WILLIAM HUGHEY, DAVID HUMPHREY, JOSEPH KELLER, JOHN McINTOSH, ISAAC MORGAN, ABRAHAM OVERLEES, EDMUND PAR-ROTT, JAMES QUINN, THOMAS QUINN, CATHERINE REED, WIL-LIAM REED, JOS. RODEFFER, JOHN ROBERTS, EZEKIEL SHAW, LUDWICK SHAW, IRA SMITH, JAMES SMITH, HENRY TROXELL, DAVID UMPHREYVILLE, ADAM WEAVER, PETER WEAVER, JOHN H. WILLIAMS, total $394.22. pp 320, (no page #321 or #322), 323, 324, 325, 326

Filed 24 March, 1821. Public sale of estate of THOM-AS HAMER, no date given. Buyers: ABRAHAM BRANNERMAN GEORGE C. DAVIS, WILLIAM GEORGE, WILLIAM G. GEORGE, DAYTON HAMER, WILLIAM HAMER JR, WILLIAM HAMER SR, JOHN HANEY, JOHN HOLDERMAN, ISAAC KEMP, SAMUEL KOOG-LER, JAMES LOWRY, JOHN MICKLE, SAMUEL MORGAN, DANIEL NEFF, EDMOND PURDY, JOHN S. RIGGS, WILLIAM SNODGRASS, THOMAS D. WHEELAN. Total $404.44. p 326

COMMON PLEAS (PROBATE) DOCKET BOOK E-1

Inv and appr of estate of CONRAD LECHLIDER on 28 April, 1821. Total $482.01. pp 1, 2, 3

Special session 7 May, 1821

Case 501.5. Adm of estate of JOHN YATES granted to HENRY ARNOLD. Sec: FREDERICK SHAFFER, JACOB FOUTS. Appr: CHRISTIAN JUDY, HENRY ZELLER, HENRY MOYER. p 3

Filed 9 June, 1821. Inv and appr of estate of DANIEL HEISTAND, total $314.37. (CHRISTIAN SHIVELY served

in place of ISAAC SHIVELY who was out of the county.)
Public sale on 30 March, 1821. Buyers: HENRY APPLE,
DAVID CROWLE, JACOB DELOR, DAVID HARDMAN, CHRISTIAN
HEASTON, DANIEL HEASTON, JACOB HEASTON, JACOB HEIST-
AND, MARY HEASTON, JONAS HOOVER, JAMES HUNT, WILLIAM
JONES, REUBEN LONG, JACOB MIKESELL, PHILIP MIKESELL,
SAMUEL MOON, DAVID OLINGER, JOEL PRESSELL, JAMES
QUINN, DANIEL RAZOR, JACOB RESOR, JOHN REESON, DANIEL
REPP, JACOB SHIVELY, HENRY TETOR, JOHN TURNER, SAMUEL
ULRICH, ELIZABETH WILAND, JACOB WILLIAM, CHRISTIAN
WINEBRENNER, JACOB WINEBRENNER, JOHN WITT total
$74.87. Property kept by widow = $9.37. Debts due
from DANIEL HECK, JAMES HUNT, JOHN KINSEY, JACOB
MIKESELL, PETER MIKESELL, JOHN OLINGER, JACOB
WILLIAMS. pp 3, 4, 5, 6, 7, 8

Special session 2 July, 1821

Case 502. Adm of estate of WILLIAM LUCE granted to
BENJAMIN ARCHER & JUDITH LUCE. Sec: THOMAS CLAWSON,
EDWARD MITCHELL. Appr: PETER SUNDERLAND, HENRY
STANSEL, BENJAMIN MALTBIE. p 8

Debts due estate of JOHN YATES of German Twp on 30
June, 1821 by HENRY ARNOLD & PETER IZOR. Total
$156.01. pp 8, 9

Inv and appr of estate of WILLIAM VANDERSLICE on 10
Feb, 1821, total $231.31. Public sale, undated; buy-
ers: POMPEY ALLEN, SAMUEL BUCHER, JOHN BIMEN, WILLIAM
EAKER, DENNIS ENSEY, WILLIAM GILLESPIE, PETER GRAHAM,
DANIEL ISELY, JAMES KANE, DAVID LEHMAN, JOHN LEHMAN,
FREDERICK LIVERINGHOUSE, HENRY MARQUART, JOHN MILLER,
ISAAC MORGAN, SAMUEL MORGAN, GEORGE NEWCOM, FREDERICK
OX, H.G. PHILLIPS, GEORGE BRETSINS, JACOB PROTSMAN,
WILLIAM ROADS, JACOB SHARTLE, LAWRENCE SHELL, TIMOTHY
SQUIRE, CHRISTIAN STRONK, DANIEL STUTSMAN, FREDERICK
ULMER, ADAM WEAVER, DANIEL WOLF, ASA WORDEN, total
$272.97. pp 9, 10, 11, 12, 13

Inv and appr of estate of JOSEPH C. SILVER on 6 Dec,
1820. Total $122.87, sworn before MOSES GREER, JP.
School accounts against STEPHEN AYRES, ENOCH BOWEN
estate, SILAS BROADWELL, H. BROWN, SOPHIA COOPER,
JAMES DANIEL, JOHN DODSON, JOHN FENNEMORE, C.R.
GREENE, D. GRIFFEN, GEORGE HARRIS, J. HART, JAMES
HENDERSON, WILLIAM HUFFMAN, J. JOHNSON, M. PATTON,
DANIEL PIERSON, MRS. REGANS, G.W. SMITH, NATHAN SIL-
VER, MRS. SQUIER, --STONESIFER, ALEXANDER WHITE plus
judgement against PETER MIKESELL; total $456.97. pp
13, 14, 15

Filed 16 July, 1821. Inv and appr of estate of CON-
RAD LECHLIDER. Widow kept $39.18 in property. Pub-
lic sale on 22 March, 1821; buyers: EPHRAIM ARNOLD,
JOHN BIMEN, GEORGE CALDERWOOD, ABRAHAM ENSEY, JOHN
GANT, BARNET B. HAGERMAN, DAVID HUMPHREYVILLE, DAVID
HUSTON, SAMUEL HUSTON, DAVID JOHN, JOHN JOHN, JACOB
KARGESS, ABRAHAM KIZER, SAMUEL KISER, DANIEL LECHLI-
DER, GEORGE LECHLIDER, RUHAMAH LECHLIDER, DAVID LEH-
MAN, JACOB LEHMAN, WILLIAM MANNING, JOSEPH MERRICK,
JOHN MOLER, VANDIVER MOLER, ABRAHAM MORGAN, WILLIAM
MORRISON, CULBERTSON PATTERSON, ROBERT RIDDLE, DAVID
SHOUP, IRA SMITH, RICHARD STEPHENS, MATTHIAS VANFLEET
ALEXANDER WEAD, total $465.30. pp 15, 16, 17, 18

Notes due estate of GEORGE YOUNT from ABSALOM WOODS.
Public sale, undated; buyers: CHRISTIAN ALBRIGHT,
GEORGE BUCHANON, JACOB BURKET, RALPH CAMPBELL, SAMUEL
CAMPBELL, THOMAS CLARK, GEORGE CLYMER, ANTHONY COBLE,
JOHN CRESS, JACOB CURTIS, GEORGE FENTRESS, HENRY
FOUTS, WILLIAM GADDIS, JOHN HELLACH, DAVID HOOVER,
JACOB HOOVER, JESSE HOOVER, JOHN HOOVER, TALBERT
IDDINGS, JAMES INSCO, DENNY JAY, THOMAS JONES, MOSES
KELLY, GEORGE KIZER, DAVID LUCAS, JOHN MACEY, PAUL
MACEY, THOMAS MACEY, JOHN MARTINDALE, SAMUEL MARTIN-
DALE, WILLIAM MENDENHALL, FRANCIS MILLION, JOHN MOON-
EY, JOHN MOTE, THOMAS NEWMAN, JOHN PEARSON, WILLIAM
PEARSON, JAMES PATTON, DAVID SHEETS, JOHN SHEETS,
GEORGE SINK, JOHN STALEY, JOSEPH STALEY, LEVI STALEY,
MARTIN STALEY, JOHN STARR, JUDITH SWEET, ABNER VORE,
DANIEL WAYMIRE, DANIEL YOUNT, FREDERICK YOUNT, HENRY
YOUNT, JOHN YOUNT SR, total $485.04. Specific be-
quests to daughters (eldest) NANCY now MACEY, and
POLLY now MACEY, given before their mother's death.
pp 19, 20, 21, 22, 23, 24, 25

Term of July, 1821

Case 469. Will of CASPER STIVER. Witness: JOHN
STIVER JR, GEORGE COLEMAN. Exec: CASPER STIVER &
FREDERICK STIVER. Appr: LEWIS SHUEY, MICHAEL GUNCK-
EL, WILLIAM EMRICK. Widow BARBARA STIVER made her
election to claim legacy of the will. p 25

Case 470. Will of JOHN HEASTON. Witness: HENRY
HIPPLE who testified he saw other witness, DANIEL
HEASTON, now dec, sign the will at testator's request
Exec: Widow MARY HEASTON. Sec: HENRY HIPPLE, CHRIS-
TIAN HEASTON. Appr: JACOB OLINGER, JOHN KINSEY,
JACOB WOLF. pp 25, 26

Case 471. Will of WILLIAM HART. Witness: JOHN MOTE,
JOHN ROHRER. Exec: DAVID LEADY relinquished right;

JAMES PATTY appted exec. Appr: DAVID MAST, SAMUEL BROWN, JOHN WARNER. p 26

Case 472. Will of JACOB STEPHENS. Witness: JOHN STOUDER, JACOB FRIBERGER. Exec: MARGARET STEPHENS, SAMUEL WILLIAMSON. Appr: JOHN STOUDER, JACOB FRIBERGER, JOHN EHRSTINE. p 26

Case 473. Adm of the estate of THOMAS WESTERMAN granted to MARY WESTERMAN. Sec: THOMAS SULLIVAN, ISAAC HARRISON. Appr: THOMAS CLAWSON, JOSEPH EWING & GARDNER EWING. p 26

Case 474. Adm of estate of ADAM MILLER granted to DANIEL MILLER & JOHN MILLER (widow relinquished right). Sec: MICHAEL HAGAR, ADAM WEAVER. Appr: JOHN APPLE, GEORGE APPLE, RHINEHART SNEP. pp 26, 27

Case 475. Adm of estate of JOHN DENISE granted to MARY DENISE & SIDNEY DENISE. Sec: TUNIS VANDEVEER, OBADIAH B. CONOVER. Appr: JAMES VAN KIRK, WILLIAM CONOVER, JOHN H. SCHENCK. p 27

Heirs of MARTIN HOOVER, dec:
Case 476. ABRAHAM HOOVER 15 yrs, & ESTHER HOOVER 13 yrs, chose JOHN HISER as guardian. Sec: JONAS HOOVER. p 27

Heirs of GEORGE YOUNT, dec:
Case 477. WILLIAM YOUNT, 15 yrs, chose HENRY YOUNT JR as guardian. Sec: JOHN MACEY. p 27
(&)
Case 478. JENNY YOUNT, 13 yrs, chose WILLIAM FINCHER as guardian. FINCHER appted guardian of SARAH YOUNT, 11 yrs. Sec: GEORGE FETTERS. p 27
(&)
Case 479. JOHN YOUNT appted guardian of GEORGE YOUNT, 9 yrs. Sec: DAVID HOOVER. p 27

Admr of estate of HENRY CLARK JR requested time extension to settle estate. p 27

Admr of estate of CONRAD LICHTY requested time extension to settle estate. p 28

Admr of estate of JOHN McCABE granted time extension to settle estate. p 28

Case 480. Adm of estate of GEORGE RENNICK granted to JOHN RENNICK & GEORGE RENNICK (widow relinquished right). Sec: JOEL WESTFALL, WILLIAM VAN CLEVE. Appr: GEORGE PARSONS, ANDREW CLARK, ALBERT R. HUEY. p 28

Case 481. Adm of estate of JAMES PETTICREW granted
to JAMES PETTICREW & SAMUEL CALDWELL. Sec: HORATIO
G. PHILLIPS, WILLIAM LONG. Appr: GEORGE NEWCOM,
RICHARD MASON & JAMES CARUTHERS. p 28

Heirs of MARTIN SHOUP, dec:
Case 482. HENRY SHOUP, 19 yrs, & ELIZABETH SHOUP, 13
yrs, chose ADAM SHUEY as guardian. Sec: MARTIN
SHUEY. p 28

Heirs of DANIEL RICHARDISON, dec:
Case 483. WILLIAM BOWSER appted guardian of WILLIAM
RICHARDSON, 12 yrs, & JOHN RICHARDSON, 10 yrs. Sec:
DANIEL BOWSER. p 28

Heirs of WILLIAM MARSHALL, dec:
Case 484. LORINDA MARSHALL, 14 yrs, chose ABRAHAM
DARST as guardian. DARST appted guardian of WASHING-
TON MARSHALL, 12 yrs, & ZEPHANIAH MARSHALL, 10 yrs.
Sec: SAMUEL DIETRICK. pp 28, 29

Admr of JONATHAN HILDRETH produced settlement. Cred-
itors paid: MICAH HILDRETH, JOB HAINES, ROBT STRAIN,
H.G. PHILLIPS, JOSHUA McINTOSH, JOHN STEELE, GEORGE
GROVE, EBENEZER STEBBINS, JOHN DODSON, O.B. CONOVER,
NOAH JOHNSON. p 29

Admr of JOSEPH BLICKENSTAFF produced settlement. Widow's half = $124.76; children's half the same. p 30

Admr of THOMAS KELSEY produced settlement. Cash paid
to BENJAMIN ARCHER, WILLIAM BRADSTREET, SAMUEL
BROADAWAY, TITUS IVES, LEONARD KEEP, WILLIAM LODGE,
BENJAMIN MALTBIE, SOLOMON MILLER, MAHLON MOON, JOHN
C. MURPHY, AARON NUTT, JAMES RUSSELL, IRA SMITH,
NAT'L STRONG, JOHN WILLIAMSON, ASAHEL WRIGHT total
$86.45. pp 30, 31

Exec of WILLIAM WAUGH produced settlement. p 31

Exec of MARY DAVIS produced settlement. Cash paid to
JOHN ANDERSON, JOHN BAKER, Dr. BLODGETT, SILAS BROAD-
WELL (whiskey for sale), JOHN COMPTON, OBADIAH B.
CONOVER, ISAAC CONOVER, WILLIAM COX, CATHERINE ETTER
(nursing), JOHN M. GRAY (taxes), DAVID GRIFFIN, JAMES
HANNA, Col. HOLT (auctioneer), JOHN LEHMAN, DAVID
LINDSLEY -- "dress for girl and taking her to Circle-
ville", JOSHUA McINTOSH, JAMES I. NESBIT (taxes),
JOSEPH C. SILVER "in beef for funeral sermon", WIL-
LIAM VAN CLEVE (road taxes), DANIEL WOLF. Notes due
estate from JOHN BAKER, WILLIAM COX, ISAAC HIRE, JOHN
LEHMAN, DAVID LINDSLEY, WILLIAM NICHOLAS (absconded),

WILLIAM ROTH, CHARLES RUCKLE (absconded), JONATHAN
STUTSMAN, ALEX WHITE; total, $897.19. pp 31, 32, 33

Admr of GEORGE LANE produced settlement. Cash paid
to VINCENT ANTONIDES, WILLIAM CONOVER, WILLIAM CRAIG
(coffin), LEWIS DAVIS, JOHN DENISE, SIDNEY DENISE, Dr
BENJAMIN DUBOIS, DANIEL DUBOIS, JACOB HARKRADER, WIL-
LIAM LONGSTREET, GEORGE LOY, DANIEL MILLER (taxes),
Rev FRANCIS MONFORT, JOHN N.C. SCHENCK, JOHN SHUPERT,
JOHN TREON, TUNIS D. VANDERVEER, JOSEPH VANNOTE (for
grave digging), AUKEY WIKOFF, JOHN WIKOFF. Notes due
estate from VINCENT ANTONIDES, BENJAMIN BARKALOW,
LEWIS BASTEDO, JOHN COMPTON, PETE CONOVER, LEWIS DAV-
IS, HENDRICK LANE, ADAM SPITLAR, MOSES VAIL, total
$3743.95. Debts which cannot be collected: SAMUEL
DENISE, Widow PENROD, GEORGE SMOCK, JOHN VANTILBURGH,
EZEKIEL VANNOAT, RACHEL VANNOTE, total $96.80. pp
33, 34, 35

Admr of estate of THOMAS HAMER directed to pay
balance due on land contract to U.S. govt. p 35

Case 485. CONRAD KAUFFMAN appted guardian to GEORGE
HORNER, an idiot 15 yrs old, & JOHN HORNER, 10 yrs,
heirs of JOHN HORNER, dec. Sec: GEORGE WEIMAR. p 36

Case 486. THOMAS CARPENTER, 18 yrs, heir of HOPKINS
CARPENTER, dec, chose JOSEPH PEIRCE as guardian. p 36

1 Aug, 1821. Admr of TALLMAN HALL granted time extension to settle estate. p 36

Exec of DANIEL C. COOPER granted time extension to
settle estate. p 36

Filed 3 Aug, 1821. Inv and appr of estate of GEORGE
RENNICK on 1 Aug, 1821. Total $289.12. Widow kept
property, total not given. p 36, 37

Filed 1 Sept, 1821. Inv and appr of estate of JOHN
DENISE on 1 Aug, 1821. Total of $944.91 included
notes due from BENJAMIN BOWERS, WILLIAM CONOVER,
SIDNEY DENISE, H. LANE, J.H. SCHENCK, JOSEPH VANNOTE,
THOMAS VANNOTE, JAMES WHITFIELD. Widow kept $320.81
in property. Public sale on 28 Aug, 1821; buyers:
WILLIAM G. ANDERSON, ANN BARKALOW, DERRICK BARKALOW,
WILLIAM BARKALOW, ZEBULON BARKALOW, JACOB BILMAN,
EDEN BURROWS, HENRY CATRICK, CHARLES CATROW, JOHN
CHAMBERS, JOHN CHRISTOPHER, GARRET CONOVER, WILLIAM
G. CONOVER, CHRISTOPHER COON, JOHN COX, WILLIAM COX,
LEWIS DAVIS, SIDNEY DENISE, JOHN EGGONS, WILLIAM
ELY, GEORGE ERGENBRIGHT, GEORGE HALL, JAMES KERR,

HENRY KINSEY, GILBERT LANE, GEORGE LOY, JACOB LOY, JAMES MARLOTT, JOHN MARSH, SAMUEL MAXFIELD, AUKEY McCABE, JOHN NEWMAN, JOSEPH PITMAN, JOHN ROBBINS, EDWARD RUCKHILE, HORTENSE SCHENCK, JOHN H. SCHENCK, ELISHA SHEPHERD, JOHN SHEPHERD, HENRY SHOUTS, BENJAMIN VANDERVEER, GARRET VANNATER, JOSEPH VANNOTE, THOMAS VANNOTE, MICHAEL VANTILE, JOHN WIKOFF, total $616.17. pp 37, 38, 39, 40, 41, 42, 43, 44

Special session 15 September, 1821

Case 487. Will of CHARLES WELBAUM. Witness: HENRY ROOF, DAVID STUDYBAKER. No exec named in will. Adm granted to CHARLES WELBAUM JR & DAVID WELBAUM. Sec: HENRY ROOF, JACOB SMITH. Appr: JOSEPH FLORY, HENRY FLORY, MARTIN WIBRIGHT. p 45

Case 488. Adm of estate of JOHN DUNCAN granted to RICHARD DUNCAN & JOHN BIGGER (widow relinquished right). Sec: PETER SUNDERLAND, AMOS IRWIN. Appr: DANIEL WILSON, JOSEPH EWING, JOHN HORNER. p 45

Filed 4 Oct, 1821. Inv and appr of estate of CASPER STIVER on 13 Aug, 1821. Total $4785.98. p 45, 46, 47

Filed 22 Oct, 1821. Inv and appr of estate of WILLIAM HART. Total $177.75. Debts due from JOHN BAKER, SAMUEL BROWN, JESSE HOOVER, ABRAHAM PUTERBAUGH, JACOB SWANK, ANDREW WAYMIRE, JOHN WERTZ. pp 47, 48

Inv and appr of estate of THOMAS WESTERMAN on 22 Oct, 1821. Total $205.12. pp 48, 49

Inv and appr of estate of ADAM MILLER, total $1048.00 Notes due estate from ABRAHAM ANZT, GEORGE GROVE, MICHAEL HAGAR, SAMUEL HAGAR, JONATHAN KERSHNER, HENRY ROBINSON. Public sale on 31 Aug, 1821; buyers: MICHAEL ALSPACH, GEORGE APPLE, JACOB APPEL, JOHN APPEL, JOHN BAUM, ADAM BOLENDER, BENNET CARTER, JESSE CLARK, WILLIAM CLARK, L.C. COTTOM, DANIEL CRAMER, JACOB CRULL, JACOB FAASNAUGHT, JACOB HART, PETER HETZEL, HENRY HILT, JOHN HISER, JOHN HORNER, DANIEL ISELEY, DANIEL KELLY, MATTHEW LEASE, DANIEL MILLER, JOHN MILLER, MARGARET MILLER, JOSEPH MULLINDORE, HENRY RADER, THOMAS RYAN, GEORGE SHAFER, CHARLES SMITH, RHINEHART SNEP, JOHN STEWART, PETER STOCK, DAVID UMPHREYVILLE, BENJAMIN WALTERS, ADAM WEAVER, CALEB WILCOX. Total $686.17. pp 49, 50, 51, 52, 53, 54

Inv and appr of estate of JOHN HEISTAND of Jefferson Twp, sworn before JOHN HOUTZ, JP, on 22 Oct, 1821. Total $118.87. pp 54, 55

Filed <u>30 Oct, 1821.</u> Inv and appr of estate of JAMES PETTICREW of Washington Twp on 31 Aug, 1821. Total $459.31. Public sale on 10 Oct, 1821; buyers not named. Total $598.10. pp 55, 56, 57

<u>Term of October, 1821</u>

Case 489. Will of EMROY HOUGHTON. Witnss: MOSES SIMPSON, WILLIAM ATKIN. Exec: AARON BAKER. Sec: MOSES SIMPSON, JOHN LEHMAN. Appr: NOAH JOHNSON, THOMAS ROYER, ELISHA BRABHAM. p 58

Case 490. Will of DAVID PHOUTZ. Witness: JACOB WIBRIGHT, JOHN BURKET. Exec: ANDREW PHOUTZ, DAVID HOOVER. Appr: JACOB WIBRIGHT, DANIEL RASOR, PHILIP BARTMESS. p 58

Case 491. Adm of estate of JOSEPH HAWVER granted to JACOB GLOSSBRENNER & JOHN BAKER. Sec: DANIEL RAZER, DAVID BAKER. Appr: JAMES EWING, DAVID HOOVER, JACOB WIBRIGHT. p 58

Case 492. Adm of estate of GEORGE BRETSINS granted to AARON BAKER. Sec: MOSES SIMPSON, JOHN LEHMAN. Appr: NOAH JOHNSON, ELISHA BRABHAM, THOMAS BOYER. pp 58, 59

Case 493. Adm of estate of DANIEL SCHNEPP granted to PHILIP SCHNEPP & JOHN SCHNEPP. Sec: GEORGE APPLER & DANIEL ISELEY. Appr: ADAM BOLENDER, JOHN APPLE, PETER HETZEL. p 59

Case 494. Adm of estate of GEORGE GEPHART granted to HENRY GEPHART JR (widow relinquished right). Sec: HENRY GEPHART, CHRISTOPHER SHUPPERT. Appr: JACOB WEAVER. DAVID MILLER, JACOB HARKRADER. p 59

Case 495. MARGARET STIVER & ADAM SWINEHART appted guardians of SOLOMON STIVER 5 yrs, ABSALOM STIVER 4 yrs, ANNA MARIA STIVER 2 yrs, & CATHERINE STIVER, 9 months, minor heirs of JOHN STIVER, dec. Sec: FREDERICK RIDGELEY, JOHN KETZER. p 59

Case 496. JACOB GEPHART, 16 yrs, minor heir of JOHN GEPHART, chose JOHN SNEPP as guardian. Sec: PHILIP SNEPP. p 59

Admr of estate of CHRISTIAN WELDY granted time extension to settle estate. p 59

Inv and appr of estate of CHARLES WELLBAUM of Madison Twp on 22 Sept, 1821. Total $589.38. Debts due from

DANIEL DIETRICK, SAMUEL HAGAR, PETER HELVISTON, GEORGE KUNS, HENRY RHUFF. Public sale on 11 & 12 Oct, 1821; buyers: LOAMI ASHLEY, DAVID BOWEN, DANIEL BURKET, HENRY COFFMAN, JOHN CONNOR, LUDWICK COY, JAMES CRAWSON, PETER FETTERS, JOSEPH GARVER, JACOB GRIPE, JOHN GRIPE, JOHN HITTLE, FREDERICK HOLSAPPLE, WILLIAM KELLY, GEORGE KUNS, JOSEPH MIKESELL, DANIEL MUNDHENK, DANIEL MURRY, DAVID MURRY, ELIZABETH MURRY, BENJAMIN NICHOLS, WILLIAM NICHOLS, JACOB OVERHOLSER, CONRAD OVERLEESE, HENRY OVERLEESE, DANIEL OX, THOMAS J. PATTERSON, JAMES PATTON, PETER PEPPINGER, NATHANIEL PORTER, MICHAEL RAGER, JOHN REESE, GEORGE RODEBAUGH, HENRY RODEBAUGH, GEORGE RODEBUSH, HENRY ROOF, PETER ROOF, DANIEL SMALL, GEORGE SMITH, HENRY SMITH, JACOB SMITH, DAVID STUDEBAKER, AARON VANSCOYCK, DANIEL WARNER, ABRAHAM WELBAUM, CHARLES WELBAUM, CHRISTIAN WELBAUM, DAVID WELBAUM, HENRY WELBAUM, MARTIN WEYBRIGHT, GEORGE WITTERS total $661.26. pp 59, 60, 61, 62, 63, 64, 65, 66, 67, 68, 69

Inv and appr of estate of JOHN DUNKINS on 10 Oct, 1821 by DANIEL WILSON, JOHN HORNER & JOSEPH EWING, filed by admr RICHARD DUNKIN (case 488). Total of $552.75. Note due from JOHN SHRYROCK. Public sale, no date given; buyers: DAVID ARCHER, SAMUEL ARMSTRONG ROBERT BIGHAM, JOSEPH COLEMAN, FRANCIS DILTS, BENJAMIN DUNKIN, BETSEY DUNKIN, PETER DUNKIN, RICHARD DUNKIN, WILLIAM DUNKIN, JOSEPH LEACH, JAMES McCLURE, MAHLON MOON, AARON NUTT SR, EPHRAIM PETTIT, SAMUEL PROARD, MOSES A. REED, ISAAC REEDER, JACOB SNOWDEN, JOHN WELLER, DANIEL WILSON, IVY WRIGHT, total $370.12 pp 69, 70, 71, 72, 73

Case 497. Adm of estate of GEORGE HORNER granted to CATHERINE HORNER & PETER SHAFFER. Sec: FREDERICK WOLF, DANIEL MUNDHENK. Appr: PHILIP LONG, HENRY SHAFFER, JOHN SWANK. p 74

Case 498. Adm of estate of JACOB BRUMBAUGH granted to MARGARET BROMBAUGH & JOHN BROMBAUGH. Sec: SAMUEL HAGAR, GEORGE BROMBAUGH. Appr: DAVID KINZEY, PAUL FREAM, NICHOLAS SMALL. p 74

Case 499. ABRAHAM WELBAUM, 18 yrs, minor heir of CHARLES WELBAUM, chose PETER FETTER as guardian. Sec: SAMUEL HAGAR, HENRY LEEDES. p 74

1 November, 1821. Case 500. Adm of estate of JOSEPH PEIRCE granted to JOSEPH H. CRANE (widow relinquished right). Sec: GEORGE NEWCOM, GEORGE GROVE. Appr: ALEXANDER GRIMES, EBENEZER STEBBINS, BENJAMIN VAN CLEVE. p 74

Case 501. Adm of estate of ISAAC PEIRCE granted to JOSEPH H. CRANE. Sec: GEORGE NEWCOM, GEORGE GROVE. Appr: ALEXANDER GRIMES, EBENEZER STEBBINS, BENJAMIN VAN CLEVE. p 74

Inv and appr of estate of MICHAEL EMRICK on 24 Nov, 1820. List of property kept by widow CHRISTIANA EMRICK total $304.40. Public sale on 24 Nov, 25 Nov & 2 Dec, 1820. Buyers: SAMUEL ANDREW, JACOB BOWER, JOHN BROSS, CHARLES CATROW, THOMAS CATROW, GEORGE CLENCY, HENRY CLINE, JACOB COY, FREDERIC DECHANT, JOHN CASPER DILL, JOHN DYNNINGER, BURREL EAKER, BEN-JAMIN EAKINS, ABRAHAM ELY, JACOB EMINGER, ABRAHAM EMRICK, CONRAD EMRICK, GEORGE EMRICK, HENRY EMRICK, JACOB EMRICK, JOHN C. EMRICK, WILLIAM EMRICK JR, SAMUEL FRAME, GEORGE GENGER, ANTHONY GEPHART, JOHN GOOD, VALENTINE GOOD, JACOB GROVE, DANIEL GUNCKEL, JOHN D. GUNCKEL, MICHAEL GUNCKEL, FREDERICK HEFFNER, JAMES HENDERSON, PHILIP HOLER, NICHOLAS HOLLAR, WIL-LIAM HUMBERT, CONRAD ISELEY, DANIEL ISELEY, JOHN JUDY HENRY KEISTER, JACOB KELLER, MICHAEL KENNY, JOHN KETSER, CHARLES KOUCKER, GODFREY KOUCKER, JOHN LATOU-RETTE, JONATHAN LINDEMUTT, GEORGE LOY, JACOB MILLER, MELCHOIR MILLER, ADAM NAVE, WILLIAM ODELL, ADAM OLER, WILLIAM OLER, DANIEL OSWALT, CHRISTOPHER SEILER, FREDERICK SHAFFER, JACOB SHAFFER, PETER SHAFFER, DAVID SHOWER, JOHN SMALLEY, MICHAEL SNIDER, BENJAMIN STIVER, FREDERICK STIVER, JOHN STIVER JR, DAVID STRAN GEORGE STROUB, JOHN STUMP, ELI SULGROVE, JACOB SWANK, JOHN TUMPAW, JOHN WAGNER, JACOB WHITENER, GEORGE WIDERS, PHILIP WOLF, JAMES YOUNGER, JACOB ZEHRING. Total $871.94. pp 75, 76, 77, 78, 79, 80, 81, 82, 83, 84, 85

Public sale of estate of WILLIAM LUCE. Buyers: BEN-JAMIN ARCHER, DAVID ARCHER, THOMAS BEER, JOHN BOWSER, JAMES BUCKLES, ROBERT BUCKLES, GOLDSMITH CHANDLER, JOSIAH CLAWSON, THOMAS CLAWSON, BOSWELL COLOM, JOSEPH FISK, JOHN HAINES, STACY HAINES, JOHN HARRIS, ETHEL KELLOGG, DENNIS LANE, BENJAMIN LUCE, JUDITH LUCE, JOHN H. MARTIN, JOHN McNEIL, EDWARD MITCHEL, AARON NUTT, DANIEL REEDER, JAMES RUSSEL, JOHN SHANKS, HENRY STANSEL, PETER SUNDERLAND. Total $337.48. pp 85, 86, 87, 88, 89

5 November, 1821. Case 502/503. Will of HENRY ZEHRING. Witness: JOHN FOX, LEWIS MEARS. Exec: JACOB GEPHART. Appr: JOHN FOX, LEWIS MEARS, FREDE-RICK HOOVER. p 89

Case 504. Adm of estate of PETER EAGLE granted to JACOB EAGLE & WILLIAM LONG (widow relinquished right)

Sec: MICHAEL HILLEGAS, DANIEL GEPHART. Appr: JAMES CAROTHERS, TOBIAS WHITESEL, RICHARD MASON. p 89

Case 505. Adm of estate of JOHN STEWART granted to RICHARD CAMPBELL. Sec: CHARLES SMITH, WILLIAM M. SMITH. Appr: JOSEPH EVANS, ISAAC MAKINNIS, JOHN FURNACE. p 89

Case 506. Adm of estate of ELIZABETH GEPHART granted to JOHN HUNTER. Sec: JACOB GEPHART, ABRAHAM TROXEL. Appr: MICHAEL HOOBLER, DANIEL SHOWERS, JOHN A. RANK. p 90

Case 507. CATHERINE GEPHART, 13 yrs, minor heir of ELIZABETH GEPHART, dec, chose ABRAHAM TROXELL as guardian. Sec: JACOB GEPHART. p 90

Case 508. DAVID WOODROW, 18 yrs, son of JAMES WOODROW, dec, chose ABRAHAM CONOVER as guardian. p 90

Case 509. WILLIAM VAN CLEVE appted guardian of his daughter, CATHERINE VAN CLEVE, heir of -- MILEY, dec. p 90

Admr of estate of ABNER GARARD produced settlement. Cash paid to DAVID ARCHER, HENRY BACON, WILLIAM BLAIR, HENRY BROWN, JOHN CAMPBELL, PETER CODDINGTON, HENRY CURTNER, GEORGE C. DAVIS, WILLIAM ELSBERRY, JOHN FRILL, JOHN GAMBLE, JONATHAN GARARD, ISAAC HARRISON, BENJAMIN HILLMAN, JOHN R. IRONS, TITUS IVES (tax), BARTON R. KEEP, ELIHU KELLOGG, WILLIAM LODGE, ELIZABETH LONG, WILLIAM LONG, BENJAMIN MALTBIE, WILLIAM MORRIS, EDMUND MUNGER, REUBEN MUNGER, WARREN MUNGER, AARON NUTT (auctioneer), LEVI NUTT (digging grave), JAMES RUSSEL, ROBERT SCOTT, ROBERT J. SKINNER (printing ads), IRA SMITH (tax), EBENEZER STIBBINS (coffin), ASAHEL WRIGHT, JONATHAN WRIGHT, GEORGE ZELLERS. pp 90, 91, 92

Admr of ABRAHAM TEAGARDEN produced settlement. Cash paid to ABRAHAM BRANNERMAN, JACOB CRULL, CRITTON STOKER, HENRY ENOCH JR, HENRY ENOCH SR, total $80.20. p 92

Admr of MATTHIAS SWARTZLEY produced partial settlement and requested time extension to settle estate. Cash paid to HENRY BOOMERSHINE, MARY BOOMERSHINE, PETER BOOMERSHINE, ADAM BUTT, JOHN COLEMAN, JOHN HOLMES, JOHN MYERS, FRANCIS PATTERSON (tax), HENRY SHEIDLER (coffin), JOHN SILVER, JOHN STIVERS (auctioneer), ABRAHAM SWARTZLEY, HENRY SWARTZLEY, WILLIAM YOUNG, total $97.58. p 93

Admr of JOSHUA WHITE granted time extension to settle
estate. p 93

Admr of JOHN STAVER granted time extension to settle
estate. p 93

Admr of HENRY CLARK granted time extension to settle
estate. p 93

Admr of GEORGE LANE produced payment of $329.59 by
JOHN H. SCHENCK. p 94

Admr of LUCEANNA ZIEGLER produced settlement. Cash
paid to SAMUEL BOOKER, SOPHIA COOPER, THOMAS CREAGER,
C.R. GREENE, MARIA GREENE, JOB HAINES, ASA JOHN, SAM-
UEL KING, MORGAN LODGE, CORNELIUS LOW, ABRAHAM MORGAN
CORNELIUS MORGAN, JOHN MORGAN, MATTHEW PATTON/coffin,
SAMUEL PEIRCE, R.J. SKINNER/printing funeral tickets,
Dr STEELE, C. WESTFALL. pp 94, 95

Exec of EBENEZER WEAD produced settlement. Sold land
to JAMES RIDDLE. Cash paid to JOHN BONNER, BENJAMIN
CRABBS, JOHN CRABBS, ALEXANDER DEAN, Dr HAINES, ABRA-
HAM HOSIER, JOHN McCOY, JAMES RIDDLE, ALEXANDER WEAD,
JAMES WEAD, JOHN WEAD, ROBERT WEAD, total $1212.94.
pp 95, 96

Admr of estate of GABRIEL SWINEHART produced settlement. $335.24 in property kept by widow. Cash paid
to JAMES GRAHAM, JOHN MILLER, GEORGE LOY, JOHN
PAULLY, total $335.29. pp 96, 97

Case 510. THOMAS KING appted guardian of ELIZABETH
DOVEY PARKS, 10 yrs, heir of ROBERT PARKS, dec. Sec:
SAMUEL BRIER. p 97

Inv and appr of estate of ISAAC PEIRCE on 4 Nov, 1821
included notes due from W.K. CLOUGH, JAMES TURNER.
Total $2014.10. pp 97, 98

Inv and appr of estate of JOSEPH PEIRCE on 9 Nov,
1821. Widow HENRIETTA E. PEIRCE allowed $600 for
support of family for 1 yr. Share in estate of ISAAC
PEIRCE = $2014.10. Share in estate of LUCEANNA ZEIG-
LER estimated to be $11,450.00. pp 98, 99

Special session 22 December, 1821

Case 511. Adm of estate of ABRAHAM COUTNER granted
to JOHN COUTNER. Sec: WILLIAM EMRICK, JONATHAN LIN-
DAMOUTH. Appr: DANIEL GUNCKEL SR, CHRISTOPHER EMRICK
& MICHAEL GUNCKLE. p 100

Case 512. Will of BENJAMIN VAN CLEVE. Witness: JEROM HOLT, CONKLING MILLER. Exec: MARY VAN CLEVE, WILLIAM VAN CLEVE, JOSEPH H. CRANE. Appr: AARON BAKER, GEORGE NEWCOM, JOHN FOLKERTH. p 100

Case 513. Adm of estate of ROBERT GIBSON granted to ROBERT WEAD. Sec: H.G. PHILLIPS, HENRY STODDARD. Appr: DAVID HENDERSON, AARON RICHARDSON, JAMES ELLIOT. p 100

Special session 4 January, 1822

Case 514. Will of JACOB COOK. Witness: HENRY STOD-DARD, JAMES ETTICOTT. Exec: GEORGE NEWCOM, ASHER BROWN. Appr: ABRAHAM GARST, NOAH JOHNSON, WILLIAM BOMBERGER. p 101

Inv and appr of estate of JACOB BRUMBAUGH of Randolph Twp on 24 Nov, 1821 by NICHOLAS SMALL, DAVID KINZEY & PAUL FRAME. Total $303.25. List of property kept by widow MARGARET BROMBAUGH = $95.62. Public sale on 21 Nov, 1821; buyers: DANIEL BROMBAUGH, DANIEL COFFMAN, HENRY COFFMAN, JAMES CROSSIN, GEORGE FETTERS, JACOB FLORY, JOHN FLORY, DAVID HOOVER, DAVID KINSEY, DAVID MASTERS, DANIEL OCKZ, JACOB OVERHOLSER, ADAM RODA-BAUGH, ABRAHAM SIFE, JACOB SPITLAR, PHILIP STUDABAKER JACOB STUTSMAN, VALENTINE TOWMAN, DANIEL VARNER, total $136.14. pp 101, 102, 103, 104, 105

Filed 21 January, 1822. Inv and appr of estate of DAVID PFOUTZ of Randolph Twp, total $309.76. Sworn before JACOB GLOSSBRENNER, JP, on 15 Jan, 1822. Debts due from PETER FETTERS, ANDREW PFOUTZ total $84. pp 106, 107

Filed 22 December, 1821. Inv and appr of estate of ROBERT GIBSON on 22 Jan, 1821, total $39.50. Debts due estate from JOHN CAMPBELL, JONATHAN MUNGER, WIL-LIAM WILEY, BENJAMIN VAN CLEVE, JOHN GROVE total $1305.75. pp 108, 109

Admr of WILLIAM VANDERSLICE presented debts due es-tate by JANE ABBOTT/rent due, STEPHEN C. AYRES, JOHN BAKER, BENJAMIN BAYLESS, ELISHA BRABHAM, SILAS BROAD-WELL, JOHN BURNS, JOHN COMPTON, L.C. COTTOM, HENRY CURTNER, G.C. DAVIS, LEWIS DAVIS, DAVID FIRDON, GEORGE GROVE, GEORGE HARRIS, JACOB LEHMAN, JOHN LEH-MAN, PETER LEHMAN, HENRY MARQUART, JOSHUA McINTOSH, SAMUEL MILLER, WILLIAM MURPHY, WILLIAM OWENS, FREDE-RICK OX, WILLIAM PATTERSON, DAVID REID, HENRY STALEY, JONATHAN STUTSMAN, WILLIAM WATTON, GEORGE WOLLASTON total $1874.57. Notes found, supposed to be joint

property with BENJAMIN BAYLESS, due from JAMES BAR-
NETT, E. BRABHAM, SILAS BROADWELL, ISAAC CONOVER,
JOHN FOLKERTH, JAMES HANNA, MOSES HATFIELD, DAVID
HUMPHREYVILLE, JOHN KNOTT, JOHN IMERICK, THOMAS
MORRISON, ALEX SIMPSON, WILLIAM M. SMITH, WILLIAM
TYLER total $361.05. Accounts due from MATTHEW PAT-
TON, JOHN BURNS, ALEXANDER GUY & D.C. COOPER total
$408.96. pp 109, 110, 111, 112, 113

Public sale of estate of ROBERT GIBSON on 19 Jan,
1822. Buyers: ROBERT GIBSON JR, HENRY STODDARD,
ROBERT WEAD total $17.75. pp 113, 114

Inv and appr of estate of GEORGE BRATSUS of Dayton
Twp on 6 Nov, 1821. Total $808.14. Public sale on
13 Nov, 1821; buyers: AARON BAKER, WILLIAM BLODGET,
ELISHA BRABHAM, LEWIS BROADWELL, WILLIAM COX, NAT'L
DANFORTH, MOSES HATFIELD, JOHN LEHMAN, HENRY MARQUART
LUDWICK SHAW, ALEXANDER SIMPSON, MOSES SIMPSON, EDWIN
SMITH, GEORGE SNIDER, BENJAMIN VAN CLEVE. Total of
$87.10. (SEE CASE 492) pp 114, 115, 116, 117

Filed 30 January, 1822. Inv and appr of estate of
EMROY HOUGHTON on 2 Dec, 1821, total $119.12. p 118

Inv and appr of estate of GEORGE GEPHART on 23 Nov,
1821. Total $1053.84. Public sale on 27 Nov, 1821;
buyers: JOHN ANTONIDES, VINCENT ANTONIDES, GEORGE
ARGENBRIGHT, PETER BULLINSBACH, MICHAEL CODRAMAN,
CHRISTIAN EMRICK, HENRY FOX, CATHERINE GEPHART, EMAN-
UEL GEPHART, GEORGE GEPHART JR, HENRY GEPHART JR,
HENRY GEPHART SR, JACOB GEPHART, JOHN GEPHART, MARY
GEPHART, JACOB HARKRADER, ADAM HARTZEL, FREDERICK
HEFFNER, JOHN HOFFMAN, DAVID HOOVER, WILLIAM HIPPLE,
JOHN LIGHTCAP, DANIEL MILLER, PETER MILLER, SAMUEL
MOON, JONATHAN MORRIS, PETER PENROD, PHILIP REPLOGEL,
JOHN H. SCHENCK, JOHN SHARRIT, CHRISTOPHER SHUPERT,
JOHN SHUPERT, DANIEL STETLER JR, GEORGE STONER, JOHN
STONER, ADAM WEAVER, JOHN WEAVER, MICHAEL WEAVER,
JACOB WINABRENNER. Total $570.32. pp 124, 125, 126

Inv and appr of estate of ELIZABETH GEPHART of Jeff-
erson Twp on 14 Nov, 1821. Total $81.56. Public
sale on 16 Nov, 1821; buyers: JOHN BAKER, PETER
BAKER, DANIEL BOWSER, BURL EAKERS, DANIEL GEPHART,
JACOB GEPHART, JOSEPH GEPHART, JOHN GETTER, JAMES
HILDERBRAND, SAMUEL HILDERBRAND, ELY HOOVER, JOHN
HUNTSINGER, JOSEPH JOHNSON, PETER KAYLOR, JOHN MINER,
JOHN A. RANK, MOSES RENFROW, DANIEL SHIDLER, DAVID
SHOWERS, JOHN SHRIDER, FREDERICK STIVER, GEORGE
STROUP. pp 127, 128, 129

Inv and appr of estate of DANIEL SNEP of Dayton Twp on 8 Nov, 1821. Including note due from JOHN WALTZ, total of $413.10. Public sale on 9 Nov, 1821; buyers: GEORGE APPLE, JOHN APPLE, JOHN BARNHARD, RICHARD BECK, DEWALD BOUGARD, ADAM BOWLANDER, JESSE CLARK JOHN CRULL, JACOB HETZEL, PETER HETZEL, JOHN HILDERBRAND, JOHN HILT, JOSEPH HOKE, JOHN HORNISH, DANIEL ISELY, JACOB KAYLOR, JOHN MILLER, BENJAMIN NICHOLAS, PARRY PEASE, MARTIN SHUEY, MICHAEL SMITH, JOHN SNEP, JOHN SNEP JR, LEONARD SNEP, PHILIP SNEP, Widow SNEP, PETER STOCK, GEORGE STROUP, ABRAHAM TOBIAS, JACOB TOBIAS, GEORGE WEAVER, COBB WILCOX, JOHN WOODRING, FELIX ZESLEY. Total $459.68. pp 129, 130, 131, 132, 133, 134, 135

Filed 26 Feb, 1822. Inv and appr of estate of GEORGE HARNER of Perry Twp. Total $173.75. pp 135, 136, 137

Inv and appr of estate of HENRY ZERING of Washington Twp on 24 Nov, 1821. Total $307.02. Public sale on 13 Nov, 1821; buyers: JAMES AKIN JR, JACOB BUTT, JOHN CLEIGH, JOHN CONSOLVER, SAMUEL COLE, JOHN CRAITON, JAMES CRUTHERS, JAMES DUNKERLY, JOHN FOX, ANDREW GEPHART, GEORGE GEPHART, JACOB GEPHART, WILLIAM HAFFNER, FREDERICK HUBS, WILLIAM JOHNSTON, WILLIAM LONG, JACOB MATTHEWS, DAVID MAXWELL, ROBERT McCORD, LEWIS MEASE, DAVID MILLER, ISAAC MYERS, PETER RICHARD, DAVID SCHENCK, PETER SHAFFER, HENRY SHELL, MARTIN SHUEY, ANDREW SMALL, JOHN TAYLOR, PETER TREON, DANIEL UNGARY SOLOMON WHITESELL, CHRISTIAN ZEARING, DANIEL ZEARING. Total $259.50. pp 137, 138, 139, 140, 141, 142

Inv and appr of estate of PETER EAGLE of Washington Twp on 20 Nov, 1821 by JAMES CROTHERS, RICHARD MASON & TOBIAS WHITESELL. Total $241. Public sale on 17 Dec, 1821; buyers: JACOB BENNER, JOHN BETSON, FREDERICK CLAWSON, SAMUEL COLE, BENJAMIN COLEMAN, DANIEL CROOMER, JAMES CRUTHERS, GEORGE EAGLE, HENRY EAGLE, JACOB EAGLE, WILLIAM EAGLE, DANIEL GEPHART, JOHN GEPHART, JOHN GRAFF, MICHAEL HILLGAP, HENRY HILT, DANIEL KINGERY, JOHN KIRGER, GEORGE LOY, MICHAEL LYDY, RICHARD MASON, ROBERT McBRIM, HENRY MILLER, PHILIP MILLER ABEL MORROW, ISAAC MYERS, GEORGE PARSONS, BENJAMIN SCOTT, JOHN SMITH, ABRAHAM VORHEES, JOHN WALTS, TOBIAS WHITESELL, JACOB WISE. Total $368.59. pp 142, 143, 144, 145, 146

Inv and appr of estate of JOSEPH HAWVER of Randolph Twp on 2 Nov, 1821. Total $115.00. Debts due from ANDREW BOYD, JACOB EDWARDS, JOHN SMITH, GARRET THOMSON, LEVI FALKNER, ANDREW WAYMIRE; total $311.16. pp 146, 147

Inv and appr of estate of ABRAHAM KASTNER of Dayton Twp on 12 Jan, 1822. Total $540.66. Public sale on 19 Jan, 1822; buyers: DAVID ALSPACH, MICHAEL ALSPACH, HENRY BEASLEY, HENRY BECHLER, LATONIAS CAPPER, GEORGE CLENCY, JAMES CLOYD, JOSHUA CLOYD, PETER DECHANT, JOHN DIGMAN, JACOB DININGER, JOHN DININGER, CONRAD EMRICK, HENRY EMRICK, CHRISTIAN ESPIESS, JACOB FRYE, JOHN GENGER, JOHN D. GUNCKEL, JACOB HAWS, JOSEPH HOKE, JOHN KASTNOR, JOHN KNAUSE, GADFREY KOUCKER, LEONARD LENGEL, JONATHAN LINDAMOUTH, FREDERICK NEWHARD, PHILIP OHLER, JACOB SCHAEFFER, HENRY SMITH, MICHAEL SNIDER, TIMOTHY SQUIER, JOHN STIVER JR, GEORGE STUMP, JOHN STUMP, JACOB SWANK, CONRAD TREHYSEUR, JOHN VANTERER. Total $289.29. pp 148, 149, 150, 151, 152, 153

Public sale of estate of JOSEPH HAWVER on 15 Nov, 1821; buyers: ADAM BARTMESS, JOHN BECKER, DAVID CEDY, JOSEPH DODSON, PHILIP EDWARDS, JAMES EWING, PETER FETTER, JACOB GLOSSBRENNER, ABRAHAM HOOVER, DAVID HOOVER, JOSEPH MARTIN, JACOB MILLER, THOMAS J. PATTERSON, JAMES PATTON, PETER SILER, ABNER VON, JACOB WEYBRIGHT, FREDERICK WOLF, JACOB ZOOK. Total $108.63. pp 153, 154, 155

Inv and appr of estate of WILLIAM WATKINS on 15 Jan, 1822 by JOHN DICKENSHEETS, EDWARD MITCHEL, JESSE LOW. Total $85.87. pp 155, 156

Inv and appr of estate of JACOB COOK on 14 Jan, 1822. Total $273.12. Debts due estate from DAVID ALSPACH, JOSIAH CLAWSON, JACOB H. CRULL, JOHN DIXSON, CHARLES FOREMAN, WILLIAM GEORGE, ROBERT GIBSON, PETER W. GRAHAM, HENRY KELHNER, GEORGE KUNS, JOHN KUNS, ISAAC MORGAN, TOBIAS RITTER, HENRY ROADS, JOSEPH SPARKS, TIMOTHY SQUIER, HENRY TROXELL, JACOB WINEBRENNER, PHILIP WOLF, ASA WORDER. Total $370.37. pp 156, 157, 158

Term of Febuary, 1822

Case 515. Adm of estate of PHILIP COLE granted to WILLIAM LONG (widow relinquished right). Sec: MICHAEL HILLGAP, JACOB GEPHART. Appr: ISAAC HARRISON, LEVIN HATFIELD, EDWIN SMITH. p 159

Case 516. Adm of estate of DANIEL DAVIS granted to CATHERINE DAVIS. Sec: WARREN MUNGER, JACOB EATON. Appr: DAVID HENDERSON, RALPH WILSON, ROBERT STRAIN.

Case 517. Adm of estate of JOSEPH BROWN granted to DAVID LINDSLY & RACHEL BROWN. Sec: TIMOTHY SQUIER,

COMMON PLEAS (PROBATE) DOCKET BOOK E-1

ELISHA BRABHAM. Appr: DAVID REED, H.G. PHILLIPS, ABRAHAM DARST. pp 159, 160

Case 518. Adm of estate of ANNA MOTE granted to JOSEPH KESLER. Sec: ANDREW HOOVER, HENRY KESLER. Appr: THOMAS NEWMAN, GEORGE SINKS, DAVID HOOVER. p 160

Case 519. Will of OBADIAH RITTER. Witness: JOHN SWISHER, DANIEL RESOR. Exec: CATHERINE RITTENHOUSE, JACOB GLOSSBRENNER. Appr: JOHN SWISHER, ANDREW FOUTZ, AARON THOMSON. p 160

Case 520. Will of JONATHAN WATKINS. Witness: LIVAMES ALLEN, LAWSON ALLEN. Exec: DAVID WATKINS, JEREMIAH ALLEN. Appr: SAMUEL BROADAWAY, JOSEPH SEUELL, JAMES MAJOR. p 160

Case 521. Will of JACOB BROADSTONE. Witness: JOHN WERTZ, JOSEPH MIKESELL. Exec: CHRISTIAN BROADSTONE. Appr: JOHN WERTZ, JOSEPH MIKESELL, HUGH CALHOUN. pp 160, 161

Case 522. Will of HENRY KINSEY. Witness: GEORGE OLINGER, WILLIAM WAGGONER & JACOB OLINGER. No exec named in will. Adm granted to JOHN KINSEY & GEORGE OLINGER. Sec: JACOB WOLF, JACOB CAYLOR. Appr: PHILIP MIKESELL, JACOB OLINGER, CHRISTIAN SWISHER. p 161

Case 523. JACOB KINSEY 17 yrs & JOSEPH KINSEY 15 yrs heirs of JOHN KINSEY, dec, chose JACOB MULLENDORE as guardian. MULLENDORE also appted guardian of LEWIS KINSEY 13 yrs, NOAH KINSEY 11 yrs, POLLY KINSEY 8 yrs DAVID KINSEY 6 yrs, JONAS KINSEY 5 yrs, & SUSANNAH KINSEY 2 yrs, heirs of JOHN KINSEY. Sec: PHILIP GUNCKEL. p 161

Admr of HENRY HART granted 1 yr to settle estate.

THOMAS KING, guardian of ELIZABETH DOVER PARKS, heir of ROBERT PARKS, petitioned for previous guardian JOSEPH PARKS to show accounts, deliver monies & other property due ELIZABETH. p 162

Case 524. Will of JOHN FOUTZ. Witness: ADAM OHLER, HENRY MOYER. Exec: FREDERICK FOUTZ & JACOB FOUTZ. Appr: HENRY MYERS, HENRY ARNOLD, FREDERICK SHAFFER. p 162

Case 525. Adm of estate of ALEXANDER BARKSHIRE granted to LETHA BARKSHIRE & THOMAS D. WHEELING. Sec: JOHN S. RIGG, JAMES STEELE. Appr: EDWARD McDERMOT,

JAMES GRIMES, ALEXANDER STEWART. p 162

Case 526. Will of JACOB ULLERY. Witness: DAVID
MILLER, DANIEL MILLER. Exec: DAVID MILLER, SAMUEL
STUTZ. Appr: JOHN ERSTINE, JOHN STOUDER, HENRY
HATFIELD. p 163

Case 527. HENRIETTA MARIA VAN CLEVE 16 yrs, MARY
CORNELIA VAN CLEVE 14 yrs, & SARAH SOPHIA VAN CLEVE
12 yrs, heirs of BENJAMIN VAN CLEVE, chose WILLIAM
VAN CLEVE as guardian. Sec: JAMES HENDERSON. p 163

Admr of THOMAS HAMER granted until Sept term to
settle estate. p 163

Admr of GEORGE RHOADS produced settlement. "paid
widow's third before her death". Balance $369.60
remains. p 163, 164

Admr of HENRY CLARK JR produced settlement. Widow's
third = $124.79; children's share $249.50. Cash paid
to ANDREW CLARK, HENRY DIEHL, SAMUEL HAGER, ADAM MIL-
LER, JOSEPH C. SILVER, IRA SMITH, EBENEZER STEBBINS,
BENJAMIN VAN CLEVE, JACOB WOLF, total $126.07. pp
164, 165

Admr of estate of JOHN McCABE granted time extension
to settle estate. p 166

Admr of estate of JOHN KINSEY produced settlement.
Widow recvd $1098.18. Cash paid to Dr. B. DUBOIS,
JOHN ETER, JAMES M. GRIMES, JOHN HOLMES, HENRY SHIDE-
LER, ABRAHAM STONER, J. VANSKOYCK. Total $45.57. pp
166, 167

Admr of PETER GEPHART produced settlement. Cash paid
to PHILIP GUNCKEL, H. BACON, GEORGE GEPHART, GEORGE
MOYER, JOHN STUMP, JOHN SNEP, DAVID REED, JOHN COMP-
TON, BENJAMIN DUBOIS. Total $61.20. pp 167, 168

Admr of estate of ABRAHAM TEAGARDEN granted time
extension to settle estate. p 168

5 March, 1822. Admr of JAMES SHAW produced settle-
ment. Widow kept $48 in property. Cash paid to
JAMES BLACK, JOSHUA COLLETT, ALEX EDWARDS, GEORGE
NEWCOM as admr for GEORGE FRIBERGER, JOHN HOLDERMAN,
LEVI JENNINGS, HUGH McFADDEN, JAMES MILLER, JOHN MIL-
LER, JAS.I. NESBIT, JOHN REED, JOHN SHAFFER, A. TIB-
BALS. pp 168, 169

Admr of PETER LEHMAN produced settlement. Widow kept

$12 in property. Cash paid to JOHN MILLER, JAMES SHELL & to GEORGE NEWCOM, admr, for trips to Miami County, total $843.13. p 170

Case 528. HENRIETTA E. PEIRCE, widow, was apptd guardian of MARY PEIRCE 10 yrs, DAVID ZEIGLER PEIRCE 8 yrs, JEREMIAH HUNT PEIRCE 3 yrs & JOSEPH PEIRCE, 1 yr, heirs of JOSEPH PEIRCE, dec. Sec: JOSEPH H. CRANE, JAMES STEELE, HENRY BACON. p 171

Case 529. HENRY BROWN appted guardian of CHLOE LATOINO, 11 yrs, heir of FRANCIS LATERNO, dec. $36 held by former guardian, now dec, JOHN REGANS. Sec: HENRY STODDARD. p 171

Admr of ALEXANDER HUSTON produced settlement. Cash paid to JACOB ABBOTT, SAMUEL ARCHER, JOHN BRADFORD, CHRISTIAN CREAGER, THOMAS CREAGER, JOHN DODSON, ROBERT EDGAR, EDWARD HUSTON, JOHN KING, JAS. I. NESBIT, AARON NUTT, WILLIAM PATTERSON, HENRY REGH, ADDISON SMITH, CHARLES SMITH, JOHN STOKER, GEORGE ZIMMERMAN, total $89.73. Balance of $144.69. pp 171, 172

Public sale of estate of HENRY CLARK JR on 19 June, 1819. Buyers: AMOS CLARK, ANDREW CLARK, HANNAH CLARK, JESSE CLARK, SAMUEL HAGER, JOHN HIZER, ALBERT R. HUEY, DAVID MILLER, THOMAS QUINN, GEORGE RENNIX, JOSEPH C. SILVER, IRA SMITH. Total $110.86. p 173

Admr of THOMAS HAMER produced settlement. Cash paid to Dr BLODGETT, SAMUEL BRINGHAM, GEORGE CIMERMAN, JOHN COMPTON, JAMES DAVIS, WILLIAM EAKER, C.R. GREENE, GEORGE GROVE, DAYTON HAMER, WILLIAM HAMER, WILLIAM HOFFMAN, JOHN HOUZER, JOHN KERR, JAMES LOWRY, H. MARQUART, E. PURDY, ELIZ. SPRAGUE. pp 173, 174,175

no page #176, #177

Filed 9 March, 1822. Inv and appr of estate of DANIEL DAVIS on 9 March, 1822. Total $21.12. p 178

Public sale of estate of GEORGE HORNER on 27 Nov, 1821; buyers: CHRISTIAN BROADSTONE, DAVID DATCH, JOHN FLOID, THOMAS FLOID, TOBIAS HOWARD, CATHERINE HOERNER HENRY HORNER, JOHN HORNER, MICHAEL HOERNER, PHILIP LONG, DANIEL MUNDHENK, LEWIS MUNDHENK, ISAAC NORMAN, JOHN PIPINGER, JOSEPH REICHARD, JOHN RICHARD, SAMUEL RICHARD, THOMAS ROCK, CHRISTOPHER SEILER, PETER SHAFFER, ADAM STAEBER, JOHN SWANK. Total $71.88. pp 179, 180, 181

Filed 20 April, 1822. Public sale of estate of

DANIEL DAVIS. Buyers: SAMUEL BOOGER, ELISHA BRABHAM, LEWIS BROADWELL, O.B. CONOVER, JOSEPH H. CONOVER, LEWIS DAVIS, WILLIAM DAVIS, JOSEPH DODSON, C.R. GREENE, THOMAS MORRISON, E. STIBBENS, JACOB VANNIMAN, JOSEPH VANNIMAN, total $17.56. p 182

Debts owed to estate of WILLIAM HART from: JACOB BANESLER, DANIEL BECKER, JOHN BECKER, PHILIP CRAFT, HENRY HART dec, HENRY KESSLER, DAVID LUDY, CHRISTIAN MOYER, JACOB ZOOK, total $1347.84. p 183

Special session 2 April, 1822

Case 530. Will of CATHERINE SUMAN. Witness: JOHN H. BRANDENBURG, WILLIAM SUMAN. Exec: JACOB SUMAN. Appr: DAVID WORMAN, JACOB SHROYER, DAVID LEHMAN. p 183, 184

Inv and appr of estate of JOHN FOUTS on 11 March, 1822. Total $157.25. pp 184, 185

Filed 19 May, 1822. Inv and appr of estate of ALEX BARKSHIRE. Total $119.56. Widow's allowance = $25. List of property at house of WILLIAM BARKSHIRE when appraised at a total of $25.50; refused to surrender items to apprs. Debt of $20 due to CHARLES STEPHENS. Public sale on 27 March, 1822; buyers: LETHY BARK-SHIRE, GEORGE BEARDSHIRE, JAMES DAUGHERTY, WILLIAM MURPHY, JAMES PETTICREW, EDMUND PURDY, JOHN READ, JOHN S. RIGGS, THOMAS D. WHELAN. Total $58.30. pp 185, 186, 187, 188

Filed 28 May, 1822. Inv and appr of estate of JOSEPH BROWN of Dayton Twp. Total $200.50. Public sale on 30 March, 1822; buyers: AARON BARKSHIRE, ELISHA BRAB-HAM, LEWIS BROADWELL, NELSON BROWN, JOHN BUCHER, JOHN BURKES, LEWIS COSTLER, ISAAC DAVIS, JOHN GARDNER, ALEX GRIMES, JOHN HARSHMAN, PETER LEHMAN, MICHAEL MARLEY, JOSHUA McINTOSH, WILLIAM McKEIG, J. PATT-ERSON, THOMAS J. PATTERSON, DAVID PARROTT, THOMAS J. PETTICREW, JAMES RIDDLE, SAMUEL RITTER, JACOB SIMMER-MAN, ROBERT J. SKINNER, GEORGE SNIDER, THOMAS SNOD-GRASS, JOHN TAYLOR, JOHN VAN CLEVE. Total $163.27. pp 189, 190, 191, 192, 193

Inv and appr of estate of JONATHAN WATKINS on 22 March, 1822. Total $474.71. pp 194, 195

Inv and appr of estate of OBADIAH RITTENHOUSE of Ran-dolph Twp on 28 Feb, 1822, made by AARON THOMSON, JOHN SWISHER, ANDREW FOUTS. (SEE CASE 519) Total of $76.06. Debts due from JOHN COFFEY, ROBERT L. HEGAN,

PETER RITTENHOUSE, JAMES WATTS total $273.25. Public sale on 14 March, 1822; buyers: DAVID ANGLE, JOHN COFFIN, JAMES CRAWSON, JESSE FARMER, PETER FETTER, ANDREW FOUTZ, JACOB GLOSSBRENNER, ANDREW HOOVER, DAVID HOOVER, MARTIN HOWE, THOMAS NEWMAN, JOHN PECK, NATHANIEL PORTER, CATHERINE RITTENHOUSE, JOHN RITTENHOUSE, JOHN SMITH, JACOB STANGER, DAVID STUTSMAN, JOHN SWISHER, AARON THOMSON, GARRET THOMSON, MOSES THOMSON, JACOB WERNER, JACOB WEYBRIGHT, FREDERICK WOLF. Total $75.02. pp 197, 198, 199

Inv and appr of estate of HENRY KINSEY on 13 March, 1822. Total $433.01. Public sale on 15 March, 1822; buyers: JACOB CAYLOR, JAMES CUNNINGHAM, THOMAS DYRER, DANIEL HARDMAN, DAVID HARDMAN, JOHN HARRIS, JOHN HART, PETER HECKMAN, CHRISTIAN HEISTAND, JOHN HISER, JACOB HOLDERMAN, CHRISTIAN HOLLAR, AARON KAYLOR, ABRAHAM KAYLOR, ABRAHAM KINSEY, JOHN KINSEY, JOHN MAXELL, JAMES MILLER, BENJAMIN NICHOLAS, DAVID OBLINGER, GEORGE OBLINGER, JACOB OBLINGER, JOHN REDICK, DANIEL REISER, JOHN REISER, DANIEL REPP, JOHN ROBINS, ROBERT SCATTER, WILLIAM SHANEFELT, PETER STOCK, JOHN TURNER, JACOB WAGAMAN, WILLIAM WAGGAMAN, JOHN WEISER, JACOB WILLIAMS, JACOB WINEBRENNER, JACOB WOLF, SUSANNAH WOLF, JOHN YOCHEA. Total $286.36. pp 200, 201, 202, 203, 204, 205, 206, 207, 208

Case 531. Will of JOHN NYWANGER. Witness: JOSEPH BARTMESS, JOHN WERTZ. Exec: DAVID KRIDER. Appr: JOHN WERTZ, MICHAEL BAKER, JACOB MICHAEL. p 209

Case 558. ELIZABETH SHAFFER, 18 yrs, heir of JACOB SHAFFER, dec, chose HENRY SHAFFER as guardian. Sec: PETER SHAFFER, PHILIP GUNCKEL. p 209

Case 532. JEREMIAH M. JACOBS, 15 yrs, heir of MARK JACOBS, dec, chose ANDREW D. BRIER as guardian. Sec: JOHN FOLKERTH. p 209

Case 533. Adm of estate of JOHN RIGGS granted to MARY RIGGS. Sec: GEORGE NEWCOM, JOHN FOLKERTH. Appr: WILLIAM EAKER, GEORGE W. SMITH, ABRAHAM DARST. p 210

Inv and appr of estate of ANNA MOTE of Butler Twp on 9 March, 1822. Total $159.06. Public sale on 11 March, 1822; buyers: DAVID ANGEL, JOHN BONNER, ABRAHAM BRADY, RALPH CAMPBELL, JOHN COFFEE, JOHN COX, JOSHUA COX, JAMES CROSSEN, JOHN DICKSON, JACOB GLOSSBRENNER, FREDERIC HOLLINGER, ANDREW HOOVER, DAVID HOOVER, JACOB HOOVER, MARY HOOVER, NOAH HOOVER, MATHIAS HUNTSINGER, WILLIAM JONES, HENRY KESLER, JOSEPH KESLER, JOSEPH KESLER JR, JONATHAN MOTE,

THOMAS NEWMAN, WILLIAM NEWMAN, NATHANIEL PORTER, EVE
RUP, DAVID SHEETS, JOHN SHEETS, MARTIN SHEETS, JOHN
SWITZER, JACOB TUCKER, DAVID WAYMIRE, FREDERICK WOLF.
Total $176.70. pp 210, 211, 212, 213, 214, 215

Admr of CONRAD LECHLIDER granted time extension to
settle estate. p 215

Inv and appr of estate of CATHERINE SUMAN on 5 April,
1822. Total $180.87. Memo of property kept by SARAH
SUMAN. Public sale on 12 April, 1822; buyers: JACOB
ABOLD, JOHN BONNER, GEORGE BRADFORD, SAMUEL BRADFORD,
JOHN BRANDENBURG, DAVID BURNS, BENJAMIN BUSH, JAMES
J. CLIMER, CORNELIUS CREAGER, LUKE DARNEY, JOHN DEEN,
CASPER DEVILBIS, JOHN ENSEY, LUKE FISK, SAMUEL HOLMES
DANIEL JORDAN, DAVID JORDAN, ISAAC KEMP, JACOB KEMP,
JOSEPH KEMP, DAVID LEHMAN, SOLOMON LEHMAN, NATHANIEL
LEWIS, DANIEL LICHLIDER, WILLIAM MANNING, MICHAEL
MARLEY, HENRY McGRAW, JOSEPH MERRICK, VANDERVEER MOR-
GAN, JOSEPH PARKS, JAMES RIDDLE, ADAM RIKE, GEORGE P.
SAVAGE, LAWRENCE SHELL, JOHN SHELLABARGER, DAVID
SHOUP, JOHN SIFERT, JOSEPH SPARKS, WILLIAM STEVENS,
JOHN STONEBERGER, WILLIAM STONEBERGER, PETER SUMAN,
SAMUEL SUMAN, HENRY SWEADNOR, SAMUEL TALES, JOHN WIL-
SON, WILLIAM WILSON. pp 215, 216, 217, 218, 219, 220

ROBERT STRAIN, father of ROBERT STRAIN JR, dec,
refused adm of son's estate. Adm granted to DAVID
REID. Sec: ABRAHAM DARST, GEORGE W. SMITH. Appr:
JOHN COMPTON, ALEXANDER GRIMES, WILLIAM CLARK. p 221

11 June, 1822. Admr of GEORGE RENNIX produced settlement. Widow's third = $88.12. Cash paid to JOHN
FOLKERTH, A. DARST, B. WILLIAMS, LUTHER BRUEN, WILLI-
AM M. SMITH, Dr WILLIAM BLODGET, JESSE CLARK, total
$43.65. Balance of $132.59 remains. pp 221, 222

Adm of estate of CHRISTOPHER CURTNER granted to HENRY
CURTNER. Sec: WILLIAM SOURBRAY, WILLIAM CLARK. Appr:
SAMUEL WATTON, WILLIAM EAKER, ABRAHAM DARST. p 222

HENRY ARNOLD, admr of estate of JOHN YATES, produced
settlement. Cash paid to HENRY ZELLER, HENRY MOYERS,
CHRISTIAN JUDY, PHILIP GUNCKEL, PETER IZOR, total
$36.63. pp 222, 223

Admr of MATTHIAS SWARTZEL produced settlement. Widow
kept $36.37 in property. Cash of $1 paid to JAMES M.
GRIMES. Balance of $86.63 remains. pp 223, 224

Filed 13 Aug, 1822. Inv and appr of estate of JOHN
NYSWANGER of Randolph Twp on 4 June, 1822. Total

$76.37, sworn before JOHN RORER, JP. Debts due from
JACOB GRIPE, HENRY HUNTSINGER, JOSEPH KESLER, FREDE-
RICK STEVENS, DANIEL WARNER total $71.94. Public sale
on 3 Aug, 1822; buyers: JOHN BOWER JR, DANIEL BURKET
WILLIAM BYERS, MARY CRAWSTON, AMOS EDWARDS, JAMES
EDWARDS, BARBARA HEFFELMAN, DAVID KRIDER, GEORGE NYS-
WANGER, JOHN NYSWANGER, SAMUEL NYSWANGER, DANIEL OCKS
CORNELIUS PIPPINGER, JOHN PIPPINGER, DANIEL RORER,
FREDERICK SMITH, LEWIS STEWART, PHILIP STOVER, JOHN
SWANK, CHARLES WELBAUM, JOHN WERTZ. Total $62.49.
pp 224, 225, 226

Filed 16 Sept, 1822. Inv and appr of estate of
ROBERT STRAIN JR on 13 June, 1822. Total $12.50.
Public sale on 4 July, 1822; buyers: DAVID REID,
JOHN PROTZMAN. Total $8.62. p 227

Term of September, 1822

Case 535. Adm of estate of CHRISTOPHER MASON (widow
relinquished right) granted to AMOS OBLINGER, SOLOMON
MASON. Sec: CHRISTIAN OBLINGER, JACOB HOLLER. Appr:
SAMUEL HEISTON, JOHN DEEL, ABRAHAM HORNER. p 228

Case 536. Adm of estate of DANIEL MILLER granted to
DAVID MILLER, JOHN MILLER (widow relinquished right).
Sec: STEPHEN MILLER, JOHN BECKER. Appr: JOSEPH
HARTER, JOHN BROWER, HENRY OLDFATHER. p 228

Case 537. ELI SUMAN, 16 yrs, minor heir of ISAAC
SUMAN, chose JACOB SUMAN as guardian. Sec: JAMES
RIDDLE. p 228

Case 538. Adm of estate of PETER SHERMAN granted to
HENRY HILT. Sec: JOHN NEIBLE, GEORGE SHAFFER. Appr:
JACOB HETZEL, FREDERICK WALTZ, DAVID LAMME. p 228

Case 539. Adm of estate of JOHN COX granted to WILL-
IAM COX. Sec: JACOB WEISENER, THOMAS THORNTON. Appr:
STEPHEN KENNEDY, JOHN BARNET, JOHN HOLLINGSWORTH. p
228

Case 540. Will of ISAAC GRIFFITH SR. Witness: JAMES
MILLER, JAMES ARCHER, JOSEPH ARCHER. Exec: (widow
relinquished right). Adm granted to ISAAC GRIFFITH
JR. Sec: JAMES MILLER, SAMUEL ARCHER. Appr: JAMES
ARCHER, JOSEPH JOHNSON, SAMUEL LONGSTREATH. p 229

Case 541. Will of FREDERICK ULMER. Witness: JAMES
RUNYON, HENRY MARSHALL. No exec appted by will. Adm
granted to DANIEL MUNDHENK. Sec: JAMES RUNYON,
HENRY MARSHALL. Appr: JOSEPH MIKESELL, SAMUEL GRIPE

COMMON PLEAS (PROBATE) DOCKET BOOK E-1

& JOEL FOUTZ. p 229

Case 542. SALLY EAGLE, 15 yrs, heir of PETER EAGLE, dec, chose DANIEL GEPHART as guardian. Sec: JACOB EAGLE. p 229

Case 543. EDWARD COLEMAN, 16 yrs, chose GEORGE C. DAVIS as guardian. p 229

Case 544. Will of CONRAD KNIFE. Witness: DANIEL MUNDHENK, JOEL FOUTZ. No exec appted by will; widow relinquished right. Adm granted to JOSEPH MIKESELL. Sec: DANIEL MUNDHENK, ABRAHAM DARST. Appr: JOEL FOUTZ, DANIEL WAGGONER, HENRY HAUSER. p 230

Case 545. Will of JOHN RUBY. Witness: PHILIP WOLF, PHILIP FOUTZ. Exec: CHRISTIAN MISENER, surviving exec, SAMUEL KINNAMON being dec. Appr: HENRY APPLE, PHILIP SCHLIFER, LUDWICK FOUST. REBECCA RUBY, widow of said JACOB, elected to take provisions under the will in lieu of dower. p 230

Case 546. WILLIAM COX appted guardian of JACOB COX, 2 yrs, minor heir of JOHN COX, dec. Sec: THOMAS THORNTON, JACOB WISENER. p 230

Widow of CONRAD KNIFE elected to take will provisions in lieu of dower. p 231

Case 547. Will of JOSEPH CRIPE. Witness: DAVID UL-RICH, HENRY HIPPLE. Exec: MAGDALENA GRIPE, SAMUEL ULRICH. Appr: DAVID SHIVELY, ISAAC ULRICH, SAMUEL WISE. Widow elected provisions of the will in lieuof dower. p 231

Admr of WILLIAM HART granted time extension to settle estate. p 231

Admr of JOHN BRADFORD granted time extension to settle estate. p 231

GEORGE SCHOERER, 17 yrs, chose ABRAHAM DARST as guardian. Sec: DANIEL WOLF. p 231

Admr of JOHN DUNKIN granted time extension to settle estate. p 231

Admr of HENRY ROGER produced settlement. Cash paid to HENRY ARNOLD, Dr BLODGET, ENIX CRUNCHMAN, HENRY HIPPLE, JOSEPH MIKESELL, HENRY NURSE, Dr. POWEL, GEORGE SHANK, NATHAN STUTSMAN, total $54.76. pp 231, 232

Term of September, 1822 continued

Exec of JOHN WAGGONER produced settlement. p 232

ADAM STIVER, adm of estate of JOHN STIVER, produced settlement. Cash paid to PHILIP BOTTS, DAVID CATHCROFT, CHRISTIAN COOK, ANDREW CRAMER, LEWIS DAVIS, BENJAMIN DUBOIS, PETER HECK, JOHN HOLMES, JOSHUA D. ISER, PHILIP ISER, ROBERT LAZURE, GEORGE LOY, DAVID MEIN, STEPHEN MILLER, JOHN REINIGER, FREDERICK RIDGELY, CATHERINE SCHNAP, JACOB SHAFFER, HARRY SHIDELER (coffin), THOMAS SNIDER, FREDERICK STAVER, HENRY STAVER, JACOB STAVER, JOHN STIVER JR, ABRAHAM SWARTZEL, HENRY SWARTZEL, J. VAN SCHOYCK, ADAM SWINEHART, JACOB SWINEHART, ANTHONY YOST total $841.66. pp 233, 234

Exec of DANIEL HOOVER JR presented settlement. Cash paid to GEORGE LINKS, DAVID HOOVER (auctioneer) & ADDISON SMITH. pp 234, 235

OBADIAH F. CONOVER, adm of GARRET CONOVER, produced settlement. Cash paid to POMPEY ALLEN, AARON BAKER, JOS BROWN, ELIJAH CONVERSE, G.C. DAVIS, ABRAHAM DARST WILLIAM EAKER, ROBERT GIBSON, JOHN M. GROVE, JONATHAN HARSHMAN, DAVID HAWTHORN, A.B. LAWTON, DAVID LINDSLEY ROBERT McCLEARY, JOHN MILLER, WILLIAM MILLER, JOHN PATTERSON, R.J. SKINNER, HENRY & JAMES SLAUGHT, G.W. SMITH, IRA SMITH, GEORGE SNIDER, ALEX WHITE, DANIEL WOLF, JACOB WORMAN, total $289.85. pp 235, 236

Exec.of ISAAC MILLER produced settlement. Cash paid to widow & to BENJAMIN HARDMAN, total $10.04. p 237

Exec of JOHN McCABE produced settlement. Cash paid to DAVID DUNCAN, ROBERT McREYNOLDS, JOHN TULLIS, HENRY ROBINSON, SAMUEL SCOTT, H.G. PHILLIPS (funeral expenses), JAMES WELCH, total $55.00. p 237

Admr of THOMAS HORNER granted time extension to settle estate. p 237

Case 548. HENRY ZEARING, 15 yrs, heir of HENRY ZEARING, dec, chose JACOB GEPHART as guardian. GEPHART also appted guardian of SAMUEL ZEARING, 12 yrs, heir of HENRY ZEARING. Sec: WILLIAM LONG. p 238

Case 549. FANNY ZEARING appted guardian to heirs of HENRY ZEARING: CATHERINE 9 yrs, MARIA 8 yrs, ELIZABETH 7 yrs, DAVID 5 yrs, SUSANNAH 3 yrs, & HANNAH 9 mo. Sec: EMANUEL GEPHART. p 238

Case 550. SARAH MORGAN 15 yrs, heir of CHARLES MORGAN, dec, chose DAVID HUSTON as guardian. Sec: LUTHER BRUEN. p 238

FANNY ZEARING, widow of HENRY ZEARING, chose will provisions in lieu of dower. p 238

Filed 1 October, 1822. Exec of CHARLES MORGAN produced settlement. Cash paid to LUTHER BRUEN, JAMES BUCHANON, JACOB DARST, WILLIAM EAKER, ABRAHAM ENSEY, JOHN FOLKERTH, JOB HARRIS, DAVID HUSTON, DAVID JOHN, ABRAHAM MORGAN, GEORGE PATTERSON, WILLIAM PATTERSON, HENRY RIKE, SOLOMON SHOUP, RICHARD STEVENS, WILLIAM WATTON total $225.73. pp 238, 239

Admr of TALLMAN HALL granted time extension to settle estate. p 239

Admr of GEORGE BRETZINS granted time extension to settle estate. p 239 (SEE CASE 492)

Filed 19 June, 1822. Inv and appr of estate of JACOB ULERY of Madison Twp on 8 April, 1822. Total $369.68, sworn before MOSES GREER, JP. pp 240, 241

Case 560. Adm of estate of SAMUEL BEERS granted to DAVID LINDSLEY (widow relinquished estate). Sec: JOHN COMPTON, HENRY BACON. Appr: LUTHER BRUEN, DAVID REID, JOHN FOLKERTH. p 242

Special session 2 November, 1822

Case 551. Will of HENRY YOUNT. Witness: BENJAMIN HUTCHINS, STEPHEN MACEY. Exec: DANIEL YOUNT, ANDREW YOUNT. Appr: ISAAC COOPER, BENJAMIN HUTCHINS JR, JOHN CURTIS. p 242

Case 553. Adm of estate of RICHARD BACON granted to HENRY BACON. Sec: GEORGE GROVE, WILLIAM EAKER. Appr: WILLIAM BOMBERGER, JOSEPH HOLLINGSWORTH, DAVID REID. p 243

Case 554. Adm of estate of GEORGE HUFFMAN granted to GEORGE OLINGER (widow relinquished right). Sec: JOHN KINSEY, ABRAHAM KINSEY. Appr: JACOB OLINGER, DAVID HARDMAN, CHRISTIAN SHIVELY JR. p 243

Filed 13 November, 1822. Inv and appr of estate of JOSEPH GRIPE on 30 Sept, 1822. Total $896.75. Sworn before HENRY HIPPLE, JP. pp 243, 244, 245, 246

Inv and appr of estate of FREDERICK ULMER of Perry

COMMON PLEAS (PROBATE) DOCKET BOOK E-1

Twp on 9 Nov, 1822. Total $57.99. p 246

Case 555. Adm of estate of JACOB ZEARING granted to
DAVID ZEARING (widow relinquished right). Sec: JOHN
KRIDER, ABRAHAM DARST. Appr: JACOB PROSS, JOHN PROSS
& MICHAEL STUMP. p 247

Filed 26 November, 1822. Inv and appr of estate of
RICHARD BACON. Total $100.06. Public sale, buyers:
JOHN BACON, SAMUEL BACON, JOS. HOLLINGSWORTH, total
$82.68. pp 247, 248

Inv and appr of estate of JOHN COX of Randolph Twp on
19 Oct, 1822 ("except $26.00 taken for suppport of 1
year old son...) total $79.19. Debts due estate from
SAMUEL JACKSON, JACOB STUDEBAKER, MARTIN HOW. Public
sale on 7 Nov, 1823; buyers: NELSON BROWN, DAVID COX,
JOHN COX, JOSEPH COX, WILLIAM COX, WILLIAM DODSON,
SAMUEL ENSELY, JOHN FARMER, JAMES GADDIS, JOHN HOL-
LINSWORTH, MARTIN HOW, JACOB MILLER, HENRY PITSENBER-
GER, JACOB PITSENBERGER, JOHN STOUDER, STEPHEN STUTS-
MAN, JACOB THOMAS, NEHEMIAH THOMAS, WILLIAM THOMAS,
ELI THORNTON, JACOB WISENER, FREDERICK WOLF, total
$89.10. pp 249, 250, 251

Case 556. Will of JOHN CAYLOR. Witness: ISAAC
SHIVELY, MICHAEL RITTER. Exec: Widow SALOMA CAYLOR,
JOHN CAYLOR. Appr: JOHN HISER, LEONARD HIER, ISAAC
SHIVELY. p 252

Special session 7 December, 1822

Case 557. Adm of estate of FREDERICK WAYMIRE granted
to ISAAC HUTCHINS & JOHN CURTIS (widow relinquished
right). Sec: BENJAMIN HUTCHINS, ANDREW YOUNT. Appr:
ISAAC COOPER, WILLIAM FARMER, STEPHEN KENNEDY. p 252

Case 558 recorded on page 209, this book. p 252

Case 559 recorded on page 221, this book. p 252

Case 560 recorded on page 242, this book. p 252

Case 561 recorded on page 133, book A. p 252

Case 562 recorded on page 157, book C. p 252

Inv and appr of estate of JOHN MORGAN of Dayton Twp
on 8 Oct, 1822. Total $541.87. pp 253, 254, 255

Filed 20 December, 1822. Inv and appr of estate of
JOHN S. RIGGS on 25 July, 1822. Total $428.12. List

of property kept by widow = $156.50. Public sale on 6 Aug, 1822; buyers: SAMUEL ARCHER, WILLIAM BARK-SHIRE, JOHN BEARD, GEORGE BEARDSHEARER, JOSEPH BOSSON SAMUEL BRIER, THOMAS DANIELS, JAMES DAUGHERTY, GEORGE C. DAVIS, JAMES FRENCH, WILLIAM GEORGE, JAMES HENDER-SON, JOHN HOOVER, ALBERT R. HUEY, ISAAC HUNTSINGER, ALLEN JONES, JOSEPH KENNEDY, WILLIAM KENNEDY, JOHN KERR, WILLIAM MASON JR, JAMES McDERMOT, JOSEPHUS MEEKER, JAMES L. MILLER, JOHN MORE, SAMUEL MORGAN, ADAM NEFF, LEWIS NEFF, ANDREW PARSONS, ABRAHAM POWERS HENRY PROTZMAN, EDMUND PURDY, ABRAHAM REED, JOHN REED MARY RIGGS, HENRY ROBINSON, PETER SCHLOSSER, LUDWICK SHAW, JACOB STRADER, JACOB SWIGART, DANIEL WAGGONER, JOHN WAGGONER, JOHN WOLF, total $257.56. pp 255, 256 257, 258

Inv and appr of estate of CONRAD KNIFE of Perry Twp on 4 Nov, 1822. Total $273.75. Public sale, buyers: ABRAHAM BARRICK, WENTLE BUTT, HUGH COLHOUN, JOEL FOUTZ, MICHAEL HAGAR, JACOB HARSHBARGER, DAVID HOOVER, JOHN KING, JACOB KNIFE, JOSEPH MIKESELL, JOSHUA MILLS, PETER SUMAN, DANIEL WAGGONER, DAVID WAGNER, HENRY WELBAUM, total $44.59. pp 259, 260, 261

Filed 3 Jan, 1823. Inv and appr of estate of SAMUEL BIERS of Dayton on 4 Oct, 1822 by apprs LUTHER BRUEN, DAVID REID, JOHN FOLKERTH, signed admr DAVID LINDSLEY total $83.75. Debts due estate from THOMAS RUE, DAV-ID LEHMAN. Public sale of estate of SAMUEL BEERS on 4 Nov, 1822; buyers: STEPHEN ALLEN, HANNAH BIERS, EPHRAIM BROADWELL, G.D. DAVIS, JOHN LEHMAN, JOHN LINDLEY, THOMAS MORRISON, E. STIBBENS, DANIEL STUTS-MAN, total $66.73. pp 261, 262

Filed 7 Jan, 1823. Public sale of estate of JOHN MORGAN on 29 Oct, 1822; buyers: PHILIP BARRET, DAN-IEL BORAF, SAMUEL BRADFORD, GEORGE CALDERWOOD, JACOB COY, ISAAC DARST, JOHN DODDS, DENNIS ENSEY, JONATHAN HAGLIN, DAVID HUSTON, ASA JOHN, DAVID JOHN, JAMES JOHN, LEMUEL JOHN, WILLIAM JOHN, JOSEPH KELLER, LEWIS KIFER, DANIEL KILER, JACOB LEHMAN, ALEXANDER LOGAN, WILLIAM MASON, JOHN McCABE, WILLIAM McCANLESS, VAN-DERVEER MOLER, ABNER MORGAN, ABRAHAM MORGAN, BARBARA MORGAN, MURREL MORGAN, SARAH MORGAN, SARAH MORGAN JR, VINSART MORGAN, GEORGE PATTERSON, JOHN PRUGH, JOHN RIKE, JONAH B. SMITH, IRA SMITH, RICHARD STEPHENS, MICHAEL SWIGART, PETER SWIGART, DEBORAH TUCKER, JOHN WEBB, JOHN WEBLE, JAMES WILKERMAN, SAMUEL WISER, total $612.68. List of property kept by widow = $70.80. pp 262, 263, 264, 265, 266

Filed 11 January, 1823. Inv and appr of estate of
CHRISTOPHER MASON of Jackson Twp on 15 Oct, 1822.
Total $402.37. Public sale on 1 Nov, 1822; buyers:
GEORGE HALLER, JACOB HALLER, JOHN HARSHBARGER, DAVID
HECK, SAMUEL HEETER, SAMUEL HEISTAND, JOSHUA HOOVER,
RICHARD KINNAMON, JACOB KUNS, JOHN KUNS, JACOB KLING-
ER, DAVID MASON, JOSHUA MASON, MICHAEL MASON, SOLOMON
MASON, MARTIN MIKESELL, JOHN NAVE, AMOS OBLINGER,
WILLIAM THOMAS, JACOB VANNIMAN, JACOB WAGONECK, total
$251.01. pp 267, 268, 269, 270

Filed 12 Febuary, 1823. Inv and appr of estate of
DANIEL MILLER of Jackson Twp. Total $247.04, sworn
before HENRY SHIEDLER, JP. Public sale on 30 Sept,
1823; buyers: JOHN BUCHER, JOHN BURGHER, ABRAHAM
MILLER, DAVID MILLER, ELIZABETH MILLER, JACOB MILLER,
JOHN MILLER, JONAH MILLER, SAMUEL MILLER, STEPHEN
MILLER, total $373.91. Debts due from JOHN BURGHER,
WILLIAM FARMER, Widow HENDERSON, MICHAEL HUBLER,
ABRAHAM MILLER, JACOB MILLER, JOHN MILLER, ISAAC
MILLER, JACOB OVERHOLSER, total $1162.32. pp 271,
272, 274, 275, 276 -- no page #273

Inv and appr of estate of JACOB ZEARING of German Twp
on 20 Nov, 1822. Total $384.15, sworn before JOHN
HOUTZ, JP. Debts due from DANIEL CLARK, JOHN CRIDER,
FREDERICK NEWHARD, CHRISTIAN ZEARING, total $40.37.
Public sale on 6 Dec, 1822; buyers: GEORGE AURT,
SAMUEL BARKLETT, JAMES CALLAWAY, WILLIAM CHAMBERS,
ASHER DAVIS, JOHN DENISE, HENRY DUCKWALL, PHILIP
EISENHOWER, JOHN ETTER, JONAS FOUTS, JOHN GANGER,
JOHN HARTER, JOHN HECK, JOHN KANDNER, JOHN KNAUS,
HENRY KLINE, SAMUEL LEFLER, JACOB MILLER, FREDERICK
NEWHARD, JOHN ODELL, GODLEAB OHLER, DANIEL OSWALT,
JACOB PROSS, JOHN PROSS, JOHN REAM, FREDERICK SHAF-
FER, ABDENEGO STEVENS, CHRISTIAN WARVEL, GEORGE WIS-
TER, HENRY WISTER, JACOB WISTER, SAMUEL RIGHT, FREDE-
RICK WOLF, CHRISTIAN ZEARING, DAVID ZEARING, Widow
ELIZABETH ZEARING, HENRY ZELLER total $445.25. pp
277, 278, 279, 280, 281

Filed 24 Feb, 1823. Inv and appr of estate of PETER
SHERMAN of Washington Twp on 15 Oct, 1822. Total of
$143.87, sworn before DAVID LAMME, JP. Debts due
from DANIEL CRAMER, JACOB HETZEL JR, JACOB HETZEL SR,
HENRY HILT, JOSEPH HOCH, THOMAS HOWARD, WILLIAM HUST-
ON, DANIEL ISELY, ROBERT J. LAMME, JOHN NEIBLE,
GEORGE PARSONS, JOHN TAYLOR, PETER TOWNSLY, CALEB
WILCOX total $279.54. Public sale on 15 Sept, 1822;
buyers: ANTHONY CHEVALIER, JACOB HETZEL, PETER HET-
ZEL, HENRY HILT, JOSEPH HOUGH, JACOB IFERT, GEORGE
NUTTS, JACOB SHAFFER, JOSEPH SHAFFER, DANIEL WHISLER,

total $173.39.   Signed by admr HENRY HILT.   pp 282, 283, 284

Inv and appr of estate of JOHN CAYLOR on 29 Nov, 1822. Included notes due from DAVID BEINARD, DAVID CAYLOR, JOHN CAYLOR JR, JOSEPH CAYLOR, PETER CAYLOR, DAVID OVERHOLSER. Public sale on 13 Dec, 1822; buyers: ADAM BOLANDER, JOHN BYERLY JR, ABRAHAM CAYLOR, DANIEL CAYLOR, DAVID CAYLOR, JACOB CAYLOR, PETER CAYLOR, SAMUEL CAYLOR, SOLOMON CAYLOR, JACOB CAUFFMAN JESSE CLARK, DEWOLT CROWEL, JOHN FISHER, ROBERT GIBSON, JACOB HALDERMAN, JOHN HANNA, DANIEL HARDMAN, JOHN HARMEST, PETER HECK, HENRY HEATER, JOHN HISER, DANIEL ISELY, JOHN JOKEY, JOHN KAYSER, JOHN KELLY, JOHN KINSEY, DAVID LASSLEY, JACOB LICHTY, JOHN LOY, JACOB MIKESELL, ABRAHAM MILLER, JOSEPH MILLER, JONATHAN MYER, JOHN NICELY, BENJAMIN NICHOLAS, ELI NOFFSINGER, JOEL PRESSEL, DANIEL REP, ISAAC SHIVELY, JACOB SHIVELY, GEORGE SNELL, PETER STOCK, HENRY TROXELL, WILLIAM TYLER, ABSOLEM WESTFALL, DANIEL WETS CHRISTIAN WINEBRENNER, PETER WOLF, total $472.76. pp 284, 285, 286, 287, 288, 289, 290, 291

Term of Febuary, 1823

Case 563. HANNAH GRIPE, 16 yrs, heir of JOHN GRIPE, dec, chose STEPHEN ULLERY as guardian. Sec: HENRY METZKER. ULLERY appted guardian of STEPHEN GRIPE, 9 yrs, heir of JOHN GRIPE, dec. p 292
&
Case 564.   HENRY METZKER appted guardian of DAVID GRIPE 7 yrs, & ELIZABETH GRIPE 11 yrs, heirs of JOHN GRIPE, dec. Sec: STEPHEN ULLERY. p 292

Case 565. Adm of estate of VALENTINE HUFFMAN granted to ELIZABETH HUFFMAN. Sec: DANIEL HOLINGER, WILLIAM M. SMITH. Appr: WILLIAM BARKSHIRE, ALEXANDER STEWART, EDWARD McDERMET. p 292

Admr of GEORGE YOUNT granted time extension to settle estate. p 292

Case 566. Adm of estate of JAMES VAN KIRK granted to SIDNEY DENISE (widow relinquished right). Sec: O.B. CONOVER, H.G. PHILLIPS. Appr: JOHN H. SCHENCK, TUNIS VANDERVEER, JOSEPH VANDERVEER. pp 292, 293

Admr of JOHN DENISE allowed 1 yr to settle estate. p 293

Admr of ROBERT GIBSON allowed 1 yr to settle estate. p 293

Case 567. DANIEL WELDY, 15 yrs, heir of CHRISTIAN
WELDY, dec, chose GEORGE GEPHART as guardian. Sec:
DANIEL GEPHART. GEORGE GEPHART appted guardian of
JACOB WELDY, 11 yrs, heir of CHRISTIAN WELDY. p 293
&
Case 568. HENRY McGRAW appted guardian of MARY ANN
WELDY 8 yrs, REBECCA WELDY 5 yrs, & HENRY WELDY 2 yrs
heirs of CHRISTIAN WELDY, dec. Sec: DAVID HOOVER.
p 293

Case 569. Adm of estate of JACOB SHEPHERD granted to
JOHN H. SCHENCK (widow relinquished right). Sec:
WILLIAM LONG, SYDNEY DENISE. Appr: JOSEPH CRANE,
JAMES CROTHERS, FREDERICK NUTTS. p 293

Case 570. JAMES MILES appted guardian of AARON MIKE-
SELL 12 yrs, & ABRAHAM MIKESELL 10 yrs, heirs of JOHN
B. MIKESELL, dec. Sec: JOSEPH MIKESELL, CHARLES WEL-
BAUM. p 294

Admr of CHARLES WELBAUM allowed 1 yr to settle estate. p 294

Admr of GEORGE HORNER allowed 1 yr to settle estate.
p 294

Inv and appr of estate of HENRY YOUNT. Total $623.38.
Public sale on 18 Nov, 1822; purchasers: RICHARD ARM-
STRONG, LEWIS BARLEY, JOHN BEIRD, NELSON R. BROWN,
WELCOME CAHOON, ISAAC CAMPBELL, LEWIS CANBY, ISAAC
COOPER, PETER CORTNER, JOHN COX, JOHN CURTIS, JOSEPH
DAVIS, WILLIAM DAVIS, CONRAD DODRAN, ENOCH FARMER,
WILLIAM FARMER, THOMAS GADDIS, WILLIAM GADDIS, JOHN
HELMICH, ABRAHAM HOFFMAN, GEORGE HOFFMAN, DANIEL
HOOVER, DAVID HOOVER, BENJAMIN IDDINGS, ARCHILOUS
JOHNSON, ELIJAH JOHNSON, STEPHEN JONES, JONATHAN JUS-
TIS, WILLIAM KENNEDY, JACOB LINKS, DAVID MAST, JOHN
MAST, SAMUEL MAST, SAMUEL MORE, JOSEPH MORSE, ASA H.
MURREL, JONATHAN NEWMAN, JOHN NORTH, NATHAN PERRY,
JOHN REED, BENJAMIN RUSSEL, CHARLES SHAW, DAVID
SHEETS, JOSHUA SWALLOW, DANIEL WAYMIRE, DAVID WAYMIRE
SOLOMON WAYMIRE, JACOB WISENER, ALEXANDER YOUNT,
ANDREW YOUNT, DANIEL YOUNT, HENRY YOUNT, SAMUEL YOUNT
total $684.80. Debts due estate from JAMES BROWN,
ISAAC DAVIS, CONRAD DODRAN, WILLIAM GADDIS, DANIEL
HERMAN, STEPHEN JACKSON, MOSES KELLY, EDWARD KINDLEY,
STEPHEN MACEY, JAMES McCANLESS, SAMUEL MILLIKAN,
VALENTINE NISHWITZ, WILLIAM PECK, JOHN ROACH, JACOB
STALEY, FRED STEVENS, THOMAS THORNTON, ISAAC WAYMIRE,
VALENTINE WAYMIRE, JOHN A. WILLIAMS, DANIEL YOUNT,
total $1769.97. pp 294, 295, 296, 297, 298, 299,
300, 301

Inv and appr of estate of GEORGE HUFFMAN on 19 Nov, 1822. Included notes due from A. DARST, WILLIAM FAR-MER, C.R. GREENE, GEORGE GROVE, CHRISTIAN HEISTAND, JOSEPH KELLER, DAVID KIMMEL, JAMES LANIER, HENRY MARKWOOD, JACOB PACHT, WILLIAM M. SMITH, CHRISTOPHER TAYLOR, JACOB WOLF, total $927.77. Public sale on 22 & 23 Nov, 1822; buyers: DAVID ALSPACH, ALANSON ASH-LEY, HENRY BABCOCK, SAMUEL BECKMAN, DANIEL BURGET, JOHN CAUFMAN, PETER CAYLOR, ELISHA CRANSTON, DANIEL GORDON, JACOB HALDERMAN, BENJAMIN HALL, JACOB HEIST-AND, SAMUEL HILDERBRAND, HENRY HIPPLE, JOHN HISER, Widow HUFFMAN, DANIEL ISELY, DAVID JEFFRIES, DANIEL JORDON, SAMUEL KAYLOR, JOHN KINSEY, ABRAHAM KISER, ANDREW KISER, JOHN MAXWELL, SAMUEL MOOR, BENJAMIN NICLOUS, GEORGE OLINGER, JACOB OLINGER, JAMES OLIVER, DANIEL REPP, DANIEL RIGIRT, DAVID RIFFLE, SOLOMON SANFORD, JACOB SHIDELER, JOHN B. SMITH, GEORGE SNIDER JOHN STOCK, GEORGE STONER, JOHN TURNER, WILLIAM WAG-GONER, MICHAEL WEAVER, CALEB WILCOX, ISRAEL WILLIAMS, JACOB WILLIAMS, WILLIAM WILLIAMS, CHRISTIAN WINEBREN-NER, JACOB WINEBRENNER, JACOB WOLF, JACOB YOCHEA, JOHN YOCHEA, total $424.52. pp 301, 302, 303, 304, 305, 306

Inv and appr of estate of FREDERICK WAYMIRE on 13 Dec 1822. Total $573.47. Property kept by widow = 11.20. Debts due from ABRAHAM HOOVER & JOEL HUTCHINS total $21.83. Public sale, undated. Buyers: JOHN BAKER, ALEXANDER COX, JOSHUA COX, GEORGE CRIPES, JOHN CURTIS NOAH DAVENPORT, JOSEPH DAVIS, JAMES ENSLEY, ENOCH FARMER, JESSE FARMER, JOHN FARMER, WILLIAM FARMER, ABRAHAM FRY, WILLIAM GADDIS, JOHN HOOVER, BENJAMIN HUTCHINS, ISAAC HUTCHINS, JOSHUA HUTCHINS, MERIDA HUTCHINS, OBADIAH JONES, STEPHEN JONES, BENJAMIN JUS-TIS, STEPHEN KENNEDY, JOHN MOTE, JOHN PECK, NATHAN PERRY, JOHN RATCLIFF, AARON RITTENHOUSE, THOMAS ROGERS, BENJAMIN RUSSELL, MARTIN STAYLEY, JESSE SWAL-LOW, WILLIAM THOMAS, DOLLY WAYMIRE, SOLOMON WAYMIRE, GREEN WILCOX, JACOB WISENER, DAVID YOUNT, HENRY YOUNT, PETER YOUNT, SOLOMON YOUNT, total $447.14. pp 307, 308, 309, 310, 311, 312, 313

Case 571. FOUNTAIN SCOTT CONNELLY, 16 yrs, chose mother PAMELA CONNELLY as guardian. p 313

Case 572. SALLY McWHINNEY appted guardian of JAMES, age 11, & WILLIAM, age 9, minor heirs of JOHN McWHIN-NEY, dec. p 313

Filed 3 March, 1823. Admr of MICHAEL EMRICK produced settlement. Cash paid to HENRY CLINE, CONRAD EMRICK, HENRY EMRICK, JOHN EMRICK JR, WILLIAM EMRICK JR,

EPHRAIM HEARSER, FREDERICK FISHER, NICHOLAS HALLER, CONRAD ISLEY, CHARLES KOUCKER, GODFREY KOUCKER, JONATHAN LINDENMUTH, HENRY MOYER, CHS. OHLWINE, FRED SHAFFER, JOHN SHOLLY, JOHN SHUTER, JOHN STUMP, CHRIST TAYLOR, JOHN WAGGONER, FRED WOLF total $692.75. Cash recvd from PETER BUXTEN, GEORGE BYER, JOHN CHRIST, PHILIP HALLER, GODFREY KOUCKER, JACOB LOY, R.J. SKINNER, JOHN STIVER, JOHN TREON. Balance of $900.22. pp 313, 314, 315

Admr of MARGARET ROBINSON produced settlement. Balance of $12.80 remains. p 315

Admr of JOHN MURRAY granted time extension to settle estate. p 316

Admr of JAMES SHAW produced settlement. Balance of $17.87 remains. p 316

Admr of ISAAC MILLER produced settlement. Balance of $1.88 remains. p 316

Admr of ENOCH BOWEN produced settlement. Cash paid to POMPEY ALLEN, WILLIAM BLODGET, SILAS BROADWELL, WILLIAM EAKER, WILLIAM GILLESPIE, C.R. GREENE, JOSHUA GREEN, MOSES GREER, ALEX GRIMES, JOB HAINES, BOWEN JOHN, JACOB JOHN, THOMAS KING, JOHN MILLER, ELIZABETH MURRAY as admr of JOHN MURRAY, SAMUEL NEWCOM, FRANCIS PATTERSON, JOSEPH POWEL, ROBERT SKINNER, JOSEPH C. SILVER, total $311.63. pp 316, 317

Admr of DANIEL DAVIS allowed 1 yr to settle estate. p 318

Admr of JOHN GILE produced settlement. Cash paid to STEPHEN ARCHER, admrs of ZACARIAH ARCHER, ABRAHAM BRANNERMAN, OBADIAH CONOVER, ADAM DEAM, HENRY DEAM, ELEANOR FRENCH, ISAAC GRIFFITH, GEORGE GROVE, SIMON HENSLEY, WILLIAM HUFFMAN, BETSEY McCREA, JACOB NIGH, PETER NIGH, JOHN REED, ROBERT STRAIN, SAMUEL THOMSON coroner, JAMES TOMPLIN, NATHANIEL WILSON, RALPH WILSON, total $196.58. p 318

Admr of ABNER GARARD allowed 1 yr to settle estate. p 319

Admr of JOSEPH C. SILVER allowed 1 yr to settle estate. p 319

Admr of DAVID SQUIER produced settlement. $268.14 in property kept by widow. Debts due estate from GEORGE GROVE, CONKLIN MILLER. Cash paid to AARON BAKER,

COMMON PLEAS (PROBATE) DOCKET BOOK E-1

Term of March, 1823 continued

JOHN BOWERS, ISAAC DAVIS, JOHN DODSON, DAVID DUNCAN, Dr CHARLES ESTE, JOHN FOLKERTH, DANIEL FULLER, JONAH GROVER, ALEX'R GUY, JEROM HOLT, JOSEPH HAMMILL, N. HUNT, SMITH LANE, JOHN LEHMAN, DAVID LINDLEY, JAMES LODGE, ANTHONY LOGAN, JONATHAN MAYHALL, JONATHAN MORGAN, THOMAS MORRISON, EDWARD NEWCOM, admr of WILLIAM NEWCOM, JAMES NOLAN, JOHN PATTERSON, MATTHEW PATTON, JOHN PERRINE, JOHN REGANS, ADDISON SMITH, GEORGE SNIDER, TIMOTHY SQUIER, WILLIAM STEWART, JOHN TREON, total $1258.79. pp 319, 320, 321

Exec of CASPER STIVER allowed 1 yr to settle estate. p 321

Case 573. Will of JANE ABBOTT proven by witnes JOHN STAFFORD. p 321

Admr of LUCEANNA ZIEGLER produced final settlement. Cash paid to THOMAS CLARK, WILLIAM COOPER, D.K. ESTE, MARIA GREENE, SOPHIA C. LOWRY, JOHN READ (taxes), ALEX WHITE (tombstone for grave of WILLIAM ZIEGLER), balance of $4062.28 remains. p 322

Admr of CONRAD LICHTY produced final settlement. Widow kept $39.18 in property. Cash rcvd from EPHRAIM ARNOLD, JACOB DARST. Cash paid to JOHN BONNER, GEORGE BRADFORD, GEORGE CALDERWOOD, WILLIAM EAKER, Dr HAINES, JONA. HARSHMAN, ASA JOHN, JAMES KINCANNON, ABRAHAM KISER, SAMUEL KISER, JOHN MOLER, JAMES I. NESBIT, EDWARD NEWCOM, WILLIAM PATTERSON, LAWRENCE SHELL, Dr TREON, THOMAS WHITE, total $507.48. pp 323, 324

Exec of D.C. COOPER produced settlement. Cash paid to JOHN BAKER, JOHN COMPTON, JOHN DODSON, DAVID FOLAND, ALEXANDER GRIMES, ABRAHAM B. LAWTON, JOSHUA McINTOSH, JOHN H. PIATT, JAMES PIPER, GEORGE SNIDER, DAVID STOUT, JONA. STUTSMAN, total $4047.23. pp 324, 325

Case 574. Will of CATHERINE JORDA. Witness: DANIEL GRIPE, JACOB GRIPE. Exec: CHRISTIAN ARNOLD. Appr: DAVID KRIDER, MARTIN WEYBRIGHT, FREDERICK HOLLZAPPLE. p 325

Admr of ALEXANDER BARKSHIRE allowed 1 yr to settle estate. p 325

Admr of GEORGE BRATSUS returned estate as insolvent. Court ordered payment of 30 cents on the dollar.

Cash rcvd from - BROADSTONE, JOSEPH CLYMER, J. FOLKERTH, ADAM GARLOUGH, J. HARSHMAN, J. McINTOSH, THOMAS SNODGRASS, HENRY STOVER, total $109.26. Cash paid to Dr. WILLIAM BLODGET, ADAM GARLOUGH, D. LAMME, GEORGE SNIDER (auctioneer). Accounts held against estate by WILLIAM BATRON, LEONARD BROADSTONE, WILLIAM HUFFMAN, MICHAEL MARLEY, JOHN LEHMAN, H.G. PHILLIPS, JAMES RITCHIE, JACOB SHARTEL, GEORGE SNIDER, DANIEL WOLF total $124.60. pp 326, 327 (SEE CASE 492)

Admr of ABRAHAM REED produced final settlement. Widow's half = $162.53. Cash paid to POMPEY ALLEN, O.B. CONOVER, DAVID GRIFFEN, G.S. HUSTON, MATTHEW PATTON, G. SNIDER, Dr JOHN STEELE, J.H. WILLIAMS, JOHN YOUNG, total $71.37. Recpt dated 9 Feb, 1824: rcvd of admr AARON BAKER $54.44 in full the right of dower of my wife CATHERINE which with former rcpts makes $162.54, signed MOSES B. ROBERTS. p 328

Admr of ABRAHAM TEAGARDEN produced settlement. Cash paid to SOLOMON CROSS, PETER NYE, GEORGE W. SMITH, IRA SMITH (taxes), total $21.15. p 329

Filed 4 April, 1823. Inv and appr of estate of JACOB SHEPHERD on 1 March, 1823. Property did not excede widow and children's maintenance for 1 year. p 329

Inv and appr of estate of CATHERINE JORDIE on 28 March, 1823. Total $58.03. Public sale, buyers: CLEM ARNOLD, ISAAC ARNOLD, JOHN ARNOLD, FRED BARNDER, DANIEL CRIPE JR, EMANUEL CRIPE, JACOB CRIPE, ROBERT GIBSON, SAMUEL GRIPE JR, DANIEL HOLSAPPLE, JOS. MIKESELL, ABRAHAM RARICK, DAVID RAUF, DAVID REPLOGLE, JACOB REPLOGLE, JOHN REPLOGLE, DAVID SUMMERS, PETER SUMMERS, HENRY WELLBAUM, FRED WEYBRIGHT, MARTIN WEYBRIGHT, HENRY WILLIAMS, total $62.09. pp 330, 331, 332

Filed 2 May, 1823. Inv and appr of estate of VALENTINE HUFFMAN. Total $78.12. Public sale, no date given; buyers: WILLIAM BARKSHIRE, JARNA DAUGHTERY, ABRAHAM FROLINGER, DAVID FROLINGER, JAMES HANLEY, ADAM PURDY, JOHN REED, JACOB WAGGONER, ANDREW WESTFALL, ELIZABETH WODMAN, total $26.98. p 333

Term of May, 1823

Case 575. GEORGE WASHINGTON KENNEDY, 15 yrs, chose WILLIAM M. SMITH as guardian. p 334

Case 576. Adm of estate of JOHN WAYMIRE granted to FREDERICK WAYMIRE & ISAAC WAYMIRE (widow relinquished

right). Sec: WILLIAM GADDIS, STEPHEN KENNEDY. Appr:
JOHN BARNETT, JOHN STOUDER, JESSE FARMER. p 334

Case 577. MARY HOOVER, 15 yrs, heir of DANIEL HOOVER
JR, chose JOHN HOOVER as guardian. Sec: GEORGE LINKS
p 334

Case 578. JOHN HOOVER appted guardian of SALLY HOO-
VER 12 yrs, & SUSANNAH HOOVER 9 yrs, heirs of DANIEL
HOOVER JR, dec. Sec: GEORGE LINKS. p 334

Case 579. DANIEL KELSEY, 17 yrs, heir of THOMAS KEL-
SEY, dec, chose WILLIAM WATKINS as guardian. Sec:
DANIEL WATKINS. p 334

Case 580. GEORGE WOLF, 14 yrs, heir of GEORGE WOLF
(who died in Cumberland Co, PA) chose PETER TREON as
guardian. Sec: JOHN STEWART, ADAM SHUEY. p 335

Inv and appr of estate of JAMES VAN KIRK. Included
accounts due from JOHN COMPTON, JOHN McILWAIN, JAMES
MORLATT, ELISHA SHEPHERD, JOHN VANDERVEER, AUKEY
WIKOFF, BENJAMIN WOODBERRY, total $628.41. Widow
kept $211.50 in property. Public sale on 20 March,
1823; buyers: THOMAS ANDERSON, ANDREW BAIRD, DERRICK
BARKALOW, JOHN CHAMBERS, JOHN COMPTON, WILLIAM CONOV-
ER, WILLIAM D. CRARY, SAMUEL DENISE, SIDNEY DENISE,
LEWIS DAVIS, MATTHEW FRANK, JAMES KERR, GEORGE LOY,
JOHN LOY, DAVID MILLER, JACOB MILLER, HENRY PAINE,
PETER PENROD, SAMUEL PENROD, AMOS POTTER, GARRET A.
SCHENCK, JOHN H. SCHENCK, BENJAMIN SCOTT, JOHN SUTPHE
JOSIAH THARP, BENJAMIN VANDERVEER, JOSEPH VANNOTE,
THOMAS VANNOTE, JAMES WHITFIELD, TYLER WOOLERY,
total $323.68. pp 335, 336, 337, 338

Case 581. Will of JOSIAH GUSHWAGH, proven by witness
DANIEL MONNBEC. p 338

Case 582. Will of HENRY BROWN. Witness: JOSEPH H.
CRANE, DAVID REID. Exec: HENRY STODDARD, JAMES HEN-
DERSON, CATHERINE P. BROWN. Appr: JAMES STEELE, WIL-
LIAM EAKER, LUTHER BRUEN. p 339

Will of JOSIAH GUSHWAGH proven by witness SIMON MYERS
Exec: PETER GUSHWAGH, DAVID GUSHWAGH. Appr: MICHAEL
HILLEGAS, GEORGE COLEMEN, CHRISTIAN SHUPERT. p 339

Admr of JACOB STUTSMAN granted time extension to settle estate. p 339

ROBERT SCOTT, exec of SOLOMON HOLLINGSWORTH, produced
settlement. Widow kept $171.00 in property. Cash

paid to JOHN ARCHER, ANDREW BAILEY (tax), DAVID BROWN, JAMES H. CAMPBELL, PETER CODINGTON, STEPHEN COVERT, JAMES CRAFT, JOHN EDWARDS, JOS. FISK, R.J. GRAHAM, BENJAMIN JONES, ABNER KELSEY, WILLIAM J. LODGE, CALEB MILLER, MAHLON MOON (coffin), AARON NUTT (auctioneer), AZARIAH PUGH (grave digging), Dr ROSS, JOHN RUSSELL, Dr STRONG, JOHN WILLIAMSON (city tax), ASAHEL WRIGHT, total $643.12. pp 339, 340

Admr of ENOCH BOWEN given until next term to produce settlement. p 340

Admr of ANN MOTE produced settlement. Cash paid to DAVID HOOVER, JACOB HOOVER, GEORGE LINKS, JOHN MOTE, THOMAS NEWMAN, total $20.21. Balance of $152.55 remains. p 341

Admr of JAMES PETTICREW produced partial settlement, given 1 yr to settle estate. pp 341, 342

End of BOOK E-1

INDEX: names in text may have variant spelling

INDEX: names in text may have variant spelling

INDEX: names in text may have variant spelling

Byman/Bimon, John 225 230
231
Cab, Nahell 69
Cahoon, Welcome 259 Will-
iam 155
Calderwood, George 231
256 262
Caldwell, Samuel 140 178
233
Calhoun, Hugh 245 256
John 140 William 86 96
106 107 186
Callendine, Christian 40
Callaway, James 257
Cammack, James 48 73 83
93
Camp, Joseph 176
Campbell, Archibald 153
Isaac 259 James 212 265
John 31 106 129 130 140
156 177 179 239 241
Patrick 156 Ralph 231
249 Richard 239 Robert
144 188 204 Samuel 231
William 76
Can, George 32
Canardy, Joseph 215
Canby, Lewis 259
Cane, Jacob 205
Cannon, James 5
Capper, Latonias 244
Caringer, John 175
Carney/Kerney, Shem 147
159 166 187
Carothers/Cruthers, James
157 222 233 239 243 259
Carpenter, Hopkins 195
234 Joseph 121 Thomas
234
Carr, James 211 John 177
212 Moses 177
Carrington, Peter 210
Carroll, Jacob 225
Carter, Bennet 206 235
Carvell, William 181
Carver, Christian 82 Ja-
cob 182 John 169 Sam-
uel 169
CASLER, see KESLER
Cason, Thomas 120 122
Casper, John 167
Cassaday, George 193 John

193 Peter 193 Thomas 76
CASTOR, see KASTER
CATEROW, see KETTEROW
Cathcroft, David 253
Catrick, Henry 234
Cattin, James 225
Cavender, John 129 Samuel
39 42 205
CAYLOR, see KAYLOR
Cecil, Zacariah 144
Cedy, David 244
Chamberlain, Abraham 205
James 217 John 120
Chambers, John 234 264
William 138 257
Chandler, Goldsmith 205
218 238
Charlton, Robert 215 217
Chatham, James 50 84 112
141 170 193 197 206 218
Chenoweth, William 7 29
42
Chervy, William 32
Chester, John 32
Chevalier, Anthony 126
127 128 140 143 156 257
Charles 85 87 134
CHRIBE, see CRIPE & GRIPE
Chrisman, Daniel 48
Christian, Ludwick 82 83
103
Christopher, John 234
Churchwell, Richard 32
CISSEL, see SISSEL
Clapmire, Abraham 17
Clapp, John 7
Clark, Amos 93 206 213
247 Andrew 200 206 232
246 247 Daniel 223 257
David 34 Hannah 247
Henry 43 49 134 137 139
177 200 206 207 208 212
213 232 240 246 247
Isaac 27 79 99 122 144
James 155 178 186 225
Jesse 49 102 104 137
141 144 200 206 217 221
235 243 247 250 258
John 147 151 187 208
Joseph 122 Julianna 207
Polly 193 Rebecca 208
Robert 34 38 39 58 140

272

INDEX: names in text may have variant spelling

Gibson continued
  253 258 263 Samuel 88
Gilchrist, Robert 8 139
  141 153 202 214
Gile/Guile, John 3 85 141
  179 181 193 201 261
  Nancy 179
Gill, John 8
Gillespie, George 3 8 150
  Henry 142 James 10 14
  15 98 116 118 119 135
  138 143 144 155 156 215
  John 186 217 220 Joseph
  134 135 150 178 205 217
  Neal 50 William 141 155
  156 186 195 220 227 230
  261
Gillingham, James 32
Gilliland, John 77
Givens, James 147 Samuel
  122
Glass, Sarah 100
Glossbrenner, Jacob 216
  225 236 241 244 245 249
Glover, Elias 29
Glympse, Emanuel 195
Gondy, Polly 213
Good, John 179 238 Valentine 238
Goodlander, Henry 202 Jacob 180 219
Goodspeed/Goodstead, Gideon 156 186 206
Goodwin, Thomas 150
Gordon, Daniel 260 James
  174 John 34 156 Lewis
  135 195 Richard 156
  William 63 214
Gosney, Fielding 172 178
  186 195 198 204
Graff, John 243
Graham, Archibald 21 129
  132 134 139 153 154 174
  216 James 240 Jonas 88
  91 Peter 220 225 230
  R J 265 Robert 80 83
  104 160 165 Thomas 63
Grant, Elijah 107
Gray, Jane 92 113 135 155
  186 John 233 Mary 113
  Rachel 98 135 140 Richard 81 92 98 112 113

  135 140 143 144 148 155
  159 Robert 98 104 113
  135 143 151 203 William 113
Greabill, John 225
Greade, James 159
Green, Charles 84 127 181
  186 195 197 202 212 227
  230 240 247 248 260 261
  John 185 225 Joshua 261
  Maria 240 262 Timothy
  156 William 198
Greer, Aaron 27 John 7
  174 Joshua 174 218 Moses 230 254 261 Ruth 27
Gregg, Sarah 3 Smith 4 36
  61 64 119 156 196
Griffin, D 230 Daniel 9
  12 16 19 25 28 40 48 53
  63 David 175 186 188
  194 196 220 233 263 Isaac 66 William 36 48
Griffith, Eleazar 99 102
  174 176 186 217 Isaac
  102 207 251 261
Griggsby, John 124 136
Grimes, Alexander 186 205
  227 237 238 248 250 261
  262 Archibald 154 156
  James 174 176 215 224
  246 250 Joel 224 John
  36 58 70 86 90 96 121
  122 127 128 134 139 140
  145 147 150 156 186 189
  197 198 202 219 227
  Samuel 129
Grindle, Pete 166
GRIPE, see CRIPE
Gripe/Gribe, Barbara 202
  Catherine 188 228 Daniel 188 194 214 262 David 258 Elizabeth 258
  Hannah 258 Jacob 97 142
  164 174 194 216 237 251
  262 John 55 74 152 164
  165 166 188 216 228 237
  258 Joseph 152 165 188
  254 Josiah 165 Magdalena 252 Samuel 65 74 93
  170 182 251 263 Stephen
  258
Grissum, David 77

INDEX: names in text may have variant spelling

INDEX: names in text may have variant spelling

INDEX: names in text may have variant spelling

INDEX: names in text may have variant spelling

INDEX: names in text may have variant spelling

McShoney, Robert 151
McWasson, William 211
McWhinney, James 260 John
  260 Sally 260 William
  260
Mears, Lewis 238
Mease, Lewis 243
Medard, George 210
Medsker, Adam 185 Andrew
  187 188 189 228 Henry
  188 219 228 258 Jacob
  220
Meeker, Joseph 5 141 147
  151 158 199 256
Mein, David 253
Memnall, Ellis 11
Mendenhall, Mordecai 123
  William 231
Mengele/Mingle, Jacob 217
  John 102 130 217 224
Mercer, Henry 166 Jona-
  than 214
Merdshall, Caleb 166
Merrick, Joseph 231 250
Messer, Edward 176
Mettard, Frederick 217
METZGER, see MEDSKER
Michael/ Mikel, Barbara
  159 Fergus 157 Henry
  217 Jacob 148 150 249
  John 182 229 Solomon
  168 208
Middleton, Isaac 173
Mikesell, Aaron 259 Abra-
  ham 259 Andrew 185 188
  198 220 228 George 36
  Jacob 168 217 230 258
  John 2 3 20 36 52 60 62
  64 65 70 76 116 117 124
  125 128 131 136 142 146
  149 174 178 185 186 191
  192 195 197 202 206 216
  259 Joseph 117 154 191
  216 237 245 251 252 256
  259 263 Martin 220 257
  Peter 78 88 156 203 205
  230 Philip 144 146 164
  165 168 170 178 184 192
  198 202 213 217 220 228
  230 245 Valentine 167
Miles, Abraham 182 Enoch
  210 Enos 152 167 185

214 James 8 36 41 48 63
  78 82 117 129 141 259
  John 166 Sarah 140
Miley -- 239
Milhollen, Jonathan 134
Miller, Aaron 134 139 166
  169 170 177 180 182 183
  203 214 Abraham 118 136
  141 151 168 182 188 190
  220 257 258 Adam 232
  235 246 Alexander 220
  Caleb 265 Catherine 71
  228 Charles 205 Christ-
  ian 88 137 146 149 178
  182 190 214 Christianna
  110 Conkling 52 77 78
  80 88 103 139 150 151
  157 186 193 241 261
  Daniel 36 71 106 107
  116 117 118 122 125 126
  127 128 131 136 138 139
  142 146 163 165 169 170
  182 202 217 223 232 234
  235 242 246 251 257 Da-
  vid 40 50 51 71 76 128
  134 136 137 139 142 150
  151 154 163 165 169 170
  172 173 174 182 187 191
  194 198 236 243 246 247
  251 257 264 Elizabeth
  257 George 194 196 Hen-
  ry 243 Isaac 66 73 112
  131 135 188 190 191 218
  228 253 257 261 Jacob
  99 117 119 130 135 142
  143 148 157 159 162 168
  169 170 171 174 179 195
  223 238 244 255 257 264
  James 2 3 5 9 11 14 16
  18 20 31 36 42 43 45 47
  50 62 65 80 83 88 89
  115 116 117 118 119 123
  139 141 176 179 188 203
  207 215 246 249 251 256
  John 3 4 10 15 17 26 28
  29 36 43 55 59 61 63 64
  70 87 88 89 93 106 107
  110 115 116 117 118 122
  123 124 126 127 129 131
  132 133 134 136 137 138
  141 142 143 144 148 151
  162 163 170 174 180 190

296

INDEX: names in text may have variant spelling

Miller continued
191 192 193 194 195 196
199 203 204 212 216 221
225 228 230 232 240 243
246 247 251 253 257 261
Jonah 257 Jonas 185 190
216 Jonathan 167 Joseph
179 223 258 Margaret
201 235 Melchior 125
217 238 Michael 192 198
Moses 142 146 190 191
Peter 242 Philip 146
173 175 208 243 Robert
14 15 139 146 176 192
Samuel 110 182 224 225
241 257 Solomon 218 233
Stephen 223 251 253 257
Susannah 131 142 Tobias
170 William 38 50 138
141 150 208 225 253
Milligan, James 21 26 60
125 126 127
Millikan, Samuel 259
Million, Francis 268 182
231
Mills, Elijah 138 Jacob
229 Jeremiah 98 160 164
Joshua 256 Lewis 229
Milman, Adam 167 185 207
208 214 Jacob 225
Miner, Abraham 191 Henry
182 John 242
Minnich, George 86 90
John 224 Leonard 159
228
Minniear, Abraham 15 74
78 104
Minton, Jacob 217 Mathew
157 160 166 217
Misener Christian 191 252
Mitchell, David 68 Edward
15 75 77 116 118 132
168 184 201 205 228 230
238 244 James 179 Sarah
116 William 184
Moler, John 231 262 Van-
deveer 231 256
Mong, Godfrey 157
Monfort, Francis 234 Pet-
er 136 203
Monro, Amos 70
Montawnie, Elijah 150

Montgomery, Elizabeth 112
173
Moon, Christian 220 Mahl-
on 233 237 265 Samuel
225 230 242
Mooney, John 231 Rebeckah
94 William 188
Moore, Benjamin 118 Bus-
tard 25 Charles 24
Francis 118 Hugh 191
John 105 256 Margaret
101 Robert 77 Samuel 4
9 11 12 32 44 260 Will-
iam 121
Morgan, Abner 256 Abraham
212 231 240 254 256
Barbara 256 Charles 17
53 61 126 183 220 224
226 254 Cornelius 240
Isaac 219 227 229 230
244 James 204 John 217
220 226 240 255 256
Jonathan 139 142 262
Joshua 154 Murrel 256
Samuel 154 229 230 256
259 Sarah 254 256 Simon
210 Thomas 179 Vander-
veer 250 Vinsart 256
Morlatt, James 211 264
Morningstar George 77 142
Morris, David 9 17 24 30
James 139 145 John 70
Jonathan 187 242 Nancy
145 Travis 70 William
239
Morrison, Daniel 186 Eph-
raim 30 James 206 Moses
204 Thomas 198 224 242
248 256 262 Samuel 2 9
10 20 25 26 27 29 30
William 221 222 231
Morrow, Abel 243 James
102 158
Moses, -- 9
Mote, Anna 245 249 265
David 184 Jeremiah 41
48 136 Jesse 155 157
166 184 John 136 168
182 184 204 208 211 231
260 265 Jonathan 20 26
249 Rhoda 184 William
184

INDEX: names in text may have variant spelling

INDEX: names in text may have variant spelling

Patton continued
145 148 174 186 192 195
204 226 227 230 240 242
262 263
Patty, Charles 87 89 209
David 158 James 158 232
Pauley, John 20 74 121
122 130 240
Paulus, Abraham 74 157
162 Christina 74
Peace, Warren 190
Pease, Parry 243
Pearson, Amelia 155 211
Benjamin 155 Hannah 163
James 209 John 231 Jo-
seph 154 155 Powel 209
William 163 180 209 231
Peck, John 249 260 William
186 259
Peery, William 4
Pelham, Samuel 214
Pence, John 191
Pendleton, Thomas 77
Peney, Samuel 77
Penrod, Catherine 187 211
Peter 159 187 211 217
242 264 Samuel 217 264
Widow 215 234
Penther, Frederick 82
Penticost, John 10 15
Pepinger, John 149 182
Peter 237
Perrine, John 262
Perry, Martha 73 Nathan
259 260 Samuel 74 90
Petrimoulx, John Baptiste
21 34
Petticrew, James 3 99 115
121 141 150 155 157 159
170 176 177 223 233 236
248 265 John 71 103 Ro-
bert 150 Thomas 248
Pettifish /   Peterfish,
Christian 99 George 195
Pettit, Alex 88 Ephraim
180 237 James 168 John
205 M S 160 N S 156
Pew, Alexander 76
Phares, Washington 68
Phillips, Elizabeth 171
177 George 94 Horatio
31 35 50 51 80 81 89 97

108 127 128 134 137 140
148 153 155 156 157 158
159 173 183 186 187 192
193 194 195 198 203 204
209 212 222 224 227 228
230 233 241 245 253 258
263 Ralph 81 101 Will-
iam 177
Phillipson, Jacob 47 60
Simon 60
Piatt, John 219 262
Pickelsimer, Jacob 13
Picket, John 49
Pierce/Peirce, David 247
Edward 77 Henrietta 240
247 Isaac 238 240 Jere-
miah 247 John 195 224
Joseph 31 35 41 80 98
99 104 127 164 169 186
192 193 198 215 224 234
237 240 247 Mary 247
Samuel 240
Pierson, Daniel 195 204
225 226 230 George 186
Piker, D 96
Piper, James 150 262
Pipinger, Cornelius 251
John 247 251
Pitman, Joseph 150 187
211 235
Pitsenberger, Henry 255
Jacob 134 174 255
Plessinger / Playsinger,
George 174 188 Jacob
188 212 221
Plotter, Nicholas 160
Plummer, Philemon 108 124
154 John 124 Sophia 108
Pogue/Poke, John 120 122
Samuel 120 122
Pontius, Abraham 142 196
211 220
Popes, Nathaniel 195
Porter, Frederic 216 Jam-
es 20 26 37 39 42 118
John 199 Joseph 10 15
Nathaniel 237 249 250
Robert 190 William 179
Potter, Amos 264
Potts, Samuel 187 211
Powell, Barbara 172 Dr
252 Jonathan 172 194

301

INDEX: names in text may have variant spelling

INDEX: names in text may have variant spelling

Rike/Reick continued
217 256
Rinker, Elijah 181
Ritchie, James 86 89 104
106 150 263 John 125
128 129 133 137 143 160
Rittenhouse, Aaron 260
Catherine 245 249 Gar-
ret 169 James 34 John
174 175 177 179 181 188
190 204 227 249 Obadiah
248 Peter 249 Rachel
174 William 154 174 190
204
Ritter, John 134 139 169
170 198 219 Michael 198
255 Obadiah 245 Samuel
248 Tobias 244
Roach, John 199 259 Will-
iam 156
Robb, Capt B 34 John 39
78 79 82 121
Robbarts, Job 247
Robert(s), Catherine 263
Charles 96 Conrad 172
194 Jesse 96 John 205
210 229 Margaret 147
Moses 263 Samuel 172
Robertson, Henry 184 John
211 Margaret 150 Robert
86 147 151 194
Robins, Aaron 212 Benja-
min 2 116 119 120 123
148 160 209 Daniel 133
John 211 235 249 Jona-
than 146 169 Levi 212
Richard 160 168 Timothy
130 211 Thomas 150 153
Robinson/Robison, Andrew
127 128 140 Daniel 16
121 Elizabeth 128 Henry
122 209 212 213 224 253
256 Hezekiah 31 35 40
48 50 55 96 97 104 213
220 Hugh 16 Jacob 5 16
James 157 John 121 Mar-
garet 127 128 261 Rob-
ert 127 128 131 150 157
Thomas 15 185 186 Will-
iam 28 29 34 35 62 65
121 122 199
Roby, John 139 157 160

Rock, Thomas 247
Rockenfields, Aaron 159
168 Joseph 210
Rockhill, William 217
Rodebaugh, Adam 136 143
151 163 172 174 194 241
David 174 188 George
237 Henry 237 Peter 165
219
Rodeffer, Joseph 173 198
219 229
Rodehamel, Jacob 129 135
160
Rodeheffer Samuel 191 195
Roe, Charles 36 41 48
Roger(s)/Rager, Alexander
132 Henry 154 252 James
132 Michael 168 185 198
208 209 210 217 237
Thomas 260 William 109
Rohrer/Rour Catherine 166
Christian 122 Daniel
182 216 251 Jacob 109
166 177 185 191 John
109 148 166 182 209 231
251 Joseph 5 6 68 69
105 117 148 150 151 194
197 204 Mary 166
Rollins, Jonathan 122
Roman, Jacob 77
Roof/Rhuff, Adam 82 112
Daniel 70 82 112 152
Henry 82 209 235 237
Jacob 187 223 Matthew
187 Peter 74 81 90 112
209 237
Roos, Nicholas 194
Rop, Ignatius 118 125 128
Ross, Aston 130 138 Dr
265 John 130
Rossman, John 150 177 178
Roth, William 225 234
Rothamel, Henry 212 224
Jacob 212
Roudebush, George 82 185
212 237
Rouser/Rowzer, Martin 96
103
Royer, George 206 209
Henry 142 182 206 209
Thomas 236
Ruby, Jacob 161 183 188

304

INDEX: names in text may have variant spelling

Thomson continued
120 121 127 129 131 135
142 172 173 174 195 204
206 227 229 Matthew 50
Moses 50 88 157 204 249
Neal 50 Polly 50 Samuel
4 6 7 8 9 13 15 18 19
36 39 42 82 115 116 121
129 135 142 147 261
Thomas 178 William 50
182
Thorkell, Henry 11
Thornbright, Amos 178
Thornton, Eli 255 Thomas
251 252 259
Thrall, Anna 192 198 Jo-
seph 151 Nathaniel 157
Richard 170 192 198 222
Samuel 151
Tibbals, Asher 210 214
246 Noah 31 35 210
Tiffin, Edward 13
Tilly, William 32 34
Tipner, John 183
Tittle, George 195 Jacob
223
Tobias, Abraham 243 Jacob
243
Todd, George 28 Isaac 66
John 157 William 72
Toff, Aaron 183 Abraham
183
Tommis, Samuel 47 56 83
93
Tomplin, James 261
Toppin, William 31
Torrens, David 130
Towman, Valentine 241
Townsley, Peter 257
Trager, Samuel 224
Trant, Jacob 205
Traxter, Sirus 131
Trehyseur, Conrad 244
Treon, John 159 160 178
194 210 219 220 234 261
262 Michael 159 167 217
Peter 159 168 189 202
211 243 264
Trevor, John 220
Trine, Christian 125 126
Troxell, Abraham 66 71
79 110 131 143 149 163

164 167 174 175 177 178
196 202 208 209 210 213
216 221 239 Henry 229
244 259 Jacob 168 Will-
iam 184
Troyer, Daniel 151 223
John 134 178
Tryer, Daniel 162
Tucker, Deborah 256 Jacob
250 James 103 John 106
177 Margaret 177 Mary
154
Tull, Charles 31 35 50 58
86 123 124 188 198
Tullis, Aaron 26 John 176
212 213 220 224 225 253
Jonathan 18 82
Tummelstous, Nathan 199
Tumpaw, John 238
Turnbarger, William 168
Turnbull/Ternbill, Jacob
179 William 132
Turner, James 240 John
230 249 260
Tyler William 204 242 258
Ullery/Ulrich, Daniel 151
David 33 74 112 186 210
252 George 117 Isaac
165 186 188 190 252 Ja-
cob 246 254 John 66 106
186 188 190 228 Joseph
165 Samuel 33 146 164
165 188 216 230 252
Stephen 61 66 68 188
191 210 258
Ulmer, Frederick 230 251
254
Ulright, Matthew 68
Ungary, Daniel 151 243
Michael 159
Updegraff,John 258
Vail, Moses 130 215 234
William 187
Vanarsdal, -- 178 Corne-
lius 49 139 145 Janet
118 119 126 John 10 15
26 36 48 49 67 117 118
119 126 145 147 William
28 93 119 126 129
Vance, John 77 125 Micha-
el 224
Van Cleve, Benjamin 2 4

312